USING

microsoft® Visio® 2010

Chris Roth

que®

800 East 96th Street, Indianapolis, Indiana 46240 USA

Using Microsoft® Visio® 2010

ISBN-13: 978-0-7897-4297-1
ISBN-10: 0-7897-4297-7

The Library of Congress Cataloging-in-Publication Data is on file.

Printed in the United States of America
Fourth Printing: May 2013

Trademarks

Warning and Disclaimer

Bulk Sales

Que Publishing offers excellent discounts on this book when ordered in quantity for bulk purchases or special sales. For more information, please contact

U.S. Corporate and Government Sales
1-800-382-3419
corpsales@pearsontechgroup.com

For sales outside of the U.S., please contact

International Sales
international@pearson.com

Associate Publisher
Greg Wiegand

Acquisitions Editor
Loretta Yates

Development Editor
Abshier House

Managing Editor
Kristy Hart

Project Editor
Andrew Beaster

Copy Editor
Chuck Hutchinson

Senior Indexer
Cheryl Lenser

Proofreader
Debbie Williams

Technical Editor
John Marshall

Publishing Coordinator
Cindy Teeters

Interior Designer
Anne Jones

Cover Designer
Anna Stingley

Compositor
Nonie Ratcliff

Contents at a Glance

Media Table of Contents

To register this product and gain access to the Free Web Edition and the audio and video files, go to quepublishing.com/using.

The following chapter can be accessed online at quepublishing.com/using:

Table of Contents

The following chapter can be accessed online at quepublishing.com/using:

About the Author

Chris Roth has always enjoyed creating pictures of any kind and absolutely enjoys the combination of computer technology with graphics. He has been working with Visio since The Beginning in 1992, when he was part of the Visio 1.0 team at then-extant Visio Corporation. Since then, he's continuously been busy helping customers incorporate diagrams, drawings, and visualizations into their daily business and to develop custom graphical solutions based on Visio.

A Microsoft Visio MVP since 2002, he has presented sessions at several Visio conferences and has written more than 250 articles about Visio for his "Visio Guy" website (www.visguy.com), which he launched in 2006.

Originally from Seattle, he currently lives with his wife and baby daughter in Munich, Germany. Away from family, laptop, and relaxing Bavarian beer gardens, he plays trombone with the TT Orchestra and the wind ensemble Pullacher Blasmusik.

Dedication

For those who think that diagrams, drawings, and pictures make the world a more interesting place and use visualizations in their daily work, or wish that they could...

Acknowledgments

Many thanks to the Que Publishing team for their help, understanding, and patience and to the Visio team at Microsoft for promptly answering nitpicky technical questions. Three cheers to Visio veteran John Marshall (the *original* Visio MVP) for his give-it-to-me-straight technical editing. Finally, huge hugs to my family for putting up with always-on working hours and the distracted state of mind that book authoring causes.

We Want to Hear from You!

As the reader of this book, *you* are our most important critic and commentator. We value your opinion and want to know what we're doing right, what we could do better, what areas you'd like to see us publish in, and any other words of wisdom you're willing to pass our way.

As an associate publisher for Que Publishing, I welcome your comments. You can email or write me directly to let me know what you did or didn't like about this book—as well as what we can do to make our books better.

Please note that I cannot help you with technical problems related to the topic of this book. We do have a User Services group, however, where I will forward specific technical questions related to the book.

When you write, please be sure to include this book's title and author as well as your name, email address, and phone number. I will carefully review your comments and share them with the author and editors who worked on the book.

Email: feedback@quepublishing.com

Mail: Greg Wiegand
Associate Publisher
Que Publishing
800 East 96th Street
Indianapolis, IN 46240 USA

Reader Services

Visit our website and register this book at quepublishing.com/using for convenient access to any updates, downloads, or errata that might be available for this book.

Introduction

Visio has been around since 1992, delighting office workers everywhere by enabling them to easily incorporate insightful business diagrams and drawings into their daily work.

Every day, millions of Visio users create illustrative org charts, block diagrams, flowcharts, process flows, and network diagrams. And thanks to foresight by the original designers, they even create scaled drawings such as space plans, office plans, site plans, network rack elevations, and the like.

Some users enhance their diagrams with data, hyperlinks, and even custom add-ins. They publish these diagrams to internal or external web or SharePoint sites and create departmental tools out of diagrams. The breadth of disciplines touched by Visio diagrams, and the depths to which users create Visio solutions, is astonishing and inspiring.

Visio 2010 ups the ante with one of the biggest upgrades ever. It's full of goodies like the new, friendly Ribbon user interface; lots of process-diagramming enhancements for making connecting, arranging, and aligning easier; juicy live previews that show you how your changes will look before you make them; enhanced CAD interoperability, improved data-visualization features; and some really cool tools for adding structure to your diagrams.

If you compare today's Internet and computing world to that of 10 or 15 years ago, you'll notice an explosion in graphics. Not only has the expectation of quality graphics grown, but the staggering amount of data that we have at our fingertips necessitates the use of pictures to understand it. Indeed data visualization has not only become a buzz word but also a serious career path.

Amidst all this, Visio occupies a curious position. It's not a "fancy grapher" that can create interactive animated web-based spiraling data visualizations that dance to lounge music. Its foremost function is creating connected diagrams and scaled 2D drawings, which are data visualizations of a different kind and have plenty of utility and value by themselves.

But because elements in Visio drawings can be linked to data and that data can be visually highlighted within Visio, it also has a place on the modern data visualization stage. If you imagine displaying alert icons on overloaded servers in a network diagram, highlighting office space that is underused or overpriced in red, or simply showing informational text that can quickly be gleaned by users, you literally get the picture.

At any rate, the importance of visual communication is growing, and Visio can be a big part of the very visual future.

How This Book Is Organized

My goal in writing this book was to demonstrate the essentials of Visio diagramming, highlight labor-saving shortcuts, expose the quirks, and hint at advanced techniques for those aspiring to be power users.

Visio's visual nature makes it easy to figure out a lot of the basics, but its long history (including eight years of life before being acquired by Microsoft!) and astonishing breadth and depth have resulted in a few less-than-obvious features, a few oddities, and hidden power.

Luckily, *Using Visio 2010* comes with web-hosted companion videos, which I think are particularly important and helpful for a graphics application—seemingly long and complicated sets of step-by-step instructions can suddenly become clear as day after watching a video!

Visio 2010 comes in three editions, Standard, Pro, and Premium. Although most of this book focuses on the things you can do with Visio 2010 Standard, Chapters 7, "Working with Data," 8, "Tips for Creating Specific Types of Diagrams," and 10, "Sharing, Publishing, and Exporting," do touch on a few features available only in Pro and Premium. I've tried to make it as clear as possible which features are available only in certain editions.

With *Using Visio 2010* you will learn how to

- Efficiently assemble connected drawings such as flowcharts, org charts, and network diagrams from premade libraries of shapes and manage the connection, layout, and arrange the shapes in those diagrams.
- Manage, search, and create shape libraries, plus incorporate graphics from external sources in your diagrams.
- Organize, annotate, and add structure to your diagrams using containers, callouts, multiple pages, backgrounds, titles, and layers.

- Find, recognize, and utilize all of the special features that make Visio shapes SmartShapes that are superior to clipart.
- Incorporate data into your diagrams, report on the data, link to external sources, and add visualizations based on that data.
- Control your output by printing in a multitude of ways, including reduction, enlargement, and printing to large-format paper.
- Share your diagrams in numerous ways, including e-mailing, exporting to PDF and other formats, and publishing to the web and to SharePoint sites.
- Program very basic Visio SmartShapes and write simple macro code to automate Visio programmatically.

Using This Book

This book allows you to customize your own learning experience. The step-by-step instructions in the book give you a solid foundation in using Microsoft Visio 2010, while rich and varied online content, including video tutorials and audio sidebars, provide the following:

- Demonstrations of step-by-step tasks covered in the book
- Additional tips or information on a topic
- Practical advice and suggestions
- Direction for more advanced tasks not covered in the book

Here's a quick look at a few structural features designed to help you get the most out of this book.

- **Chapter objective:** At the beginning of each chapter is a brief summary of topics addressed in that chapter. This objective enables you to quickly see what is covered in the chapter.
- **Notes:** Notes provide additional commentary or explanation that doesn't fit neatly into the surrounding text. Notes give detailed explanations of how something works, alternative ways of performing a task, and other tidbits to get you on your way.
- **Tips:** This element gives you shortcuts, workarounds, and ways to avoid pitfalls.

LET ME TRY IT Let Me Try It tasks are presented in a step-by-step sequence so you can easily follow along.

SHOW ME Show Me videos walk you through tasks you've just got to see—including bonus advanced techniques.

TELL ME MORE Tell Me More audios deliver practical insights straight from the experts.

Special Features

More than just a book, your USING product integrates step-by-step video tutorials and valuable audio sidebars delivered through the **Free Web Edition** that comes with every USING book. For the price of the book, you get online access anywhere with a web connection—no books to carry, content is updated as the technology changes, and the benefit of video and audio learning.

About the USING Web Edition

The Web Edition of every USING book is powered by **Safari Books Online**, allowing you to access the video tutorials and valuable audio sidebars. Plus, you can search the contents of the book, highlight text, and attach a note to that text, print your notes and highlights in a custom summary, and cut and paste directly from Safari Books Online.

To register this product and gain access to the Free Web Edition and the audio and video files, go to **quepublishing.com/using**.

In this chapter, you learn about Visio's exciting versatility and capabilities. You create your first basic flowchart, see what features are new in Visio 2010, and learn the differences between the three editions of Visio 2010. You learn how to navigate Visio's user interface and some essential shortcuts for working more quickly.

1

Introducing Visio 2010

What Is Visio?

Did a box or DVD inscribed with "Visio 2010" just land on your desk? If so, you may be wondering, "What is Visio?"

If you ask around, you're likely to get short, quick answers—all of them different.

The responses I hear often go like this:

"It's a flow-charter!"

"Visio? Oh, that's a network diagramming tool."

"We use it for org charts."

All these answers are correct, but often people think of Visio as a tool for just one purpose. Visio is a versatile application for creating rich and diverse diagrams. With Visio, you can create an astonishing variety of visualizations that span a vast number of subjects, disciplines, and professions.

One of the early tenets of Visio philosophy, in existence since 1992, is that most people don't have the time or inclination to draw. Instead, they should *assemble* diagrams from preexisting, task-specific shapes.

In Visio, groups of related shapes are organized in *stencil* libraries. To start, you choose a Visio *template* appropriate to your discipline. A template opens with a preformatted drawing page, along with a set of stencils that contain the shapes you need to complete your diagram.

All you have to do is drag and drop!

TELL ME MORE **Media 1.1—About the Author and Why He Loves Visio**

Access this audio file through your registered Web Edition at ***my.safaribooksonline.com/9780132182683/media.***

Getting Started: Creating a Simple Flowchart

Visio is visual in nature and you will intuitively understand it if you *just do something*. Rather than discussing theory, let's just roll up our sleeves and get to diagramming.

Although Visio is capable of many types of diagrams, flowcharts and connected diagrams are its bread and butter. So we'll start with a simple flowchart. The idea is to assemble a diagram using premade task-specific shapes. You start with template that serves up a blank page and a palette of appropriate shapes.

For creating a flowchart, the process goes like this:

- Choose a template from the Backstage area.
- Drag shapes onto the page, connecting as you go.
- Add text to the shapes and branching connectors.
- Ensure that all steps are properly connected.
- Add a background and title.
- Choose a theme to add color and style to your diagram.
- Save or publish the diagram.

SHOW ME **Media 1.2—Creating a Simple Visio Flowchart**

Access this video file through your registered Web Edition at ***my.safaribooksonline.com/9780132182683/media.***

Now you try it! Create a flowchart, similar to the one made in the video, which is shown in Figure 1.1.

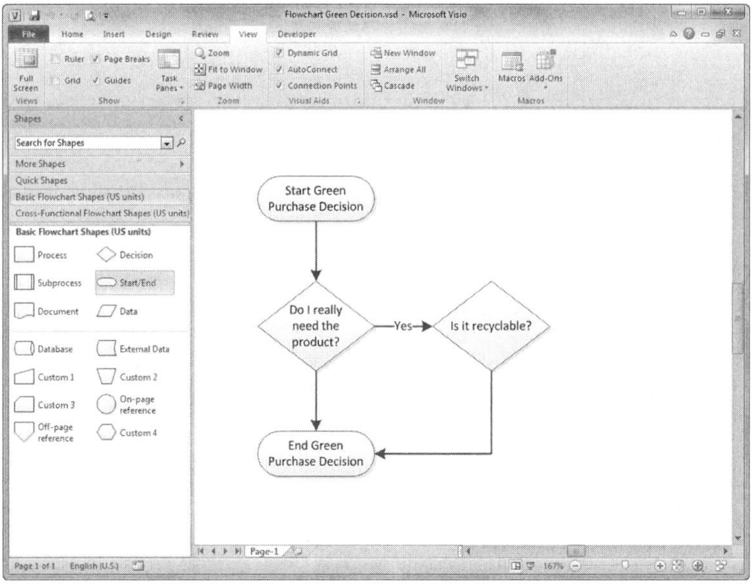

Figure 1.1 *A simple flowchart that depicts an environmentally-friendly decision-making process.*

LET ME TRY IT

Creating a Simple Visio Flowchart

1. Choose a template from the Backstage area. Go to File, New.
2. In Template Categories, click the Flowchart icon.
3. Inside the Flowchart category, click Basic Flowchart and then click the Create button on the far right. Alternatively, just double-click on Basic Flowchart.
4. From the Basic Flowchart Shapes stencil on the left, drag the Start/End shape onto the page. After you drop it, note the blue resizing handles indicating that the shape is selected.
5. With the shape still selected, start typing the text: "Start Green Purchase Decision". Adding text to Visio shapes is simply a matter of selecting and typing.

6. Hover over the Start shape until you see blue arrows pointing in all four directions. Then, mouse-over the bottom arrow until you see the mini-toolbar that displays four shapes.
7. Click on the diamond. A Decision shape is inserted directly below the Start shape, and a connector is added between them.
8. The Decision is now selected, so go ahead and type "Do I really need the product?" as its text.
9. Click-and-drag the Decision shape to move it around. Notice how the connector stays glued between the Start and Decision shapes.
10. Hover over the Decision shape until the blue arrows appear. Pause over the right arrow, then click the diamond in the mini-toolbar. Another Decision shape is added to the right of the first one, with a connector glued to both shapes.
11. Enter the text "Is it recyclable?" for the new Decision shape.
12. Click on the connector between the two Decisions to select it, then type "Yes". Connectors are normal shapes that you can select and add text to, just like the flowchart steps.
13. Hover over the first Decision shape until the blue arrows appear. You don't have to select it to get the arrows. Then go to the bottom arrow and click the Start/End shape that appears in the mini-toolbar. A Start/End shape is dropped and connected to the diamond.
14. Enter the text "End Green Purchase Decision" for the new shape's text.
15. Select the newly-added connector, then type "No" for its text. Your flowchart is almost complete. Notice that there is one connector missing, however. The second Decision shape needs to be connected to the End shape.
16. Hover over the second Decision shape until the blue arrows appear. This time click and drag the bottom arrow to the End shape. It is like you are pulling a connector out of the Decision shape. When you are over the End shape and see red highlighting around it, let the mouse up. A connector between the two shapes is created!
17. To spruce up the diagram, you can add backgrounds and change themes. Click on the Design tab in the Ribbon at the top of the window.
18. In the Backgrounds group, click the Backgrounds drop-down button. Click the World background. A background graphic of a map of the world is added to your flowchart. Note the new page tab at the bottom of the window that says "VBackground-1." Background graphics are added to

background pages, which we will discuss in Chapter 2, "Working Around the Diagram."

19. Note the Themes group on the Design tab, which shows several color and effect schemes. Pause your mouse over each item and see how your diagram changes. This is Live Preview in action. You can "try before you buy," so to speak, as Visio shows you how each theme will appear, before you actually click.

20. Notice the controls on the right side of the theme gallery. They let you scroll to more themes, or show a drop-down list so that you can select from a wider variety at once. Pick a theme that appeals to you. Notice how the fill color, shading, line-style, and text for the flowchart shapes and the background all tastefully change in unison.

Your first Visio flowchart is now complete, congratulations!

What Kinds of Diagrams Can Visio Create?

If you purchased Visio 2010 Premium, you have 65 templates at your disposal, right out of the box. Visio 2010 Professional has a few less templates; 62. Visio 2010 Standard is the least expensive edition, which comes with 24 templates.

You've already seen Visio's template gallery that appears when you start Visio. In Figure 1.2, note that there are several Template Categories that take you to related sets of templates.

If you click through each template category, you discover that Visio can handle an impressive variety of diagrams. In Table 1.1, I've done the work for you and compiled a list of the templates that come with the Premium edition of Visio 2010. If you have the Pro or Standard editions, some of these templates won't be available to you.

You can download even more templates from Office.com, and there are numerous websites that offer templates and shapes for free and for purchase. Here are a few of them:

Visio Guy (www.visguy.com) Chris Roth, Visio MVP

Visio Information (visio.mvps.org) John Marshall, Visio MVP

visLog (visualsignals.typepad.co.uk) John Goldsmith, Visio MVP

bVisual (davidjpp.wordpress.com/) David Parker, Visio MVP

Visimation (www.shapesource.com) Many different shapes and templates, some free, some for purchase.

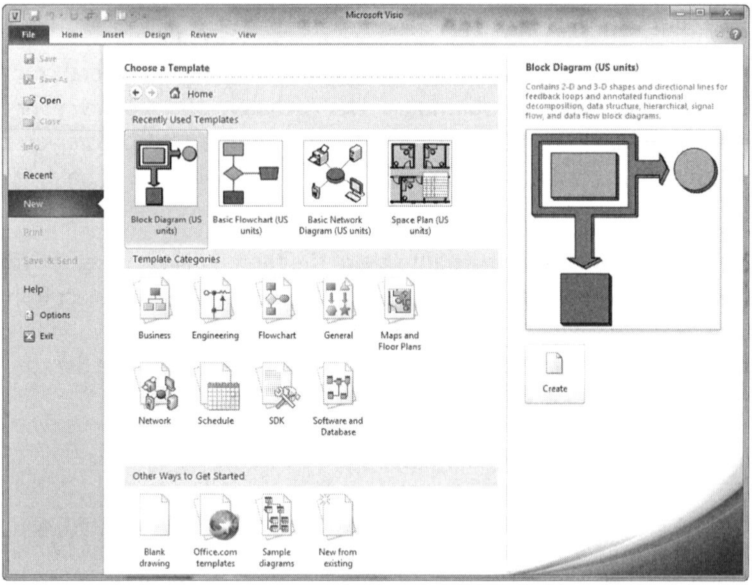

Figure 1.2 *Visio 2010's template gallery enables you to choose a template and quickly start diagramming.*

Table 1.1 Visio 2010 Premium Edition's Templates

Audit diagrams	Brainstorming diagrams
Cause-and-effect diagrams	Charts and graphs
EPC diagrams	Fault tree analysis diagrams
ITIL diagrams	Marketing charts and diagrams
Organizational charts	Pivot diagrams
Six sigma diagrams	TQM diagrams
Value stream maps	Basic electrical diagrams
Circuits and logic diagrams	Fluid power diagrams
Industrial control systems	Part and assembly drawings
Piping and instrumentation diagrams	Process flow diagrams
Systems diagrams	Diagrams to lay out furniture arrangements in your house and office
Cell-phone tower networks	Solar panel layout
Numerous organizational chart solutions	Exit paths for fire-safety procedures
Basic flowcharts	BPMN diagrams
Cross-functional flowchart (Swimlane) diagrams	IDEF() diagrams

Table 1.1 Visio 2010 Premium Edition's Templates

Microsoft SharePoint workflow diagrams	SDL diagrams
Workflow diagrams	Block diagrams
Perspective block diagrams	Directional maps
3D directional maps	Electrical and telecom plans
Floor plans	Home plans
HVAC control logic diagrams	HVAC plans
Office layouts	Plant layouts
Plumbing and piping plans	Reflected ceiling plans
Security and access plans	Site plans
Space plans	Active directory diagrams
Basic network diagrams	Detailed network diagrams
LDAP directory diagrams	Rack diagrams
Calendars	Gantt charts
PERT charts	Simple timelines
COM and OLE diagrams	Conceptual website diagrams
Data flow diagrams	Data flow model diagrams
Database model diagrams	Enterprise application diagrams
Program structure diagrams	UML model diagrams
Website maps	Wireframe diagrams

Just about every job or discipline can benefit from some form of visualization to help with designing, planning, configuring, brainstorming, and analyzing. There is likely some way Visio can help in just about every case.

And if there's no template or shape set for your need, you can always create your own.

ABOUT VISIO SMARTSHAPES

One characteristic that makes Visio special, and Visio diagramming more powerful, is SmartShape technology. Visio shapes can be much more than just symbols or clip-art. Shapes can have a variety of special features that make them more useful.

Shapes can employ parameterized geometry that help them to behave more intelligently. For example, the Start/End shape that you used in "Creating a Simple Visio Flowchart" maintains tasteful circular ends no matter how wide or narrow you make the shape. Clipart or images simply warp as you stretch them and look rather ugly. Similarly, the Document shape on the Basic Flowchart Shapes stencil maintains a consistent page tear, no matter how tall you make the shape.

SmartShapes can also carry data fields that can be linked to external data, used in reporting, or even control the appearance of the shape.

Some shapes have special yellow control handles that let you visually change the way a shape looks. Imagine being able to change the long and short hands on a clock shape just by pulling on control handles! Other shapes let you reposition the text block by pulling a control handle. This saves you the bother of going to the Home tab and getting the Text Block tool just to move shape text around.

And shapes can have custom right-click actions in their context menus that allow you to fine-tune appearance or invoke other advanced functionality.

You learn a lot more about how smart Visio shapes can be, and how to find the additional features, in Chapter 6, "Working with Individual Shapes."

Examples of What Visio Can Do

That huge list of templates in Table 1.1 gives you a good idea of the kinds of diagrams you can produce with Visio. Plus, you'll absorb a thorough understanding of Visio's capabilities while working through this book.

Since Visio is all about visualization, it is almost a crime to use words to describe what it can do. Instead, why not *see* for yourself what Visio can do. Try going to www.bing.com/images or www.google.com/images and typing "Visio." You'll get an eyeful.

In my experience with Visio, I've noticed three general groups of diagram types: connected diagrams, block diagrams, and measured drawings. This categorization is not hard and fast, but it might help you to better understand the Visio ecosystem.

Connected Diagrams

Connected diagrams consist of boxes or nodes connected by lines. They include flowcharts, network diagrams, mind maps, database diagrams, UML diagrams, wiring schematics, organizational charts, and more. Connected diagrams make heavy use of Visio's connector feature, along with layout and routing and other process-related features.

The organizational (org) chart in Figure 1.3 shows the breakdown of various energy sources. A huge portion of all Visio drawings are connected diagrams, and most of them are flowcharts, org charts, or network diagrams

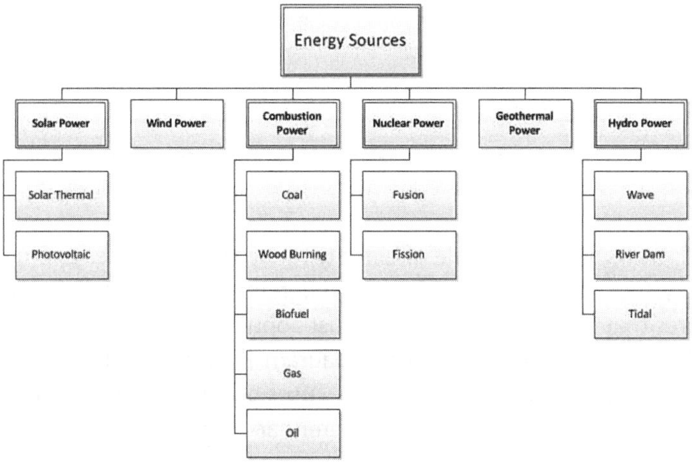

Figure 1.3 *An organizational chart can illustrate any hierarchy, not just the reporting structure of company personnel.*

Block Diagrams

Block diagrams is kind of a catchall name for anything that isn't a connected diagram or measured drawing. Many diagrams don't use connecting lines to establish relationships; they convey meaning through size, position, color, styling, and graphics instead.

Block diagrams benefit from Visio's easy-to-use drag-and-drop interface. Drawing from a large library of shapes, or even images from the Internet, you can easily pull and push shapes around the page and resize and format them in an infinite number of ways.

Figure 1.4 shows a block diagram that represents the same hierarchy as in Figure 1.3. In this diagram, the hierarchy flows from outermost elements to innermost elements. This diagram uses Visio 2010's new Containers feature, which you'll learn about in Chapter 3, "Organizing and Annotating Diagrams."

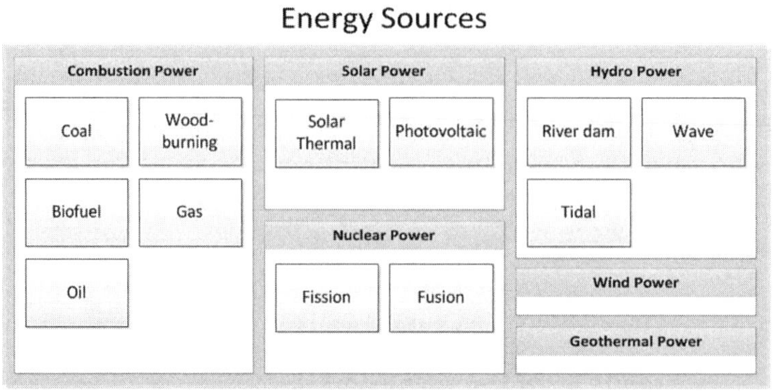

Figure 1.4 *Structure and meaning come from shape and position in a block diagram.*

Figure 1.5 shows a different style of block diagram that illustrates energy flow in a solar-cell system. This illustration is vastly different from the previous one and underscores that block diagrams can be just about anything. Although this example could easily have been a connected diagram, it uses a 3D effect to enhance the visual and add weight to the shapes. It also uses position to help illustrate sunlight coming down from the sky, as well as different arrow thicknesses to suggest quantities of energy loss through each step in the system.

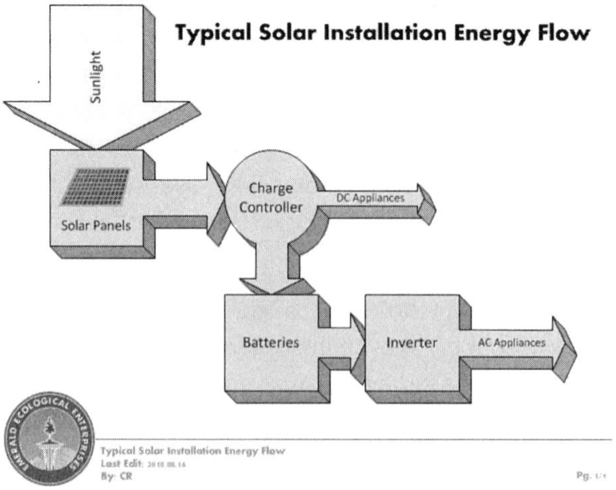

Figure 1.5 *The flow of energy in a typical solar installation, block diagram style.*

Measured Drawings

You can create measured, or scaled, drawings in Visio as well. They include office plans, space plans, site plans, elevation views, network rack diagrams, and plant layouts.

Measured drawings represent real-world, physical objects. For that reason, you work in a scale, such as 1:50 or 1" = 1′ – 0". Visio does the math for you, so you can think in real-world units and not waste time converting in your head.

When you drop a sofa shape into an office plan, like the one in Figure 1.6, you see in the status bar that the sofa shape is 7 feet long, even though it occupies only an inch or two on your screen!

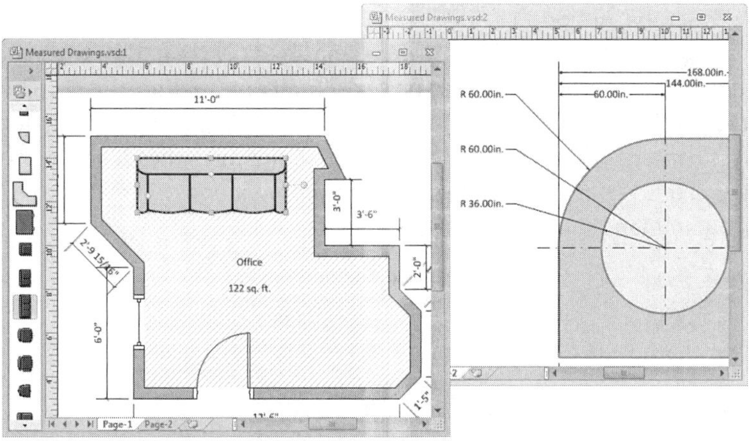

Figure 1.6 *Two different measured drawings, using dimension line shapes to indicate size. Note the status bar for the selected sofa shape indicates that it is 2 ft. 6 in. x 7 ft. The drawing is scaled, and the size of objects is reflected in real-world measurements.*

Of course, your diagrams can cross over category boundaries to use techniques and features from all three. For example, you could add network equipment shapes to a map of the USA and connect them. Each connector's text could display the distance between each piece of equipment, which could be significant for transmission times or signal loss. In such an example, you have a connected network diagram which uses block diagram positioning to convey geographical information, while distance information incorporates elements of scaling and real-world dimensions.

What Visio Isn't

Visio isn't a replacement for high-end CAD tools, it's not a 3D design tool, and you'll want to retain the folks in the graphic arts department when you need artistic visuals created with tools such as Adobe Illustrator.

I make that statement with fingers crossed behind my back, though. Visio can work very close to the 2D CAD realm, especially technical drawings that use a lot of symbols. Plus, Visio has built-in features that allow interoperation with AutoCAD files.

With a bit of creativity, you can produce some very artistic and attractive diagrams or drawings. And for the technically adept, Visio's SmartShape capability and programmability allow you to customize and automate Visio in ways that never cease to amaze.

Figure 1.7 shows a fictional company logo that I created for a few of the illustrations in this book. Although it was created in Visio, it represents atypical use of Visio. The mountain, tree, and tower were painstakingly created by tracing over imported images. Because Visio has no text-on-a-curve feature, the circular "Emerald Ecological Enterprises" text required complicated ShapeSheet programming to achieve. Chapter 11, "Developing Custom Visio Solutions," introduces the curious among you to the basics of ShapeSheet development and other ways to customize Visio programmatically.

Figure 1.7 *A company logo created with Visio requires power-user fervor and programmer's techniques to achieve.*

Understanding Visio 2010 Editions

As you've gathered already, Visio 2010 comes in three versions: Premium, Pro, and Standard.

Standard is the most inexpensive of the three and has the fewest features. It ships with 24 templates and despite sounding lean still offers first-class tools for creating flowcharts, network diagrams, block diagrams, office layouts, and more. This book is mainly targeted at users of Visio 2010 Standard, but I point out important features of the other editions where it seems appropriate.

The **Professional** edition adds a lot more content, with 62 templates. These templates dive deeper into the details of networking, engineering, software design, and floor and space planning, not to mention Pivot Diagrams. Many of these templates come with add-ins that bring additional functionality and features. With Pro, you also get Link Data and Data Graphics, which help you link data to shapes and then visualize that data via data-driven callouts, bar graphs, icons, and colors. Data graphics are discussed at the end of Chapter 7, "Working with Data."

Visio Premium is the top-end and most expensive edition that contains *everything*. You get 65 templates. On top of what Pro offers, there are templates for creating SharePoint workflows, BPMN diagrams, and Six Sigma diagrams. Premium also offers a slick SharePoint publishing feature (Visio Services for SharePoint 2010), automated creation of subprocesses, and diagram validation for process flows.

Documents created with all editions can be opened and edited by all other editions. The differences are mainly in the predefined content and editing tools for interacting with shapes and diagrams. For example, a Standard user can open a Visio Pivot Diagram and even select, move, and delete shapes. But they can't expand and contract nodes, or automatically change views, ordering and filtering the way a Pro or Premium user can.

What's New in Visio 2010?

Visio has been around since 1992, so you might have tinkered with older versions. If you haven't seen Visio for a while, you're in for a treat, as the list of improvements for 2010 is quite impressive.

Updated User Interface

Visio 2010 joins the rest of Microsoft Office by incorporating the Fluent UI user interface. This is comprised of the controversial Ribbon, the Quick Access Toolbar, the Backstage area and an improved status bar.

The Ribbon is a graphical version of the menu system that groups functions and features by task, is easy to scan visually, and reduces clutter by showing only those controls relevant to the current task. Love it or hate it at first, I think the Ribbon will grow on you. You'll learn more about the Fluent UI later in this chapter.

The new Shapes window is more efficient and compact. Stencils now have a selection of favorite shapes called Quick Shapes, and you can see all the Quick Shapes from open stencils in one convenient view.

Also new is the fantastic Live Preview feature, which lets you "try before you buy." Live Preview shows you how your diagram will look before you actually click on formatting control. You can now inspect how changes to line, fill, shadow, text, alignment, layout, and themes will look before you actually apply them.

Enhanced Diagramming Features

The improved Dynamic Grid shows you handy orange lines and arrows that help you align and equally space shapes as you drag.

New Container and List shapes allow you to associate related shapes together and add meaningful structure to diagrams without resorting to grouping. Shapes that belong to Containers are moved, duplicated and deleted with their Container.

Callout shapes are improved and smarter. They attach to shapes and move with them, making annotation of your diagrams easier and more efficient.

Connecting shapes is easier than ever. A mini toolbar gives you access to four Quick Shapes in the drawing area, so you don't even have to drag from a stencil. When shapes are deleted, associated connectors are also deleted. When steps are inserted into a flow, existing shapes are automatically slid out of the way to make room for the newcomer.

Auto Align & Space magically makes your flowcharts tidy by aligning and equally spacing shapes, and minimizing kinks in connectors.

The AutoSize page feature lets your connected drawings wander endlessly. As your diagram spills over the edge, new page tiles are added so that you never run out of paper.

Inserting, reordering, and managing pages is improved; much more can be accomplished from the page tab bar.

You now have finer control when pasting shapes. Pasting from the menu with Ctrl+V pastes shapes at their original location, while pasting via right-click drops them at the mouse location.

Content-specific Improvements

Users of all editions of Visio 2010 will enjoy improved swimlane management in cross-functional flowcharts. By using new Container and List shapes, reordering and inserting lanes is easier than ever.

If your organization uses SharePoint 2010, it comes with a Visio Process Repository site template that makes it easy to check process diagrams in and out and deal with versioning. You can interact with the repository directly from within Visio 2010.

For sharing information with the engineering department, Visio 2010 offers improved AutoCAD compatibility that allows you to import, save, and work with files from AutoCAD 2008.

Visio Pro Enhancements

Moving up the edition chain, Visio Pro adds the new Data Graphics Legends feature, which lets you instantly create visual legends that explain the meaning of Data Graphics applied to your shapes. This is especially useful for understanding icon sets and color by value Data Graphics.

Pro also includes the new Wireframe Diagrams template. It lets you create medium-fidelity user-interface designs for prototyping the look and layout of your software and Internet projects.

Visio Premium Enhancements

In addition to the gains of Visio Pro, Visio Premium users get even more!

New Subprocess functions make it easy to simplify complicated process flows. For example, at the click of a button, Visio will move a selected set of steps to a subpage, replace them with a single Subprocess shape, and then hyperlink it to the subpage. Single complicated flowcharts get broken into manageable, understandable pieces.

The new SharePoint Workflow diagrams template lets you create workflows that can be exported to SharePoint designer to aid in site creation. You can also import workflows and Visio will generate a diagram, so you can pass files back and forth between Visio and SharePoint Designer.

The BPMN Diagram template enables you to create business process diagrams that adhere to the Business Process Modeling Notation 1.2 standard.

Visio Premium introduces new diagram validation technology. You can now check process diagrams against a set of rules to ensure consistency and completeness.

Violations are brought to users' attention in the Issues window, which makes it easy to find and correct errors.

The new Six Sigma diagrams template allows you to create Six Sigma flowcharts and House of Quality diagrams.

With Visio Services for SharePoint 2010, you can publish interactive, data-connected diagrams to SharePoint 2010 sites. Users can view the diagram in a browser, even if they don't have Visio installed. They can pan and zoom the diagram and follow hyperlinks in shapes. When data changes, shapes update to reflect the changes.

Getting Around in Visio Using the Fluent UI

Fluent UI is Microsoft's name for the new way of piloting its flagship applications. The Fluent UI is composed of the Ribbon, Backstage area, Quick Access Toolbar, and the status bar. I think of it as the "controls around the edge" of the application window.

The Ribbon is the most noticeable component of the Fluent UI. If you've been using Office 2007 for a while, the Ribbon is nothing new for you. However, if Visio 2010 is your first upgrade in a while, you could be in for a shock!

The Ribbon

As PC applications got more and more complicated, the number of cascading menus and toolbar icons became unwieldy. Microsoft's answer was to invent the Ribbon.

The Ribbon is a hybrid system that combins menus and toolbars. You click what used to be main menu items but are now called "tabs," and the entire toolbar space switches to display tab-specific functions.

Each tab's controls and buttons are organized into groups. I find that the controls are often bigger and easier on the eyes, and the overall effect is less visually confusing. But getting used to the Ribbon might take some time if you're used to the older system of cascading menus and toolbars.

Ribbon Tabs

Visio 2010 Standard has six Ribbon tabs: File, Home, Insert, Design, Review and View. Visio Pro adds the Data tab, and Visio Premium adds the Process tab on top of that. You can see them in Figure 1.8.

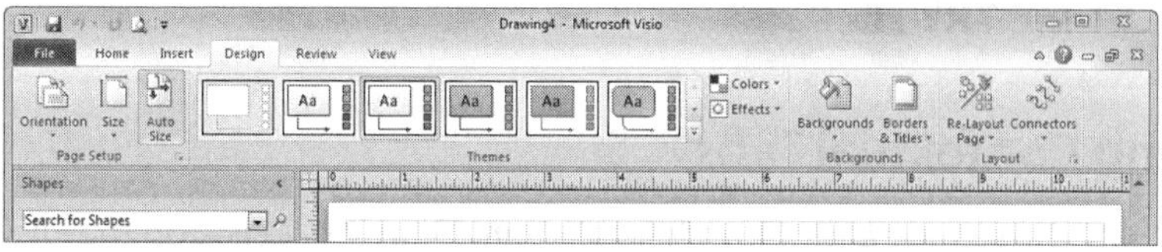

Figure 1.8 *Visio 2010 Standard's Ribbon, with the Design tab selected.*

There are a few more tabs that appear under certain circumstances. These are called contextual tabs. Visio 2010 has four of these: Picture Tools, Ink Tools, ShapeSheet Tools, and Container Tools.

Contextual Ribbon Tabs

Contextual tabs appear when their functions apply to the shape or shapes that you are working with in the Visio drawing window. For example, you can import photos into Visio and move them around like other shapes. When you select an image shape, the Picture Tools tab appears which offers image-specific functions. Figure 1.9 shows the Picture Tools contextual tab.

Figure 1.9 *The Picture Tools tab appears when the imported image is selected.*

If you look closely at Figure 1.9, you notice that "Picture Tools" is actually above a tab called "Format." Contextual tabs can appear as sets of tabs. You may have seen Excel 2010's Chart Tools set, which contains three tabs. All of Visio 2010's contextual tab sets only have one tab.

LET ME TRY IT

Showing Contextual Tabs

1. Start with a new Basic Flowchart diagram. Start Visio, click on the File tab, then click New in the left sidebar. Click Flowchart in the Template Categories area, then double-click Basic Flowchart. A new, blank, unsaved drawing appears with flowchart shapes in the stencil on the left.
2. Get an image to bring into your Visio drawing. Start your favorite web browser, and browse to a site with images. Right-click an image and choose "Copy" or "Copy Image."
3. In Visio, right-click anywhere on the drawing page and choose Paste. The image you copied from the web appears as a highlighted shape in your drawing. In the Ribbon, note the Picture Tools contextual tab appears.
4. Click Format under Picture Tools if it is not already selected. Notice the various image-specific controls that appear in the Ribbon, such as Brightness, Contrast, and AutoBalance.
5. Create several copies of your image. A shortcut for duplicating shapes is to hold down the Ctrl key, then drag a shape. This creates a copy at the point where you let up the mouse button.
6. Select all of the copies of your image. Hold down the Shift key, then click on each image. Or simply hold down the left mouse button and drag a rectangle around all of the shapes. You should see pink selection rectangles inside of an overarching blue rectangle, which indicates that multiple shapes are selected.
7. Click the Insert tab on the Ribbon.
8. Drop-down the Container list in the Diagram Parts group, and select any item. Your images have now all been assigned a Container. Note the Container Tools contextual tab appears.
9. Keep the Container shape selected. If you deselect it accidentally, note that you can select it only by clicking on its header or on its border, but not on blank space inside. Still on the Design tab, click the Heading Style drop-down button on the right side of the Container Styles group. Notice how the container's heading changes as you move the mouse over each item. That's Live Preview in action. You can click an item to change the heading for your container, or click a blank area in the drawing to cancel the operation and make no changes.

You've just seen two contextual tabs, and created your first Container. If you drag it around the page, notice that all of the shapes inside move along with it. You'll learn more about Containers in Chapter 3, "Organizing and Annotating Diagrams."

Template-specific Ribbon Tabs

There are also template-specific tabs that add extra functionality to particular drawing types. Look for them on the far right of the Ribbon. Depending on the template you open, and the edition of Visio you have, you might see these tabs: Brainstorming, Org Chart, Cross-functional Flowchart, Process Engineering, Plan, Calendar, Gantt Chart, Timeline, Database, UML, Web Site Map.

Template-specific tabs have commands that make sense for just that diagram. For example, the Organization Chart template adds the Org Chart tab and has buttons for rearranging subordinates. These functions wouldn't make sense for flowcharts or office plans, so it's nice they only appear with org charts.

Ribbon Controls

Most of the controls on the Ribbon tabs are familiar. You need no introduction to buttons, toggle buttons, drop-down lists, and so on. Two controls are worth a few words, however: galleries and dialog box launchers.

Galleries present visually rich lists of items. They can be dropped-down to reveal all or most of their contents, as shown in Figure 1.10. When not expanded, they show one row of items, as you saw in Figure 1.9. If there is a particular row of items in the gallery that you like, you can scroll to it using the scroll bars on the right side of the gallery, and it stays put. You don't have to drop-down the gallery any more to get to your favorites.

In the pre-Ribbon era, three dots at the end of a menu item told you that a dialog would pop up if you clicked it. How many menu items like "Options..." have you seen in your life?

In Visio 2010, you still see the ellipsis at the end of drop-down lists and in right-click menus, but you don't see "..." anywhere on the Ribbon itself. Instead, look for the dialog box launcher control, which is a tiny box with a diagonal arrow, located in the lower-right corner of a group of controls.

In Figure 1.10, the Page Setup group and Layout group each have a dialog box launcher control. Click this box, and a dialog pops up, offering a full set of options that were too numerous to stuff into the group.

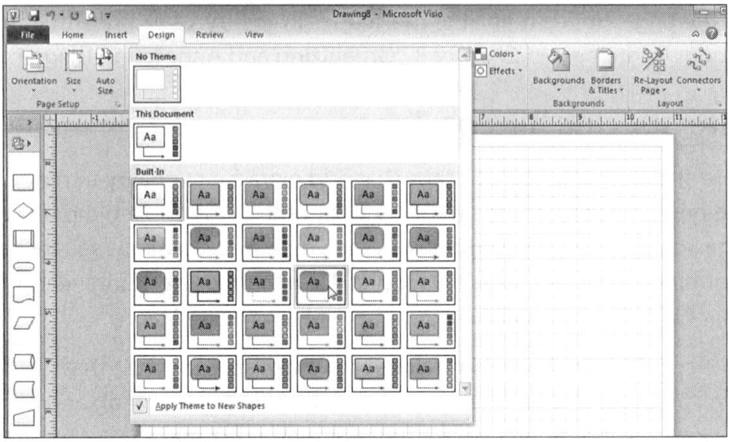

Figure 1.10 *The theme gallery in its expanded state. Note also the dialog box launcher controls in the Page Setup and Layout groups.*

Customizing the Ribbon

You can create custom Ribbon tabs and groups that contain your favorite commands. Start by choosing File, Options then clicking Customize Ribbon in the Visio Options dialog that appears. Alternatively, right-click anywhere on the ribbon and choose "Customize the Ribbon."

You see a big list of commands that can be filtered by picking an item from the "Choose commands from" drop-down list. Select a command from the list, then select a target group within a main tab from the list on the right. Click Add, and the command is added to the group.

You can't add commands to Visio's built-in groups, so you have to add a custom group to an existing tab, or create an entirely new tab with custom groups.

Notice also the nifty Reset and Import/Export buttons. If you make a mess of your Ribbon, it's easy to return it to its original state. And if you create the perfect customization, you can export an XML file to share with your coworkers, or just keep it as a backup.

If you need more screen real estate while diagramming, you can collapse the Ribbon so just the tab names are visible. Click the arrow at the far right of the window, next to the Help question mark. Now your Ribbon looks a like a main menu from an old-style application.

If you click a tab, its full set of controls appears long enough for you click one of them.

Finding Commands in the Ribbon

If you've been using Visio for years and the old menus and toolbars are firmly ingrained in your bones, you might have trouble finding commands.

Fortunately, Microsoft and others have tried to ease the pain by providing look-up systems and other menu-to-Ribbon translating tools. The following article points you to several resources for bridging the menu-to-ribbon gap:

- Menus to Ribbons: Find Commands in Office 2010 at www.visguy.com/2010/06/23/menus-to-ribbons-find-commands-in-office-2010/

There is also help from within Visio.

1. Go to the Customize Ribbon screen.
2. Choose "All Commands" from the "Choose commands from" drop-down list.
3. Pause the mouse over items in the list. A ToolTip will appear indicating where the item is located, or that it isn't in the Ribbon.

For example, hovering over "Size & Position" reveals the tooltip: "View Tab | Show | Size & Position (SizeAndPostionWindow)."

However, hovering on "Reset Connector" reveals: "Commands Not in the Ribbon | Reset Connector (ResetConnector)." Meaning you won't find it in the Ribbon, but can find it in the "Commands Not in the Ribbon" list, even though you have already found it in the "All Commands" list.

The Quick Access Toolbar

Although the Ribbon does a good job of grouping related tasks together, you will find that there are certain functions that you need to use a lot—so much so that the two steps of clicking on a Ribbon tab and then searching for a function becomes tiring and annoying.

Luckily, you can add your favorite and most frequently used functions to the Quick Access Toolbar.

The Quick Access Toolbar is a little row of icons located just above the Ribbon, on the left side of the Visio application window. By default, it shows the save, undo, and redo commands.

There are a number of ways to add functions to the Quick Access Toolbar:

1. Right-click on any Ribbon control and select Add to Quick Access Toolbar.
2. Right-click anywhere on the ribbon or Quick Access Toolbar and choose Customize Quick Access Toolbar. This opens a chooser dialog that lets you add commands from a list on the left to the set of Quick Access Toolbar commands on the right.

For example, sometimes I work with imported images in Visio and need to do a lot of cropping. The Crop tool is located on the Picture Tools contextual tab, which appears only when you select an image. Furthermore, the Crop tool goes away as soon as I select a different shape, reverting to the Pointer tool. Putting the Crop tool on the Quick Access Toolbar saves me the trouble of repeatedly selecting the Picture Tools tab just to get to the Crop tool.

Removing commands from the Quick Access Toolbar is similar to adding them:

1. Right-click on a Quick Access Toolbar icon and choose Remove from Quick Access Toolbar.
2. Right-click anywhere on the Ribbon or Quick Access Toolbar and choose Customize Quick Access Toolbar. In the chooser dialog, highlight commands in the list on the right, and click the Remove button.

You can also customize the Quick Access Toolbar by using the drop-down arrow at the right end of the Quick Access Toolbar. You can see the arrow just after the Crop tool in Figure 1.11. This Customize Quick Access Toolbar list offers a fixed selection of popular commands that you can quickly check on or off, including New, Open, Save, Email, Quick Print, Print Preview, Spelling, Undo, Redo, and Open Recent File.

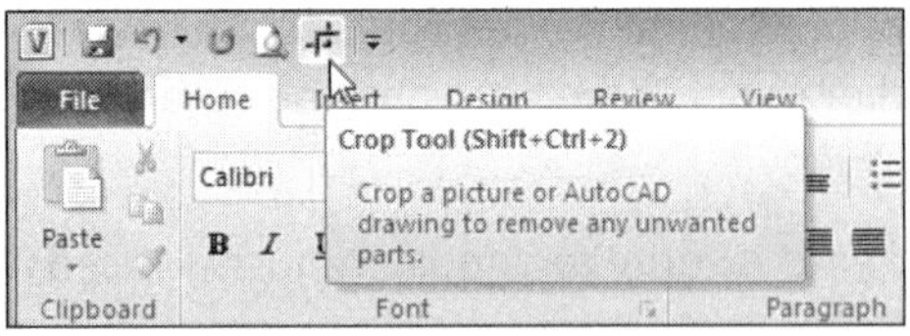

Figure 1.11 *The Quick Access Toolbar with Print Preview and the Crop tool added to it.*

From this list, you can also change the position of the Quick Access Toolbar. It can be placed either below or above the Ribbon. Placing the Quick Access Toolbar below the Ribbon makes a lot of sense. Because Quick Access Toolbar functions are ostensibly used often, putting them closer to the drawing area saves you time and movement. But you use up more screen real estate than a top-oriented toolbar, which makes efficient use of the mostly-empty window header.

Right-click Context Menus

Consistent with Windows and Microsoft applications in general, you can get a lot done by right-clicking in Visio. The context menu that appears when you right-click a shape offers many useful functions including cut, copy and paste, grouping, containing, managing front-to-back positioning, and hyperlinking. There are also cascading menu items that lead you to various data-related features and to the line, fill, and text formatting dialogs.

You also see a mini-toolbar above the context menu that gives you visual access to many common formatting functions, including font family, size and style, front-to-back controls, and line, fill, and text formatting drop-downs.

Finally, many Visio SmartShapes have custom items in the context menu. For example, flowchart shapes have options that restore shapes to default sizes or cause shapes to automatically expand to accommodate increasing amounts of text. Other shapes offer choices for fine-tuning appearance or selecting from a variety of built-in symbols.

If you're an avid right-clicker, you'll find plenty of useful stuff in Visio's context menus. If you're not, you might consider becoming one!

The Backstage Area

One oddball tab in the Ribbon doesn't behave like the others: the File tab. Clicking File opens a full-page screen called the Backstage area. You've been there already. You see it when you start Visio, and you visit it when you start a new drawing, or save a modified one.

Once in the Backstage, you navigate by using the list of items on the left. Some items pop up dialog boxes, others change the contents of the pane on the right. Figure 1.12 shows the Help area of the Backstage.

The Backstage area is your Visio command center—a place to handle all your non-drawing operations. Here's a quick list of things it helps you to do:

- Starting new drawings and opening existing files
- Saving files
- Setting document information such as Creator, Title, and so on
- Reducing file size and removing sensitive information from documents before distribution

- Printing
- Publishing to the Web, PDF, or exporting to other formats
- Sending as email attachments
- Accessing Help
- Setting numerous options
- Exiting the application

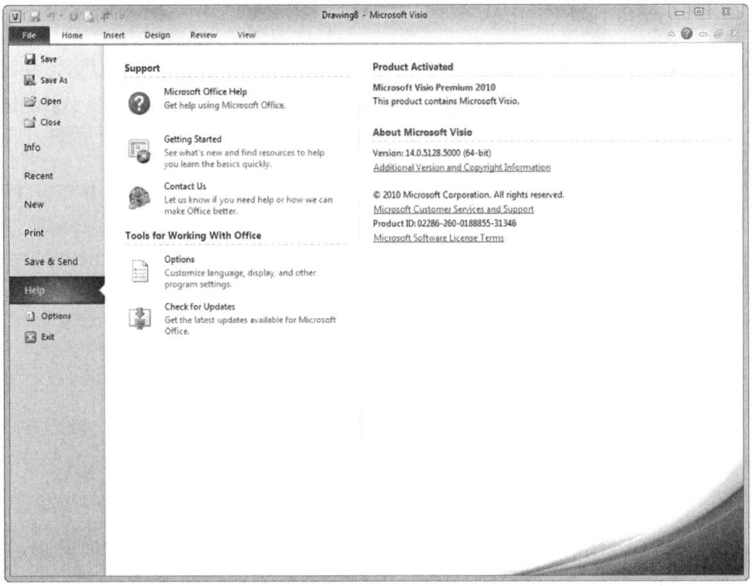

Figure 1.12 *The Backstage area, with Help selected.*

We'll revisit the Backstage numerous times throughout this book and discuss individual features in detail.

Status Bar

The status bar runs across the bottom of the Visio application window. Its elements are very similar to what you see in other Microsoft Office applications.

On the left side are mostly informational items. Here you find a readout that tells you:

- Which page you are on out of total page count
- The width, height and angle of the selected shape

- The current language setting, such as English (U.S.)
- A button for recording macros in the Visual Basic for Applications (VBA) programming language. VBA is the same language used for macros in all the other Office applications.

On the right side of the status bar are controls that help you with zooming, panning, and managing windows. From left to right, you see the following items, as shown in Figure 1.13:

- Normal and Full Screen view toggle buttons
- Numerical Zoom level button (such as 50%, 100%, 200%)
- Zoom level slider control
- Fit Page to Current Window button
- Show Pan & Zoom window toggle button
- Switch Windows button

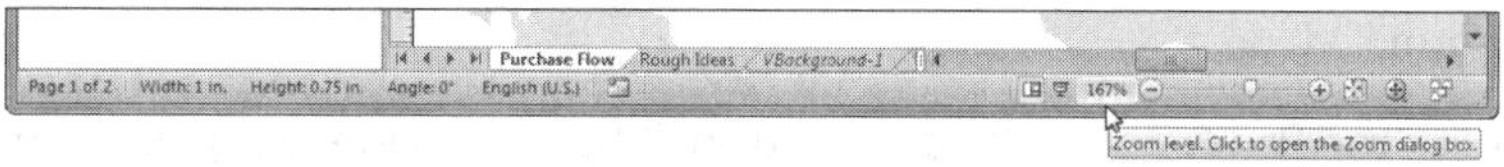

Figure 1.13 *Visio's status bar with the Zoom Level control's ToolTip showing.*

As with most things Visio and Microsoft, if you're not sure what something does, just pause your mouse over it and a ToolTip displays.

SHOW ME **Media 1.3—Panning and Zooming a Diagram Using the Status Bar and Pan & Zoom Window**

Access this video file through your registered Web Edition at ***my.safaribooksonline.com/9780132182683/media.***

LET ME TRY IT

Panning and Zooming a Diagram Using the Status Bar and Pan & Zoom Window

1. Start with an existing sample drawing, supplied with Visio. Go to File, New.
2. At the bottom of the screen, under "Other Ways to Get Started," click "Sample diagrams." A selection of pre-drawn samples appears in the Choose a template gallery.

3. Double-click "IT Asset Management." A new, unsaved copy of the sample opens. You can tell that it is unsaved because you see a name like "Drawing1" at the top of the Visio window.
4. In the lower-left of the status bar, note that you are on "Page 1 of 3."
5. Select any shape in the drawing area. The shape's width, height, and angle are displayed in the status bar. Select a differently-sized shape and watch the values change.
6. Drag the zoom slider on the right of the status bar. Notice how the drawing details get larger or smaller as you drag towards the "+" or "-".
7. Click the zoom Level Button. It's to the left of the "-", and has a number with "%" after it. The Zoom dialog appears, allowing you to choose from standard zoom levels or enter a custom value.
8. Click the Full Screen button to the left of Zoom Level. The Visio drawing occupies the entire screen. Note that clicking in full screen mode advances to the next page in the document. Right-click to go to the previous page, a specific page, or exit full screen mode. You can also type Esc to return to normal view.
9. Click the Pan & Zoom Window button. It has the magnifying glass icon with the arrows inside. The Pan & Zoom task pane appears, showing a thumbnail of the current page's contents.
10. You can drag the Pan & Zoom window around, dock and anchor it to sides of the Visio window, or leave it floating. Take a moment to drag it around and see how it snaps into place as you near sides and corners of the drawing window.
11. You can zoom using the vertical slider in the Pan & Zoom window. Notice the red rectangle that appears and shrinks as you increase the zoom level. At the same time, the contents of the drawing window are also zoomed.
12. You can zoom by directly resizing the red rectangle itself. Just pull on a side or corner to make it bigger or smaller. As it grows, Visio zooms the drawing out. As it shrinks, the you zoom in.
13. To pan the drawing, drag the red rectangle around the Pan & Zoom window.

Working in the Visio Drawing Window

You've seen the pleasant-looking Fluent UI and likely found it very similar to other Microsoft Office applications. Now let's turn our attention to the Visio-specific elements of the user interface, most of which you find inside of the Visio drawing window.

Figure 1.14 shows a flowchart where the user has decided to add network shapes to visually accent particular steps. Let's take a brief tour of the elements in the window.

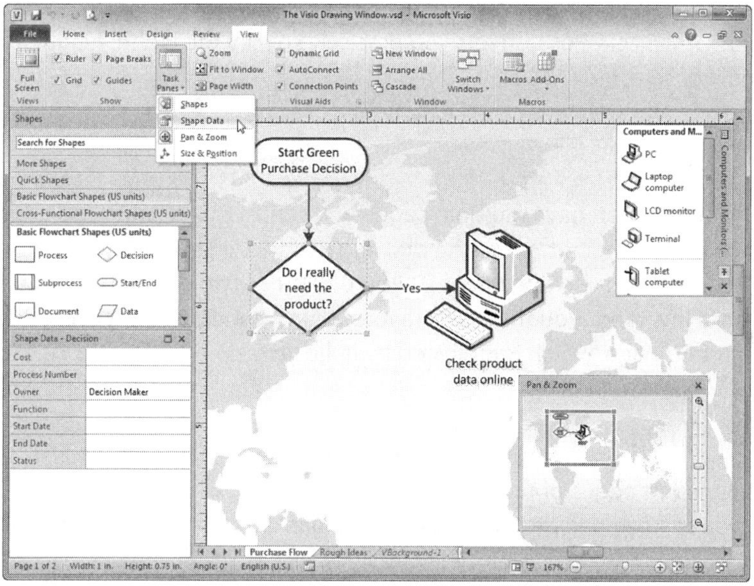

Figure 1.14 *Stencils on the left of the drawing window serve up shapes for your diagrams.*

Task Panes

Visio has several task pane windows that organize shapes and help you to edit diagrams. The figure shows the expanded Task Panes drop-down list which lets you show and hide four different mini-windows.

Docked to the left side of the window is the Shapes task pane, which manages open stencils and their Quick Shapes, offers a search bar and access to more stencils via More Shapes. The Basic Flowchart Shapes stencil is currently showing, but clicking on other stencil tabs reveals the contents of other stencils.

You can tear off stencils and float them or dock them to other sides of the window. In Figure 1.14, you see that the Computers and Monitors stencil has been torn off and docked to the upper right corner of the window.

The Shape Data window is docked at left, beneath the Shapes window. Shape Data displays data fields for selected shapes and also allows you to edit their values. In Figure 1.14, you see process-related Shape Data fields for the selected diamond shape.

In the lower-right corner, you recognize the Pan & Zoom task pane from the previous Let Me Try It exercise. It is floating freely, and isn't docked.

The last task pane in the drop-down list is the Size & Position, which is not showing in Figure 1.14. Size & Position lets you precisely specify the width, height, position, and angle of selected shapes.

Page Tabs

Visio documents can have multiple pages. You can easily navigate and add pages using the tabs at the bottom of the drawing window, just as you navigate sheets in an Excel workbook. The document in Figure 1.14 has two pages, but three tabs. "Purchase Flow" and "Rough Ideas" are foreground pages, while "VBackground-1" is a background page, which is indicated by italic text.

Ruler & Grid

The top and left edges of the drawing area in Figure 1.14 display the ruler. This allows you to keep perspective when zooming in and out, and is particularly useful for scaled drawings such as office layouts. You can pull horizontal and vertical guides out of the rulers to which shapes can be glued (not shown). This makes it easy to keep a whole row of shapes lined up.

Not shown in Figure 1.14 is the grid, but you likely saw it when you created your first flowchart. The grid is helpful for quickly aligning shapes both visually and via snapping. Unfortunately, graphics on background pages obscure the grid.

Notice in Figure 1.14 that the View tab is showing. In the "Show" group, check boxes allow you to hide and show the Ruler and Grid.

Multiple Drawing Windows

The View tab contains the "Windows" group that has controls which let you manage multiple windows. You can open multiple documents in Visio, or open multiple windows to the same document—even to the same page. Being able to switch windows or arrange them is vital, and the controls of the Windows group help you to do this.

Getting a Handle on Shapes

Continuing our march from outermost user-interface elements to innermost, we finally land on the drawing page itself, where you manipulate shapes by dragging on handles.

You have noticed the selection handles that appear around shapes when you select them. Handles let you know that a shape is selected, and they also let you change the size and rotation shape.

Selection handles are blue, but they can turn red when they are glued to other shapes and gray when they are locked.

Some shapes have extra control handles, which are yellow. These let you graphically manipulate individual parts of a shape.

You will experience quite a variety of shape handles as you use Visio. But don't worry about memorizing them all or wondering what they all do. You can just select a shape, pull on a handle, and see what happens. If you don't like the result, just hit undo.

There are two types of resizing handle sets, which depend on the shape's purpose. "2D shapes" are box-like and have handles altering width, height, and rotation angle. Shapes such as lines, connectors, and arrows are called "1D shapes." They have handles that let you change location of their begin and end points. The rotation angle follows naturally from the placement of these ends.

Generally, you manipulate shapes using the Pointer Tool, which you will find in the Tools group on the Home tab. But there is a bit of overlap in tool functionality. If you are using other tools, such as the Rectangle, Ellipse, Connector, Pencil or Line tool, you can still pull on handles and edit shapes to some extent. Generally it is easiest to use the Pointer tool, however.

SHOW ME **Media 1.4—A Whirlwind Tour of Visio Shape Handles**
Access this video file through your registered Web Edition at ***my.safaribooksonline.com/9780132182683/media.***

2D Shape Handles

Figure 1.15 shows how the mouse cursor looks when dragging a shape and manipulating its 2D handles. You can independently resize the width and height of a shape by pulling the square handles at the midpoint of each side.

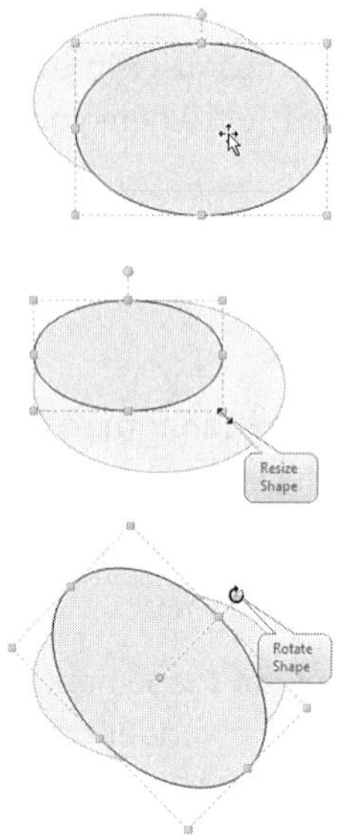

Figure 1.15 *Crosshairs indicate that you can move a shape. Eight square handles let you change the width and height, and the "lollipop" lets you rotate a shape.*

You can also change width and height simultaneously by pulling one of the corner handles. Visio preserves the aspect ratio of the shape when you pull on a corner, so that the width to height proportion is preserved. Holding the Shift key while dragging a corner handle overrides this behavior.

You rotate a shape by dragging the "lollipop" handle, shown at the bottom of Figure 1.14. Note the rotation point that appears when you mouse-over the rotation handle. You can also move this point and change the center of rotation for the shape.

1D Shape Handles

Some shapes are defined by starting and ending points, with width and height taking a secondary role. Arrows, lines and connectors are typical examples of shapes that make sense as "1D."

Figure 1.16 shows several 1D shapes. Notice that all three have square handles at either end. These are the Begin and End handles that define where the shapes start and end. The empty square is the Begin, and the shaded square is the End.

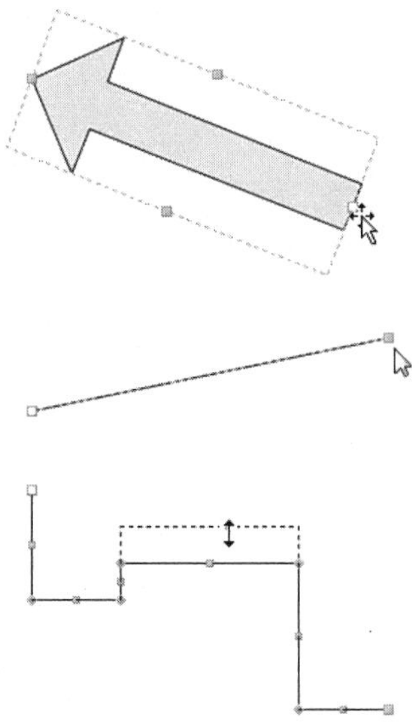

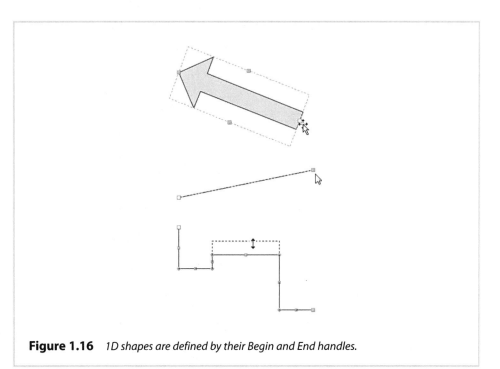

Figure 1.16 *1D shapes are defined by their Begin and End handles.*

You also see two height handles on the arrow shape, that let you adjust its thickness, but the line shape doesn't have height handles. The connector at the bottom has several handles at each vertex and midpoint which let you fine-tune its path. These are specific to connectors only, and you learn more about these in Chapter 6, "Working with Individual Shapes."

The ends of 1D shapes can be glued to other shapes and connection points, so that they stay connected when the other shapes are moved around. When shapes are glued, their handles turn red, indicating that they are attached. You learn more about connecting, glue and connection points in Chapter 4, "Connecting Shapes."

Control Handles

Some shapes have extra parts that can be adjusted, in addition to width, height and angle, or begin and end points.

These shapes employ Control Handles, which appear as little yellow diamond handles. You can pull on them to adjust a wide variety of extras that Visio shapes might have. If you see a control handle, but aren't sure what it's for, you can pause the mouse over it to reveal a tip that tells you more about the handle's purpose.

Figure 1.17 shows several shapes that have control handles, and illustrates their helpful ToolTips.

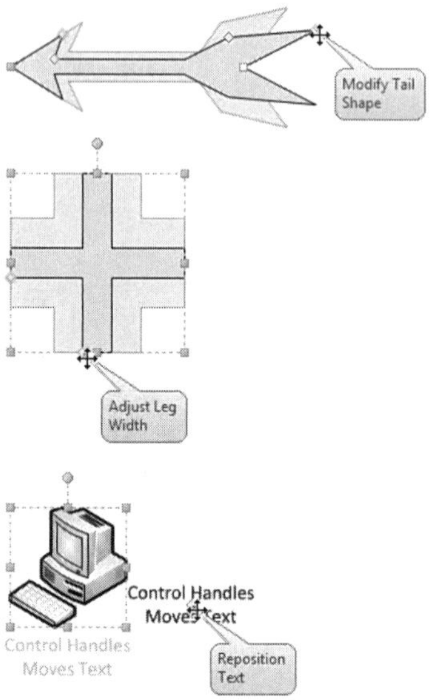

Figure 1.17 *These shapes employ control handles to change geometry or reposition text.*

Vertex Handles

If you select a shape using the Line, Pencil, Freeform, or Arc tools, you see vertex and midpoint handles. With the line tool, you will only see the vertices at each corner of the shape. With the pencil tool, you will also see midpoints that let you adjust the curvature of a segment, as seen in Figure 1.18.

Other Shape Handles

Occasionally, a shape designer will lock a shape from being resized in a particular direction. If you see gray selection handles, then they are locked. When you mouse-over them, you won't see the arrow cursor that tells you that resizing is possible.

Some shapes consist of simpler shapes grouped together. To get at the "sub-shapes," you can subselect individual members. Visio presents slightly different handles for subselected shapes. You learn more about subselecting in Chapter 3, "Organizing and Annotating Diagrams."

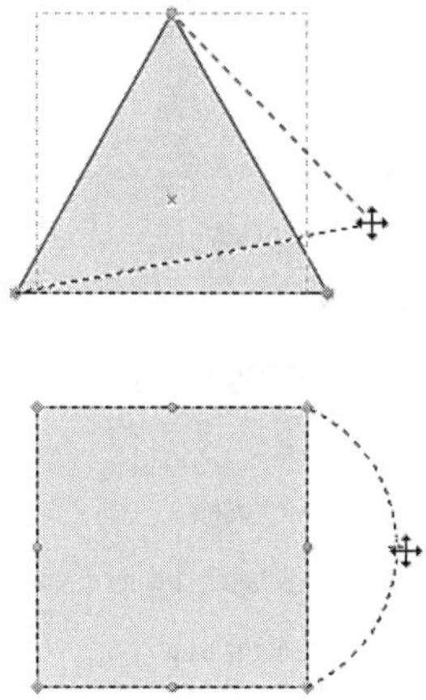

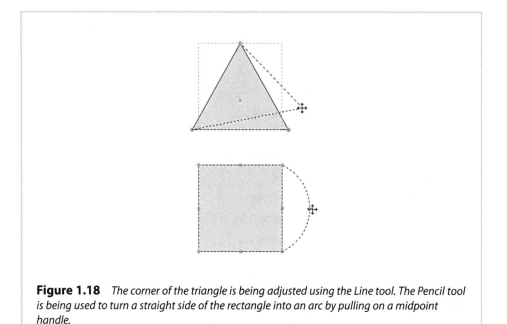

Figure 1.18 *The corner of the triangle is being adjusted using the Line tool. The Pencil tool is being used to turn a straight side of the rectangle into an arc by pulling on a midpoint handle.*

Working Faster with Keyboard Shortcuts

It may seem odd to talk about power user keyboard shortcuts in an introductory chapter, but with Visio, I feel it is important. Over the years, I've watched many beginners struggle with Visio and noticed their mixed feelings toward the application. The main problem was awkwardness when moving around the drawing and manipulating shapes. Trying to do everything with toolbar buttons and scroll bars was difficult, distracting, and unnecessary.

In Visio, you need to constantly zoom in and out, pan to different locations, and adjust shapes. If you can't do these fluidly and without thinking, you become distracted from the task you really wanted to accomplish. It makes you tired and cranky! For these reasons, I introduce a set of "magic" keyboard shortcuts and techniques that alleviate awkwardness and help your diagramming flow more naturally. You involve your non-mouse hand to operate modifier keys and become a Two Handed User. It can make the difference between night and day!

So take a few moments to try out and master these keyboard shortcuts. Become a two-handed user and stop consciously thinking about how to move around the diagram. Seriously! Stop reading and learn at least the first ten items in Table 1.2.

Table 1.2 Top Keyboard Shortcuts for Working Faster with Visio

To Do This	Do This
Zoom in	Ctrl + Shift + Left Click
Zoom in	Ctrl + Roll forward
Zoom out	Ctrl + Shift + Right Click
Zoom out	Ctrl + Roll backward
Zoom to area	Ctrl + Shift + Left drag rectangle
Select all shapes on a page	Ctrl + A
Select multiple shapes	Shift + click on each shape
Select multiple shapes	Left mouse drag rectangle around desired shapes
Deselect shapes	Click a blank area of the page
Deselect shapes	Press ESC
Duplicate shapes	Select shapes, then press Ctrl + D
Duplicate shapes	Select shapes, then Ctrl + drag
Edit existing shape text	Double-click the shape. If this doesn't work, select the shape and press F2.
Repeat an action	Press F4 to repeat the last action. Great for repeating a duplication over and over.
Return to the Pointer Tool	Press Ctrl + 1
Save your diagram	Ctrl + S
Explore special features of SmartShapes	Right-click the shape. This is a good habit to develop, as you never know what you might discover!

Summary

In this chapter, you learned what Visio is, what it does, and how to do it. You were introduced to the editions and new features of Visio 2010, and you learned the incredible variety of diagrams that can be created with Visio.

You jumped right in by creating your first flowchart and experienced Visio's easy-to-use drag-and-drop diagramming metaphor. In a matter of minutes, you were able to drag pre-made master shapes from a stencil onto a drawing, connect the steps, add text to them, and quickly assemble a simple decision-making flowchart.

You were introduced to Visio's user-interface from the outside in, starting with the Fluid UI, the Ribbon, Backstage area, Quick Access Toolbar, moving on to Visio-specific task panes and window elements, and finally seeing the variety of selection and resizing handles that allow you to manipulate shapes on the page.

Finally you were exposed to essential keyboard shortcuts that will speed your navigation of diagrams and make it second nature.

In this chapter, you learn how to manage and work with templates, drawing files, documents, pages, backgrounds, themes, stencils, and master shapes.

2

Working Around the Diagram

You will spend the majority of your Visio life dropping, moving, resizing, formatting, connecting, and adding text to shapes. But all that work will be easier if you understand the bits and pieces that surround the diagram and complete the Visio story.

Getting Started with a New Drawing

You can create a new Visio document in several ways. You briefly saw the template gallery and used the Basic Flowchart template in the preceding chapter. Now, take a look at templates and the various other ways to start new diagrams.

Navigating the Template Gallery

When you start a new Visio drawing, the first place to go is the Backstage area. Click File and then select New from the list on the left, and you see Visio's template gallery, as shown in Figure 2.1.

Right away, you notice the major areas of this screen. From top to bottom in the middle panel are: Recently Used Templates, Template Categories, and Other Ways to Get Started. On the right, there's a big preview area, with a Create button underneath that screams "Click Me!"

Templates that you frequently access will appear in the Recently Used Templates at the top, but all templates can be found using Template Categories in the middle.

One thing can be a bit confusing at first. When you are at the top level, the icons in Template Categories appear blue and have a "sheet of paper" look. These icons serve as folders that contain more templates. Click one, and you drill down into the folder and see a list of templates for that category.

Figure 2.2 shows the template icons inside the Maps and Floor Plans category for Visio Premium. If you have the Standard edition, you see only three templates.

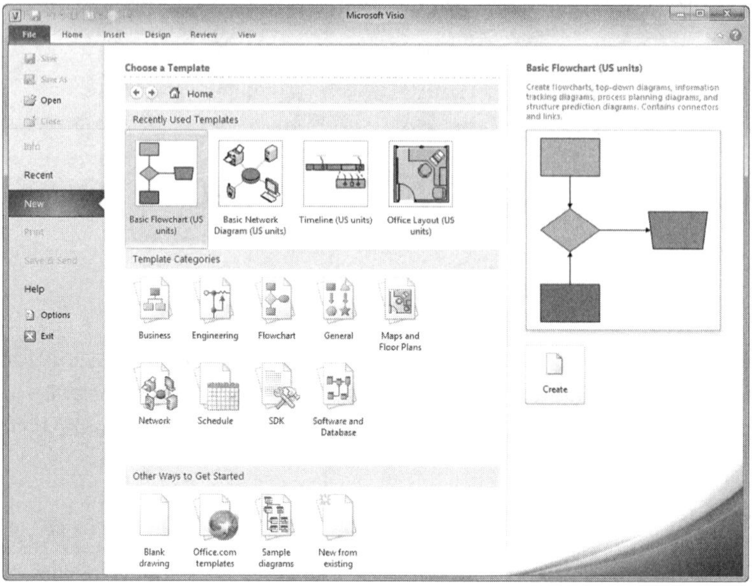

Figure 2.1 *The Home view of Visio 2010 Premium's template gallery.*

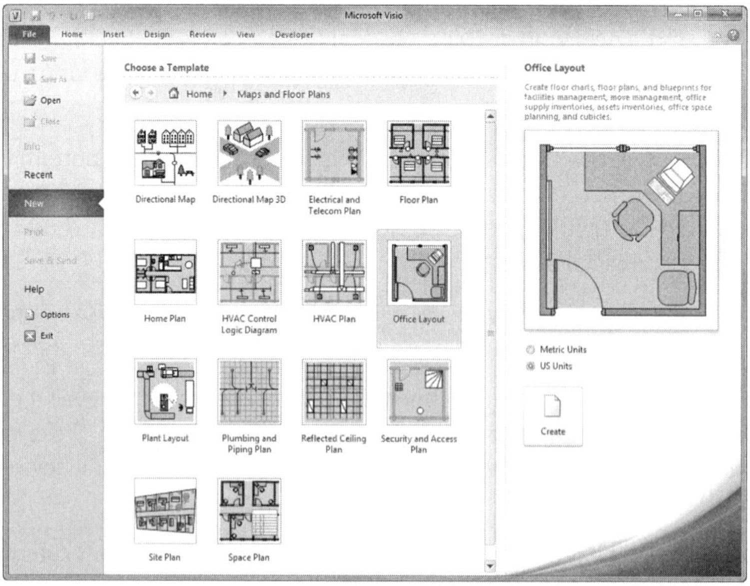

Figure 2.2 *Diving into Visio 2010 Premium's Maps and Floor Plans template category gallery.*

Inside a category, the blue icons and the Template Categories bar disappear. In roughly the same place, you now see larger, more-detailed, full-color icons that represent actual templates. It can take a bit of time to get used to this difference: Big, colored icons represent actual templates; smaller blue icons with document motifs represent template categories at the higher level. Take a moment to contrast Figures 2.1 and 2.2.

When you click on a template icon, the preview area shows a zoomed view of the icon, along with a description of the template. This gives you a clear idea of what you can create with the template. To start, just click the Create button or double-click the template icon itself. A new, unsaved copy of a drawing based on that template then appears in the Visio drawing window.

If the category doesn't have the template you need, you can go back one level by clicking the Back button near the top of the page or by clicking the Home button. From there you can dive into a different category of templates.

Just above the Create button are two radio buttons: Metric Units and US Units. Most of the world outside the United States uses A4-sized paper with millimeters or centimeters as the measuring system, instead of 8 ½" × 11", letter-sized paper measured in inches.

If you select Metric Units before clicking Create, your template opens with a metric ruler and grid, A4 paper, and shapes created to be metric friendly.

What Happens When You Start from a Template?

When you start a drawing from a template, a few things happen:

- You get a new, "blank" document that is an unsaved copy of the original template.
- The document's rulers, grid, measuring system, and page size are appropriate to the drawing type and unit system you've chosen.
- Several stencils are opened that present you with palettes of shapes for completing the drawing. Stencils are separate files in themselves but are conveniently displayed in the Shapes area in docked, stacked panels.
- A custom add-in Ribbon tab might be loaded, as discussed in Chapter 1, "Introducing Visio 2010." Some templates require extra functionality from add-in modules. These modules often add an extra tab on the far right of the Ribbon for accessing their functions. For example, the Organization Chart and Cross-Functional Flowchart templates open with custom Ribbon tabs that give you access to special features.

Templates don't have to be blank. It makes a lot of sense for a template to have titles, borders, company logos, background pages, and some starting shapes already on the page to get you up and running even more quickly. However, almost every template that comes with Visio 2010 starts out with a blank page. Not to worry, you can create your own templates and pre-add common diagram elements to the page. This not only enforces consistency but saves you time as well.

There is also no requirement that templates load a custom Ribbon tab or open any stencils. But most templates open at least one stencil.

Creating a Blank Drawing

Sometimes you need to sketch a quick concept with simple rectangles, circles, ellipses, and text. For these quick rough-diagram situations, I often start with a blank drawing and simply use the Rectangle and Ellipse tools in the Tools group on the Home tab. No templates, no stencils!

SHOW ME **Media 2.1—Quickly Sketching with Blank Drawings**
Access this video file through your registered Web Edition at ***my.safaribooksonline.com/9780132182683/media.***

LET ME TRY IT

Creating a Quick Sketch in a Blank Drawing

1. Click the File tab to get to the Backstage area (refer to Figure 2.1).
2. Click New in the left column.
3. Double-click Blank Drawing at the bottom of the screen, under Other Ways to Get Started. You should see a new, blank drawing, which is unsaved and has no stencils open.
4. Locate the Drawing Tools in the Tools group on the Home tab, as shown in Figure 2.3. The drop-down to the right of the Pointer Tool contains six drawing tools: Rectangle, Ellipse, Line, Freeform, Arc, and Pencil.
5. Create shapes using the Rectangle and Ellipse tools. You use these tools by clicking on the page and then holding down the mouse button while you drag. When you release the mouse button, you've created a shape.

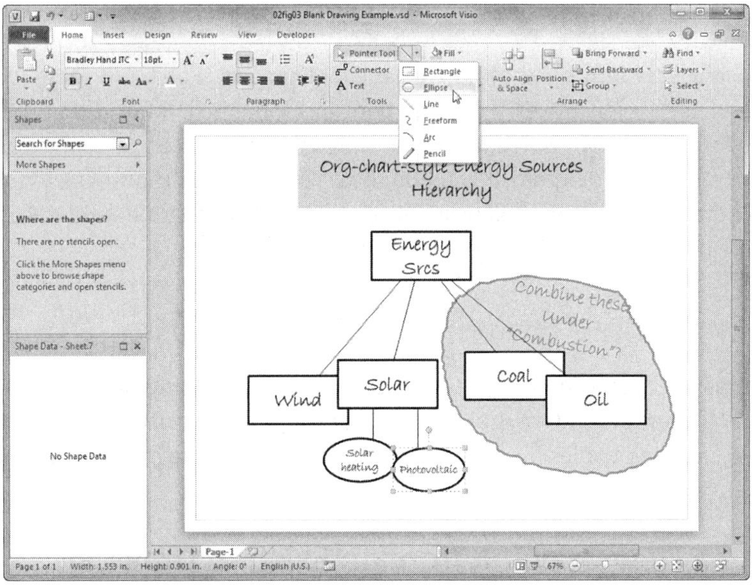

Figure 2.3 *The beginning of an idea. Drawing tools on the Home tab enable you to quickly scratch out an informal diagram. The connectors were changed to the straight style by right-clicking them. The Freeform tool created the sketchy outline around coal and oil.*

6. To constrain rectangles to squares and ellipses to circles, hold down the Shift key while dragging with the corresponding tool.
7. Select some of your shapes and then type some text on them.
8. Use the Connector Tool in the Tools group to connect your shapes together. Notice the red highlighting around a shape when you mouse over it with the Connector tool. This indicates that your connector will be glued to the shape, so that the connector stays attached to the shape automatically. To change a connector's style, just right-click it. You see choices for right-angled, straight, and curved.
9. Experiment with line, fill, and text formatting by right-clicking your shapes and using the mini formatting toolbar. There are also plenty of formatting options on the Home tab. The lines are also shapes, and you can change the format of the line, including adding different line ends.
10. Try creating shapes using the Pencil and Line tools. These tools also work with clicking and dragging. Repeatedly clicking and dragging adds more line or curve segments to the shape. If you release the mouse button near the starting point, Visio closes the shape so you can give it a fill color

11. Switch back to the Pointer tool as a matter of habit. This makes it easier to select shapes, move them and edit text.

I start blank drawings quite often—whenever I need to sketch out some rough ideas and need a few boxes, a circle or two, and some text. If my ideas solidify and a more formal diagram is needed, I then move to a template to create a more formal and structured diagram. If you bought Visio for a specific purpose requiring a specific drawing type, you will probably start templates. But it's good to know how to create basic shapes using the drawing tools.

Creating a New Drawing from an Existing Drawing

An alternative to starting from a template is to use an existing drawing as a basis. Visio 2010 offers several ways to start new drawings from existing drawings, creating new, unsaved copies for you and saving you the trouble of copying files in Explorer.

Starting a New Drawing from an Existing Drawing

At the bottom of the New screen, just below Other Ways to Get Started, is the New From Existing icon, also shown in Figure 2.1.

Click it to open a file open dialog in which you can browse for an existing Visio drawing on which to base your new drawing. When you find a base file, double-click it, or select and click the Open button.

Visio opens an unsaved *copy* of your original drawing. You can modify it as you like, without fear of overwriting the original drawing.

Starting a New Drawing from a Sample

The standard installation of Visio comes with several sample drawings that you can use. You can start new drawings from these samples, just as you can from existing files.

LET ME TRY IT

Starting a New Drawing from a Sample Drawing

1. Click File to get to the Backstage area.
2. Click New in the left column.

3. In the Other Ways to Get Started area at the bottom of the screen, click Sample Diagrams.

4. From the Choose a Template panel, double-click Project Timeline.

You should now see an unsaved copy of the Contoso Pharmaceuticals sample timeline. You can safely play around with this drawing and experiment with the shapes without damaging the original.

You can tell when you've opened a copy of a drawing by looking at the title of the Visio window. If you see "Drawing1," "Drawing2," and so on, your drawing is unsaved—unless, of course, you've explicitly saved your drawing with a name like "Drawing1." I hope you usually give your files more meaningful names!

Starting a New Drawing from a Recent Drawing

Another convenient way of starting new drawings is to use the Recent feature. Instead of going to the New page, click Recent in the Backstage area. You see a list of files that you have previously opened.

If one of these files would make a good starting point for your next drawing, just right-click the item and choose Open a Copy, as shown in Figure 2.4.

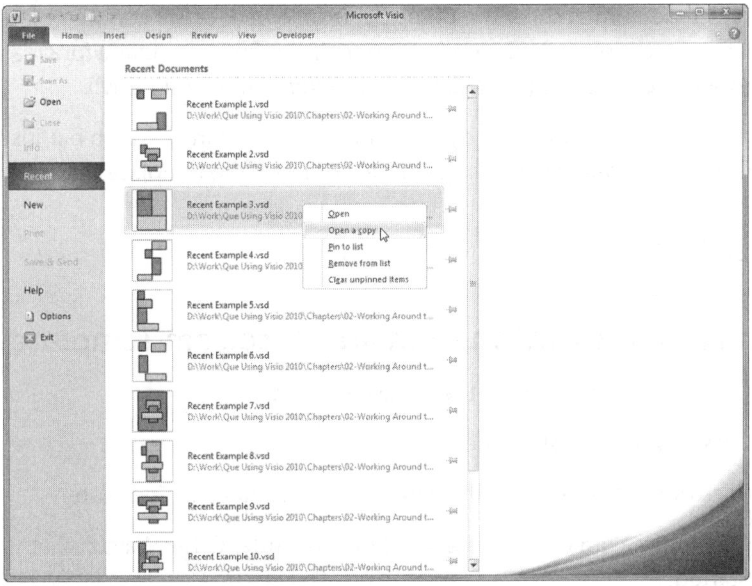

Figure 2.4 *Creating a new drawing from an existing drawing using Recent Documents.*

If you like this way of starting from Recent, you can make sure that your favorite files never disappear from the Recent list. Figure 2.4 shows a tack icon on the right side of each item in the list. The tacks let you pin files permanently to the list. Pinning recent files in this manner effectively transforms your Recent list into a "Favorites" list. Depending on your workflow, this may be a more efficient way to get started. You might never visit the New screen or the template gallery again!

Using Templates Online

A great feature in Visio 2010 is the web-integrated template-finding feature that enables you to pull templates straight from Office.com.

Under the Other Ways to Get Started area you will also find the Office.com templates icon, also visible in Figure 2.1. Clicking this button drills down into a hierarchy of templates stored and organized on Microsoft's servers.

In contrast with the content installed on your PC, the levels of online folders can be several levels deep. The Back and Forward buttons at the top of the window help you to retrace your steps and back out of subfolders. If you get totally lost, click the Home button and just start over.

Figure 2.5 shows an online template that is several layers deep in the hierarchy. The clickable breadcrumbs show the path you've followed: Office.com Templates, More Templates, Case Inserts. At the end of the trail, you find a template for creating inserts for CD jewel cases (created by some joker named Visio Guy!).

If you can't find what you want by browsing, there's a handy search bar just right of the Office.com Templates heading. Figure 2.6 shows the template search in action.

LET ME TRY IT

Starting a New Drawing from an Office.com Template

1. Click the File tab to go to the Backstage area.
2. Click New in the list on the left.
3. Click Home at the top of the window, under Choose a Template.
4. Click Office.com templates at the bottom, under Other Ways to Get Started.

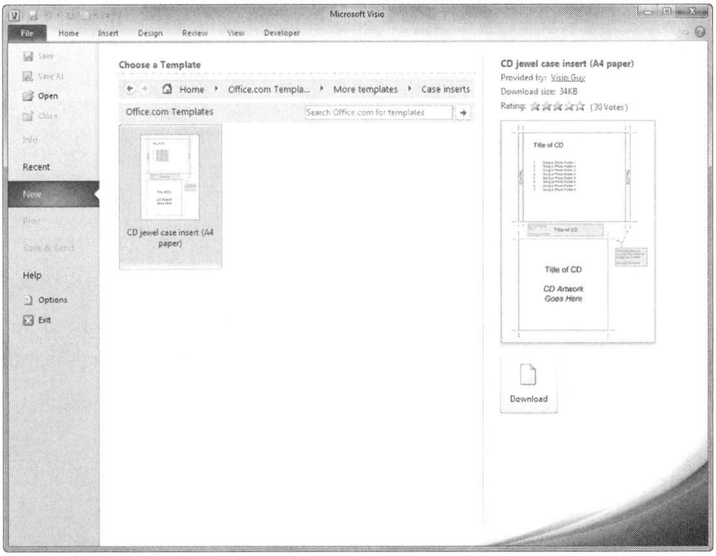

Figure 2.5 *Creating a new CD jewel case insert by starting from an Office.com template, via the Internet. Note that the path to the template is shown as "breadcrumb" buttons to the right of the Home button.*

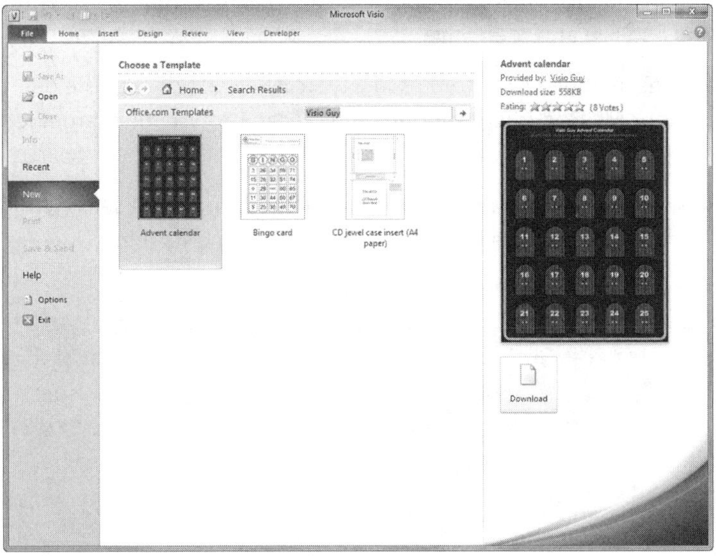

Figure 2.6 *The Office.com offerings resulting from a search on "Visio Guy."*

5. By either browsing or searching, see whether you can find some of these templates. Go ahead and open them: explore and experiment!
   - Rack Design Guideline
   - Troubleshooting flowchart
   - Process improvement
   - Map of Africa
   - Family tree
   - One week planner
6. Remember that when you open a template, you get an unsaved copy of the original. So experiment, play, and mess around to your heart's content, and have fun. You won't screw up the original!

Saving Diagrams

You don't need me to tell you that after investing hours of hard work in a diagram, you should save it. In fact, saving is a real good idea after just *minutes* of hard work!

Saving Documents Using Save As

The simplest way to save your document is to click the little disk icon in the top-left corner of the Visio application window in the Quick Access Toolbar. Pressing Ctrl+S is even faster if you like keyboard shortcuts. You can also go the more traditional route: choosing File and then Save As.

If a drawing hasn't been saved, you see a typical Save As dialog. The default save location is your My Documents folder, but you can browse for a target location from there.

If your drawing has already been saved and named, you don't see anything happen—other than maybe the hourglass cursor doing its thing.

> You can customize the default file save location if you don't like using My Documents. Just go to File, Options, Advanced tab, scroll to the bottom of the dialog and click the File Locations button. In the Documents field, paste or type the path to the place you'd rather save documents. For example, I like to dump stuff to my Desktop and then sort them out later, so my Documents field says C:\Users\Chris\Desktop\.

Saving Documents Using Save & Send

When you click the File tab, you see the familiar Save and Save As items atop the list on the left. Further down, you also find Save & Send. The Save & Send pane offers many options for saving, exporting, and sharing your diagrams in a nicely organized, easy on the eyes layout. Save & Send enables you to do the following:

- Save to SharePoint.
- Save in Visio XML format.
- Save in Visio 2000–2002 format.
- Save as a PDF- or XPS-formatted document.
- Export to various graphics formats, such as PNG, GIF, SVG, or EMF.
- Save as a web page.
- Send the file as an email attachment in Visio, PDF, or XPS formats.

You return to Save & Send in Chapter 10, "Sharing, Publishing, and Exporting," but take a moment now to peruse the options.

Configuring Auto Save

If you don't habitually hit Ctrl + S like me, you may want to have Visio automatically and periodically do the saving for you. You configure Visio's automatic saving options in the Backstage area, in the File, Options, Save panel. There you can configure automatic saving options by specifying the default file format and the AutoRecover time increment.

Finding and Managing Shapes

After you are an expert at *starting* new drawings, you will want to become proficient at finding and dropping shapes! The Shapes window is the key to finding and managing stencils and the master shapes they contain.

Navigating the Shapes Window

When you open a template, you immediately notice the big, vertical Shapes pane docked on the left. The Shapes window, shown in Figure 2.7, is your main stop when looking for master shapes to drag out into your diagram.

Much improved in Visio 2010, the Shapes window is the place for managing stencils and masters and searching for shapes.

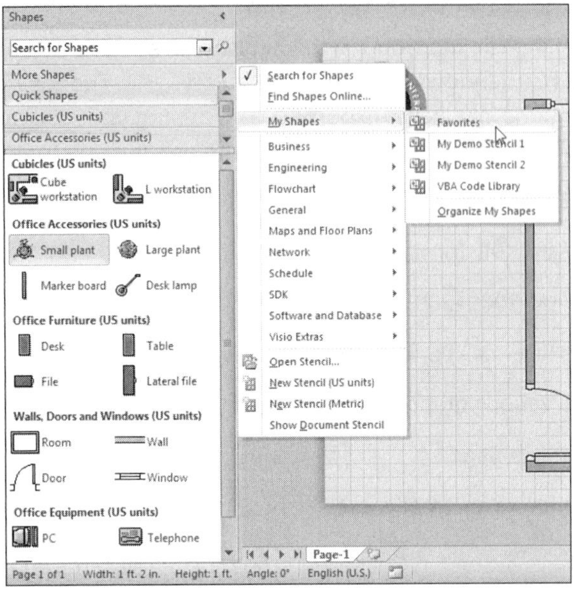

Figure 2.7 *The Shapes window for the Office Layout template and its key elements.*

From top to bottom, the Shapes window has six major parts:

- **Shapes header**—This header allows you to tear off the entire Shapes window and float it or dock it to other sides of the window, like any other task pane.

  The sideways-facing arrow also lets you collapse the Shapes window to free up more space for drawing, then re-expand it to see all the details.

  You can right-click the Shapes header to change how master icons are displayed in the Shapes panel, choosing from compact, icons-only, or verbose icon/name/description views. You can also hide the Shapes window entirely via this menu.

- **Search for Shapes field**—You can enter a keyword and search for shapes by name or description. The results are displayed in a virtual stencil that appears below in the shapes panel.

- **More Shapes**—It looks like a stencil tab, but it serves only to hold the More Shapes menu, which is expanded in Figure 2.7. More Shapes lets you access all the stencils that come with Visio, along with your favorite shapes, and other stencils on your system. You can also create new stencils from here.

- **Quick Shapes**—Clicking Quick Shapes reveals a virtual stencil that shows the Quick Shapes for each of the open stencils. We talk more about Quick Shapes in the next section.
- **Stencil tabs**—Every stencil that is open has a stencil tab in the Shapes window. Click a tab to reveal the master shapes for that stencil in the shapes area below.

  There are actually six stencils open with the Office Layout template shown in Figure 2.7, but you can see only a few of them. Note the short scrollbar to the right of the stencil tabs, which you can use to see the stencil tabs that aren't visible. You can also pull down the splitter between the stencil tabs and the shapes panel to show more stencil tabs (and fewer master shapes).

  When you click a stencil tab, it is highlighted in orange, and the stencil's masters are displayed in the panel below.

  You can pull individual stencil tabs out of the Shapes window area and dock them to other sides of the Visio window or just let them float. Figure 2.8 illustrates this. You can drag stencil tabs around to reorder them in the Shapes window, and you can close stencils by right-clicking their tabs and choosing "Close."
- **Shapes panel**—This panel shows icons for the master shapes in the selected stencil tab. If Quick Shapes is selected, the Shapes panel actually shows master shapes from several stencils.

HAVE YOU LOST THE SHAPES WINDOW?

Right-clicking the Shapes window header gives you the option of hiding the window. But after it's hidden, how do you get Shapes back?

No problem! Go to the View tab, click the Task Panes button in the Show group, and then choose Shapes in the drop-down list. Your Shapes window magically reappears.

Quick Shapes—Accessing and Managing Frequently Used Shapes

Quick Shapes show up in the Visio UI as two different entities. First, every stencil has a selection of Quick Shapes at the top. These are the favorites or most frequently used shapes for that stencil. Second, Quick Shapes is a stencil tab that you've just seen in the Shapes window.

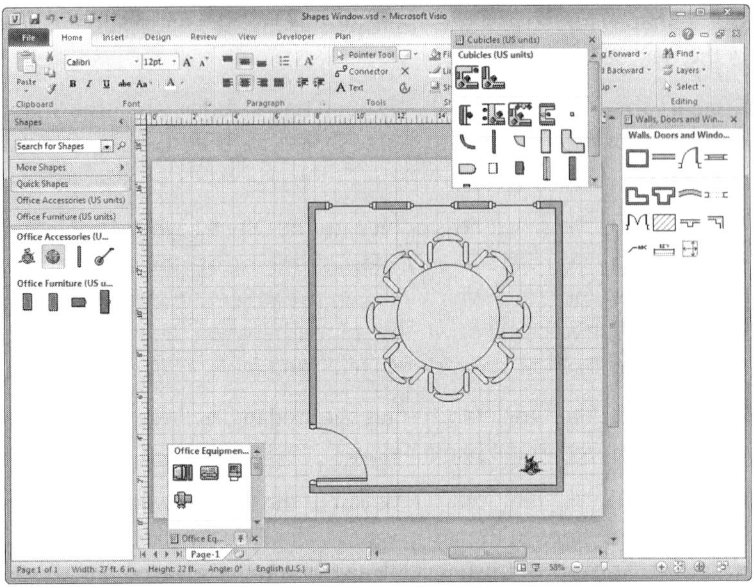

Figure 2.8 *Stencils torn away from the Shapes window, docked and floating in various places. Right-clicking the Shapes header allows you to change the way master icons are displayed. Here we see the "Icon Only" view, which is compact and efficient.*

In Figure 2.9, you can see the Quick Shapes area for the Office Accessories stencil. Look closely for the faint line just after the top four shapes. You can choose which shapes should be Quick Shapes by simply dragging them above the line, and you can demote shapes to be nonquick by dragging them below the line.

Visio remembers your Quick Shape preferences, but if you want to return things to their pristine state, just right-click a stencil's tab and choose Reset Stencil. This resets the Quick Shapes and moves each master back to its original position. So don't be nervous about playing around and trying different arrangements.

Quick Shapes is also a stencil tab in the top portion of the Shapes window. Click it, and you see the Quick Shapes from each of the open stencils. So this Quick Shapes tab isn't really a stencil that comes from a file on disk, but more of a virtual view of shapes in other stencils that are open.

Oddly, Quick Shapes shows only masters from stencils that are docked in the Shapes window. Quick Shapes from stencils floating elsewhere are not included in Quick Shapes view.

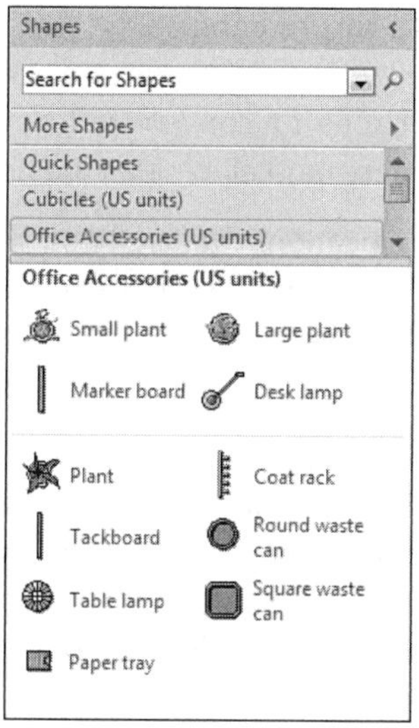

Figure 2.9 *Quick Shapes for the Office Accessories stencil.*

Quick Shapes are also used by the mini-toolbar, which lets you quickly drop and connect shapes. You encountered the mini-toolbar briefly in Chapter 1, "Introducing Visio 2010," when you created your first flowchart. You revisit it in Chapter 4, "Connecting Shapes."

Opening Other Stencils

Regardless of the template you start with, you can always open additional stencils. You can open Visio-supplied stencils or stencils that you have saved elsewhere on your hard drive.

Of course you can open stencils using the traditional File, Open dialog, but you'll find that using More Shapes is much more convenient. It gives you quick access for opening any of Visio 2010's numerous stencils. You can see how Visio categorizes various groups of stencils by looking at the expanded More Shapes menu in Figure 2.7.

The hierarchy is similar to what you see in the template gallery. Stencils are organized by the following categories: Business, Engineering, Flowchart, General, Maps and Floor Plans, Network, Schedule, Software and Database, and Visio Extras. Some categories have subcategories, but keep digging, and you'll eventually see little green stencil icons that you click to open libraries of shapes.

Figure 2.7 also shows an expanded My Shapes submenu (That's "My Shapes" under the "More Shapes" menu, it's easy to confuse the two!) As you learn to mark your favorite shapes and build up your own custom stencils, you will likely store them in the My Shapes folder. My Shapes is a convenient location for your shapes because it is built into the Visio interface, and eliminates the need to browse the file system.

If you have stencils saved in locations that aren't part of the My Shapes system, then you will need to browse to them. You can use More Shapes, Open Stencil, or use the File, Open. When the Open dialog appears, note the file type filter in the lower-right corner. Setting it to Stencil (*.vss, *.vsx) makes it easier to find stencils in folders on your PC.

If you open a stencil when no document is open or when all document windows are minimized within Visio, you get a separate stencil window, as shown in Figure 2.10. While you can't dock separate stencil windows into the Shapes area, they are useful for dragging shapes into several different documents, since they don't disappear when you switch drawing windows.

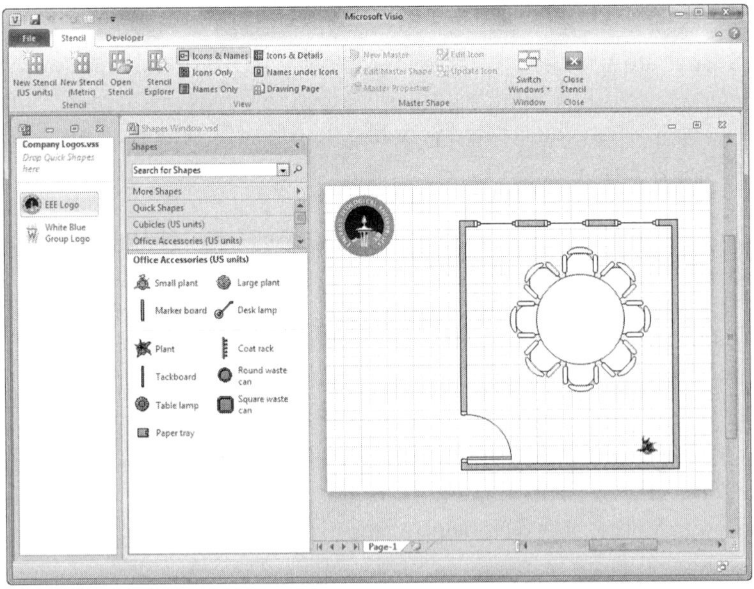

Figure 2.10 *The Company Logos stencil was opened before the Office Plan drawing. When no drawing is present, stencils open in separate, nondocked windows.*

Searching for Shapes

If you're not in the mood for painstakingly browsing each of Visio's stencils to find just the shape you need, try searching instead! The Search for Shapes text box atop the Shapes window will help you do this.

Using Shape Search

Say you need a lamp for your office plan. Just type **light** into the search box and then press Enter (or click the Start Search magnifying glass). Figure 2.11 shows how the results look:

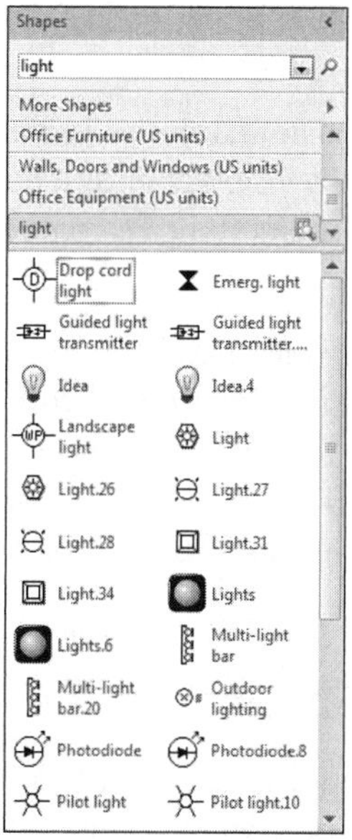

Figure 2.11 *Shape Search for the term* light *creates a temporary virtual stencil with the shapes it found.*

The results of your shape search appear as a stencil with their own stencil tab. Like Quick Shapes, this is a virtual stencil that doesn't really exist as a file but is created on the fly to hold your results.

You can drag any shape from it and then close the stencil. Alternatively, you can save it to your favorites for later use (as a real, live stencil file). Just right-click the tab and choose close or save.

After performing several searches, you might notice that the Shape Search field becoms a drop-down list filled with past search queries. If you frequently search for the same shapes, check the drop-down list and save yourself some typing.

If no shapes are found for a particular search expression, it isn't added to the search expression list. This keeps the list from getting cluttered with useless data.

Why Shape Search Results Have Funny Numbers

Figure 2.11 shows many results for the search on "light." What happened is that Shape Search dug through many stencils, looking for masters that have the word *light* in their names, keywords, or descriptions.

Within a single Visio stencil, master names must be unique. Having two masters named "Light" is not allowed, so Visio appends a number to make each name different. Even though the search results stencil is temporary, it still has to follow these rules.

If you've installed both metric-unit and US-unit content on your machine, you often get double results because Visio finds both the metric and US-units version of the shape. Visio might also find shapes from other sources, such as stencils you've downloaded or created yourself. On my machine, I've also installed Visio 2007, and Shape Search finds masters from the stencils installed with that product, too.

Saving the Results of Shape Searches Using My Shapes

You can save the results of your searches in a number of ways. You can drag single masters to your favorites stencil, save the entire results as a new stencil, and more.

LET ME TRY IT

Saving the Shape Search Results

1. Start a new drawing from the Maps & Floor Plans, Office Layout template.
2. In the search field, type **light** and press Enter. You should see results similar to those in Figure 2.11. (Note: If you don't see the Search for Shapes field, click More Shapes and check Search for Shapes.)

3. Right-click on the Idea shape (or any shape of your choosing) and choose Add to My Shapes, Favorites. The Idea master is added to your Favorites stencil.
4. To see your Favorites stencil, click on More Shapes, My Shapes, Favorites. The Favorites stencil should appear with your newly added master.
5. Right-click on the Favorites stencil's tab and choose Close.
6. To save the entire search-results stencil, right-click on the tab that says "light" and then choose Save As.
7. In the Save As dialog, set the stencil name to **My Lights.vss** and then click Save. The caption of the search-results stencil should now change to "My Lights." It is now a real, saved stencil and no longer a temporary search-results stencil.
8. Click More Shapes again and choose My Shapes, Organize My Favorites. An Explorer window opens, showing at least two files: Favorites.vss and My Lights.vss.
9. You can easily access your new stencil in the future. Because it is stored in the My Shapes folder, it is directly accessible from Visio's user interface. To retrieve it, just click More Shapes, My Shapes. You should see My Lights in the list.
10. Back in the search field, type in a new expression (in this case, **lamp**) and then press Enter. You should see several results below in the "lamp" search-results stencil.
11. Right-click the Desk lamp master and then choose Add to My Shapes, My Lights.
12. If the My Lights stencil is still open, you should immediately see a small, dark-blue disk icon on the right side of the My Lights stencil tab. The reason is that the stencil has been changed: you just added the Desk lamp shape to it. If My Lights was not open, you will see the newly-added lamp shape the next time you open the stencil.
13. Click on the My Lights tab to activate the stencil. Scroll to the bottom of the stencil. You should see that the Desk lamp master has been added to the stencil.
14. To save the updated My Lights stencil, right-click the tab and choose Save. The disk icon disappears, but a small red star opens in its place. This indicates that My Lights is open for editingso you can add, delete and rename masters.

Configuring Shape Search

You can fine-tune the way Visio searches in one of two ways:

1. Right-click the Shapes window title bar and then choose Search Options.
2. Go to File, Options, and choose the Advanced tab.

Both methods take you to the same dialog, but beware! The Advanced tab has five sections, each with a bunch of options, so you need to do some scrolling. To configure Shape Search, scroll all the way to the bottom. The second-to-last section has the options you're looking for, as shown in Figure 2.12.

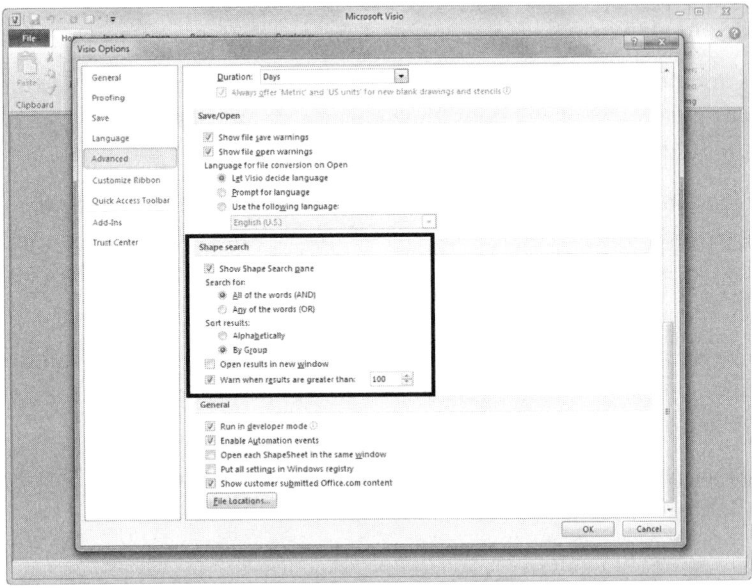

Figure 2.12 *Shape Search options in the Backstage area. Be sure to scroll to the bottom of the panel; otherwise, you won't see the options in the Shape Search section.*

The options for Shape Search are few, but one of the coolest options is the Sort Results setting. If you select By Group, your results are categorized by containing stencil, as shown in Figure 2.13.

This capability is reminiscent of how the Quick Shapes window displays shapes from each open stencil. It is easy on the eyes when there are a lot of search results, and clearly shows double results from the Metric and US units stencils.

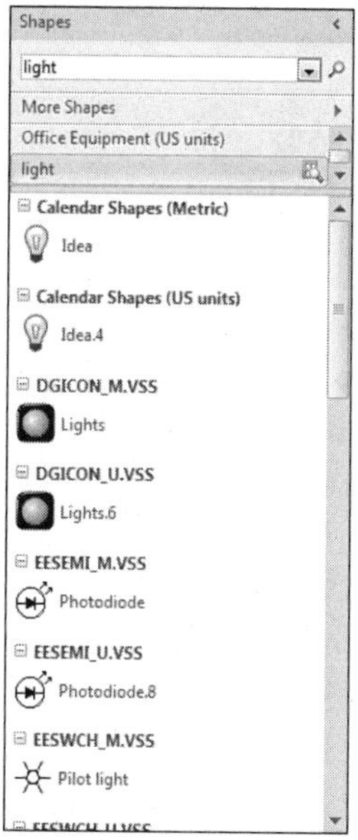

Figure 2.13 *Search-results stencil for "light," sorted by group. Note stencils ending with "_M" are metric, those with "_U" are US units, also known as imperial units.*

Knowing the stencil name is also great if you want to explore the rest of the shapes in the source stencil. Sadly, there's no shortcut that takes you straight to the original stencil. You have to go back to the More Shapes menu and dig around until you find the source stencil's name in the menus.

Saving Favorite Shapes

As you spend more time using Visio's stencils and templates, you will come across shapes that you want to bookmark as favorites.

Just as you can save shapes from a Shape Search, you can add any shape you see in any stencil to your favorites. To do so, right-click a shape in the stencil, click Add to My Shapes, and then select a stencil from the list. You can also choose to create a new stencil if Favorites is getting overcrowded, or you need sets of favorites for different diagram types.

Figure 2.14 shows the Coffee icon from the Symbols stencil being added to my Favorites stencil.

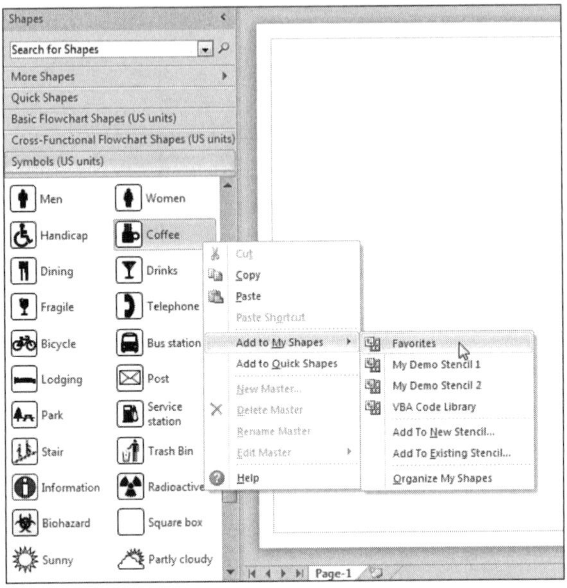

Figure 2.14 *Saving an existing master to Favorites by right-clicking and then choosing Add to My Shapes.*

Managing and Organizing Your Favorite Shapes

In the previous Let Me Try It, you briefly saw the My Favorites folder, which you can quickly get to via More Shapes, My Shapes, Organize My Favorites. This folder has special status in that its contents are shown in the My Shapes and Add to My Shapes cascading menus.

Figure 2.15 shows the expanded More Shapes, My Shapes menu, along with the corresponding Explorer window.

You can see that I've added a few stencils of my own to the My Shapes folder: My Demo Stencil 1, My Demo Stencil 2, and VBA Code Library. They also appear in the My Shapes menu.

Note that My Shapes can even contain subfolders. In Figure 2.15, you can see that I've quickly added a new folder, named (cough) New Folder. This contains the stencil named My Demo Stencil 3. This capability is great for further organizing your Favorites because subfolders just become another level of cascading menu inside the Visio interface. If you have tons of favorites and custom stencils, you can keep them sorted using subfolders but still have them handy via the My Shapes menu.

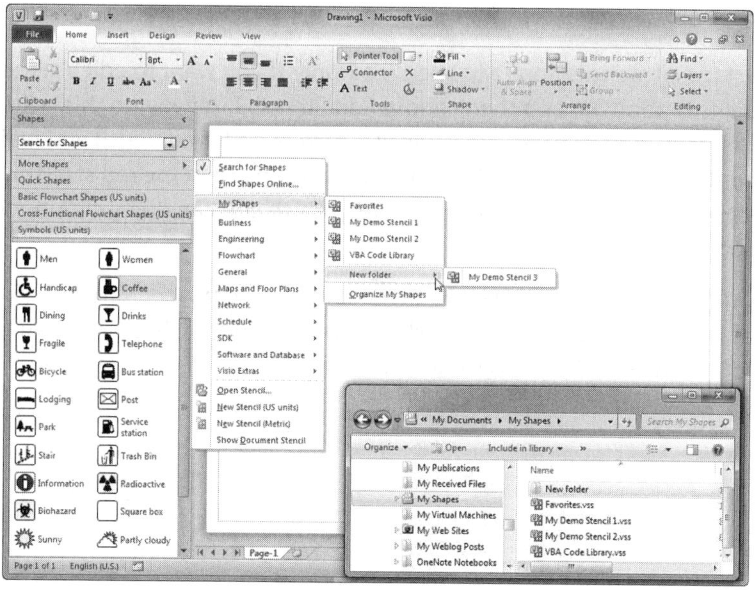

Figure 2.15 *The My Shapes menu item reflects the stencil-containing structure of the My Documents, My Shapes folder on your system.*

If you download or purchase Visio shapes from a third party, it's a good idea to put the files in the My Shapes folder. That way, they are easily accessible from within Visio. Of course, you could put them in any folder on your system, but then you need to browse to them.

> If you're a bit of a techie, you've probably wondered why I have the stencil VBA Code Library shown in the My Shapes folder. This stencil is interesting in that it doesn't contain any shapes at all. I created it solely for storing Visual Basic macros that I frequently use. I touch on VBA code in Chapter 11, "Developing Custom Visio Solutions."

Editing Existing Stencils

Using the various My Shapes mechanisms to add shapes to stencils is quick and convenient. You can also drag masters from stencil to stencil or even create new ones by dragging shapes you create from the page onto a stencil. You can also delete shapes from stencils by selecting them and then pressing the Delete key.

However, there are a few gotchas that might trip you up when you try to edit a stencil.

The first is that stencils normally open read-only. If you want to edit a stencil, right-click on its caption bar and then choose Edit Stencil. After you do this, a little red star shows up, indicating that the stencil is now open for editing. If you make changes to the stencil, a little disk icon appears in place of the red star. This icon indicates that the stencil needs to be saved, which you can do by clicking the disk icon.

The second problem is that stencils that come from Microsoft with your Visio installation cannot be edited, no matter what you click. Figure 2.16 shows a fruitless attempt to make the Symbols stencil editable.

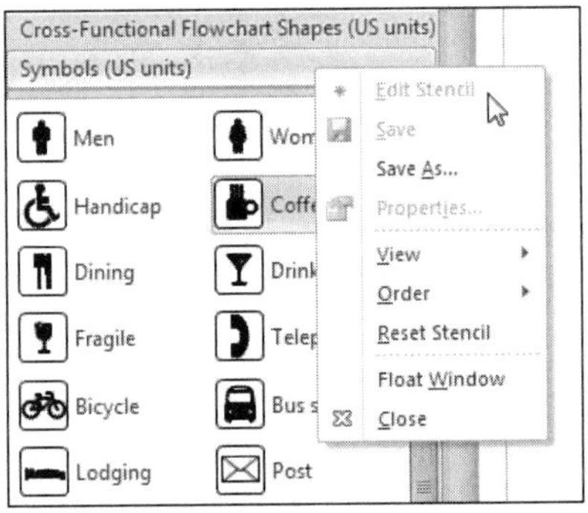

Figure 2.16 *Right-clicking the Symbols stencil's caption shows that Edit Stencil is grayed-out and not available.*

One work-around is to save a copy of the stencil and then make changes. For instance, you could right-click the Symbols caption, choose Save As, and then save it to your favorites as, say, "My Symbols." Now you can freely add and delete shapes from this stencil using the methods just discussed.

Creating a Custom Master Shape and a Custom Stencil

All this talk of editing and managing shapes and stencils might have you dreaming up your own custom libraries of shapes. So let's go over the basic steps for creating a new stencil with a new master.

LET ME TRY IT

Creating a New Stencil with New Masters

1. Create a new Blank drawing.
2. Using the Rectangle and Ellipse tools, draw a few basic forms. Position them near each other or even overlapping.
3. Format the shapes with crazy colors and line styles. Have fun, go crazy!
4. Select the Pointer tool, and select all your shapes by dragging a selection rectangle around them.
5. Group them together by pressing Ctrl+G or right-clicking Group, Group. You now have a single shape composed of several subshapes. You can save this shape in a stencil to make it easy to reuse.
6. Create a new, blank stencil. Go to More Shapes, New Stencil. You should see a new stencil window that has a name like Stencil1 or Stencil2.
7. Drag your grouped shape from the drawing page onto the stencil. You should see a new master with a name like Master.1 or Master.2.
8. Edit the name of the master by right-clicking and choosing Rename Master. Enter a name for your new shape, such as "My First Shape."
9. Notice that the stencil now shows the disk icon in the upper-right corner. This indicates that the stencil has been changed and should be saved. Click the disk to save the stencil. The Save dialog appears, showing the My Shapes folder by default. Enter a name for the stencil and click Save. The new name of the stencil now shows in the stencil tab caption.
10. You can edit the properties for your stencil by right-clicking the stencil tab and choosing Properties. There you can edit fields such as Title, Subject, Author, Manager, Company, Language, Categories, Tags, and Comments. Notice that if you customize the Title, it appears in the stencil's caption instead of the filename.
11. You can also edit the master shape itself. Double-click the master icon or right-click and choose Edit Master, Edit Master Shape. You then see a new window that shows just the innards of the master. Try changing a few colors or adding some text. When you're done, click the x to close the master window. If you made any changes, you see the alert "Update My First Shape?" Click Yes to accept your changes. Notice that the master icon visually updates to reflect your alterations.

12. Test your new master shape by dragging and dropping it onto the drawing page.

It's a good idea to group shapes together before dragging them to a stencil to create a new master. If you don't, Visio will group them when you drag them back to a drawing anyway.

It would be great if masters could deliver several disjoint shapes at once. Preconfigured sets of furniture for office cubicles would be a great example. But unfortunately masters can only deliver a single shape.

If you need to get at the pieces of a master, you can ungroup it once it hits the page. Visio will show you a warning that you are "severing" it from its master. If you created the master with the intention of ungrouping it, then all should be OK. But be warned: masters that weren't designed to be ungrouped might blow apart in surprising and unexpected ways! So be prepared to undo.

Understanding the Document Stencil

When you drag masters into a drawing, not only do you get a shape on the page, but you also get a copy of the master inside the document itself. Every document has an "internal" or "local" stencil called the *document stencil*. Working with the document stencil is considered an advanced Visio topic, but I think that understanding it helps avoid confusion down the road, and deepens your understanding of Visio.

SHOW ME **Media 2.2—Understanding External Stencils, Local Masters, and the Document Stencil**

Access this video file through your registered Web Edition at ***my.safaribooksonline.com/9780132182683/media.***

LET ME TRY IT

Working with the Document Stencil

1. Start a new diagram using the Basic Flowchart template.
2. On the Design tab, in the Themes group, click the left-most theme called No Theme to remove any theming from the drawing.
3. Click My Shapes and then choose Show Document Stencil from the bottom of the menu. A blank stencil window appears with "Document Stencil"

as its title. This internal stencil holds copies of masters dragged into the drawing, and belongs to the document itself. It isn't a separate stencil file.

4. Move the Document Stencil to the right side of the window by dragging its stencil tab. See whether you can get it to dock to the right side of the drawing window.
5. In the Shapes window, click Basic Flowchart Shapes.
6. Drag the Decision shape onto the page. You see a diamond on the page as expected, and a Decision master also appears in the Document stencil. This is the local copy of the master!
7. Drag several more Decision shapes onto the page. Select one and resize it to be narrower. Select another and type the text "A Decision."
8. Double-click the Decision master in the Document stencil. A new window appears showing just the diamond shape. This is the master editing window. (You don't have to enable the Document Stencil for editing, because it belongs to the document that you are already editing!)
9. Select the diamond and type "Yes or No?" for its text.
10. Stretch the diamond and make it wider.
11. Give the shape a gaudy fill color such as red or orange. You can do this by right-clicking and picking a color from the fill bucket drop-down.
12. Close the master editing window by clicking the "X" in the top-right corner (make sure you don't close the whole Visio application!).
13. Accept the changes by clicking "Yes" when the warning: "Update 'Decision' and all of its instances?" appears.

    Notice that the Decision shapes on the page have updated to reflect the changes you made to the master. However the shapes that you edited on the page before editing the master, don't get every single change that you made. The "A Decision" shape's text is unchanged, and the narrower shape didn't become wider. Changes made to shapes on the page override changes made to the master.

Clearly the Document stencil offers a lot of power and potential for quickly changing your documents. But let me point out a few caveats and common misconceptions.

- The stencils that open with a template are actually separate files. When a master from an "external stencil" is dropped into a document, it is copied to the document stencil, as you've just experienced. Only changes to the master in the document stencil affect shapes in the drawing. Changes to the original master in the original stencil do not affect dropped shapes.

- If you drag masters from various stencils onto a page and then delete them, there are still copies of those masters in the document stencil. This leads to mysterious file bloat: you could have a completely blank document that has a huge file size because the document stencil is full of masters that were dropped and then deleted. File, Info, Reduce File Size (discussed in Chapter 10, "Sharing, Publishing, and Exporting") can help you to detect and remove unused local masters.
- Not all changes that you make to Document stencil masters will propagate to shapes on the page. If shapes have been modified on pages, those changes take precedence over changes made inside the master, as you saw in the excercise.
- Editing Document Stencil masters seems like a great way to replace shapes. While this works to some extent, you could get some unexpected results. Small changes to masters usually propagate just fine, but complete replacement of the innards of a master can lead to surprises.

Managing and Styling Pages

Now that you know how to create new drawings and find plenty of shapes to add to them, let's look at how to create and manage pages themselves. Visio documents can contain multiple pages of different sizes, scales, and orientations. This capability is great for breaking up complex diagrams into simpler pieces or for keeping different types of diagrams together in a single project.

Inserting Pages

You might want to add pages to a Visio document for lots of reasons. Some projects require several different types of diagrams, and keeping them all in a single drawing file but on separate pages is convenient. For example, the drawings for a system installation project typically require a title page, several scaled plan and elevation views that show the site and actual views of real equipment, plus unscaled schematic and wiring diagrams that show how to hook everything up.

Other drawings are so complicated that it helps to break them down into overview and detailed views. Large organizational charts and complicated process flows benefit from using multiple pages to "drill down" in the hierarchy. For these diagrams, separate pages in a Visio document contain simplified high-level views and detailed low-level views.

Adding Pages Quickly

The fastest way to insert a new Visio page is to click the Insert Page tab on the right end of the page tab bar, as shown in Figure 2.17. If you use Microsoft Excel, this will be second nature for you.

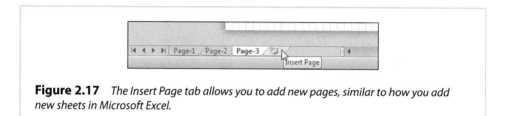

Figure 2.17 *The Insert Page tab allows you to add new pages, similar to how you add new sheets in Microsoft Excel.*

When you click this tab, a new page is added to the end of your document. The new page has the same size, scale, and orientation as the active page. You therefore get a fresh copy of whichever page is showing but without any shapes.

On the Ribbon, the Blank Page button on the Insert tab also lets you add new pages. Figure 2.18 shows the Blank Page button with expanded choices.

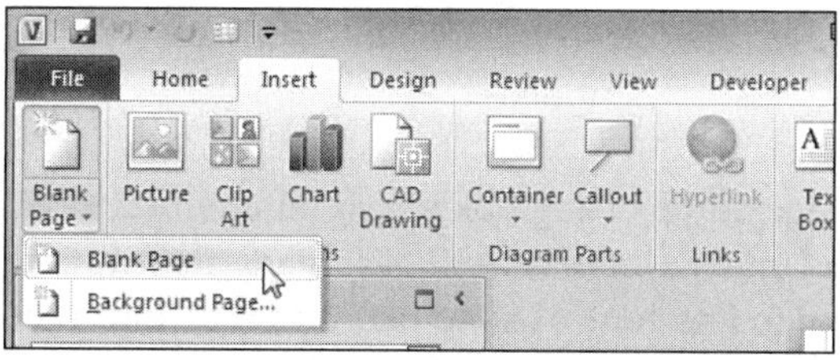

Figure 2.18 *Adding pages via the Insert tab's Blank Page button.*

Simply clicking the Blank Page button gives the same effect as clicking the Insert Page tab at the bottom of the window. Use the drop-down functionality for finer control.

Adding Pages with the Page Setup Dialog

As you become a more sophisticated Visio user, you might want more control over the pages you insert. The Page Setup dialog offers many options for specifying the name, size, scale, measuring units, layout settings, and more.

To access the Page Setup dialog, right-click a page tab for an existing page and then choose Insert. The Page Setup dialog opens, as shown in Figure 2.19.

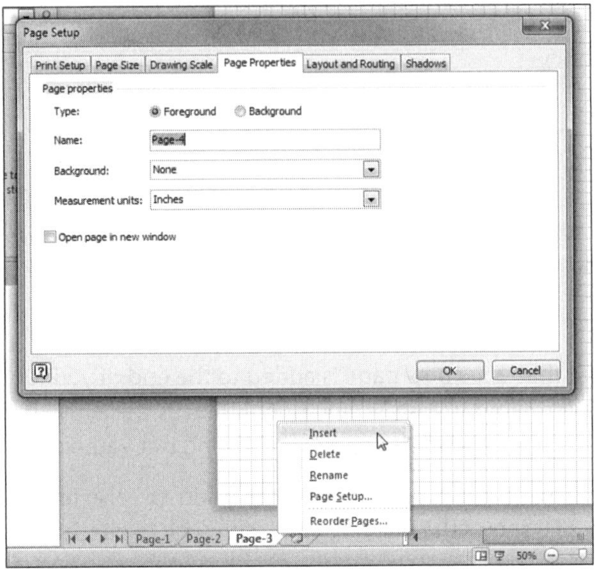

Figure 2.19 *The Page Setup dialog gives you full control over new pages, as well as existing pages. Note that this dialog has six different tabs.*

Notice that the Page Setup dialog box has six different tabs. Clearly, adding a page using this method offers a lot of control over many aspects of the new page. Page Setup can be used to fine-tune existing pages as well. Just right-click a page tab for an existing page and choose Page Setup (see Figure 2.19).

We revisit the Page Setup dialog many more times throughout the book. For now, take a few moments to familiarize yourself with the different tabs and options available in it.

SHOW ME **Media 2.3—Adding and Manipulating New Pages**
Access this video file through your registered Web Edition at ***my.safaribooksonline.com/9780132182683/media.***

LET ME TRY IT

Adding and Manipulating New Pages

1. Create a new blank drawing. It should have one page, with one page tab at the bottom displaying Page-1.
2. Quickly add several pages by clicking the Insert page tab on the right end of the page tab bar several times. Note that pages are added to the end of the document and are automatically named in order: Page-2, Page-3, Page-4, and so on.
3. Draw different shapes on each page of the document using the Rectangle or Ellipse tool. Click the page tabs to go back and forth in the document and view different pages.
4. Note the rewind, forward, backward, and fast-forward buttons to the left of the page tabs. They help you to scroll tabs when you have more pages than can be shown in the page tab area.
5. You can quickly jump directly to any page in the document by right-clicking any of these controls and then choosing a page from the list.
6. Rename any of your pages by double-clicking a page tab. This should activate text editing so you can type in a new name for the page.
7. Add a new page using the Page Setup dialog. Right-click a page tab for an existing page and choose Insert.
8. In the Page Setup dialog, type a custom name for the page. Experiment with other settings on the tab and see what features of the new page you can control. After you click OK, you should see your new page at the end of the page tab bar.
9. Change the name of another page by right-clicking its page tab and then choosing Page Setup. The name of the page should be highlighted in the Name field for you to change quickly.
10. Reorder the pages by simply dragging page tabs to and fro.

Working with Background Pages

Background pages are special pages whose content shows on foreground pages but can't be edited from the foreground. Because background pages can be shared by multiple foreground pages, they can save you a lot of work and make your documents more efficient. Common elements can be shared by many pages, and updated in only one place!

A common use for background pages is for holding titles, borders, and background art for an entire document.

LET ME TRY IT

Adding Background Pages Using Borders and Titles

1. Create a new drawing, either blank from a template or from a sample drawing.
2. Drop or draw a few shapes on the default page.
3. Click the Design tab.
4. In the Backgrounds group, select a background from the Backgrounds gallery. Notice that you now have background graphics, and a new page tab has been inserted: VBackground-1 (see Figure 2.20). The name of the new page appears in italic, and is at the right end of the page tabs, two clues that a page is a background.

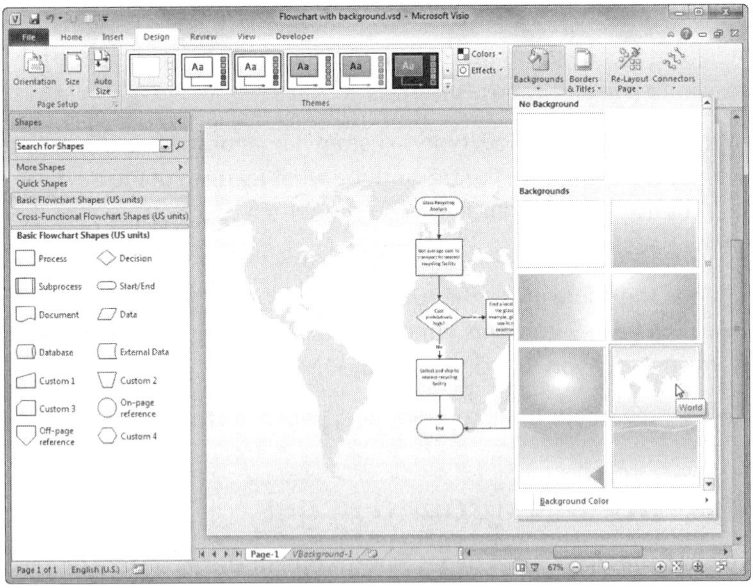

Figure 2.20 *Inserting the World background creates a new background page called VBackground-1.*

5. Add a title by selecting an item from the Borders & Titles gallery. The item appears, but no new page tab is added.
6. Try to select the border or title shapes. Notice that you can't do this. Both the background graphics and title have been added to the VBackground-1 page. They show through to Page-1 but can't be edited from there.
7. Now go to the new background page by clicking its page tab.
8. Try to select the border or title shapes. Notice that this time it works.
9. Add some more shapes to the background page. Drop shapes from stencils or just draw rectangles and ellipses.
10. Return to the original page by clicking the Page-1 tab. Notice that you can see the shapes that you added to the background page, but you can't select them from the foreground page.
11. With Page-1 active, click the Insert Page tab. You should see a new (foreground) page tab named Page-2.
12. Click Page-2's tab (if it isn't already active). Notice that the background graphics show for Page-2 as well. Remember that a background page can be shared by multiple foreground pages, and when you insert a page, the current page's settings are copied, including background page assignments.

If you look at your page tabs, you can see that your document now has three pages. When you print your document, however, only two pages will come out. The reason is that background pages don't print as separate pages, but their content prints on foreground pages that reference them.

It is worth noting that background pages can themselves have background pages. A foreground page could have a background page that in turn has another background page and so on. You can create complicated (and confusing) chains and hierarchies of background pages, several layers deep. For certain applications, this capability is quite useful, but you'll want to guard against complexity that will make maintenance and modification difficult.

Imagine you are designing different web page templates for a website. Every page in the site has the same header and footer, but some page types have different sidebars and navigation menus. In Visio, foreground pages could represent actual web pages in the site. These then reference background pages for their sidebar treatments, and those backgrounds reference the header and footer background. If you needed to change, say, the company logo in the header, you only need to edit the backmost background page, and all of the foreground pages would show that change.

In the previous example, background pages were created for you automatically. To build sophisticated structures like a layered website, you need to know how to create and assign background pages manually.

SHOW ME **Media 2.4—Adding Background Pages Manually**
Access this video file through your registered Web Edition at ***my.safaribooksonline.com/9780132182683/media.***

LET ME TRY IT

Adding Background Pages Manually

The process of manually creating background pages is a bit more involved but allows finer control. Be sure to notice the key step of *assigning* the background page to a foreground page.

1. Create a new blank drawing.
2. Click the Insert tab on the Ribbon.
3. In the Pages group, click the Blank Page drop-down and select Background Page. Alternatively, right-click a page tab and choose Insert. The Page Setup dialog appears.
4. Set the Type to background by clicking the Background radio button.
5. Enter a name for the page. Background-1 is the default, but shorter names reduce clutter in the page tab bar. I usually use something like bg1. Click OK and a new page is added. The page should be active in the drawing window, and its page tab should be at the far right.
6. On your new background page, draw a large rectangle and type **Hi, my name is Background**.
7. Return to Page-1. Notice that you do not see the shape you just created. The reason is that the background has not yet been assigned.
8. Right-click on the page tab for Page-1 and choose Page Setup. You should see the Page Setup dialog, with the Page Properties tab active.
9. In the Background drop-down, choose the name of the background page that you just created and then click OK. You should now see the "Hi my name is Background" shape showing through.

10. With Page-1 still active, click the Insert Page tab to add a new page. A new page named Page-2 should be added, and you should still see the background graphics. The new page is copied from Page-1 and retains its settings, including the assigned background.

11. Right-click Page-2 and choose Page Setup.

12. In the Background drop-down, choose None; then click OK. The background shapes should now be gone from Page-2. You have just *unassigned* the background page from Page-2.

Inserting Backgrounds, Titles, and Borders

You've seen the Design tab's Backgrounds group which contains two galleries for quickly adding backgrounds, borders, and titles to your document.

When you pick one of these elements, Visio automatically creates a background page to hold the background graphics, borders, or titles you choose. Backgrounds are easily identified by their obvious names, italic text, and positioning at the end of the page tabs.

Putting titles and other graphics on background pages makes it easier for new foreground pages to share the background graphics. The structure of your Visio document becomes similar to Backgrounds and Background styles in PowerPoint. It also makes it easier to work on foreground pages, as you don't have to worry about accidentally selecting and moving background shapes.

Backgrounds, titles, and borders that you add from the Ribbon are actual shapes dropped on the background page. You can go to the background page and manually alter them. However, many of them are designed to automatically stretch to the size of the page, or be positioned on one edge, so you might not be able to freely resize or reposition them.

If you pick new border, background or title styles from the Design tab, Visio deletes existing shapes and replaces them with new ones. You don't have to worry about creating a stack of shapes on the background page, one on top of the other.

Many of the titles have text that indicates the page number. If you look at the page number while a background page is active, you'll see something like Page 0, which can be disconcerting. Don't worry, though; the page number is an inserted field that is smart enough to change for each foreground page (go look at the foreground pages and you'll see reasonable page numbers). We talk more about inserting smart fields into text blocks in Chapter 3, "Organizing and Annotating Diagrams."

You also see the word *Title* in many of the title shapes. This field is not smart in any way, even though it would make sense to link it to the Title field from the document's properties (again, discussed in Chapter 3, "Organizing and Annotating Diagrams"). At any rate, you have to go to the background page to edit it. Just click on the background page tab, select the title shape, and then type your own title text.

Renaming Pages

Your pages don't have to be named Page-1, Page-2, and so on. You can change them to anything you like. All you have to do is double-click a page tab and type in a new name. This is the same as right-clicking a page tab and choosing Rename, but double-clicking is much easier.

You can also go to the Page Setup dialog to rename a page. Just right-click a page tab, click Page Setup, and then enter a new name in the Name field on the Page Properties tab.

Reordering Pages

Reordering pages is as simple as dragging the page tabs around, just as you would in Excel.

If your document has lots of pages, dragging tabs from one end of the document to the other can be difficult. But there's help! Right-click any page tab and choose the last menu item: Reorder Pages. In the dialog that pops up, you can reorder your pages by using the Move Up and Move Down buttons. Your pages clearly move up and down in the list box, as shown in Figure 2.21.

A great feature of the Reorder Pages dialog is the Update Page Names check box. If you leave this box checked, any pages that have the default page names (Page-1, Page-2, Page-3, and so on) are updated to reflect their new positions in the document.

In Figure 2.21 the Table of Contents page is being moved from the end to the beginning of the document. After the move, Page-1 will become Page-2, Page-2 will become Page-3, and on. But you might not want this change because the table of contents is more like a Page-0. In such a case, you should uncheck Update Page Names before moving any pages.

One last note: background pages always appear at the end of the page tab list, and can't be reordered.

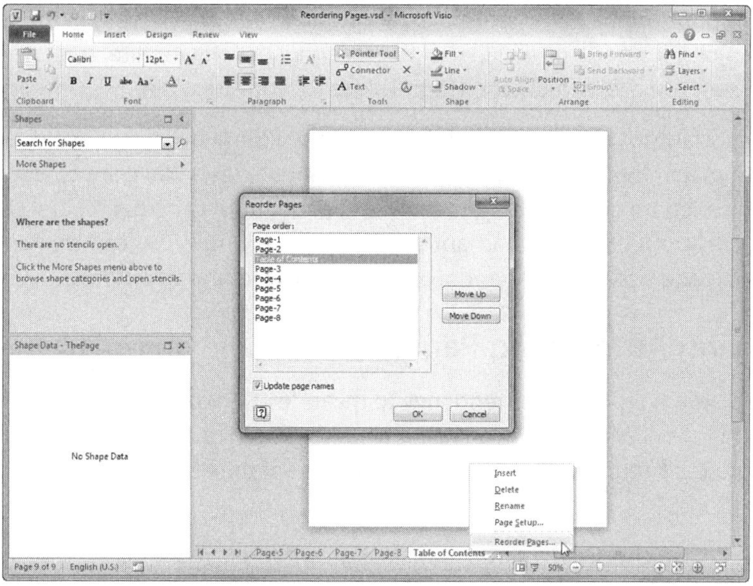

Figure 2.21 *The Reorder Pages dialog is great help when you have lots of pages to move around.*

Controlling Page Size and Orientation

You can set your Visio pages to any size and orientation you want. Perhaps you want to work with sheets that adhere to standard paper sizes, or maybe you want your page to expand ad infinitum as your drawing grows. For wide drawings, you'll want a landscape orientation; for tall diagrams, portrait.

Whatever your needs, your first stop is the Design tab. On the left you find the Page Setup group, which contains three handy buttons: Orientation, Size, and AutoSize.

Setting Page Orientation

You can set your page to landscape or portrait orientation in a snap by clicking the Orientation drop-down button. Switching between wide and tall drawing pages couldn't be easier!

Setting the Page Size

The next button in the Page Setup group, Page Size, offers you a long drop-down list full of standard office paper sizes.

Engineers and architects might want to click More Page Sizes at the bottom of the list. This pops up the Page Setup dialog, with the Page Size tab highlighted. There you can pick from Metric (ISO), ANSI Engineering, or ANSI Architectural standard page sizes. You also can enter custom values for your page size.

It is important to understand that the size of the Visio drawing surface *does not* have to match the size of the paper in your printer! When you want to print, pages can be scaled up or down to fit the printer's paper or tiled across several sheets. We talk more about this topic in Chapter 9, "Printing." For now, you can create any drawing page size you want and worry about how to print it out later.

Specifying Auto Sizing Pages

Some diagram types have a tendency to meander. Network diagrams, flowcharts, and other process diagrams can just grow and grow! For these types of diagrams, the AutoSize button is great, and saves you a lot of time horsing around with page size settings.

With AutoSize checked, your drawing just grows when you drop a shape in the blue "off-page" area. Visio automatically extends your drawing by one sheet of paper in the direction that you are working, and you never have to worry about running out of space again. If you remove all shapes from a page tile, then AutoSize will remove the tile and your page size contracts.

For some folks this feature is a scourge. The pasteboard (blue off-page area) is great for holding temporary graphics, clipboard scraps, and other temporary junk that you want to have around but don't want in the drawing itself and don't want to print. If you're the type that likes storing bits and pieces "off stage," then you will want to turn AutoSize off, which you can easily do by clicking the AutoSize button on the Design tab. Problem solved.

LET ME TRY IT

Using AutoSize Versus Manually Resizing Pages

If you create sprawling network or flowchart diagrams, you'll love AutoSize. If you like using the pasteboard, you won't like AutoSize. If you like both features, there is a happy middle ground that lets you quickly and easily resize the page at your leisure without resorting to the Page Setup dialog.

1. Start a new drawing using the Basic Flowchart template.
2. Go to the Design tab and turn on AutoSize (it is on by default for this template, but double-check).

3. Drop some flowchart shapes on the page.
4. Try dropping more shapes in the blue pasteboard area. See how Visio automatically extends the drawing surface by one page?
5. In the View tab, make sure that Show, Page Breaks is checked. As AutoSize expands your page, you see dashed lines that indicate how your drawing will be tiled when you print. This capability helps you avoid dropping shapes in awkward positions that land directly on the page break, where they might get mangled in printing.
6. Now go to the Design tab and turn off AutoSize.
7. Drop more shapes in the blue area. The page no longer expands automatically, and you can store shapes off-page in the pasteboard region. Note that shapes on the pasteboard won't print.
8. If you decide that you want to expand the drawing, there is a shortcut that lets you quickly and visually expand te page without having to reactivate AutoSize. In the drawing window, move your cursor to an edge of the drawing page—where the white meets blue. Hold down the **Ctrl** key. Your cursor should change to a double-headed resizing arrow.
9. While still pressing the Ctrl key, hold down the left mouse button and drag the border of the page to a new location. See how you can quickly resize the page to any dimensions you like?

I think that the manual page resizing is a nice middle-ground between AutoSize and Not AutoSize. One minor drawback is that you end up with completely arbitrary page sizes, instead of the integral numbers of sheets that AutoSize provides. This isn't a huge problem because you have a lot of control at print time regarding scaling and page tiling anyway. If you are adamant about having exact numbers of page tiles, however, you should use AutoSize.

Setting Page Scales

Engineers and architects create drawings that represent objects in the physical world. They use page scales to relate real-world sizes to on-paper sizes. Scales allow them to easily draw objects that are much bigger (or much smaller) than the physical paper, without doing lots of mathematical conversions in their heads.

For example, imagine your office measures 10 by 12 feet. To fit a drawing of the office onto an 8 ½" x 11" letter-sized page, those 10 feet (120 inches) have to fit onto 8 ½ inches of paper! This means that each inch on the paper has to cover at least 14.1 inches in the real world.

Dividing every measurement by 14.1 would be error prone and tedious. Luckily, Visio supports scaled drawings and automatically does the math for you! For the office plan, you could use a standard architectural scale like ½" = 1' – 0". This gives you a ratio of 1:24, meaning that 1 inch on the paper covers 24 inches of real-world space—more than enough to fit the office onto a letter-sized page. At this scale, the page represents 22 × 17 feet of real world space. That's enough for your office, a title block, and maybe some notes around the edges.

You can set the scale of a drawing by going to the Page Setup dialog and then clicking the Drawing Scale tab, as shown in Figure 2.22.

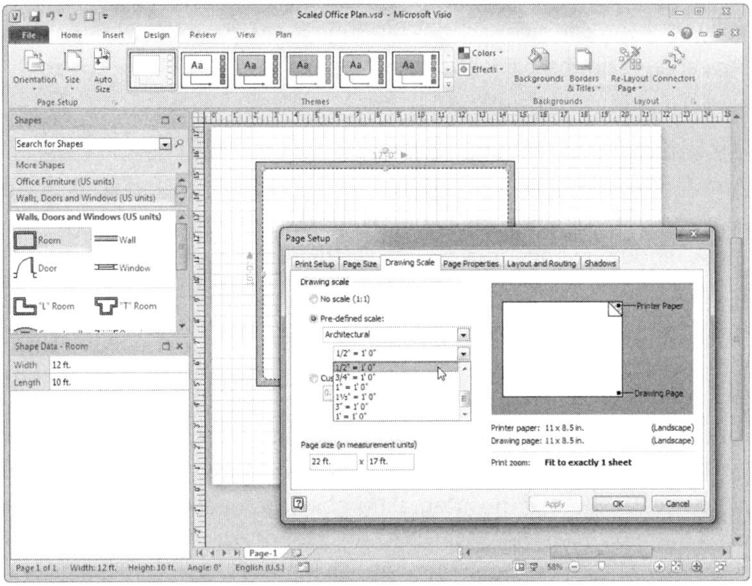

Figure 2.22 *Selecting an architectural scale for an office plan using the Page Setup dialog.*

The Drawing Scale tab has three radio buttons for configuring your page's scale: No Scale, Pre-defined Scale, and Custom Scale.

No Scale is just a 1:1 ratio. You use this scale for schematic diagrams such as flowcharts, network diagrams, and block diagrams. For measured drawings, you can choose Pre-defined Scales that follow Architectural, Civil Engineering, Metric, or Mechanical Engineering standards. Custom Scales enable you to enter any ratio you'd like. You could enter 1 cm = 1' – 2" if you want! Custom scales are good for using the paper to its fullest because using standard scales often leaves left-over space.

The Office Layout template that ships with Visio comes preconfigured with the Architectural scale of ½" = 1' – 0" (1:24) for US units and 1:25 for Metric units. The shapes that open with this template also are created to scale. For example, the Sofa shape from the Office Furniture stencil drops on your page at 7 feet × 2 feet 6 inches—a typical sofa size. You can see the size of a selected shape by looking at the status bar in the lower-left corner of the Visio application window or by looking at the Size & Position window (turn it on by choosing View, Show, Task Panes, Size & Position).

When choosing scales, note the two fields under Page Size (In Measurement Units). As you change the scale, these fields update to reflect the width and height that your page represents in the real world. This lets you double-check that the space on your page is big enough to fit the object you are drawing.

Using Themes to Change the Look of Pages and Documents

Themes allow you to change the look of a single page or all pages in your document at the click of a mouse. Using themes is much easier than formatting individual shapes, and themes help you maintain consistency in your diagram.

Some might view themes as eye-candy, but I think that themes offer more than "just a pretty face." If you are printing drafts of a diagram to a black-and-white printer, a simple, low-color theme saves toner. If, however, you want to use your drawing in a presentation or publish it to the Web, black-and-white will bore your audience. Choosing a vibrant theme can spice up your drawing and keep your viewers interested. Themes are great for matching corporate style guidelines, and Visio's themes match up with PowerPoint's, letting you seamlessly use Visio graphics in your presentations.

Using the Theme Gallery Control

You saw how easy it was to apply a theme to your first basic flowchart in Chapter 1, "Introducing Visio 2010." Let's revisit them and have a look at the details. The Design tab has a Themes group that contains a gallery of themes. Each theme shows a preview of the theme's colors, fill effects, fonts, corner-rounding, and arrowhead treatments. You can scroll the theme gallery or drop it down to see more themes.

Remember that themes have Live Preview enabled, so you can "look without buying." If you hover your mouse cursor over a theme, the drawing changes to show you how it will look with this theme. If you like the look, click the theme to apply it to your diagram. If not, move your mouse cursor away and your diagram reverts to the way it was.

LET ME TRY IT

Changing Themes for Pages and Diagrams

1. Create a new workflow diagram (located in the Flowchart template group).
2. Drop some of the snazzy workflow shapes onto the page. Add some text to the shape and make sure that a few of the shapes are connected.
3. Add a background and a title using the Backgrounds and the Borders & Titles controls on the Design tab.
4. Add a new page or two to the document using the Insert Page tab. The new pages should have the same background as the first page.
5. Copy shapes from the first page and paste them onto the new pages. You should have something similar to that shown in Figure 2.23.

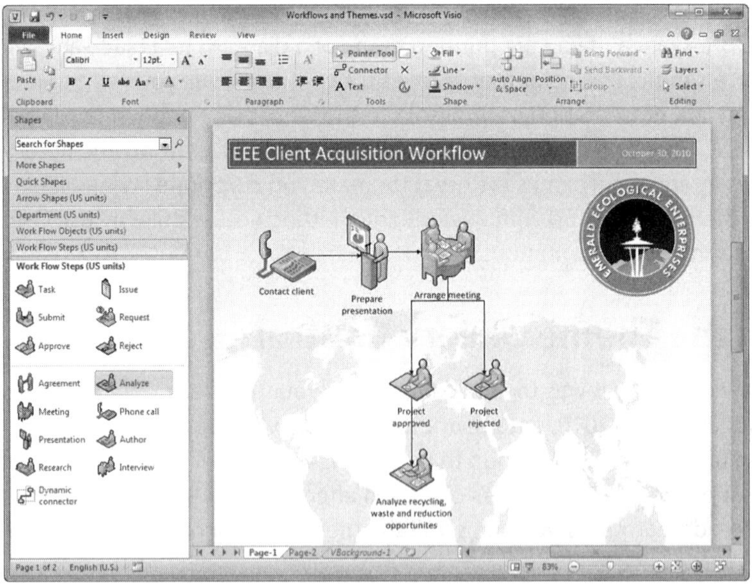

Figure 2.23 *A workflow diagram with a background page that contains background-graphics, a title, and a company logo.*

6. On the Design tab, hover over various themes in the theme gallery. Notice how Live Preview gives you a peek at what the theme will look like in your diagram.
7. Apply various themes by clicking items in the theme gallery. Notice how the colors and styles on the background page change too.
8. Notice that the stencils in the Shapes window also update to reflect the current theme.
9. Click the drop-down button for the theme gallery to reveal more themes, as shown in Figure 2.24. Notice that the theme's name appears when you pause the mouse cursor over an item.

Figure 2.24 *The expanded theme gallery. ToolTips reveal the name of each item.*

10. There are three areas in the drop-down separated by shaded bars: No Theme, This Document, and Built-in. You can click No Theme at any time to bring your drawing back to its original, "unthemed" state.
11. Visit the other pages in your document by clicking the page tabs at the bottom. Notice that the other pages have the theme that you chose.

Setting Themes, Theme Colors, and Theme Effects

To the right of the theme gallery are two small drop-down controls labeled Theme Colors and Theme Effects. Themes are actually combinations of color sets and graphical effects. Effects include fonts, fills, lines, arrowheads, and shadows.

This separation is great if, for example, you like the colors of a particular theme, but would rather have different graphical effects. Instead of looking for a different theme altogether, just drop down the Effects list and look for different combinations of line, fill, text and shadow while leaving the colors untouched.

Notice that each item in these drop-downs has a name below the icon. These make it easier to match the style of your Visio diagram to that of a PowerPoint presentation.

Visio Theme Colors match up reasonably well with those in PowerPoint, but the names of effects do not. The reason is probably that PowerPoint's effects change the layout and look of the slide in addition to graphical styles. So PowerPoint's notion of an "effect" is quite a bit different from Visio's.

Applying Themes to Pages versus Documents

Themes can be applied to all the pages in a document or to just one page at a time. If you right-click an item in the theme gallery, you see two choices: Apply to All Pages and Apply to Current Page.

These settings are sticky; whichever setting you choose becomes the default. For example, if you right-click a theme and then choose Apply to All Pages, your entire document gets the theme you clicked. The next time you click a theme, every page will change to the new theme as well! There is one tricky gotcha involved here. Themes can't be independently applied to pages that share the same background. Take the foreground pages for the document in Figures 2.23 and 2.24. These pages share the same background. If you change the theme for one page, the other page's theme changes too. It doesn't matter which Apply setting you use.

Of course, if your document has multiple pages that use different backgrounds or no background at all, you can freely apply different themes to different pages.

Themes that you use in a document show up in a short list that helps you to remember which ones you've already used. Notice the This Document area of the themes gallery (refer to Figure 2.24). If you hover over one of these items, the ToolTip tells you which pages the theme is used on, plus the theme's name. For example, you might see "Aspect colors, Simple Shadow effects: Used by page(s) 3–4." Very useful information if you have a complex document with many pages.

Preventing Theming

Sometimes, you don't want shapes to react to themes. A simple example of this is a Stop Sign shape. It should always be red with white text, and doesn't need rounded corners, transparency, or soft shadows.

You have already seen a shape that ignores themes for good reason. Take another look at Figures 2.23 and 2.24 and notice the Emerald Ecological Enterprises company logo in the upper-right corner. Regardless of the theme applied, its colors and effects remain unchanged. This is good, because we wouldn't want the corporate folks to come down on us for mangling company branding

You can easily prevent a shape from reacting to themes. Right-click it, click Format, and then uncheck Allow Themes. This works best if you choose this setting while your drawing still has No Theme applied. If your shape has already been inadvertently themed, click Remove Theme in the same submenu.

Another way to make theme-proof shapes is to format them with Standard Colors, instead of Theme Colors, which we discuss next.

Setting Color Palettes and Themes

When you format the color of a shape's line, fill, or text, Visio presents a color palette with several sections. In Figure 2.25, you can see that the drop-down palette has Theme Colors, Standard Colors, and Recent Colors sections.

You've probably noticed that theme colors change with the theme. Because of this, they have names. In Figure 2.25, you can see the ToolTip under the mouse: "Accent 1, Lighter 80%." This indicates that you are applying an "80% shade" of the "Accent 1" color to the shape.

If you explore the columns of colors in the color palette, you see that they are named White, Black, Background, Line, Fill, Accent1, Accent2, Accent3, Accent 4, and Accent 5. Because colors can float with themes, it helps to think about the name of the color and what you are applying it to. Instead of thinking, "Oh, let's make this shape's outline mauve!" you might instead think, "Hey, let's apply the theme's Line color to the outline of this shape!"

If you don't want your colors to float with the theme, use a color from the Standard Colors or Recent Colors region. This approach makes sense for things like a stop sign, where you'd want white text and a red fill, no matter the theme. You can also click on More Colors to access a full-spectrum color palette and a wider range of standard colors.

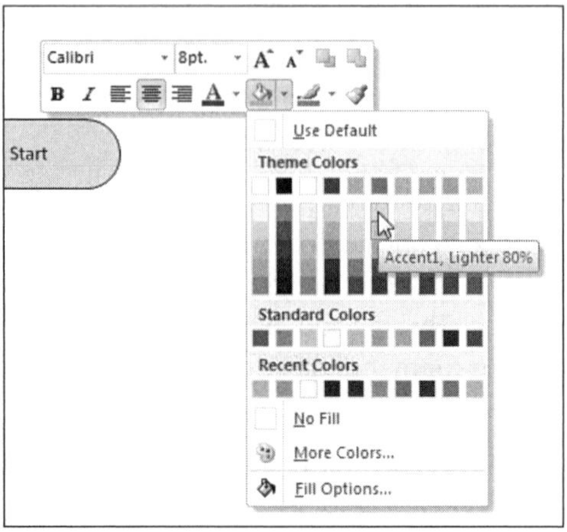

Figure 2.25 *Theme Colors change when themes change. Standard and Recent Colors remain the same.*

Using Visio Windows

Visio is a multiple-document interface (MDI) application, which means you can have several documents open at once, and all the documents are contained within Visio's main window. Contrast this with, for example, Microsoft Word, in which each document has an entirely separate window.

Visio basically has three levels of windowing:

- The main application window
- Drawing windows
- Task panes

Drawing-level windows also include group-editing windows, master-editing windows, and separate stencil windows, along with the ShapeSheet window which you learn about in Chapter 11, "Developing Custom Visio Solutions."

Task panes are generally owned by drawing windows. They can be anchored or docked to sides and corners of drawing windows, or they can freely float in space. You've seen task pane windows already, but the complete list includes the following:

- Shapes
- Stencils

- Shape Data
- Size & Position
- Pan & Zoom
- Document Explorer
- Task panes for specific templates and custom Visio solutions

Figure 2.26 shows a rather busy sampling of Visio windows. You see two different drawing windows. The workflow drawing on the left has a collapsed Shapes window, a stencil anchored to the top-right corner, the Size & Position task pane anchored to the lower-left, and a separate ShapeSheet window for the selected shape at the bottom. The directional map window on the right shows the Pan & Zoom window in the lower-left corner, in addition to an expanded Shapes window.

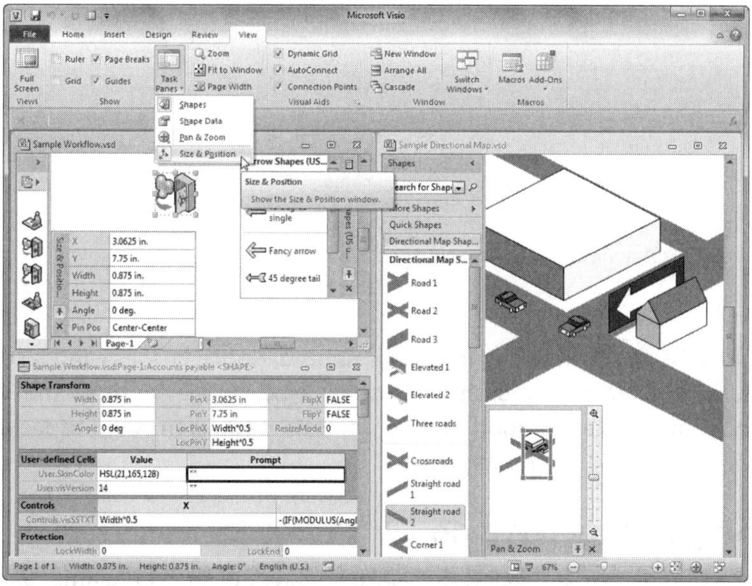

Figure 2.26 *Window soup: Multiple drawing windows are open, along with several task pane windoqs, and a ShapeSheet window.*

You can show other task panes by going to the View tab and then clicking the Task Panes drop-down button in the Show group (refer to Figure 2.26).

Managing Windows

Because of Visio's different window-within-window levels, there are a few points to consider when managing windows.

Minimizing and Maximizing Drawing Windows

Because drawing windows are inside Visio's application window, they have their own set of minimize and maximize buttons. These buttons can jump around, depending on whether or not your window is maximized.

In Figure 2.27, the drawing window is not maximized, so it has its own frame that you can tug on. Its minimize, maximize, and close controls are in the upper-right corner of the window, as you would expect.

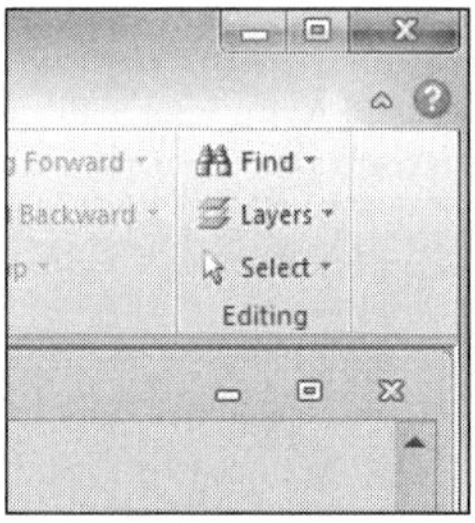

Figure 2.27 *A nonmaximized drawing window.*

In Figure 2.28, the drawing window is maximized. Notice how its window controls have jumped up to the top of the application window. They're above the Ribbon just under the Visio application window controls. If you aren't used to seeing this behavior, it can be a bit of a surprise!

Switching Between Windows

If your drawing windows are maximized, you don't see any of the other windows' frames. If they aren't maximized, they can still be hidden behind one another, and minimized windows can be easy to overlook.

There are several ways to navigate between windows:

- Pressing Ctrl+Tab cycles through the windows.
- The Switch Windows button in the lower-right corner shows a pop-up list of open windows. This is the last button in the status bar, just to the right of the magnifying glass icon. Click on it, and you can choose from windows that are

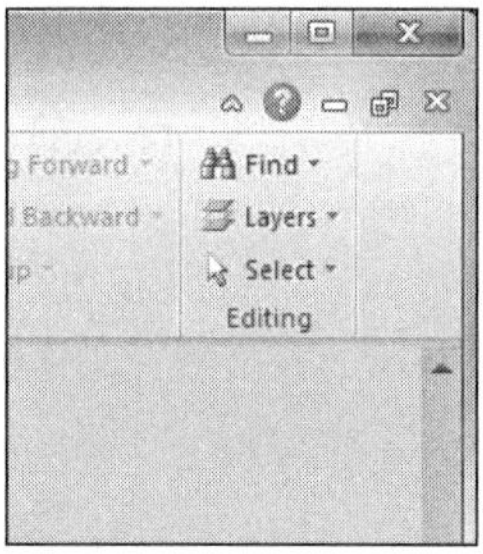

Figure 2.28 *A maximized Visio window. See how the min, max, and close controls jump up above the Ribbon?*

open in Visio. It is helpful for discovering windows you didn't think were open!

- In the Window group on the View tab, the Switch Windows button provides a drop-down list of available windows.

The View tab's Window group also contains controls for arranging and cascading all open windows. These come in handy when you have many windows open, start to lose track of them and need to tidy things up.

You can open new windows using the New Window button. This lets you look at different pages within a drawing or even compare different locations on the same page.

Positioning Task Panes

Task pane windows behave a bit differently, however. They can float in space or be docked or anchored to sides of a drawing window. When panes are docked, you will see a pin control. Clicking the pin activates auto-hide, which can save you space by collapsing the pane after a few moments of inactivity. Figure 2.29 shows task panes in their various states.

In Figure 2.29, the Shape Data window is docked to the top of the window and spans the entire drawing area. The Pan & Zoom window is anchored to the left side and autohidden. Simply drag a pane near the edge of the drawing window, and you see a snapping behavior that either anchors to the edge or docks to the full side of the window.

You can set a task pane to autohide by unclicking the pin icon, or by right-clicking and unchecking the AutoHide menu item, as the figure shows with the Size & Position pane. When you mouse over a collapsed pane, it expands so that you can access its controls.

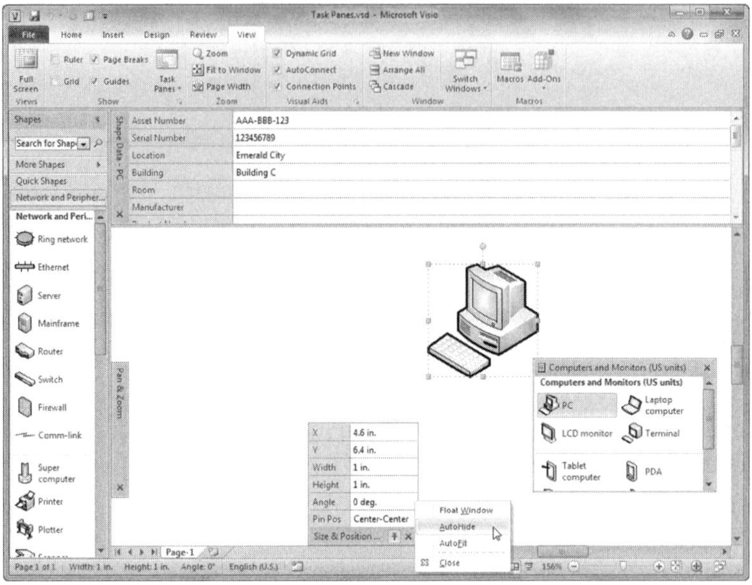

Figure 2.29 *Task panes, floating, anchored, docked, and autohidden.*

Finally, the Computers & Monitors stencil is freely floating in space. You can even drag task panes so that they float outside the Visio application window.

Using Full-Screen View

One last window option is full-screen view. With Visio's full-screen view, you see only the current page, maximized to fill your screen. No Ribbons, no scrollbars—just clean, pure Visio content.

To get to full-screen view, simply press F5 or use the Ribbon and go to View, Views, Full Screen. Press F5 again or press Esc to return to the normal Visio environment. You can also right-click anywhere and choose Close from the context menu.

Full-screen view is largely static, meaning you can't interact with the Visio drawing very much. You can't select shapes nor edit them, but hyperlinks do work, and you can page through a document.

When you're in full-screen view, clicking the screen advances to the next page. Right-clicking gives you more navigation control so that you can go forward, backward, or jump to any page within a document.

TELL ME MORE **Media 2.5—Making PowerPoint-Style Presentations with Visio**

Access this audio file through your registered Web Edition at ***my.safaribooksonline.com/9780132182683/media.***

Summary

In this chapter, you learned about Visio's supporting bits and pieces that lie beyond the graphics on the drawing page.

You saw many ways to start a new drawing. You learned how to access different stencils, search for shapes, and save the ones you like to your Favorites stencil.

In addition, you learned how to add pages to your documents and manage them. You saw the power of background pages and how to add background graphics and titles to them. You also learned that themes offer a convenient way to change the entire look and feel of a page or all pages at the click of a button.

Finally, you saw the various levels of windowing inside Visio and how to manipulate drawing windows as well as task panes.

You are now well equipped to dig into the details of diagramming with Visio 2010, which is the main focus of the rest of this book!

In this chapter, you learn about some of Visio 2010's new structured drawing features—Containers, Lists, and Callouts—that take organization and annotation beyond just text and lines on the page. This chapter also describes groups, layers, and markup and review features, which offer even more possibilities.

3

Organizing and Annotating Diagrams

Incorporating hierarchies, groupings, and classifications into your diagrams makes them easier to create, understand, and update. Because many documents are continually evolving and in need of updating, you need tools to help you annotate and comment on drawings as they change with your business.

Containers and Lists

There are many cases in which you need to visually associate shapes that are logically related. It is easy to draw a box around items and then label them with a text block, but Visio offers a better way.

Visio 2010's new Container and List shapes make organizing sets of shapes a snap. Shapes can be easily added and removed from them, and all member shapes conveniently move along with their parent containers.

Let's look at how containers and lists can add structure and organization to your diagrams.

Containers

Containers are special shapes designed to visually group other shapes together and to make it easy for you to maintain these relationships. Container shapes consist of a rectangular region where member shapes are contained, plus a title area called a *header*.

You've already seen containers in action in the "Energy Sources" block diagram that appeared in Chapter 1, "Introducing Visio 2010." Figure 3.1 shows it under construction.

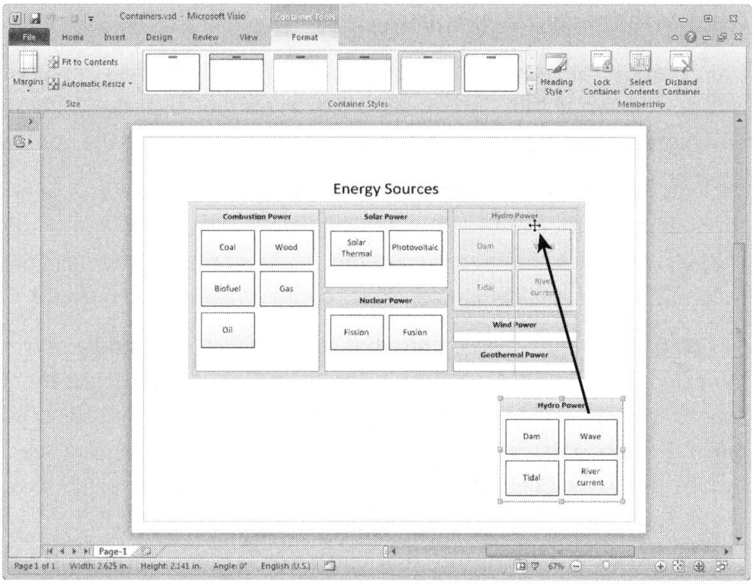

Figure 3.1 *The Hydro Power container contains member shapes lower in the hierarchy. It is being dragged into the main Energy Sources container, showing that containers can contain other containers, as well as regular shapes.*

SHOW ME **Media 3.1—Organizing Shapes with Containers**

Access this video file through your registered Web Edition at ***my.safaribooksonline.com/9780132182683/media.***

LET ME TRY IT

Organizing Shapes with Containers

Although containers are shapes, they're so cool and important that you don't access them from a stencil. Instead, they are built right into the user interface on the Insert tab. Let's look at adding shapes to and removing them from containers.

1. Start a new drawing from any template, such as the Basic Network Diagram.
2. On the Insert tab, expand the Container gallery in the Diagram Parts group.

3. Select a container item from the gallery. You should see a new container shape in the middle of your page.
4. Drag shapes from any stencil and drop them on top of the container. Notice the orange highlighting as you drag a shape over the container. This highlighting tells you that the shape will be added to the container.
5. Click on a shape in the container. Notice that it is easily accessible and not "buried" inside the container as grouping does (discussed later in this chapter). Also notice that the container is highlighted with a thin, orange outline. This tells you which container contains the selected shape.
6. Select the container shape. Note that if you click in the middle of the container, you are not able to select it. This is so that you can select member shapes without accidentally moving the container itself. To select the container, you need to click on the very edge or on the header. You see the mouse cursor changes to crosshairs when you are over a selectable part of the container.
7. Move the container by dragging it around the page. See how all the member shapes follow the container?
8. Make the container bigger or smaller by pulling on any of the eight blue resizing handles. Notice that you can't make the container smaller than its member shapes.
9. Drag a shape out of the container so that it is in a blank area of the page. This shape no longer moves with the container. Removing a shape from a container is that easy.
10. Duplicate the container several times. You can do this quickly by Ctrl+dragging. Or try selecting a container and then pressing Ctrl+D to duplicate it. No matter how you copy a container, all the member shapes are duplicated along with it; you don't need to select the member shapes at all.
11. Now delete one of the duplicate containers. All the member shapes are deleted along with the container. This is very convenient but might be unexpected the first few times you do it.
12. Right-click a container and notice the Container menu item. This contains many container-specific actions, which are also available on the contextual Container Tools tab in the Ribbon.
13. Expand the Container menu to see its subitems; then choose Disband Container. The container is deleted, but this time, the member shapes are

not deleted. This is handy if you want to get rid of the container, but keep the members.

14. Select the shapes that remain from the container that you disbanded in the previous step.
15. On the Insert tab, select a new container from the Container gallery. A new container is placed behind the select shapes, effectively "slipping a new container under" the selected shapes.

LET ME TRY IT

Changing an Existing Container

In Figure 3.1, you might have noticed the Container Tools contextual Ribbon tab. This tab is available when you have one or more container shapes selected or when shapes that belong to containers are selected. You might also have noticed the Containers context menu that appears when you right-click a container.

Let's explore some things you can do to existing container shapes.

1. Start with any drawing that has a container that contains a few shapes.
2. Select the container; then click the Format tab under the Container Tools contextual tab.
3. In the Container Styles gallery, click a new style. As you move your mouse cursor over the various styles in the gallery, notice how Live Preview shows the way your container will look, as depicted in Figure 3.2. Click a new style to change the look of your container in-place.
4. Similarly, you can change the look of the container's heading by browsing the Heading Style gallery to the right of the Container Styles gallery.
5. Resize your container so that there is lots of extra space, beyond what the member shapes require.
6. Click the Fit to Contents button in the Size group on the Container Tools tab. The extra space in the container disappears, and the container neatly and tightly encloses its members.
7. Click the Margins drop-down to the left of Fit to Size. Mouse over the various items in the list. Notice how the padding, or margins, of the container increase and decrease. If you drag member shapes near the edges of the container, orange lines will appear to help you align shapes to the margins of the container.

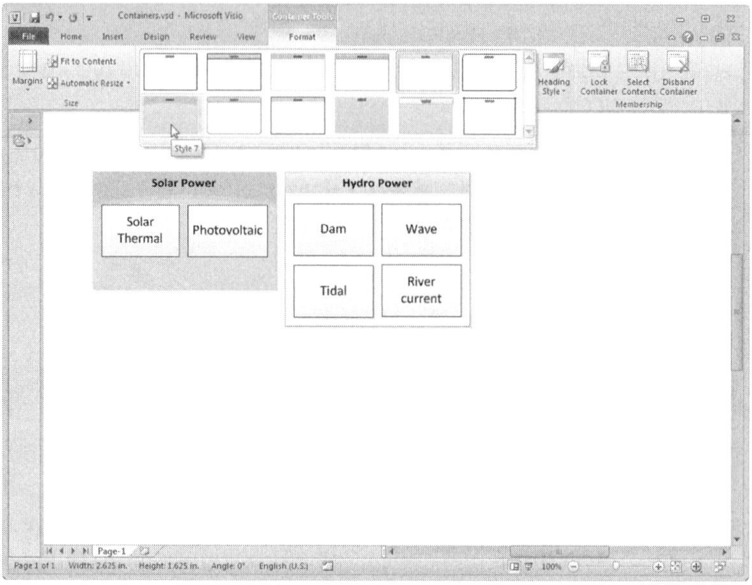

Figure 3.2 *You can change containers on the fly, in place. No need to delete the container, add a new style, and then re-add member shapes.*

8. With the container selected, click the Lock Container button in the Membership group. Now try to remove member shapes from the container by dragging or deleting them. You can't do it. If you try to move a shape off the container, the container just gets bigger and keeps the shape within its boundaries. You can click the Lock Container button again to unlock the container.
9. From the Automatic Resize drop-down, choose Always Fit to Contents.
10. Move the container's member shapes around. Notice how the container expands and contracts to accommodate the shapes. If you unlock the container, this behavior will change slightly because you will be able to remove member shapes from the container.

    With Always Fit to Contents, expanding the container is a bit tricky. If you move a member shape too far, then it will jump out of the container. If you move it partially off the edge of the container, then the container will expand. A neat trick is to select a member shape and then move it by pressing the arrow keys. The container will keep expanding as you move the shape towards the edge, but the shape won't jump out of the container.

ABOUT THE CONTAINER CONTEXT MENU

The Container context menu actually exists for all shapes. For shapes that aren't containers, however, there are only two items instead of six. They are Add to New Container and Add to Underlying Container.

The first item provides a quick way to wrap selected shapes in a container without going to the Ribbon. A default container appears around the selected shapes, and you can change its look later using the Container Tools tab. If you are creating a lot of containers, this approach can save you a bunch of time.

The second item helps in the event that a container gets slipped under a shape. This happens when a container is stretched so that it encompasses nonmember shapes or if a container is moved underneath nonmember shapes. In these cases, shapes are not automatically added to the container. Clicking Add to Underlying Container adds the shapes to the container.

Another way to accomplish the same effect as using Add to Underlying Container is to just nudge the shapes. Either grab them with the mouse and move them slightly, or nudge them with the arrow keys. For example, pressing the left-arrow key and then the right-arrow key adds the shapes to the container but returns them in their original positions.

Containers are powerful, useful, easy to use, and fun! It is important to note that they are not just boxes with text: they are structured drawing elements understood by Visio as more than just graphics. This has implications when it comes to validating diagrams against corporate standards and when programming custom solutions on top of Visio. Diagram validation is a feature available in Visio 2010, Premium edition; building custom solutions is touched on in Chapter 11, "Developing Custom Visio Solutions."

Lists

Lists are special container shapes that keep members stacked together in a single column or row. What's great about lists is that you can drag member shapes up or down in the order, and the other shapes automatically rearrange themselves in the list.

Lists don't have their own gallery, like containers, and there aren't a lot of list shapes that come with Visio. However, if you create cross-functional flowcharts, or *swimlanes*, you will run into lists.

Lists in Cross-Functional Flowcharts

Figures 3.3, 3.4, 3.5, and 3.6 illustrate how lists are used to manage the swimlanes in a cross-functional flowchart.

In Figure 3.3, a new swimlane needs to be added to hold steps that apply to TCR Inc. The figure shows how lists have a nifty "insert" feature. For vertical lists, a horizontal blue arrow and an orange line appear where a new item will be inserted.

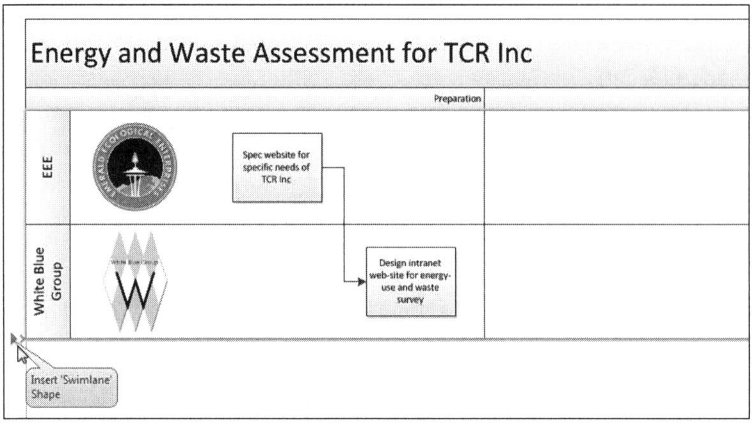

Figure 3.3 *Inserting a new swimlane into a cross-functional flowchart. When the mouse is between list items, a blue arrow and orange highlight show where a new list item can be inserted.*

Clicking the blue arrow adds the new lane, which appears in Figure 3.4. You might not see the colors in this book, so I encourage you to start a new Flowchart, Cross-Functional Flowchart drawing and experiment with inserting swimlanes.

Because Emerald Ecological Enterprises is the main contractor, its swimlane needs to be moved to the top of the process. You can simply grab the lane header and drag it to the top. Figure 3.5 shows a similar blue arrow and orange line showing where the shape will be inserted when you release the mouse button.

Figure 3.6 shows the final, rearranged swimlane. The items in the swimlane list are rearranged, and kept tightly together. You don't need to fiddle around with moving shapes apart, then pushing them back together.

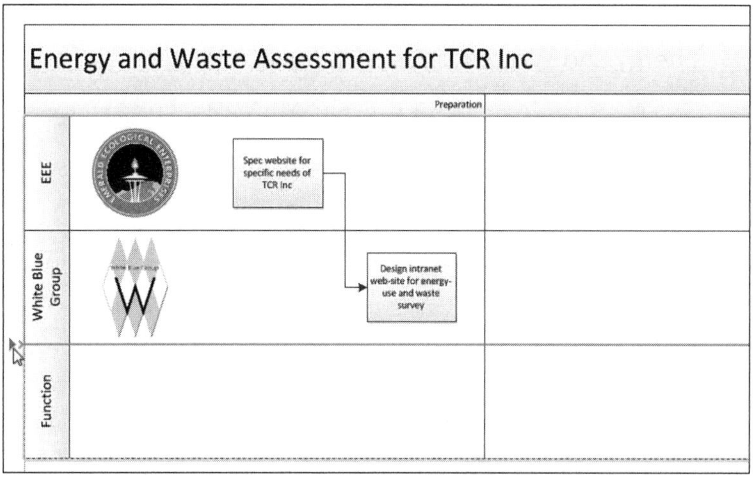

Figure 3.4 *After the insert arrow is clicked, a new lane is added to the process. The text for the lane can be immediately edited.*

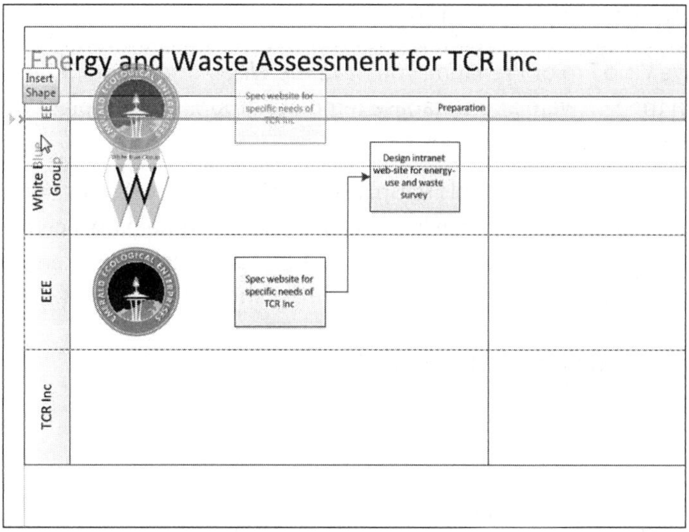

Figure 3.5 *Dragging a lane up to a higher position. Highlighting shows where the lane will be inserted.*

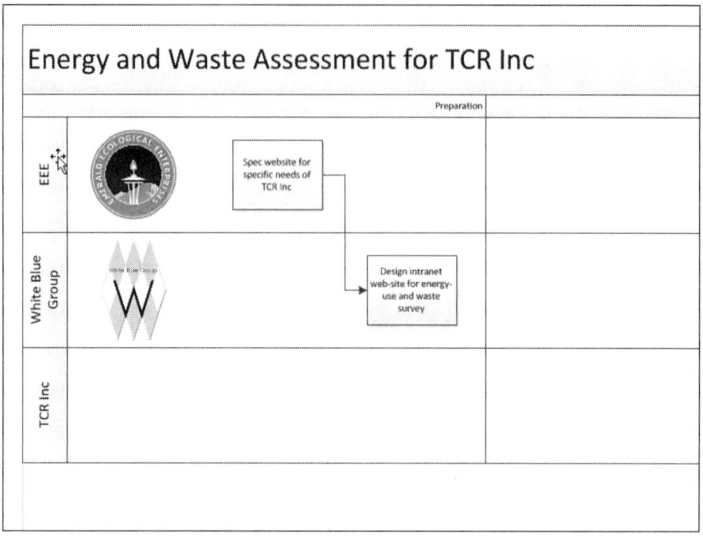

Figure 3.6 *The EEE lane is inserted above the White Blue Group lane. Notice that the shapes moved with their respective lanes, and the connector remained intact.*

Lists in Wireframe Diagrams

If you have Visio Pro or Premium, you have the Wireframe Diagram template, located in the Software and Database template group. This template enables you to create user-interface mockups.

The stencils that open with this template contain a few list shapes that you might want to experiment with. These lists are designed to contain only certain list members. If you drag shapes from the stencil to a list, only certain list item shapes can be added to the list container shapes. Table 3.1 shows the pairings.

Table 3.1 Wireframe List Shapes and List Member Shapes

List Shape	List Item Shape
Menu bar	Menu bar item
Drop-down menu	Menu item
Status bar	Status bar item Status bar icon Status bar splitter Resize grabber
Tab bar	Upper tab item Bottom tab item

Table 3.1 Wireframe List Shapes and List Member Shapes

List Shape	List Item Shape
List box	List box item
Tree control	Tree control item

But lists have the insert arrow feature, so you don't have to drag and drop in the first place. Just move your mouse until you see an insertion highlight. Figure 3.7 shows the Menu bar shape, with several menu bar items. You can see that the menu bar is a horizontal list, and that the insert highlighting is rotated at 90 degrees to what you saw earlier in the vertical swimlane list.

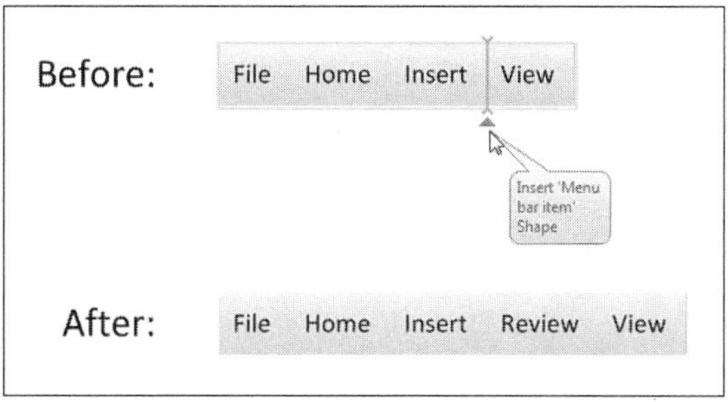

Figure 3.7 *Inserting items in a horizontal list.*

Wireframe shapes are intended for window, form, and web page design and are meant to be combined with other UI elements to build up a design. Hence, the wireframe list shapes don't have headers like containers do, because the headers would muddy the design. Without headers, though, it can be hard to find the list containers when you're working on a diagram. Figure 3.8 shows two Tree control lists full of Tree control items. You can see that when a list item is selected (in the right half of the figure) the list container is also highlighted with a thin, orange line. Click on the orange line to select the actual list shape.

You also see the familiar Container Tools contextual tab when you select a list or a list item shape. See how the Container Styles choices are slightly different for Tree control shapes? The two trees in Figure 3.8 show the different bullet styles shown in the Container Styles gallery.

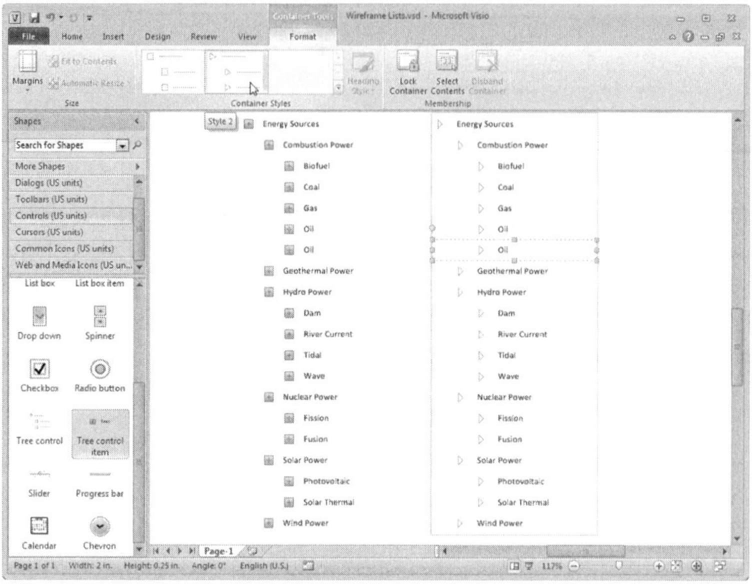

Figure 3.8 *The list container is hard to see until a member is selected. Note the Container Tools contextual tab also shows up for lists.*

Groups

Another way to keep related shapes together is to group them. Containers and lists are brand new in Visio 2010, but groups have been around since Visio's inception.

In Visio any two or more shapes can be grouped together. As your Visio experience grows, you will see that groups come in two flavors:

1. Assemblies of premade or finished shapes grouped together. Think of a set of office furniture shapes grouped together to represent a standard cubicle configuration.

2. Elemental graphical bits grouped together to form a single shape. Think of any network PC shape. There is a thick outline, a screen, a bezel, a keyboard, and some shading. These are all separate shapes, grouped together to form a single symbol.

Groups are useful and have their place, but they also cause some problems. When shapes are grouped together, they get buried inside a group shell, which hides data, makes formatting awkward, and can be confusing to users.

In fact, the shortcomings of groups provided impetus for the invention of containers and lists. Nevertheless, you should understand how groups work in Visio, and how to recognize them, as well as how and why to use them.

SHOW ME **Media 3.2—Creating Grouped Shapes**
Access this video file through your registered Web Edition at ***my.safaribooksonline.com/9780132182683/media.***

LET ME TRY IT

Creating a Grouped Shape

1. Create a new drawing from any template.
2. Drop three shapes on a page.
3. Select all three shapes.
4. In the Arrange group on the Home tab, click the Group drop-down and select Group.
5. Move the group. Note that all the subshapes move with the group. That's the point of grouping!
6. With the group still selected, choose a new fill color either from the Home tab or by right-clicking. Note that all the subshapes are colored. This is a potential drawback of groups.
7. Type some text while the group is selected. Notice that the text goes to the group, not to any of the subshapes.
8. Move one of the subshapes. To do this, you need to *subselect* a shape. First, click the group, pause for a second, and then click on one of the subshapes. You should see lighter-blue selection handles around the subshape and a dashed line around the entire group, as shown in Figure 3.9. You can now move the subshape within the group.
9. Reselect the group. To do this, first deselect everything by clicking on a blank area of the page or pressing the Esc key. Then click once on the group to reselect it.
10. Ungroup the shape. In the Arrange group on the Home tab, click the Group drop-down and then select Ungroup. You now have four shapes. Of course, you get your original three shapes back, but you also have one more "clear" shape that holds the text that you typed on the group.

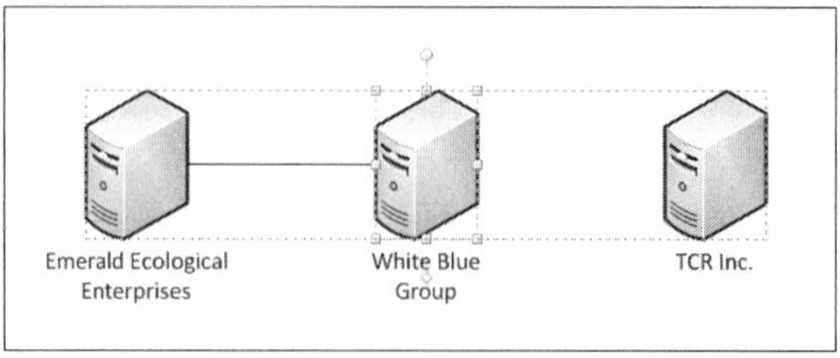

Figure 3.9 *Three network shapes grouped together, with the White Blue Group server subselected. Subselected shapes have lighter-colored handles, and a dashed line shows the parent group.*

There are some nifty shortcuts for grouping and ungrouping that will come in handy if you end up dealing with groups a lot. Shift+Ctrl+G groups a selection, and Shift+Ctrl+U ungroups a group or all groups in a selection of shapes.

If you like menus, right-clicking reveals the Group item. This item has two subitems: Group and Ungroup.

TELL ME MORE **Media 3.3—When to Use Groups**
*Access this audio file through your registered Web Edition at my.**safaribooksonline.com/9780132182683/media**.*

When to Use Groups

You should use groups in the following scenarios:

- For creating a single shape. If you are creating a shape that will be used as a single graphic, and users don't need to have access to its innards, grouping is appropriate. If your shape needs to have multiple text blocks, or details with different fill and line colors, you have to group separate pieces together.
- For temporary movement or arrangement. Perhaps you need to align a set of shapes with another set, while maintaining spacing within the set. You can quickly group your shapes together, move them around, align them, and ungroup them.
- For planned ungrouping. An example could be an office plan where you have several standard arrangements of furniture. These arrangements could be stored as grouped units on a "library" page. Users could copy an arrangement

to the floorplan page for placement in an office and then ungroup to get the individual equipment and furniture items.

You could even store such assemblies in stencils as masters and ungroup them after dropping them into a drawing. But Visio presents a warning when you ungroup masters, which can be unpleasant for users.

When Not to Use Groups

You might not want to use groups in the following scenarios:

- For creating categorical relationships. For example, you want to show which servers are in North America and which are in Asia on a network diagram. This is a good application for containers, not groups.
- If your shapes have Shape Data fields that need to be readily edited by users of your diagram. Grouping buries data fields and forces users to subselect to get at the data.
- If your shapes have other custom features such as right-click actions or control handles that users will need to manipulate. Grouping buries these features as well.
- If you expect that users of your diagram won't understand groups and subselecting subshapes.

If you are creating shapes for others to use, they might not know about subselecting within groups and might find it awkward. If you don't mind subselecting and are the only user of your shapes, then these caveats take on less importance.

Editing Inside a Group

If you want to change the look of a grouped shape, especially one that came from a stencil, you should add graphics *inside* the group. Many beginners try to ungroup a shape, add graphics, and then regroup the shape. This approach works for groups of shapes that have been temporarily grouped together, but not for custom shapes that may have special behaviors.

For example, the Server shape from the Network and Peripherals stencil is a grouped shape that has 22 Shape Data fields. It also has a special control handle that enables you to reposition its text block easily.

If you ungroup the Server shape, you destroy the text/control handle behavior and obliterate the shape data fields. Regrouping doesn't bring them back.

LET ME TRY IT

Editing Inside of a Group

1. Start a new drawing from the Basic Network Diagram template.
2. Drop a Server shape on the page.
3. With the Server selected, right-click it and choose Group, Open Server. Because every shape on the page has a different name, you might see something like Open Server.5 or Open Server.19.
4. A new window opens showing just the innards of the Server shape. You are inside the group, in a group editing window. Notice that the caption atop the Visio window has the text "<GROUP>" to remind you that you are inside a grouped shape.
5. From the Home tab, select the Rectangle or Ellipse tool and draw a shape or two on top of the server.
6. Close the group editing window by clicking the X (or "Close window" button) in the top-right corner of the window. Make sure you don't accidentally close the Visio application window!
7. You should now see your modified server from the "outside," with your additions safely inside the group.

If you like the idea of adding icons to server shapes, be sure to check out my "Visio Network Server Shape Icon Customization Tool" at http://www.visguy.com/2009/09/11/visio-server-shape-icon-customization-tool/. It uses a VBA macro to automatically perform steps 1-7 at the click of a button!

> Shape designers have a way of locking groups against subselection. Many of the master shapes in Visio's stencils are groups but, you can't subselect the member shapes. This is great, because they feel like single shapes and you don't accidentally subselect parts within the group.
>
> Designers normally don't want you to ungroup the masters they create. Nevertheless, you're free to try! Be advised, however, that you'll see a warning if you try to ungroup an instance of a master shape. Because designers incorporate various protection and behavior into their shapes, unexpected things can happen when you ungroup masters (such as subshapes jumping down to the lower-left corner of your page!). So proceed with caution, or better yet, try it out first in a test drawing that you don't intend to save.

Callouts

Callouts are blocks of text linked to a graphic via a line or other pointing visual. They are used to annotate diagrams without interrupting the flow of the main visual. A classic callout is the word balloon that you see in comics to indicate speech. You also see them in product brochures, discreetly pointing out essential features of a fancy new gadget but not distracting from the glossy visuals.

Using Visio 2010's New Callouts

In Visio, callouts can be used in innumerable ways to annotate diagrams. In Visio 2010, callouts have been upgraded significantly. They are now part of the structured diagramming features along with containers and lists and are fully integrated into the user interface.

SHOW ME **Media 3.4—Adding Callouts to Shapes**

Access this video file through your registered Web Edition at ***my.safaribooksonline.com/9780132182683/media.***

LET ME TRY IT

Adding Callouts to Shapes

1. Starting with any drawing, make sure one shape is selected. This shape will be the target of the callout.
2. In the Diagram Parts group on the Insert tab, drop down the Callouts gallery. You should see 20 or so callouts, similar to what is shown in Figure 3.10.
3. Choose one of the callouts to apply to your target shape. You can now move the callout around and type text into it, as shown in Figure 3.11. If you move the target shape, the callout follows along.
4. When you select the callout, the target shape is highlighted with a thin orange outline. This highlight is especially helpful for callouts that don't have a leader line because you can still tell which shape owns the callout.
5. Duplicate the *target* shape (not the callout) by Ctrl+dragging or pressing Ctrl+D. You should see that the callout is duplicated along with the target, as shown in Figure 3.12.

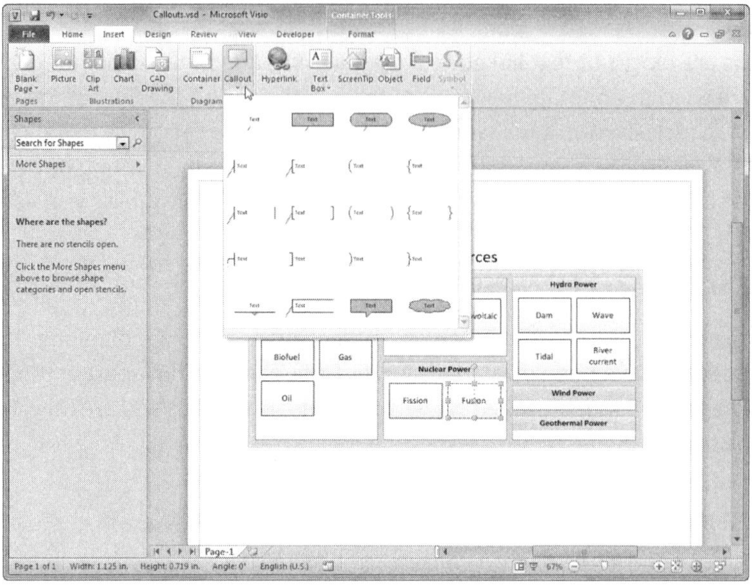

Figure 3.10 *The Callouts gallery.*

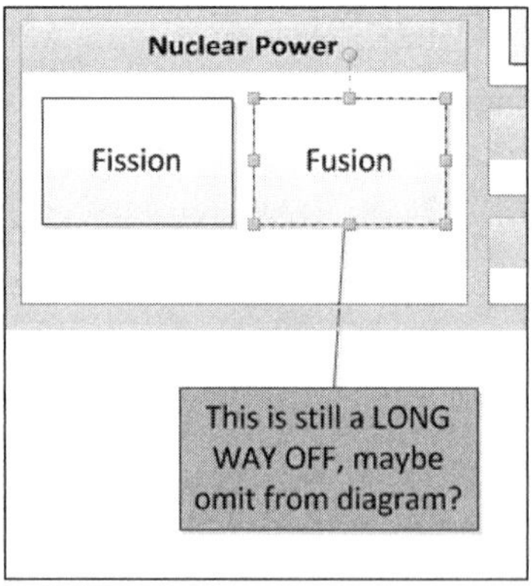

Figure 3.11 *A callout applied to the Fusion shape.*

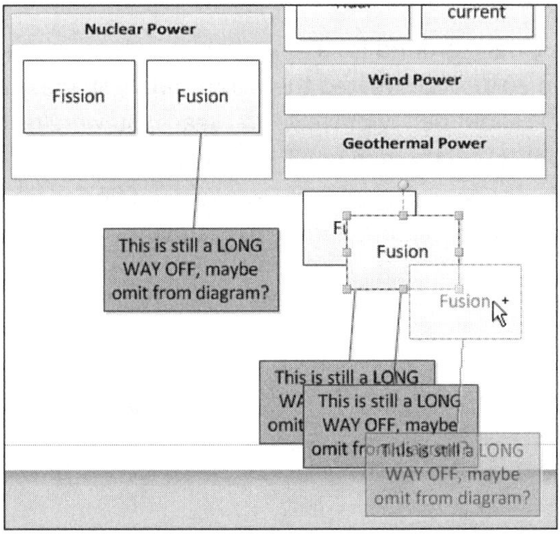

Figure 3.12 *When callout-target shapes are duplicated, callouts come along for the ride.*

6. You can change the style of the callout by right-clicking it and expanding the Callout Style cascading menu. There, you see the same 20 styles shown in the Callout gallery in step 2.
7. Note there are three more callout-specific menus below Callout Style: Orientation, Callout Line, and Resize with Text. Take some time to experiment with these functions.
8. Select the callout and notice the yellow control handle at the end of the leader line, in the middle of the target shape.
9. Move the control handle so that it is over a blank area on the page. You have now disconnected the callout from its target.
10. You can use this handle to change the callout's target shape. Drag the control handle so that it is over a different shape. Notice that as you do this, the new target is highlighted with an orange outline, indicating that it will receive the callout and become its target.
11. Move the new target shape and notice that the callout is now attached.

Using Legacy Callout Shapes

Visio callouts have been around for a long time, but they were much less sophisticated before Visio 2010. Visio treated them as ordinary shapes and didn't provide any of the special callout behavior we've just seen. You were responsible for moving them and duplicating them manually. Nevertheless, these old-style callouts are useful, and you might appreciate the variety. You can find them in the More Shapes menu, under Visio Extras, Callouts. Figure 3.13 shows a wild sampling from the Callouts stencil.

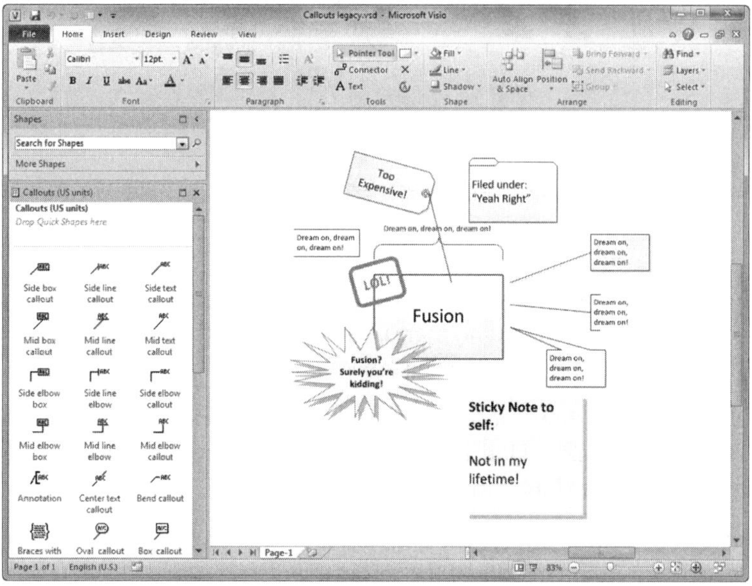

Figure 3.13 *The poor "Fusion" shape being picked on by legacy callout shapes from the Callouts stencil.*

Many of the old callout shapes are 1D shapes, which means you position each end independently, like you do with lines and arrows and connectors. You can glue callout ends to connection points on target shapes and to guides. (Guides can be pulled out of the rulers. They don't print, and you can glue shapes to them.)

The practical result is that the leader line stays glued to the target, and the text end stays put, which is sometimes exactly what you want a callout to do. Figure 3.14 shows old style callouts arranged in two columns. Each callout has one end glued to a target, the other end glued to a guide.

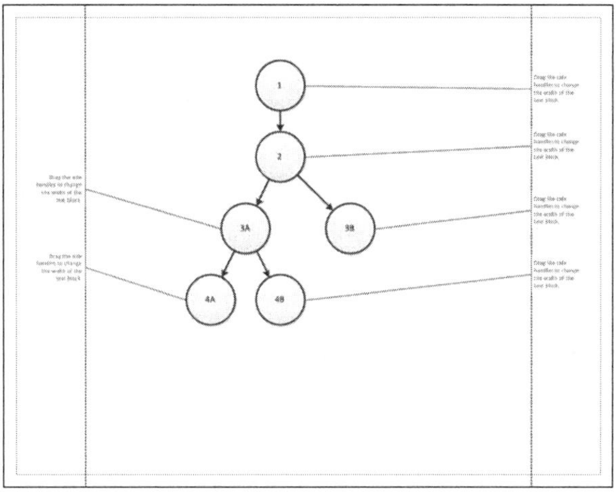

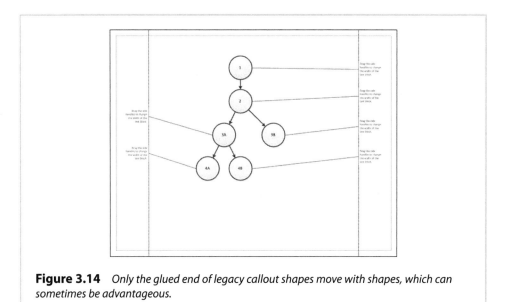

Figure 3.14 *Only the glued end of legacy callout shapes move with shapes, which can sometimes be advantageous.*

The text remains near the page edges, but the leader lines move with the target shapes. And since the text ends are glued to the guides, each column can be easily repositioned by moving a single guide. Older technology, but still quite useful!

SHOW ME MEDIA 3.5 **Cool Tricks with Legacy Callout Shapes**
Access this video file through your registered Web Edition at ***my.safaribooksonline.com/9780132182683/media.***

The Callouts stencil has three special callouts that behave much like Visio 2010 callouts, and in some ways are even smarter.

At the bottom of the stencil, you'll find Custom callout 1, Custom callout 2, and Custom callout 3. You attach them using control handles, and they move with their targets just as the new callouts do. Even better, these callouts can display Shape Data information from their targets—something Visio 2010's new callouts don't do. In this case, the "old" callouts are actually more powerful than the new ones. We can only wonder why Microsoft didn't include the Shape Data field display in the new callouts!

ScreenTips on Shapes

Visio ScreenTips offer a simple and clandestine way to add comments to your shapes. ScreenTips are just like ToolTips that you see everywhere in Windows when your mouse stops moving over some bit of the user interface.

If you hover over a Visio shape that has a ScreenTip, a little window pops up, displaying informational text for your enlightenment. Figure 3.15 shows one of these exciting ScreenTips in action.

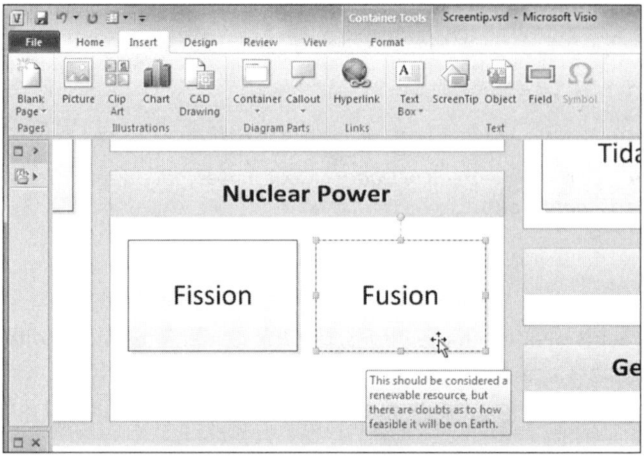

Figure 3.15 *A ScreenTip pops up when the mouse cursor hovers over a shape. Note there is no visual cue to indicate that a shape has a ScreenTip.*

ScreenTips are intended as a shape designer feature—a vehicle for communicating to users how to use the shape, or what it is for. The theory is that a forlorn user will pause in confusion over a shape, and your ScreenTip will pop up and enlighten him or her!

However, there's no reason they can't be used to enhance your diagrams creatively in a nondistracting way. The only drawback is that there is no visual clue that a shape has a ScreenTip in the first place—you have to pause over a shape to find out whether it has one.

Adding ScreenTips to Shapes

Adding a ScreenTip to a shape couldn't be easier. Just select a shape and then go to the Insert tab. In the Text group, click ScreenTip; then enter your message in the dialog that appears.

LET ME TRY IT

Adding a ScreenTip to a Shape

1. Select a shape in any drawing.
2. In the Text group on the Insert tab, click ScreenTip. You can see this Ribbon and button in Figure 3.15.
3. In the pop-up dialog that appears, type a message and then click OK.
4. Hover your mouse cursor over the shape. You should see your ScreenTip display after a second or two. Note that the shape need not be selected to show the tip.

Strategies for Using ScreenTips

ScreenTips are great because they add value to your drawing without unnecessarily cluttering it. However, they don't print and there is no visual cue that a shape even has a tip.

If you are thinking about incorporating ScreenTips into your work, consider the following suggestions to make them more discoverable and usable:

- Get in the habit of hovering over every single shape (no, I'm not serious!).
- Always append an asterisk (*) to the text of shapes that have ScreenTips.
- Add ScreenTips only to dedicated "ScreenTip shapes." For example, you could use small, brightly colored circles that have no text. Users easily see these circles, but your drawing isn't cluttered by the full text of the tip.
- Use a Callout shape as a "ScreenTip Shape." Give it no text and make the word bubble as small as possible. The tip moves along with its target shape, the user sees a small circle or square that indicates a tip, but the tip's full text doesn't clutter the drawing.
- Use dedicated ScreenTip shapes, but assign them to a nonprinting layer (discussed in the "Layers" section later in this chapter) so that they don't show up in printed output.
- Use the *Comment* feature from the Review tab (discussed in the "Markup & Review" section of this chapter). Review comments are visible to the user in a collapsed form but don't print.

ScreenTip text wraps automatically, but you might want to force a new line manually, say for a title or for some tabular information. The ScreenTip editing box doesn't accept the Return key by default, but if you hold down the Ctrl key while pressing Return, you can insert new lines as you like.

Headers and Footers

You've just seen that ScreenTips are visible only when you are editing. But sometimes you need information to appear only when printing. That's where headers and footers come in.

Word and Excel users already know that a *header* is a line of text that appears at the top of each printed page; a *footer* appears at the bottom. They are typically used to hold information such as filename, document title, or page number—information that is obvious when you are working in Visio, but not when you are holding the hard copy in your hand.

Visio provides three fixed information areas each for headers and footers. Providing a grand total of six possible fields.

You add headers and footers from the Print Preview tab of the Ribbon, which you can get to via File, Print, Print Preview. Clicking Header & Footer opens the dialog shown in Figure 3.16. Note the two columns of three fields in which you can enter information.

You can enter any text you want into each box, and you can also add field codes for dynamic information. Field codes are used for information that might change, such as the filename and date, or information that varies from page to page, such as number or name. Visio has a small set of field codes, but even so, you don't have to memorize them. The arrows to the right of each text box in the Header and Foorter dialog help you to insert them. Table 3.2 summarizes the available field codes for headers and footers.

Table 3.2 Field Codes for Headers and Footers

Field Information	Field Code
Page number	&p
Page name	&n
Total printed pages	&P
Current time	&t
Current date (short)	&d
Current date (long)	&D

Table 3.2 Field Codes for Headers and Footers

Field Information	Field Code
Filename	&f
File extension	&e
Filename and extension	&f&e

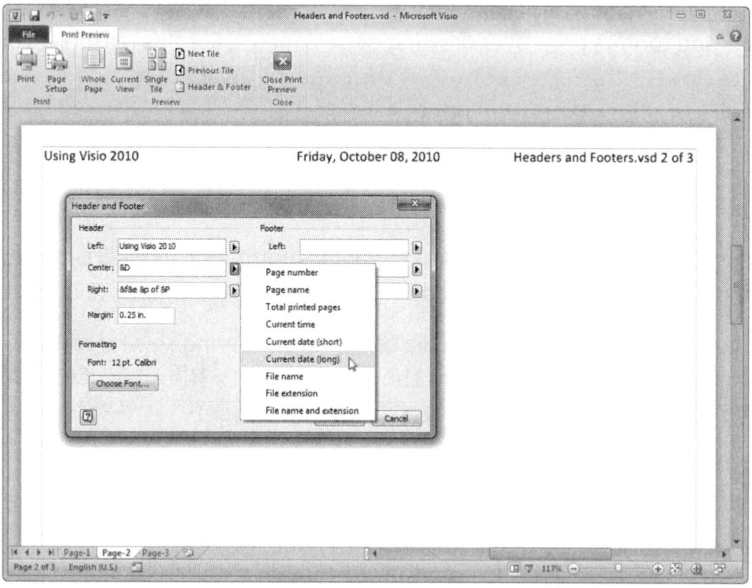

Figure 3.16 *The Header and Footer dialog, with Print Preview in the background. Notice the combination of free-form text and field codes used to build this document's three-part header.*

Some users find the set of field codes too limiting. For example, there is no code for the document's directory. The workaround is to insert fields into shapes, where the choices are much more varied and numerous. You effectively create headers and footers by using shapes placed on background pages. This is described in the next section.

You can mix text and field codes to make more readable headers. One of the most common combinations is &p plus &P which shows which page you are on, out of the number of pages in the document. Here are a few ways you might mix codes with text:

- pg &p of &P pages → pg 2 of 3 pages
- &p/&P → 2/3
- Page &p (&P total) → Page 2 (3 total)

Remember that headers and footers appear on every page in a document, but they don't show on the drawing page when you are working on your diagram. You only see them in Print Preview, on printed documents, and documents exported as PDF or XPS files.

Headers and footers print over drawing page content. For this reason, if you have graphics close to the top or bottom of the page, be aware that headers and footers might obscure them when you print.

Inserting Fields into Shape Text

Text on Visio shapes can be linked to dynamic information as well. Using the Field button on the Insert tab, you can add dynamic fields to a shape's text block.

When you click the Field button, a dialog pops up offering several categories of information that can be inserted, as shown in Table 3.3. The array of choices puts the field codes in the Header & Footer dialog to shame.

Table 3.3 Insert Field Categories for Smartening Shape Text

Field Category	Options
Shape Data	Values stored in shape data fields that might be attached to a shape
Date/Time	Date and time information indicating when the document was created, last edited, printed, or the current date/time
Document Info	File and document properties information, such as creator, description, directory, filename, keywords, subject, title, manager, company, category
Page Info	Name, page number, number of pages, and background page name (if any)
Geometry	Width, height, and angle of shape
Object Info	Developer-centric information, such as shape ID; master name; shape name; shape type; and information stored in legacy Data 1, Data 2, and Data 3 fields
User-Defined Cells	Values stored in user-defined cells stored inside the shape
Custom Formula	ShapeSheet, discussed in Chapter 11, "Developing Custom Visio Solutions"

LET ME TRY IT

Inserting Text Fields in Shape Text

1. Start a new, blank drawing.
2. Using the Rectangle tool from the Tools group on the Home tab, draw a rectangle on the page.
3. With the rectangle still selected, type the text **I am SO big by SO wide**.
4. Now replace the *"SO"* text with the actual width and height of the shape.
5. If you have deselected the shape, click the Text tool in the Tools group on the Home tab, then click your shape. You can also double-click the shape or just press F2 to get into text edit mode.
6. Use the mouse to select the first *"SO"*. These characters will be replaced with a field.
7. On the Insert tab, click the Field button in the Text group.
8. Select the Geometry category from the list on the left.
9. Click Width in the Field Name column on the right.
10. Click the Data Format button if you would like to change the number format. For instance, you can show or hide the measurement units for the field and change the number of decimals displayed.
11. Click OK until all dialogs are closed. When you stretch and shrink your shape, the field should update with the actual width of the shape. Check the status bar in the lower-left corner to compare the width values.
12. Repeat steps 6–11, but replace the second *"SO"* with the height. When you resize your shape, both the width and the height should update in the shape's text.

Inserted fields are indeed powerful, and the information that you can display has much more variety than that of headers and footers.

> You can detect inserted text fields with this simple trick: Select a shape and go into text edit mode (I like to press F2, but you can use the Text tool on the Home tab). Now press the left- or right-arrow key to move the text cursor along the text. If the cursor jumps over several characters at once, you have found an inserted field.

Of course, if the inserted field's value is only one character in length, this technique doesn't work. For decimal numbers, file paths, and dates, it is fairly effective.

Using Shapes with Preconfigured Fields

The Title Blocks stencil, located under Visio Extras in the More Shapes menu, contains many shapes that have preconfigured text fields. You can find shapes with preinserted information such as Date, Description, Drawn by, Filename, File+path, Page number, Revised date/time, Drawing scale, and Drawing title. A real timesaver indeed!

Furthermore, these shapes have a nice feature that enables you to position the field label either above the value or to the left. Just right-click the shape, as shown in Figure 3.17.

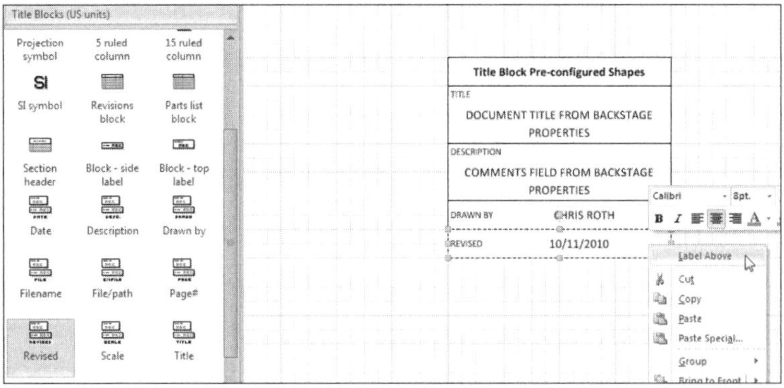

Figure 3.17 *Building a quick title block with shapes preconfigured with dynamic text information.*

Inserted fields can be used as shapes placed on background pages to perform functions similar to headers and footers. Certain fields, such as page name and page number, are smart enough to update differently for each foreground page.

Even though there is only one shape sitting on the background page, the text it displays is updated for each foreground page that references the background page.

Layers

You can add organization to your Visio documents by using layers to categorize shapes. A *layer* is a named category to which any number of shapes can be assigned.

Layers help you do things to entire categories of shapes at the click of a button. For example, you can

- Hide and show shapes
- Lock shapes from being moved, edited, and selected
- Temporarily color shapes to emphasize (and find) them
- Set shapes so that they print or not
- Quickly select all shapes belonging to a particular layer

The neat thing about layers is that unlike callouts and containers, they don't have to visually impact your diagram at all. You can assign shapes to layers, use layer operations when you need them, and then return things to their original state.

Basic Layer Skills

As with most things Visio, it is easier to describe layers after you've created and manipulated a few yourself. So let's start by creating some layers and assigning shapes to them.

LET ME TRY IT

Creating Layers

1. Start with a new, blank drawing.
2. Using the Rectangle tool, draw several rectangles; then use the Ellipse tool to draw several circles.
3. Apply a theme to the drawing to make it more interesting. In the Design tab, click the second theme in the theme gallery (Basic Colors, Basic Shadow Effects). Your shapes should now have a slight gray gradient fill.
4. Switch back to the Pointer tool and then select all the rectangles.
5. Go to the Layers drop-down in the Editing group on the Home tab.
6. Click Assign to Layer in the drop-down list. Next, you will assign the rectangles to a new layer.

7. In the Layer dialog, the New Layer should pop up automatically because you have no layers in this drawing.
8. Enter the name **Rectangular things** and then click OK. In the Layer dialog, Rectangular things should now be checked, indicating the shapes will be assigned to that layer. Click OK again to exit.
9. Now select just the circle shapes.
10. Click the Assign to Layer button again. The Layer dialog pops up.
11. Click the New button to define a new layer; then enter **Circular things** in the text field. Click OK twice to get back to your drawing.

There is a trick that lets you quickly add multiple layers at once, which is handy if you use layers often and need to create many of layers at a time. When you click the New button in either the Assign to Layer or Layer Properties dialogs, you can type in a list of layers, separated by a semicolon. For example, entering **Walls;Furniture;Equipment** in the Layer Name field creates three layers in one fell swoop.

You should now have a bunch of shapes assigned to one of two layers: Rectangular things or Circular things. Hold on to this document; we'll take the layers for a spin in the next exercise.

LET ME TRY IT

Manipulating Layers

1. Open the Layer Properties dialog by choosing Home, Editing, Layers, Layer Properties. You should see the dialog shown in Figure 3.18, which lets you control all the layers for a page.
2. Note the two layers you created earlier and the different columns. The # column shows the number of shapes assigned to each layer.
3. Uncheck Visible for one of the layers; then click Apply. The shapes on that layer should disappear. Apply lets you test settings without leaving the dialog, whereas OK makes the changes and then exits the dialog. Recheck Visible to bring them back.
4. Check Color for one of the layers; then select a color from the Layer Color drop-down list in the lower-right of the form. Click Apply, and the shapes on the corresponding layer should now be colored.

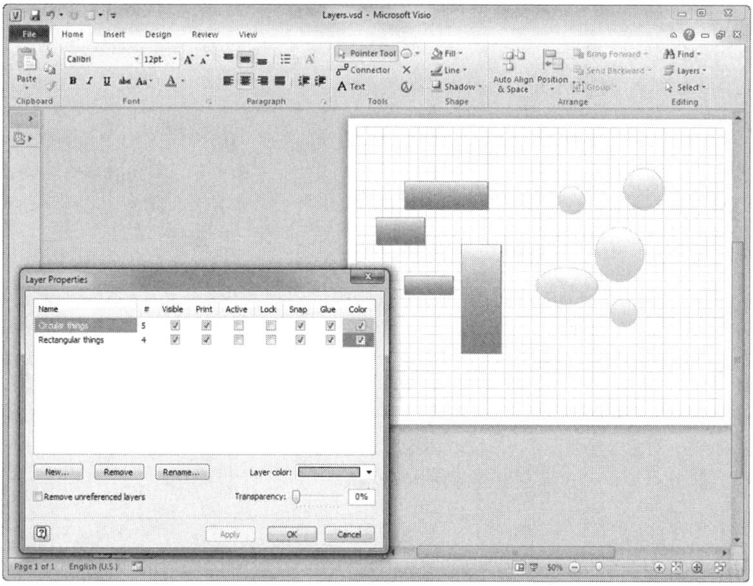

Figure 3.18 *The Layer Properties dialog. Note the shape counts for each layer in the # column. Also, each layer has been assigned a color, which can be seen on the drawing page in the background.*

Figure 3.18 shows what happens when layers are colored. This coloring is actually overlaid on your shapes. The formatting of the shapes themselves has not actually changed. When you uncheck the color boxes, your original formatting returns.

5. Check Lock for both layers; then click OK. The Layer Properties dialog disappears, and you return to the drawing. Note that you can't move any of the shapes on the page, because you locked the layers to which they are assigned.

6. Return to the Layer Properties dialog, remove all coloring, unlock all the layers, and return all layers to the visible state. Your shapes return to their natural state, unfettered by layer settings.

7. You can easily select all members of a particular layer. To do this, choose Home, Editing, Select, Select by Type.

8. In the dialog, click the Layer radio button and then check Rectangular Things. When you click OK, all the shapes on the Rectangular things layer should be selected. This is a really handy feature for complex drawings and just by itself is a good reason to assign shapes to layers!

The name Layers might make you imagine transparent sheets that can be stacked, each level showing through to the next. This is the way layers work in many CAD and graphics illustration programs.

In Visio, layers have nothing to do with Z-order (the order of shapes from back to front). You can't move one layer of shapes on top of another, because layers do not organize shapes at discreet levels. A shape can be assigned to any layer and be at any position, front-to-back-wise.

Visio shapes can belong to more than one layer, as you might have noticed from the Assign to Layer dialog. This capability makes it impossible to organize layers by Z-order.

For this reason, I like to say that Visio layers are "class, not glass." They are for classifying shapes into meaningful groups, but not for organizing them by level on metaphorical sheets of invisible glass.

To mimic the way layers work in other applications, you can create a system of background pages, since you can create chains of backgrounds with backgrounds with backgrounds. But managing and moving these can be a real pain, so I wouldn't recommend it beyond very simple cases.

Practical Application of Layers

You can see that layers offer an easy and flexible way to perform category-specific operations on shapes.

Locking shapes is a great way to protect parts of a drawing from accidentally being edited while you are working on other details. A great example of this is locking down the walls, windows, and doors of an office plan while you're working on furniture arrangements. Just as in real-life, these features are mostly immobile, whereas furniture can be rearranged more easily!

I like to use imported images in my drawings—often as backgrounds. Assigning the image to a layer and then locking it makes it much easier to work without continually selecting the image by accident. For more information on this topic, see the article "Importing Images as Backgrounds for Tracing" at www.visguy.com/2008/04/16/importing-images-as-backgrounds-for-tracing/.

As diagrams get more complex, making certain layers invisible can make your work a lot easier. If you are laying out furniture for an office or home plan, hiding layers for, say, switches, electrical outlets, and cabling removes a lot of clutter while you work. Visio will also be more responsive, since it has less to redraw every time you pan or zoom.

The ability to hide and show layers is also helpful if your drawing has many different audiences. The plumber, electrician, and facilities manager can all use the same drawing but you can print out different sets of layers for each of them.

With layer-coloring and select-by-layer, calling attention to and finding specific types of shapes are easy tasks. For large, complex drawings, these tools are invaluable.

If you've made a bunch of notes to yourself that you don't want to share with contractors or other consumers of the diagram, you can assign your callouts and other annotations to a nonprinting layer. They are visible while you're editing (so you don't forget about them), but they don't appear in the printed copies you send out into the field.

Visio Layers for Power Users

If you are excited about layers and see them as a key feature that you will be using a lot, you might be interested in a few fine points, some of which can be a bit confusing:

- Layer sets are per-page, not per-document. If you add pages to a document, you have to re-create layers on each page.
- When you copy a shape, the new copy retains its layer membership.
- If a shape is assigned to a layer and is dropped on a page that doesn't contain that layer, the layer is added to the page. You can create "layer set" shapes to make it easy to add a standard set of layers to new pages. Just create a rectangle, assign it to every layer that you need, and then drop it onto a new page. All layers are created instantly.
- The Layer Properties dialog has an Active Layer column. If you check any active layer boxes, new shapes added to the drawing page are automatically assigned to active layers—if they don't already belong to layers. Shapes that are already assigned to layers keep their settings.
- Shapes can belong to multiple layers; this affects behavior when you check and uncheck items in the Layer Properties dialog. Generally, it operates on a "positive logic" principle: if something is checked for any of a shape's layers, that attribute takes hold. So if a shape belongs to two layers, and one of them is locked, the shape is locked. To hide the shape, you have to uncheck both layers' visibility because a positive value for either layer will result in a visible shape. I generally find it easier and less confusing to limit my shapes to one layer as much as possible.

- The exception to the previous point is layer coloring. If a shape belongs to multiple layers and you want to color it via layers, all layer boxes need to be colored *and* assigned the same color. For this reason, I find that multiple layers and layer coloring do not mix well.
- If a shape is on a nonvisible layer, but the layer is set to print, the shape *will* print, even though it is invisible in Visio. This can sometimes come as a surprise. If you are a heavy layers user, get in the habit of checking Print Preview before you print.
- Many of the shapes associated with the Office Layout template are assigned to multiple layers. For instance, the Door shape is assigned to "Building Envelope" and "Door," the Wall shape is assigned to "Building Envelope" and "Wall," and the Oblong dining table is assigned to "Movable Furnishings" and "Furniture."

  This is great if you want to select shapes by varying degrees of specificity. You can select all doors and walls by selecting shapes on the "Building Envelope" layer, or just get the doors by selecting shapes on the "Door" layer. Cool!

  However, if you want to hide shapes on these layers, you have to uncheck Visible for two layers in each case. Assigning shapes to multiple layers has its pluses and minuses.

Getting to the layer dialogs via the Ribbon can become tedious if you do it frequently. To make it easier, customize the Ribbon or Quick Access Toolbar by adding a control called "Layer," which you'll see if you show All Commands in the customization dialogs. The Layer control presents a drop-down list of existing layers and lets you assign layers to selected shapes much more quickly.

Markup & Review

You've seen how callouts and ScreenTips can be used to annotate your diagrams and how layers can be used to turn details on and off.

If you have a living document for which several people need to give input, the markup and review features will be of interest, particularly comments, markup, and ink. Visio's reviewing capabilities aren't as powerful or fluid as Word's, but you might still find them useful.

Comments

Comments allow multiple users to critique a document. They are similar to ScreenTips but are more noticeable, and they aren't attached to shapes.

Comments float on the page as little yellow boxes with the initials of the commenter and an ID number. To read one, just click it and it expands to reveal its contents.

Figure 3.19 shows a diagram with comments from two different users. The comment from "BWG" is collapsed, and the comment from "EEE" is expanded so you can read the message, along with the commenter's full name and the date it was made.

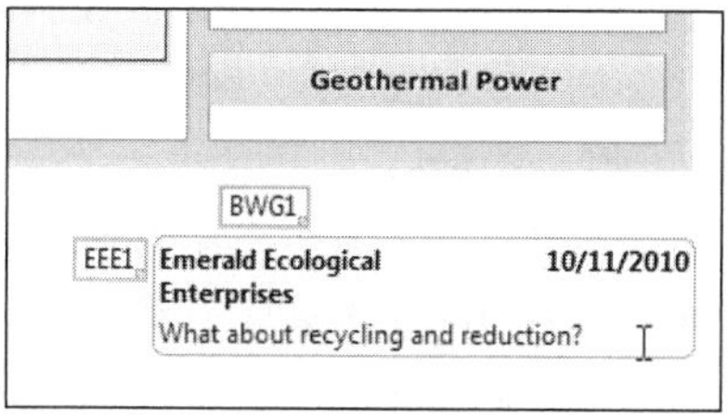

Figure 3.19 *Expanded and collapsed reviewing comments.*

LET ME TRY IT

Adding Comments to Your Diagram

1. On the Review tab, click New Comment in the Comments group. A little yellow box with your initials appears on the page, with an expanded area for adding text.
2. Enter a message in the box. As soon as you click somewhere else on the page, the comment collapses to show just the initials.
3. You can freely drag the comment box around the page and position it wherever you want.
4. If you hover your mouse cursor over the comment box, the full name of the commenter appears, along with the date the comment was last updated.

Note: The name and initials of a user are set in the File, Options, General tab, in the Personalize Your Copy of Microsoft Office area. There you see text fields for User Name and Initials.

5. If you click a comment box, it expands and the entire comment appears.
6. Notice also that in the Markup group on the Review tab, the Show Markup button is now pressed, and the Reviewing pane is visible on the right.
7. Toggle the Show Markup button on and off. Notice that your comments appear and disappear.
8. Toggle the Reviewing Pane button on and off. The Reviewing pane shows and hides itself, but your comments remain as long as Show Markup is pressed.
9. With Show Markup pressed, go to File, Print, Print Preview. Notice that the comments are not visible. Review comments do not print.

Be aware that comments are part of Visio's Review features and are visible only when the Show Markup button is pressed. This is a little confusing because comments are actually different from markup, as you see in the next section.

Markup

In Visio, markup is slightly different from the comments you just explored, even though they are related by the Show Markup button and the Review tab.

Markup consists of graphics that a user adds to a page. When you click the Track Markup button (just above the Reviewing Pane button), Visio creates a special markup overlay tab for the current user on top of the page. Any edits to the drawing made while Track Markup is pressed are put on this tab and given a color that corresponds to the user. Markup is like a hybrid of pages and layers; each reviewer gets his or her own markup overlay tab, associated with a particular page and a particular reviewer.

Figure 3.20 shows a familiar diagram that has been commented on and marked up by two users.

There's a lot going on in Figure 3.20, so let's go over the important bits, one by one:

- In the Reviewing pane, there is a history list under "Markup Page-1." This shows both comments and markup added, and which user made the modification. You can see that EEE and BWG have both added comments and shapes to the drawing.

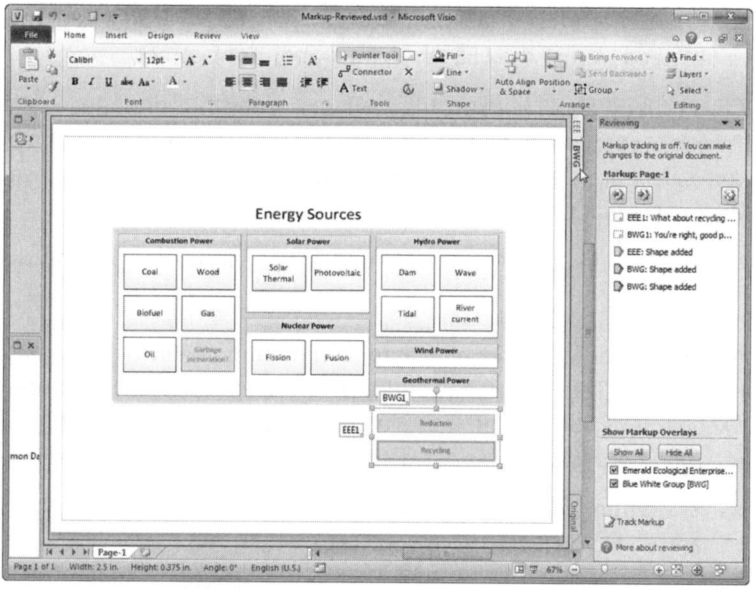

Figure 3.20 *A diagram that has comments and markup from two users. Note the two markup tabs in the upper-right corner of the page.*

- Each user has an associated color. When a user creates a shape on the page, it is shown in this color. You might not be able to see this in the printed form of this book, but user EEE is red and user BWG is blue in Figure 3.20.
- There are two tabs in the upper right corner of the drawing page, one for each user. These tabs are colored to match the red and blue of EEE and BWG, respectively.
- Along the same edge, but at the bottom, you see the Original tab. This is, of course, where the nonmarkup drawing bits can be accessed. Clicking the Page-1 tab also returns you to the regular drawing.
- Tab BWG has just been clicked. When this happens, the markup shapes from BWG are selected in the drawing page. You can see that the Reduction and Recycling boxes are selected. These boxes are also colored blue, because they were created by user BWG.
- When the BWG tab is active, only the shapes created by BWG can be selected and edited. The drawing's shapes can't be touched, and neither can EEE's markup shapes.

- Notice the shape under "Combustion Power" that says "Garbage incineration?" This shape is red and was added by user EEE. To edit this shape, you would need to click the EEE tab in the upper-right corner.
- If you turn off Show Markup, the markup overlay tabs disappear, along with the corresponding markup shapes. Alternatively, you can turn off markup from select users by checking and unchecking users in the list beneath Show Markup Overlays.
- Any visible markup will print, although comments do not print, as we discussed earlier.

The markup features for Visio are great for commenting on living diagrams that are in continuous flux. The colorization and separate overlay tabs for each user are useful and keep things tidy. I found these features to be a bit complicated at first, but if you just experiment for a few minutes, they'll start to make more sense.

What is missing from Visio markup, however, is the ability to delete shapes and Accept Changes, as you can in Microsoft Word.

If you've used Word's reviewing features, you are probably used to being able to accept or reject a change. Graphics on the markup overlay tabs are stuck in their own parallel universe, separated from the actual drawing. This has frustrated Visio users for quite some time.

The workaround is to cut shapes from an overlay tab, click the Original tab, and then paste them. Not difficult, but not as smooth as right-clicking and choosing Accept or Reject. As for deleting shapes, you can simply add a rectangle or comment that says "delete this" and hope that the document's owner takes your advice.

Ink

If you use a tablet PC or like to scribble with your mouse, you'll like Ink. Inking allows you to draw and write freehand on Visio pages. You can leave your inking as Ink entities, convert it to Visio shapes, or let Visio try to recognize your handwriting and convert it to text.

You access Ink from the Markup group of the Review tab, but your inking does not have to be part of a markup overlay; it can be used in normal drawings independent of markup and review.

When you click the Ink button, you are taken to the Ink Tools contextual tab. There you can choose to scribble with the Ballpoint Pen or Highlighter. You can change the color and weight of your ink creations and erase strokes using the Stroke Eraser. Each ink stroke that you add is combined with the previous ones into a single shape. You can click the Close Ink Shape to finish one inking entity and begin a new one.

Figure 3.21 shows two ink entities: one is text created with the Ballpoint Pen tool, and the other is a Highlighter streak over the "Energy Sources" title. To make sure the highlighter streak was not combined with the handwritten text, I used the Close Ink Shape in between.

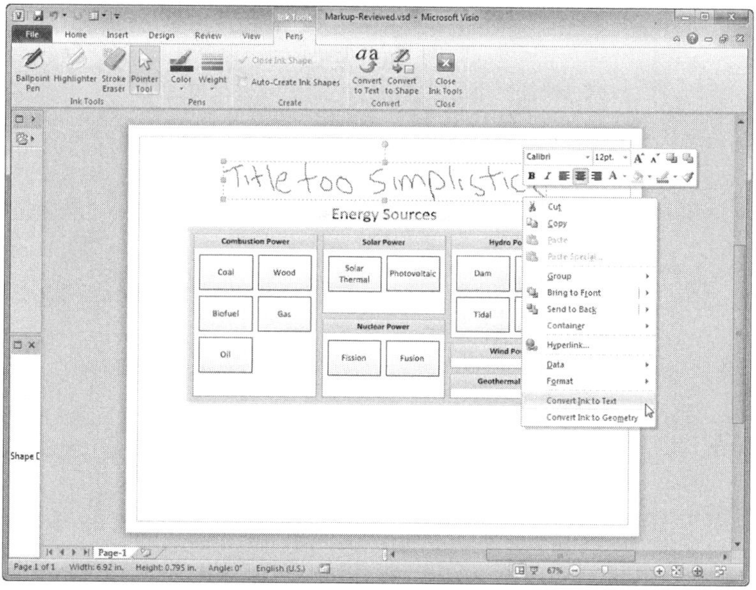

Figure 3.21 *Ballpoint pen and Highlighter entities created with Ink.*

You can also see that I've right-clicked the chicken scrawl and am ready to click Convert Ink to Text. Believe it or not, this actually worked! A moment later, a legible block of text in 12-point Calibri appeared in its place. You can also convert your ink items to Visio shapes that can be edited with the Line, Pencil or Freeform tools.

Summary

In this chapter, you saw that Visio has an abundance of features for organizing and annotating diagrams.

You learned how to keep related sets of shapes together using containers, lists, and groups and how to categorize and manipulate shapes using layers.

You also saw that headers and footers can be used to add dynamic information to pages and that inserted fields and ScreenTips can be used to do the same for shapes.

When it comes to annotating your diagrams, you have a bevy of choices. You can choose from the new Visio 2010 callouts, older callout shapes, Comments, Markup, or Ink tools.

Finally, you can control the visibility and printing of specific sets of shapes using layers or markup overlays.

In this chapter, you learn about connecting shapes together with Visio's connectors and how to use supporting features that help you complete your diagrams more efficiently.

4

Connecting Shapes

Using lines and arrows between shapes to indicate relationships is an important element in visual communication.

If you need to create org charts, business process diagrams, network diagrams, flowcharts, entity relationship diagrams, wiring schematics, or anything similar, you should have a thorough understanding of how to connect shapes in Visio.

Understanding Visio Connectors

In Visio, lines between boxes are called *connectors*. Connectors are a special class of shape, with special behaviors. They stay *glued* to shapes, so when you reposition objects, the connectors follow along. Connectors are smart enough to route around objects, as shown in Figure 4.1. They can be split to allow the insertion of new shapes, and they are deleted along with the shapes to which they are connected.

Connecting Basics

There are many ways to connect shapes in Visio 2010. To learn them all at once can be overwhelming, so let's look at a few of them right now. We cover more ways later in the chapter.

SHOW ME **Media 4.1—Basic Connecting in Visio 2010**
Access this video file through your registered Web Edition at ***my.safaribooksonline.com/9780132182683/media.***

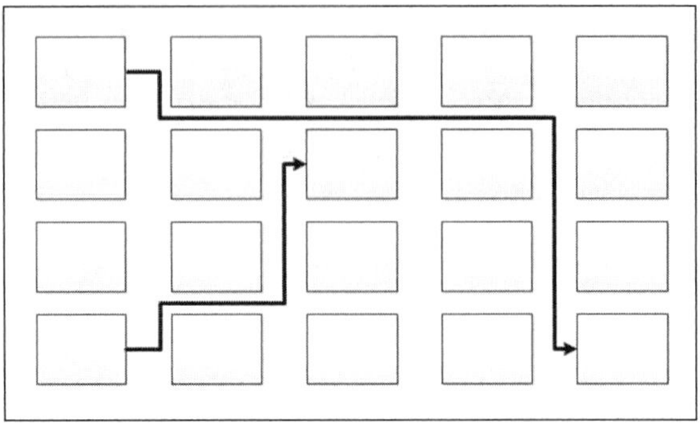

Figure 4.1 *Visio connectors showing off—avoiding the Process shapes at all costs.*

LET ME TRY IT

Basic Connecting

1. Start a new Basic Flowchart drawing.
2. Drag a Start/End shape onto the drawing page. You can enter some text, such as **Start**.
3. Notice that when your mouse cursor hovers over the shape, four blue AutoConnect arrows appear around the edges. If you move your mouse cursor over one of these arrows, you see the mini-toolbar, as shown in Figure 4.2. This feature enables you to insert one of the top four Quick Shapes from the currently visible stencil.

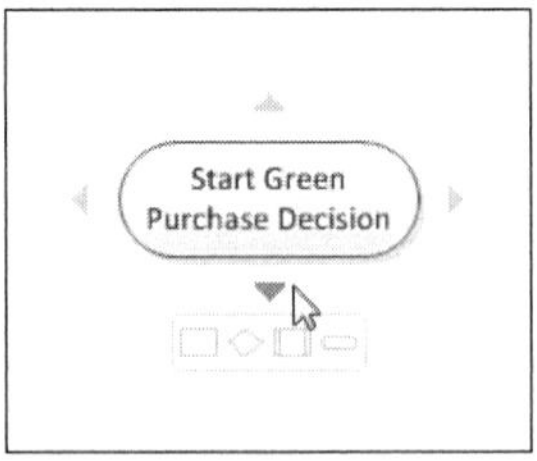

Figure 4.2 *Hovering over an AutoConnect arrow reveals the mini-toolbar, which helps you to insert and connect Quick Shapes quickly.*

4. Click on one of the shapes in the mini-toolbar. Notice that the shape is added to your diagram, aligned with the previous shape, and automatically connected.

5. Move your new shape around. Notice that the connector stays glued to both shapes. Notice also that the connector wanders around the edges of the shapes so that the nearest sides are connected.

6. Select the connector. Notice that it has two endpoint handles instead of the eight blue resizing handles that the Start/End shape and other 2D shapes have. The endpoint handles are red, indicating that the connector is glued at both ends to the other flowchart shapes. The connector also has some smaller blue handles that allow you to reposition bends and corners.

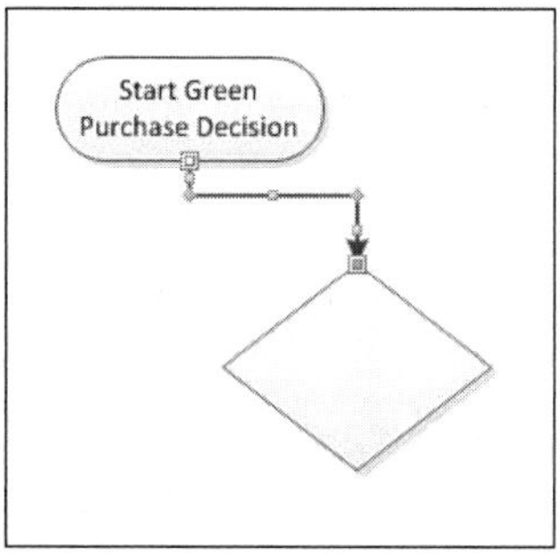

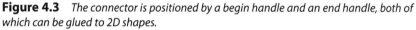

Figure 4.3 *The connector is positioned by a begin handle and an end handle, both of which can be glued to 2D shapes.*

7. Drag a Custom 2 shape onto the page, away from the other two shapes. It is below the Quick Shapes line in the Basic Flowchart Shapes stencil, so you might have to scroll the stencil window to see it. Since it isn't connected to any shapes, let's connect it to the flow using a more manual method in the next few steps.

8. On the Home tab, select the Connector tool from the Tools group.

9. Connect the Custom 2 shape to the process by clicking on one shape, dragging over another, and then releasing the mouse button. Notice the red highlights when the mouse cursor is positioned over a shape.

   A red box around the entire shape means *glue dynamically*: the connector wanders around the shape to find the nearest side. Mousing near the edges of the shape reveals small red squares with blue Xs inside, shown in Figure 4.4. Connecting to these makes *point-to-point glue*, where the connector stays attached to this point, no matter where you position the flowchart shapes.

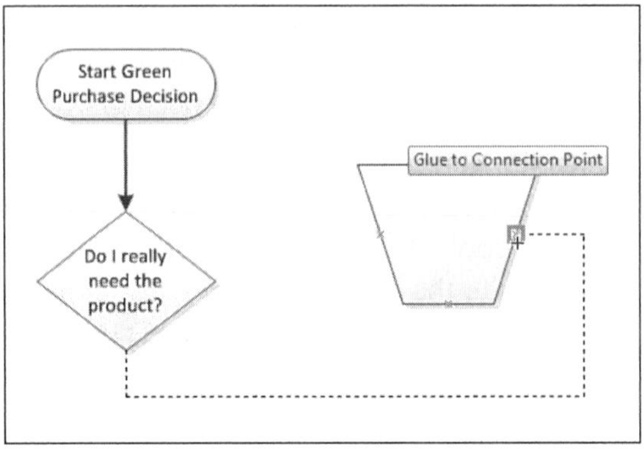

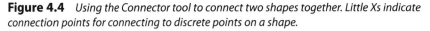

Figure 4.4 *Using the Connector tool to connect two shapes together. Little Xs indicate connection points for connecting to discrete points on a shape.*

10. Switch back to the Pointer tool, located just above the Connector tool (or just press Ctrl+1).

11. Select and delete the Custom 2 shape that you added in step 7. Notice that the connector is automatically deleted along with it!

12. Drag another shape from the stencil and drop it on the connector between the two remaining shapes. Don't drop the shape until you see red highlights on both ends of the connector.

    This highlighting tells you that Visio will automatically help you with the insertion of the step. When you let go, Visio splits the connector in two and glues the new shape to the pieces. It also dynamically slides the existing shapes out of the way to make room for the newcomer.

13. Delete the shape you just added in the preceding step. Notice that the two connectors heal to become just one. However, they do not automatically slide closer together to close the gap.

14. Drop another shape onto the page, unconnected to the others.

15. To connect it to another shape, pause the mouse cursor over the shape until the AutoConnect arrows appear. Now click and drag from one of the arrows. You can actually drag a connector out of the arrow and connect it to another shape.

16. Experiment with gluing the dangling end to a target shape using dynamic or point to point glue. Once the connector is glued, you can still select it and then grab a handle and move it to another shape or another connection point on the same shape. Try re-connecting ends of the connector to other shapes and connection points on other shapes.

Using the Connector Tool

You've just seen that you can connect Visio shapes using either the AutoConnect arrows or the Connector tool. AutoConnect is convenient because it saves you the trouble of switching tools. In some situations, though, you'll want to use the Connector tool.

Using the Connector Tool Can Be Faster

Sometimes you want to connect a bunch of shapes that are already on the page. While you can drag connectors out of the blue arrows to do this, it can be slow, because you have to pause and wait for the AutoConnect arrows to appear each time. If you've been drinking a lot of coffee, the pausing can try your patience.

Switching to the Connector tool (Ctrl+3) allows you to work more quickly. With the Connector tool, you can create many connections very quickly, without pausing and waiting for the user interface to catch up. You can work faster and with less mouse precision—a perfect combination for the caffeinated!

AutoConnect Won't Always Be There for You

If AutoConnect is turned off, you don't see the blue arrows at all. AutoConnect can be turned on and off via the View menu, in the Visual Aids group. Because some templates have AutoConnect turned off by default, you might find it quicker to create a few connections with the Connector tool instead of switching AutoConnect on, making connections, and then switching it back off again.

A common scenario occurs when superimposing wiring schematics on top of space plans and office layouts. While drawing walls, windows, and doors and laying out furniture, you *don't* want those AutoConnect arrows popping up all the time. For this reason, the Office Plan template has AutoConnect turned off by default. At some point, however, you might place PC and telephony icons on the plan and link them back to the server room. In this case, AutoConnect might come in handy, but it's just as easy to get the Connector tool in this situation.

Also, if a shape is already connected, you don't see any blue arrows on the sides where there are connectors. If you need to have multiple connectors to a shape, you have to get the Connector tool.

Multimode Tools Eliminate the Need for Switching

You might be concerned about having to switch tools a lot while creating connected drawings. This is one reason the AutoConnect arrows were invented in the first place, but most Visio tools have a bit of overlapping functionality.

With the Connector tool, you can move and resize shapes in addition to connecting to them. Pay attention to the cursor as you mouse over a shape. An S-shape with an arrow at the end means connect mode. Crosshairs indicate that you can move the shape. If you see the diagonal double-ended arrow while over a selection handle, you can resize the shape.

Similarly, the Pointer tool can be used to reconnect connectors, change the position of bends in the connector, or move the whole connector altogether. You do not have to use the Connector tool to modify existing connectors.

Connectors Are Shapes, Too!

Connectors straddle the line between built-in, special-purpose Visio features and plain old Visio shapes. Visio adds pizzazz to connectors by automatically assisting with inserting, deleting, splitting, gluing, and routing. And, of course, you have a dedicated Connector tool for creating them. The end result is still a shape on the page that you can manipulate just like other Visio shapes.

Here are a few ways in which connectors behave as regular shapes:

- You can format the line color, weight, pattern, and arrowhead style of a connector, just as you would any other line in Visio.
- When connectors are created, they are actually an instance of a master named Dynamic Connector. In fact, you might see it as a master in stencils, ready for dragging and dropping. If you've made a connection in your diagram, you will see the Dynamic Connector master in the local Document Stencil. Whether you use the Connector tool or the AutoConnect arrows, the result is that a connector *shape* is added to your drawing.
- You can select connectors with the Pointer tool (or any tool) and manipulate their various handles. You can change the position of bends in the connector or drag the ends and glue them to other shapes.
- You can add text to them by selecting and typing. When a connector has text, a little yellow control handle appears. It enables you to reposition the text easily without resorting to the Text Block tool. Flowchart fans can quickly label the connectors emanating from Decision shapes with "Yes" and "No" text, and the text follows along when the connectors reroute.
- Connectors are shapes of the 1D variety. Remember that 1D shapes are adjusted by their begin and end handles.
- You can copy, cut, paste, and duplicate connectors. They don't even have to be glued to other shapes.

- You can alter a connector's style by right-clicking. You'll see options for right-angle, straight, curved geometry, plus an option for resetting to the drawing's default connector style.

WHERE DOES THE TEXT GO WHEN A CONNECTOR IS REROUTED?

You can easily type text on a connector and reposition it using the yellow control handle. But what happens to the text when the connector gets rerouted? Depending on the position of the shapes at either end, a connector might be horizontal, vertical, or all bent up!

When you reposition the text block on a connector, Visio makes a note of how far along the connector the text is, from beginning to the end. Say you position the text near the arrowhead, 90% along the way from beginning to the end. When the connector gets rerouted, even if it has a bunch of turns, Visio preserves the location, placing it at 90% of the way along the line.

Connecting to Shapes versus Points on Shapes

You've briefly seen how connectors can be glued to shapes or points on shapes. With dynamic glue, connectors attach to a shape in general, and find the side of a shape that is nearest to the other end of the connector. With point-to-point glue, the connector is glued to a specific point on the shape, which may result in more complicated, less efficient routing.

Figure 4.5 contrasts the behavior of these two types of glue, which becomes apparent when shapes are rearranged. The open and filled dots were added to indicate point-to-point glue and dynamic glue, respectively.

If you are creating a connector with the Pointer tool, or reconnecting an end of a connector, Visio provides red box highlights to help you decide which type of glue to create.

Creating Dynamic Glue

When you mouse over a shape with the Connector tool, or drag an end of a connector over the middle of a shape, you see a bright red box around the entire shape, as shown at left in Figure 4.6.

Note that when you use the AutoConnect arrows to create connections, the connectors are dynamically glued by default.

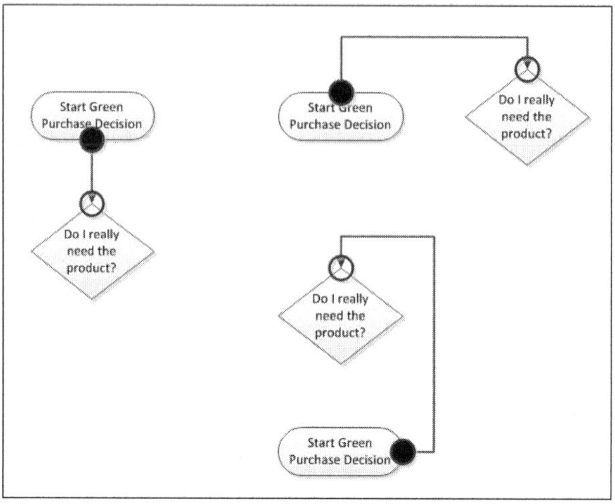

Figure 4.5 *Connector behavior for different types of glue. As shapes are moved around, dynamic glue (black dot) wanders around the Start/End shape. Point-to-point glue (open dot) stays fixed to the top-center of the Decision diamond.*

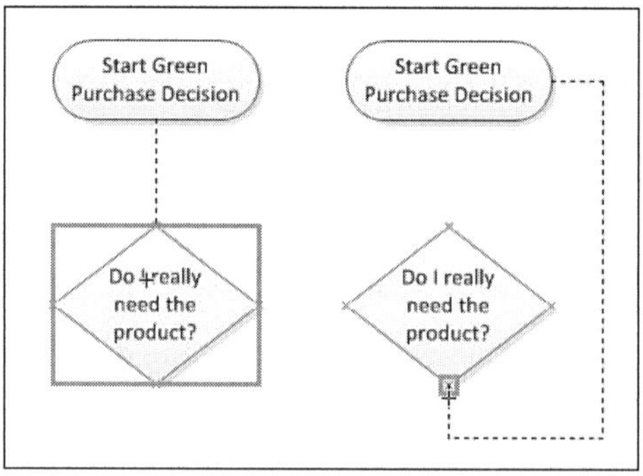

Figure 4.6 *Highlights around the decision shape indicated different types of glue as a connector is dragged toward it. At left, you see the highlight for dynamic glue. At right, the smaller box indicates a point-to-point connection.*

Creating Point-to-Point Glue

Some shapes come prebuilt with connection points to help you connect to specific points. They are often found at the midpoints on each side and in the center of a shape.

Connection points aren't always visible, but they are easy to locate while connecting. If you mouse around a shape while making a connection, you discover small red squares, as shown on the right in Figure 4.6. If you don't find them, then the target shape probably doesn't have any predefined connection points.

You can make connection points more visible by going to View, Visual Aids, Connection Points and checking the check box. Now, when you connect to a shape, the connection points for that shape appear. They are small, hard-to-see blue Xs. You might just be able to make them out in Figure 4.6.

FORCING A DYNAMIC GLUE CONNECTION

Sometimes you want to dynamically glue, but it seems as though Visio won't let you! The mouse cursor needs to be far enough away from a connection point so that Visio knows you want to make a dynamic glue connection. If a shape has a lot of points, or you are zoomed way out, however, finding a clear area of the shape can be difficult and frustrating.

If the little red squares are getting in the way of the big red rectangle, just hold down the Ctrl key while connecting. This tells Visio to ignore the connection points altogether and makes dynamic gluing possible.

Deciding Between Dynamic Glue and Point-to-Point Glue

Dynamic glue keeps your diagrams cleaner because it minimizes the routing paths of connectors. Dynamically glued shapes are more easily laid out in different arrangements. Layout is discussed in the next chapter.

Connectors establish relationships and give specific meaning to diagrams. For some shapes, connection points represent particular inputs and outputs, as shown in Figure 4.7. In this illustration, you see a schematic shape that represents ports on the laptop I'm using to write this book.

Dynamic glue is used in the top example, and you can see that it is very bad: it connects both the power source and the USB hard drive to the video-input terminal.

Convention might also play a part in your connected diagrams. Most of the flowcharts that I've seen run from top to bottom, and decision shapes often send the "Yes" and "No" branches off to the right or down. To enforce this convention, you might want to use point-to-point glue when connecting Decision diamonds in your flowcharts.

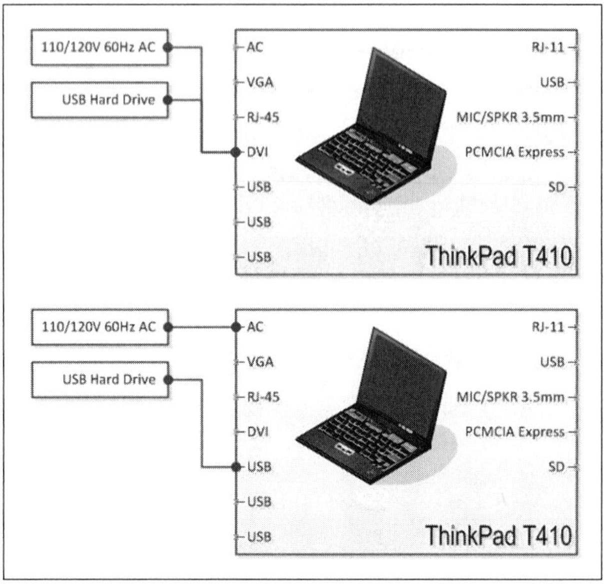

Figure 4.7 *Schematic wiring shapes demonstrate the undesirable effects of dynamic glue (top) versus appropriate point-to-point glue (bottom).*

Connecting Shapes in Multiple Ways

You've already seen a few different ways to connect shapes. Between the Connector tool and AutoConnect arrows, you should be able to get the job done.

There is, however, an astonishing variety of ways to connect shapes. Let's look at the full laundry list, and point out each method's advantages and disadvantages. Depending on your working style, you might like some methods more than others.

SHOW ME **Media 4.2—Grand Tour of Connection Options**
Access this video file through your registered Web Edition at ***my.safaribooksonline.com/9780132182683/media.***

LET ME TRY IT

How Do I Connect Thee? Let Me Count the Ways

1. Start a new drawing from the Basic Flowchart template.
2. Drop several shapes on the page.

3. Work through the methods of creating connections described in the rest of this section (until you reach "Changing the Appearance of Connectors").

Connector Tool

You've seen the Connector tool in action a few times by now. Located in the Tools group on the Home tab, you simply click on one shape and drag to another to create a connection. Red highlights help you to choose between dynamic glue or point-to-point glue connections.

AutoConnect Arrows

AutoConnect arrows that appear around a shape are subtle and unassuming, but they pack quite a punch when it comes to connection features. You'll be amazed how many different ways you can use them to create connections!

Connecting to Shapes in the Mini-Toolbar

Pausing over an AutoConnect arrow reveals the top four shapes in the active stencil. Click one of the four shapes, and it is immediately dropped and connected.

If the active stencil has no shapes appropriate for connecting, you don't see the mini-toolbar. If it has no Quick Shapes, then the first four masters will be displayed.

If no stencils are open, then you won't see the mini-toolbar at all when hovering the cursor over an AutoConnect arrow.

Clicking an AutoConnect Arrow

Clicking an arrow causes one of two things to happen:

- If there is empty space in the direction the arrow points, a new shape is dropped and connected. If a master is selected in the stencil, it is added. Otherwise, the first shape in the stencil is used.
- If there is a neighboring shape, a connection is made from the current shape to the neighbor.

Dragging from an AutoConnect Arrow

You can click and drag from an AutoConnect arrow, and pull a connector out of the shape. While you drag, it is as if you were using the Connector tool. Just drag to any target shape to complete the connection. When you release the mouse button, there's a shiny new connector, and your cursor reverts to whatever tool you were using.

Drop on AutoConnect Arrow

You can drop shapes on AutoConnect arrows to create connections. Just drag shapes from a stencil or elsewhere on the page, and pause over the shape to which you want to connect. When the AutoConnect arrows appear, you can release your shape over one of them.

The shape you dragged gets connected to the shape that you dropped it on. Plus, Visio neatly offsets it in the direction of the blue arrow that you targeted so your diagram stays orderly and organized.

Dragging, Splitting, and Deleting

There are several interesting operations that affect how connectors already on the page behave.

Dragging Connectors to Shapes

Just like any other Visio shape, you can drag an entire connector around the page by clicking on its line and dragging. Instead of just one end being repositioned, the whole connector moves, and any existing glue is broken.

While you drag, if either of the connector's ends passes over other shapes or other shapes' connection points, you see red highlighting. This lets you know that you can glue the connector to these shapes.

Dragging Shapes to Connectors

You can also drag shapes to unconnected connectors, which is the reverse of dragging connectors to shapes. If you have a connector with a free end, you can drag a shape to the free end of the connector and create a glued connection. While you drag, you see red highlighting on the connector as your shape nears the unconnected end. If the connector's end is over the middle of the shape, you see solid red squares on the connector. These indicate that a dynamic glue connection will be made. If the connector's end is near a connection point on the shape, you see open red squares, indicating imminent point-to-point glue.

Splitting Connectors

If you need to insert a step into a flowchart, Visio 2010 helps. Drag a new shape over a connector between two steps. You see solid red squares at either end of the connector, which indicate that the shape can split the connector. Figure 4.8 shows how this looks during the drop and afterward.

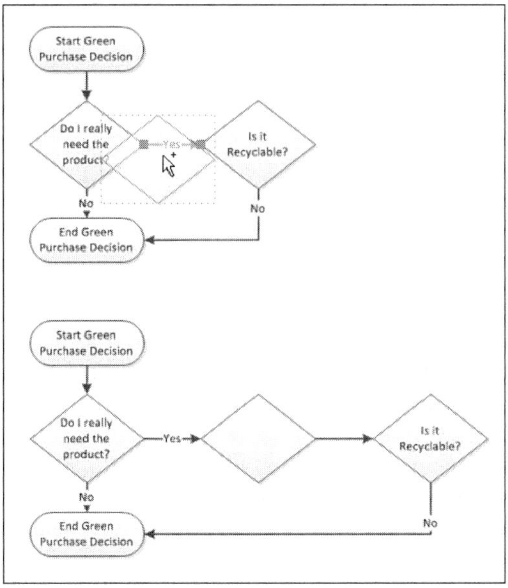

Figure 4.8 *A connector shows solid square highlights at either end (above) when it is about to be split by an incoming shape. Visio then creates two connectors from one, glues both to the new shape, and slides existing shapes out of the way to make room for the newcomer (below).*

Not all templates have connector splitting enabled. For example, the shapes in the Basic Network Diagram template do not split connectors.

For power users interested in enabling connector splitting, note that both the page and shapes need to be configured for splitting to work.

Chris Hopkins' Visilog tells you how to do it in "Splitting Your Own Connectors," which you can find at http://blogs.msdn.com/b/chhopkin/archive/2010/02/03/splitting-your-own-connectors.aspx

Deleting Connected Shapes

When you delete a shape that is connected, any connectors glued to it are also deleted. However, existing connectors that have text are not automatically deleted. Visio assumes they have special status since you have added text to them, and doesn't presume to eliminate your hard work!

If you delete a shape in the middle of a process flow, then Visio heals the gap for you automatically: the previous and next shapes are connected.

For some, auto deletion of connectors might be an annoyance. Not to worry, you can turn it off by going to File, Options, Advanced, Editing options, and unchecking Delete Connectors When Deleting Shapes.

Changing the Appearance of Connectors

Different diagrams require different styles of connectors. Line style properties add clarity, feeling, and meaning to diagrams. For example, flowcharts use arrowheads to show direction, but network diagrams depict directionless connections and don't need arrowheads. A dashed line can indicate a temporary relationship, a proposed modification, or a wireless connection.

The routing style of connectors is also important. Flowcharts look more orderly when connectors bend at right angles. Network diagrams have a more sprawling web feel when connectors are radial and straight. Mind maps (brainstorming diagrams) seem more free-thinking and flowing when connectors have curved bends. Figure 4.9 contrasts routing styles and formatting for three different types of diagrams.

Whether you are changing the formatting for a connector or the structural style of a connector, consider that there are ways to do it both for individual connectors and for the whole page.

Formatting Connectors

You can change the line color, line weight, line pattern, arrowhead style, and text characteristics of an individual connector just as you would for any other Visio shape. On the Home tab, the Font and Shape groups have plenty of controls for changing the look of a connector. You can also right-click any connector to access line, fill, and text formatting controls.

To make changes to the entire page or document, consider using themes, as discussed in Chapter 2, "Working Around the Diagram." Themes can change the look of line patterns, corner rounding, line weight, color and more. Browse the theme gallery on the Design tab to see whether one fits your needs.

You can also select all the connectors on a page and make formatting changes to them in one fell swoop. Go to Home, Editing, Select, Select by Type. In the dialog, check the Shape Role radio button and then check only Connectors. Click OK and all the connectors on the page are selected.

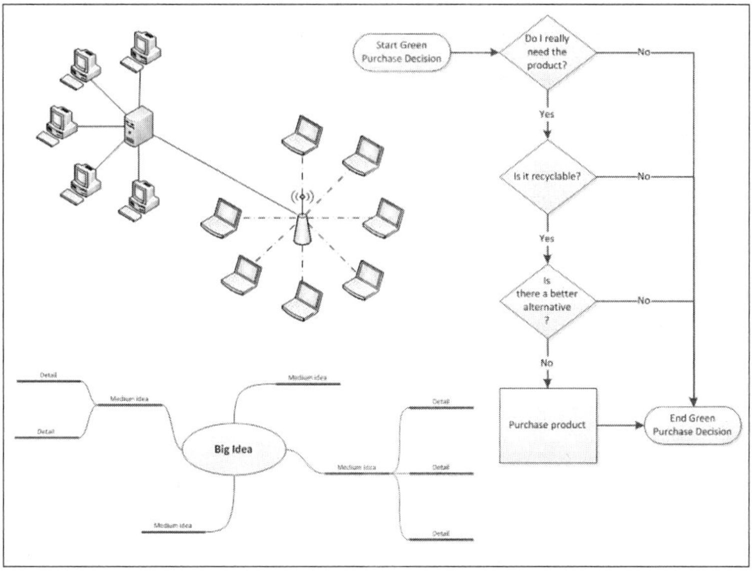

Figure 4.9 *A network diagram, flowchart, and brainstorming diagram have different routing styles and formatting that give each its own meaning and feeling.*

TELL ME MORE **Media 4.3—Connector Begins and Ends: Structure vs. Cosmetics**

Access this video file through your registered Web Edition at ***my.safaribooksonline.com/9780132182683/media.***

Changing Routing Style for Connectors

The routing style governs the geometrical path that a connector takes from beginning to end. You can quickly change the routing style for a connector by right-clicking. Near the bottom of the menu are three choices: Straight line, Right-angled, and Curved.

Figure 4.10 shows a horrid example of a flowchart that has mixed all three routing styles.

A similar set of items is available from the Connectors button in the Layout group on the Design tab. However, this button is more powerful: It applies to all selected shapes, and if none are selected, it changes all connectors on the page.

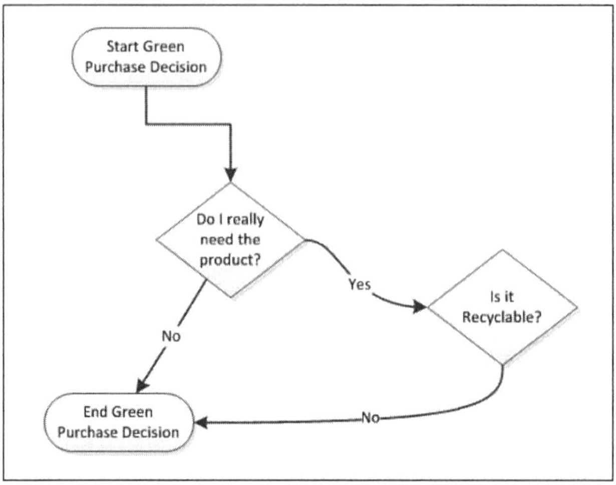

Figure 4.10 *Connectors with different routing styles—a poor expression of individuality.*

LET ME TRY IT

Changing the Routing Style of Connectors

1. Start a new drawing from the Basic Flowchart template.
2. Drop several shapes on the page and connect them together using your favorite connection methods.
3. Move the shapes so that they are not perfectly aligned and the connectors have bends.
4. Right-click a connector and choose "Straight Connector." The connector loses its bends and becomes a straight line.
5. Right-click another connector and choose "Curved Connector." The connector's bends become gently curved instead of sharply angled.
6. Deselect any shapes, then go to the Design tab. In the Layout group, click the Connectors drop-down and choose Right Angle. All of the connectors on the page revert to their original, right-angled style.
7. Select a connector, and choose "Curved Connector" from the Connectors drop-down list. Notice that only the selected shape is changed. The Connectors drop-down affects all connectors if none are selected. Otherwise, it affects only selected connectors.

For even finer control of routing settings for a page, go to the Page Setup dialog (right-click a page tab or click the dialog box launcher for the Layout group). On the Layout and Routing tab you find the Routing section, which has more settings for tuning the routing style.

Figure 4.11 shows the dialog with a Center to Center routing style. Note the Preview section on the right, which hints at how the changes affect your diagram.

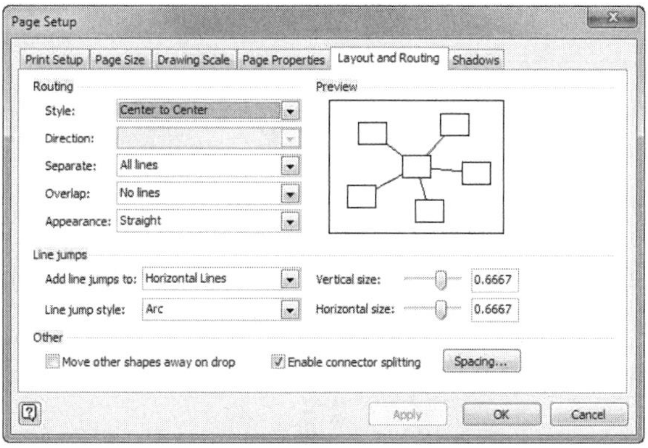

Figure 4.11 *The Layout and Routing tab for Page Setup.*

Style and Appearance are the most interesting settings to play with. Separate and Overlap settings seem like opposite sides of the same coin, and still aren't clear to me after many years of using Visio. They are intended to prevent the overlapping of connectors heading in similar directions so that separate paths remain distinct and clear.

Note that the name of the tab is *Layout* and Routing. Layout is the way shapes are arranged on the page and is discussed in the next chapter.

Controlling Line Jumps for Connectors

Some drawings have lots of crisscrossing connectors or ambiguous intersections. Consider the left half of Figure 4.12. The intersection could be where connectors crossi or where corners coincide.

The right half of Figure 4.12 shows a gap-style line jump that clears up the ambiguity. The connectors are indeed crossing over each other, not bending at the same point in space.

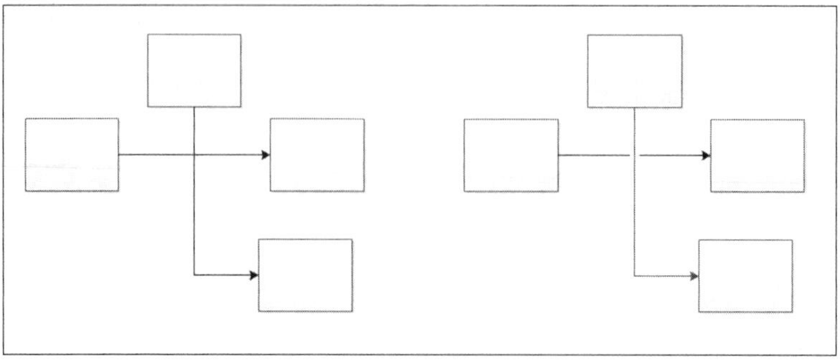

Figure 4.12 *Overlapping lines can have unclear meaning. Line jumps make intersections easier to understand.*

You might have noticed the Line Jumps section of the Layout and Routing tab, shown in Figure 4.11. The two drop-down lists in this section enable you to specify where to apply line jumps to and which style of jump to use.

Some of the line jump styles have funny names; Figure 4.13 shows six of the nine options.

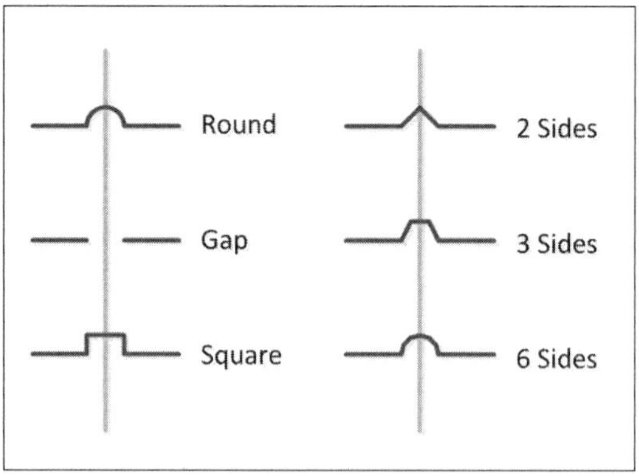

Figure 4.13 *Visio has nine line jump styles, here are six of them.*

I personally like the Gap style. It keeps things neat and clean, is easy on the eyes, and is less distracting than the Round bumps. However, in diagrams with relatively few intersections, it could be important for jumps to stand out. In this case, the Round style might be a good choice.

Note that there isn't a "no jump" style. To suppress line jumps, choose None from the Add Line Jumps To drop-down.

Manually Editing Connector Paths

With point-to-point glue and routing styles, you can get a running start at how your connectors appear and where they go. Sometimes, though, you just need more!

Fortunately, Visio's Dynamic connector has special handles at the midpoints and vertices of each leg. With these handles, you can move legs around and even add new ones.

Figure 4.14 shows connector-editing handles in action but requires further explanation.

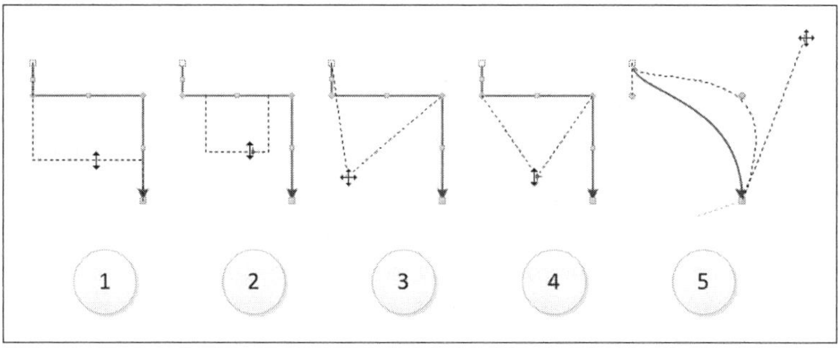

Figure 4.14 *You can alter the path of a connector by pulling on the blue handles.*

You can edit a connector's path in one of five ways as shown in Figure 4.14. Better yet, try it yourself!

LET ME TRY IT

Adding and Removing and Editing Connector Legs

1. Start a new blank drawing.
2. Select the Connector Tool from the Ribbon and draw a connector on the page.
3. Switch back to the Pointer Tool and make sure the connector is still selected.
4. Pull on the midpoint handles of each leg of the connector and note how the connector legs adjust horizontally and vertically.

5. Now hold the Shift key and pull on a midpoint handle. This adds a new set of bends to the leg, as shown in #2 of Figure 4.14.
6. Hold the Ctrl key and pull on one of the corner vertexes. This allows you to adjust the legs nonorthogonally, as shown in #3 of Figure 4.14.
7. Holding the Ctrl key while pulling a midpoint adds a nonorthogonal angle to the connector, as #4 of Figure 4.14 shows.
8. Draw a new connector somewhere on the page, right-click it and choose "Curved Connector." Notice that the handles look a bit different than for the right-angled connectors.
9. For curved connectors, Shift and Ctrl have no effect, but you can change the position of the bend by dragging the midpoint handle, and change the angle and extremity of the curve by manipulating the "tangent" handles at either end. #5 of Figure 4.14 shows a curved connector being modified.
10. If you've modified a connector to the point that it is unrecognizable, you can restore it to a manageable state. Right-click one of your mangled connectors and choose "Reset Connector." It returns to its original form, where you can start modifying it again, but this time more judiciously!

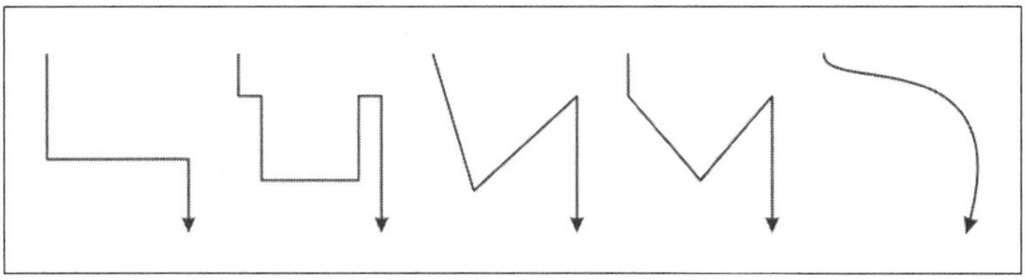

Figure 4.15 *The result of manipulations to Figure 4.14.*

Adding and Editing Connection Points

Dynamic glue is a wonderful automatic feature for drawings like flowcharts and network diagrams. As you saw with the schematic wiring example way back in Figure 4.7, however, there are scenarios where a connector should glue to a specific point on a shape.

Luckily, you can easily add connection points to shapes—after you've learned the less-than-obvious way to do it!

LET ME TRY IT

Adding and Removing Connection Points to Shapes

1. Start a new drawing from the Maps & Floorplans, Directional Map template.
2. Make sure that connection points are visible. Go to View, Visual Aids and check the Connection Points box.
3. From the Road Shapes stencil, drop the Road Square shape on the page.
4. From the Landmark Shapes stencil, drop a Factory shape on the page.
5. Return to the home tab and select the Connection Point tool from the Tools group. When you select this tool, connection points on shapes become visible. Note that the road shape has two connection points (little blue Xs) at either end, but the Factory shape has none.
6. Click on the Factory. Note that the shape has a light blue dashed line to indicate it is selected but the normal resize handles are not visible. Selected shapes look different when you are using the Connection Point tool. It is easy to overlook the selection box and inadvertently add connection points to the wrong shapes.
7. To add a connection point to the Factory, hold down the Ctrl key while clicking locations on the shape. Wherever you click, you should see a little blue X. In Figure 4.16, connection points are being added to the smoke stacks.

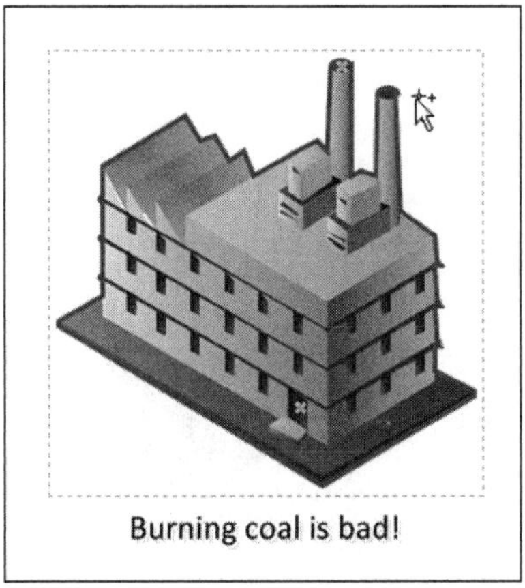

Figure 4.16 *Hold the Ctrl key and click with the Connection Point tool to add connection points to shapes.*

8. Add connection points to both smoke stacks of the Factory. To get more accurate positioning, try zooming way in (You can use the Ctrl+Shift+ Left/Right mouse click shortcuts even with the Connection Point tool).
9. Practice removing a connection point. Make sure the Factory shape is still selected and that you are still using the Connection Point tool.
10. Click on one of the existing connection points, without holding down any modifier keys. The X should turn red. If you hold down the Shift key, you can click on more points to select several at once.
11. Once the connection points are selected, press Delete to remove them.
12. Re-add the points you deleted, using the technique in Step 8.
13. To move an existing connection point, select one as you did in Step 10. Once the connection point is selected (highlighted in red), you can click and drag it to a new position. This can be a bit tricky at first. Just remember: click the shape, click the point, then click-and-drag once the point is highlighted.
14. Take your new creation for a test-drive. Using the Connector tool, glue some connectors to your shape, and perhaps create an illustration like the one shown in Figure 4.17.

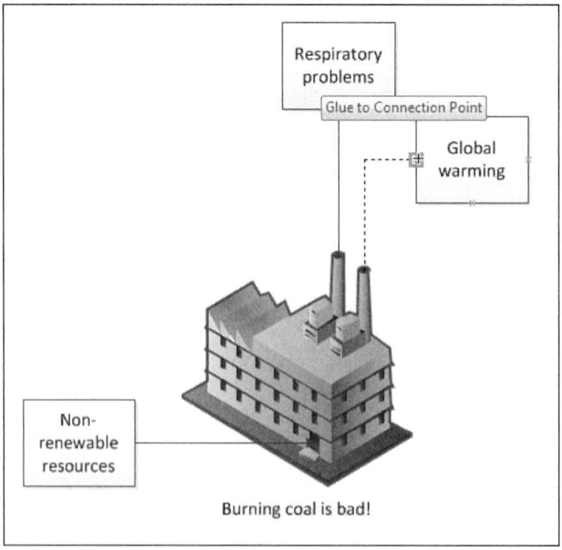

Figure 4.17 *This Factory shape has custom connection points added to its smoke stacks. Connectors can be easily glued to the points to illustrate damaging outflow.*

Note that connection points on subshapes inside groups are still accessible outside the group. If you're creating a complex shape that has many repeated elements (such as the laptop ports schematic shape shown in Figure 4.7), it is easier to create one connection point on one elemental subshape than to add several to the top-level group!

Summary

In this chapter, you learned about Visio's Dynamic connector and how it behaves like a normal Visio shape, yet receives special treatment. You learned to add connectors and connect shapes in myriad ways using the Connector tool and AutoConnect arrows.

Additionally, you saw how connectors can seek out the most efficient path using dynamic glue and how they can attach to specific points on a shape via point-to-point glue. You practiced editing these points by adding, moving, and deleting connection points on a shape. Plus, you saw how to change the routing style for connectors and how to edit the legs and vertices of individual connectors.

In this chapter, you learn how to align and arrange shapes neatly using a variety of features, and I explore Visio's automatic layout features for arranging connected diagrams.

5

Aligning, Arranging, and Laying Out Shapes

Shape position plays a big role in a diagram's meaning. Position on the page and proximity to other shapes can signify importance, order in time, or hierarchy.

Tidiness and consistency are also important. A jumbled drawing is hard on your eyes and confusing to look at. An orderly diagram dispenses with noise and lets the meaning shine through..

Aligning and Arranging Shapes

Visio 2010 has several features for keeping your shapes neatly in order. Some help you maintain tidiness while you draw; others enable you to clean up the mess afterward.

Using the Dynamic Grid to Align Shapes as You Draw

If you've noticed thin, orange lines and arrows briefly appearing as you drop shapes on the page, you've already seen the Dynamic Grid in action. The Dynamic Grid aims to prevent the mess before it happens.

SHOW ME **Media 5.1—Using the Dynamic Grid to Align Shapes in Visio 2010**

Access this video file through your registered Web Edition at
|my.safaribooksonline.com/9780132182683/media.

LET ME TRY IT

Working with the Dynamic Grid

1. Create a new drawing using the Basic Flowchart template.
2. For flowcharts, the Dynamic Grid is on by default, but you can double-check. Go to the View tab and make sure that Dynamic Grid in the Visual Aids group is checked.
3. Drag and drop a Process shape onto the page.
4. Drag a second Process shape directly to the right of the first one. As you drag, notice the orange line and arrow that appear, as shown in Figure 5.1. The horizontal line indicates vertical alignment between the shapes. The horizontal arrows indicate uniform spacing, which doesn't mean much when you have only two shapes on the page. For the first two shapes on a page, the Dynamic Grid uses a *standard spacing* that is defined for the drawing.

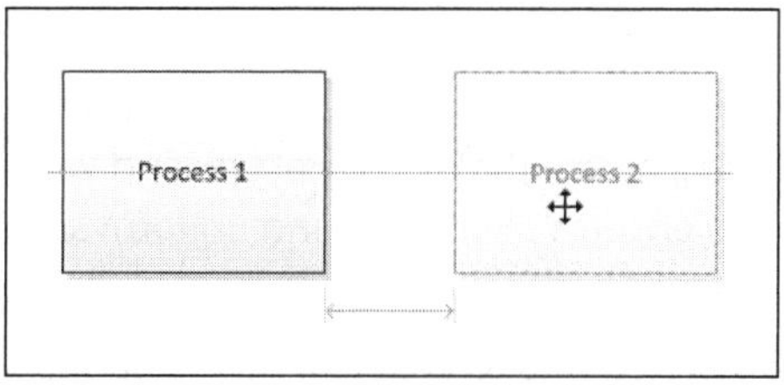

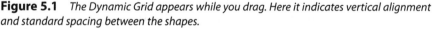

Figure 5.1 *The Dynamic Grid appears while you drag. Here it indicates vertical alignment and standard spacing between the shapes.*

5. Drag a few more Process shapes onto the page, continuing to the right. Drop them when you see the alignment line and spacing arrows, as shown in Figure 5.2. The uniform spacing arrows now make a lot more sense!
6. In a flowchart, you would normally connect as you go, which you haven't done so far. Mouse over your last Process shape and use the AutoConnect arrows to add another Process shape to the right. Notice that it is aligned vertically with the other shapes and spaced equally. Figure 5.3 shows the result; you can see that AutoConnect uses the same standard spacing as the Dynamic Grid to place new shapes.

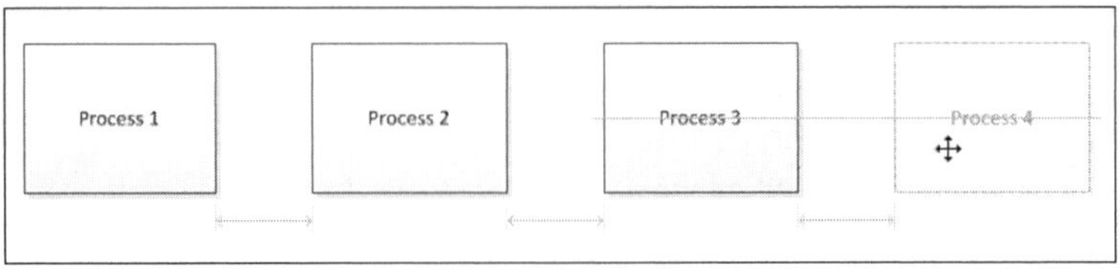

Figure 5.2 *The Dynamic Grid helps to enforce uniform spacing between shapes.*

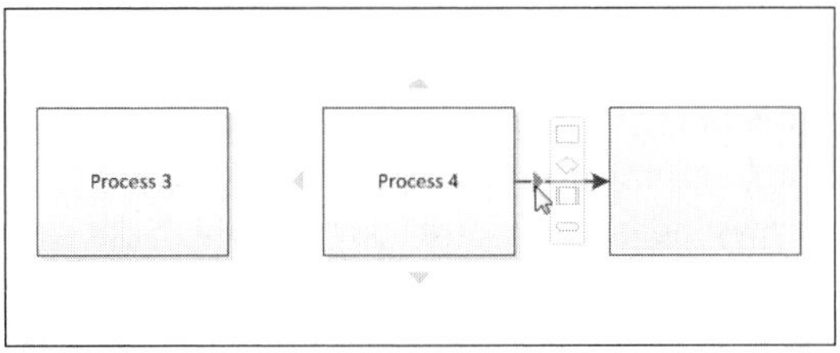

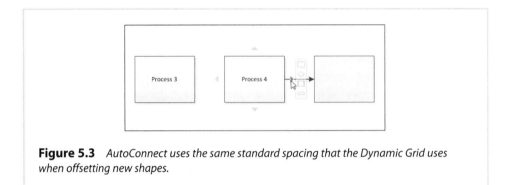

Figure 5.3 *AutoConnect uses the same standard spacing that the Dynamic Grid uses when offsetting new shapes.*

7. Drag any of the existing Process shapes so that it is below one of the others. As you drag, notice that a vertical line and vertical arrows appear. The Dynamic Grid ensures alignment and uniform spacing for vertical rows of shapes as well.
8. Drag one last Process shape so that it aligns vertically and horizontally with the shapes already on the page. You should see alignment lines and spacing arrows in both the horizontal and vertical directions, as shown in Figure 5.4.

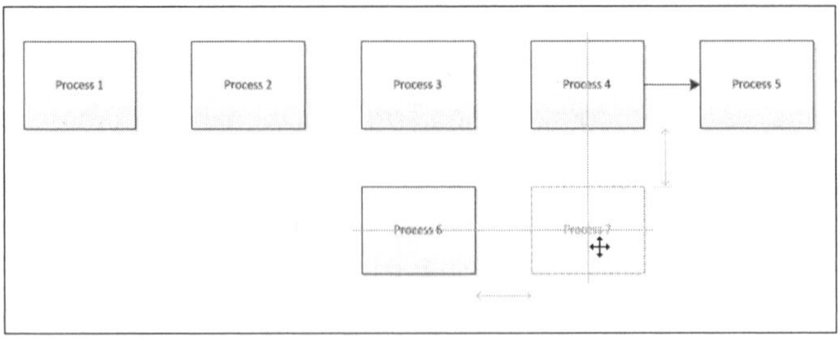

Figure 5.4 *The Dynamic Grid works in both directions simultaneously.*

Controlling Dynamic Grid Spacing

The uniform spacing used by the Dynamic Grid is flexible. Visio looks for patterns in related shapes to establish local spacing values. You effectively set uniform spacing for a region when you drop a second shape next to a first. Subsequent shapes in that area of the drawing will use that spacing. This means that you can have several different uniform spacing values on a page, as Figure 5.5 illustrates.

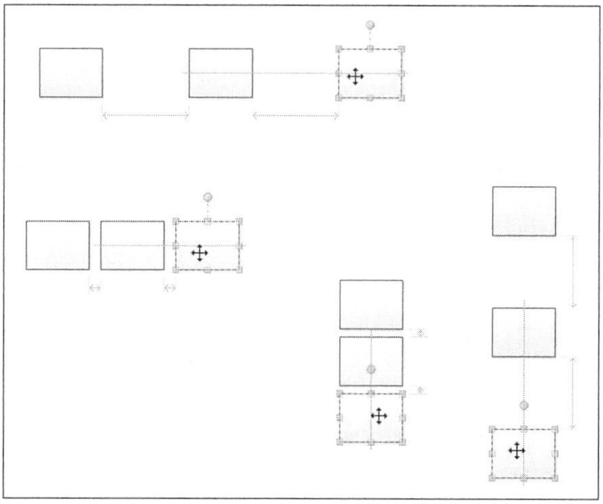

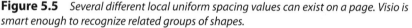

Figure 5.5 *Several different local uniform spacing values can exist on a page. Visio is smart enough to recognize related groups of shapes.*

If no grid spacing has been established or Visio detects no spacing pattern, Visio uses standard horizontal and vertical spacing values, which are defined for each page. AutoConnect always uses these standard spacing values when you insert shapes by clicking AutoConnect arrows. However, AutoConnect doesn't respect local spacing values, unfortunately.

You can change the standard spacing for a diagram. Right-click a Page tab and choose Page Setup. On the Layout and Routing tab, click Spacing. Under Space Between Shapes, you can change the Horizontal and Vertical values. Visio also uses these values for spacing shapes when automatically laying out connected diagrams, and AutoConnect uses it when adding new shapes.

Dynamically Aligning Other Parts of Shapes

When you have lots of shapes on a page that are roughly the same size, such as in a flowchart or network diagram, the Dynamic Grid is most likely to assist you with center-to-center alignment. The Dynamic Grid also can align shapes by their edges:

left, right, top, and bottom. Figure 5.6 shows a small shape being aligned to larger shapes at its top and right edges.

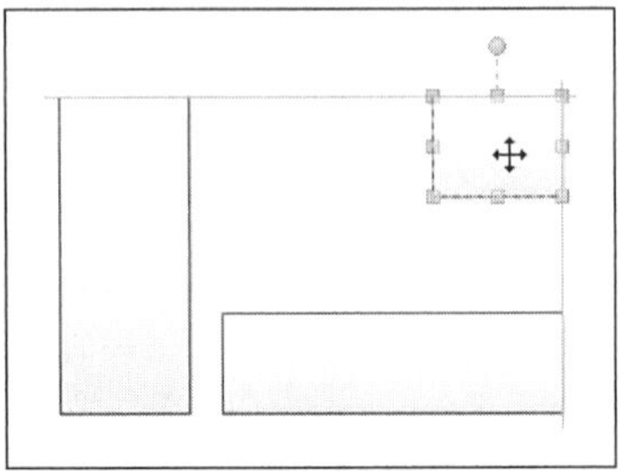

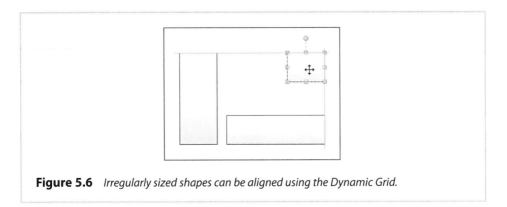

Figure 5.6 *Irregularly sized shapes can be aligned using the Dynamic Grid.*

Using Auto Align & Space to Clean Up Connected Diagrams

If you have been furiously flowcharting away, rapidly rearranging process steps and not paying attention to the Dynamic Grid, you might find yourself with a rather disheveled flowchart.

To save you the trouble of straightening everything one shape at a time, Visio 2010 has added the Auto Align & Space button. Located in the Arrange group on the Home tab, this button wonderfully straightens out your diagrams, as illustrated in Figure 5.7.

Auto Align & Space has no options or settings or drop-down submenus. Just click that big button and POW! Your connected diagrams instantly get straightened out. Auto Align & Space operates on only the shapes you select, but if no shapes are selected, it tidies up the whole page.

While AutoConnect and the Dynamic Grid make it easy to maintain clean diagrams while you draw, I think Auto Align & Space nicely rounds out the feature set. It allows you to work lightning fast and concentrate on the information in your diagram, knowing that cleanup can be effectively taken care of later. Also, if you have AutoConnect or the Dynamic Grid turned off for whatever reason, Auto Align & Space is still there to help you out afterward.

TELL ME MORE **Media 5.2—Tricking Auto Align & Space into Tidying-up Non-connected Shapes**

Access this audio file through your registered Web Edition at ***my.safaribooksonline.com/9780132182683/media.***

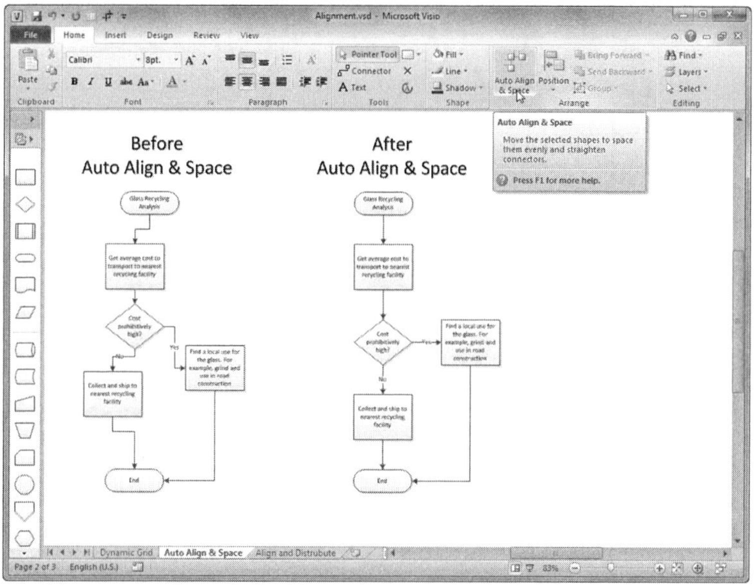

Figure 5.7 *The messy flowchart on the left is cleaned up with a single click of the Auto Align & Space button.*

Aligning and Distributing Shapes Using Position Functions

Just to the right of the Auto Align & Space button is the Position drop-down button, which contains elemental functions for aligning, distributing, rotating, and flipping shapes. Figure 5.8 shows all of Position's items and subitems.

Though Dynamic Grid, Auto Align & Space, and AutoConnect decrease the need for many of these functions, some diagrams are too complex for the Dynamic Grid. Also, some non-connected diagram types, such as office plans, aren't suited for Dynamic Grid, AutoConnect, or Auto Align & Space. In these cases, the functions under Position are especially useful.

TELL ME MORE **Media 5.3—Figure 5.8 is a Visio Drawing!**
Access this audio file through your registered Web Edition at ***my.safaribooksonline.com/9780132182683/media.***

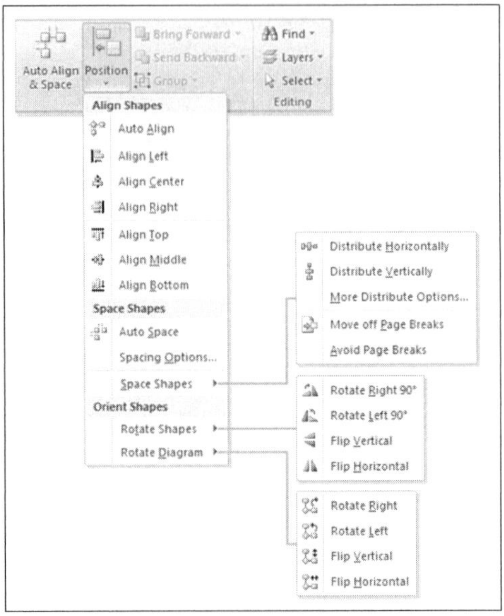

Figure 5.8 *The Home, Arrange, Position menu and its submenus.*

Aligning Shapes

You can align shapes by their left, right, top, or bottom edges as well as their horizontal and vertical centers.

LET ME TRY IT

Practice Aligning Shapes

1. Start a blank drawing and draw several differently sized rectangles on the page.
2. When you align the shapes, they can get bunched together so that some obscure others. If you give them a transparent fill, you can still see all the shapes, even if they become stacked.

   Select all the rectangles, click the Fill drop-down, and choose Fill Options at the end of the list. The Fill dialog appears, and lets you select a color and set a transparency level among other things. Try setting a 50% transparency for your rectangles.

3. Shapes are aligned to the primary selection, or first shape in the selection. When you select multiple shapes, the primary selection is the shape with the thicker magenta outline. You can explicitly control which shape is the primary selection by doing this:

   a. Click the shape that you want to be the primary shape—the one that the other shapes will align to.

   b. Hold down the Shift key.

   c. Drag a selection rectangle around the rest of the shapes, or click each one individually while continuing to hold the Shift key.

4. Drop-down the Position button in the Arrange group on the Home tab. Slowly mouse over the first seven menu items that deal with alignment (they are the ones below the Align Shapes header in bold). Live Preview shows how each alignment option will affect your shapes. Figure 5.9 demonstrates how two of these alignment operations work.

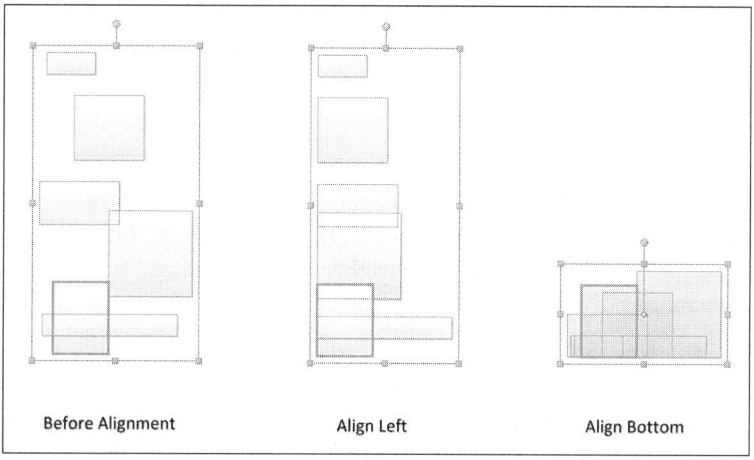

Figure 5.9 *Using the alignment functions of the Position drop-down. Note the box with the thicker selection highlight in the bottom-left corner. This is the primary selection, to which the other shapes get aligned.*

Distributing Shapes

If you need a set of shapes to be equally spaced, the distribute functions can help. You find them in the Space Shapes group within the Position drop-down. For veteran PC users, "space" seems to be the Visio 2010 verb for what used to be called "distribute."

Figure 5.10 shows a practical application of shape distribution (spacing). The left half of the image shows horizontal and vertical reference line shapes that aren't nicely distributed. The goal is to create a grid so that a coordinator can communicate locations within a building to contractors; for example, "The elevator at C-4 is due for regular maintenance."

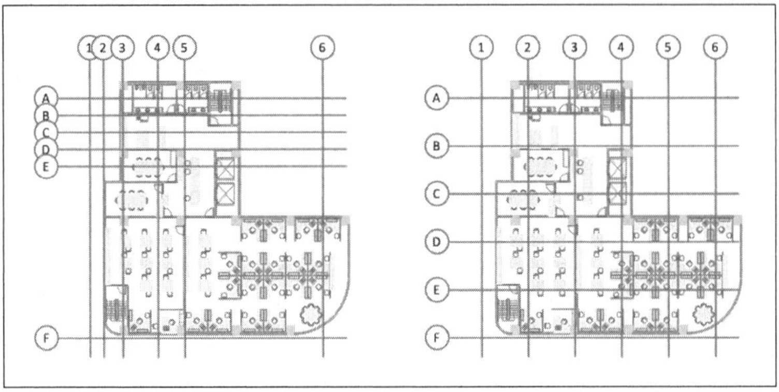

Figure 5.10 *Distributing zone shapes horizontally and vertically to create a reference grid for an office plan.*

Manually positioning the reference shapes is difficult and time consuming, and the Dynamic Grid's uniform spacing features aren't quite right for this task. You could use the Size & Position dialog to numerically specify locations for the shapes, but the Space Shapes functions, make this a simple task.

The key is to place the shapes roughly in order and then make sure the first and last shapes span the appropriate region. In Figure 5.10, shapes 1 and 6 are at the horizontal extremes of the plan, and shapes A and F are at the vertical extremes. The remaining shapes just need to be spaced equally between them.

To distribute each set of shapes, simply select all shapes that you wish to equally space, and then click Position, Space Shapes, Distribute Horizontally, or Distribute Vertically. The distribute functions calculate the necessary shape-to-shape spacing required to evenly distribute the selected shapes between the extremes.

If you need to space the shapes a specific distance from each other, you can use the Position, Spacing Options command. This presents a dialog where you enter precise horizontal and vertical measurements. Oddly, it seems to work only with connected diagrams; it would be a great feature for organizing grids of nonconnected shapes, too!

You might have noticed two familiar-sounding items under Space Shapes that I haven't discussed: Auto Align and Auto Space. They simply break down Auto Align & Space function into separate components so that you can line up shapes or space them equally apart.

Rotating Shapes

At the bottom of the Position menu is the Orient Shapes group with two curiously similar-sounding items: Rotate Shapes and Rotate Diagram.

The items under Rotate Shapes enable you to rotate a selection of shapes as a single unit. You can also mirror the shapes in the horizontal or vertical direction using the flip commands.

Rotate Diagram sounds confusing. Isn't that the same as Rotate Shapes? If you are mathematically inclined or an Excel expert, you will understand that Rotate Diagram *transposes* shapes. It rotates the *positions* of the shapes, but not the shapes themselves.

Figure 5.11 contrasts Rotate Shapes and Rotate Diagram. Note that Rotate Diagram applies only to connected shapes.

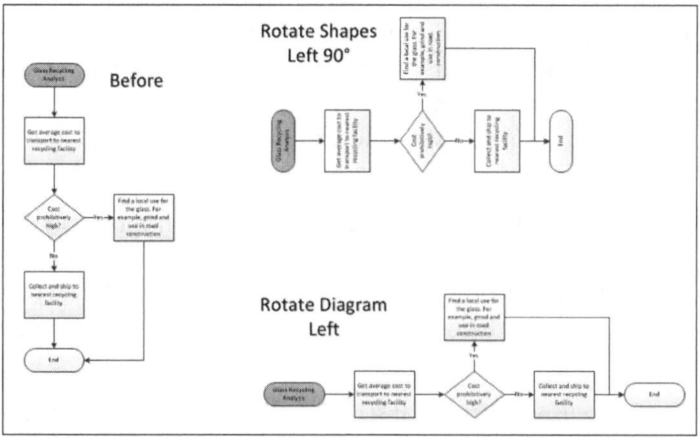

Figure 5.11 *Shapes rotated using Rotate Shapes and transposed using Rotate Diagram.*

Using the Grid, Ruler, and Guides

Visio has a few other elements that are useful for keeping diagrams straight and orderly. The grid, ruler, and guides have been around since the first release of Visio and are starting to be considered old-fashioned.

Although the newer Dynamic Grid and Auto Align & Space features are snazzy and impressive, they are most useful for connected diagrams. The grid, ruler, and guides are still great for measured drawings, block diagrams, user-interface mockups, and other unconnected drawings.

You can show or hide the grid, ruler, and guides using check boxes in View, Show. Let's discuss what they are used for so you can better decide whether to turn them on or off in the first place.

Grid

Visio's grid gives you quick visual and tactile feedback for aligning shapes and maintaining consistency. As you draw and resize shapes, your cursor snaps to the grid.

This feature makes it easy to create shapes that have identical or similar sizes, and makes it easy to abut shapes against each other. Because Visio doesn't have any kind of abutting function, "designing shapes that fit the grid" goes beyond a compulsion for senseless order and makes it easy to place them against each other.

The blocks in Figure 5.12 demonstrate the usefulness of fitting to the grid. Because all the squares are exactly 1 inch × 1 inch, it is easy to snap the arrow shapes against their edges. If the squares had nongrid sizes like 1.05 inch × 1.2875 inch, it would be difficult to accurately slide the arrows against them, and the diagram would look sloppy.

You should be aware of a few quirks about the grid. When you zoom in and out, the grid changes such that you always see roughly the same number of squares. Because of this, it is easy to forget how far in you are zoomed. To keep your perspective, pay attention to the numbers on the ruler and the size of selected shapes in the status bar.

If you really want a fixed grid, click the dialog box launcher for the View, Show group. There, you can specify custom fixed units for both the ruler and the grid, and the grid won't vary as you zoom in or out.

Just because the grid is visible doesn't mean that you will snap to it. This is usually the case, but you can turn grid snapping on and off via the Snap & Glue dialog. You access it by clicking the dialog box launcher in the View, Visual Aids group.

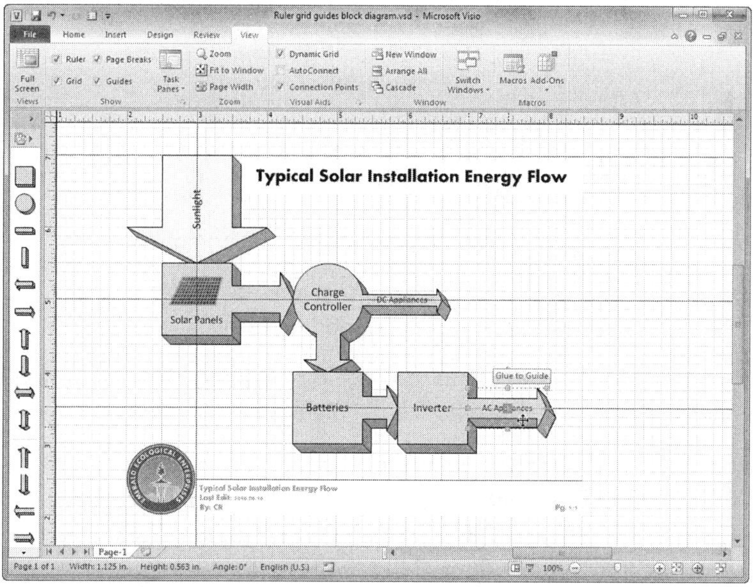

Figure 5.12 *A block diagram with the ruler, grid, and guides in action.*

Ruler

The ruler appears along the left and top sides of the drawing window and helps you maintain perspective while zooming in and out. The ruler displays coordinates from the lower-left corner of the page, in the size and units of the drawing scale, not the size of the paper.

You can change the zero point of the ruler by Ctrl+dragging from the top-left corner where the rulers intersect to any point on the page. This capability is useful for measured drawings such as office plans, site layouts, or mechanical drawings. You can reset the origin by double-clicking the ruler intersection.

Guides

Guides are used to provide visual cues for horizontal and vertical alignment and as tools for repositioning shapes aligned in columns and rows.

You pull guides out of the rulers, as needed. They look like blue, dashed infinite lines in the horizontal or vertical directions. They don't print, and you can glue shapes to them.

In Figure 5.12, the four guides are just barely visible. Three are horizontal and one is vertical. They help to highlight the major axes of the diagram but also make adjustments easier because shapes are glued to the guides. In the figure, the AC Appliances arrow is being glued to the guide.

LET ME TRY IT

Gluing Shapes to Guides

1. Start a new diagram using the General, Block Diagram template.
2. Double-check that the grid, ruler, and guides are visible. If they aren't, go to View, Show and check the corresponding boxes.
3. Drag a horizontal guide onto the page by dragging from the ruler at the top of the page. You see a horizontal blue dashed line on the page.
4. Drag the 2D Double Arrow master onto the page and glue it to the guide. As you position the shape over the guide, note the red handles that appear. These indicate that you can glue the shape to the guide. You can glue the center or the edges of the shape to the guide.
5. Drag the 1D Double Arrow onto the page and glue it to the guide, too. This shape is 1D and has different handles than the 2D Double Arrow you dropped in step 4, but they nevertheless glue to the guide.
6. Move the guide up and down. Note how the shapes follow along.
7. Pull one end of the 1D Double Arrow off the guide. Notice that the handle is now blue instead of red. It is no longer over the guide and, therefore, no longer glued to the guide.
8. Move the guide up or down again. Only one end of the 1D shape follows along, but the 2D shape remains glued.
9. Add a vertical guide by dragging from the ruler at left.
10. Drag an Arrow box master onto the page and glue it to both guides. You can glue any corner of the box or its center to both guides at the same time. You see red handles indicating glue in both directions.
11. Move both guides. If you've properly glued the Arrow box to both of them, it should follow the guides in the horizontal and vertical directions.

Nudging Shapes

Two keyboard tricks will help you get shapes aligned when they are off by just a little bit.

You can nudge shapes up, down, left, or right by tapping any of the arrow keys while shapes are selected. If you hold the Shift key while nudging, the shapes move in even finer increments.

The distance moved is in pixels, not a specific distance on the page. So if you are zoomed way out, nudging moves the shapes further than when you are zoomed way in. This is very much an "eyeballing it" feature. If your drawing demands precision, nudging might not be the best way to get shapes properly positioned.

Controlling Front-to-Back Positioning

You've learned about a range of features for horizontally and vertically arranging and aligning your shapes, but other than a brief mention in Chapter 3, the third dimension has been neglected.

As you create shapes, the most recent ones appear "on top." They obscure any previously-created shapes that happen to be in the immediate area. However, you don't have to carefully plan the order in which you add shapes to a diagram because you can easily manage their Z-order. Z-order is just a mathy way of saying front-to-back order. If *X* is horizontal and *Y* is vertical, *Z* is into and out of your computer screen!

In your travels around the Visio interface, you've likely seen four commands for dealing with Z-order: Send Backward, Send to Back, Bring Forward and Bring to Front.

Bring Forward and Send Backward move shapes in or out in the Z-order by one level, whereas Bring to Front and Send to Back move shapes all the way out or in.

There are several places to get at them, including:

- Home, Arrange group
- Right-click context menu for any shape
- Shift+Ctrl+F to bring a selection of shapes to front
- Shift+Ctrl+B to send a selection of shapes to back

Note that when you group shapes together, you effectively create a new shape (the group), which ends up on top. Even if all the group's members were behind other shapes to start, they end up on top. Also, subshapes within a group must belong to the same Z-order pocket and can't be interwoven. So subshapes inside of a group can't be both in front of and behind other shapes on the page.

CONTAINERS AND Z-ORDER

When it comes to shape Z-order, containers offer an exception. Containers (covered in Chapter 3, "Organizing and Annotating Diagrams") know they serve as frames and backgrounds for other shapes. Even if you add a container on top of existing shapes, Visio sensibly places it behind those shapes. It wouldn't do to hang a picture frame in front of the pictures, now would it?

Send to Back also behaves differently within containers. If you send a shape to back, it appears behind other shapes within the container but isn't behind the container itself. If you use Send to Back a second time, however, the shape *does* disappear behind the container. Because the shape still belongs to the container and moves around with it, you may never see the shape again!

If you think you've "double-sent" shapes behind a container, don't worry. Just select the container itself and send it to back. Any shapes lurking in Z-order purgatory again become visible on top of the container!

LET ME TRY IT

Enhancing a 3D Block Diagram Using Z-order

1. Start a new diagram using the General, Block Diagram template.
2. In the Shapes window, activate the Blocks Raised stencil.
3. Ensure that the grid is visible. If it isn't, go to View, Show and check the Grid check box.
4. Drop the Right Arrow shape. Resize it and marvel at how well behaved it is. The 3D "shadow" and arrowhead maintain proper proportions and don't stretch as clip art would. This is Visio SmartShape behavior at its best.
5. For fun, give it a new fill color and notice that the 3D part automatically takes a darker shade of the color you choose. More smarts in action.
6. Drop the Square Block shape.
7. Move the arrow so that it abuts the edge of the square. With the grid activated, this should be easy to do. Notice that the extrusion from the square obscures part of the arrow and looks visually incorrect.
8. Right-click the arrow and choose Bring to Front. Alternatively, right-click the square and choose Send to Back. The extrusions should no longer conflict, and your block diagram starts to look better.

9. Notice that the square and the arrow do not blend together because of the line between them and (perhaps) the different fill color.
10. Make the square the same color as the arrow. First, select the arrow and then click the Format Painter button in the Home, Clipboard group. Finally, click on the square. The square should now have the same formatting as the arrow.
11. Heal the line between the two shapes so that they seamlessly blend together. Right-click the arrow shape and choose Open Tail. The line at the base of the arrow should disappear, and the two shapes should flow together, much like the raised block shapes in Figure 5.12. Open Tail only works if the arrow is on top of the square, z-order-wise.

Laying Out Shapes

Layout refers to the arrangement of shapes in a connected diagram. If you think about the way flowcharts, org charts, and network diagrams are typically laid out, you notice a difference in style that helps with the meaning and organization of each diagram type.

When you connect shapes together using the skills you developed in Chapter 4, "Connecting Shapes," you actually impart meaning to the diagram that Visio can glean to automatically lay out your diagram. In this section, you explore the features, options, and tips for laying out connected diagrams.

Using Visio's Layout Features

If you look at Figure 5.13, you see a well-connected diagram that needs help. Surprisingly, this diagram has enough information to determine the hierarchy of the system. The top-level shapes have been rigorously connected to the next level of shapes, on down the chain. Connectors are glued so that the 1D Begin handle is at the superior shape, and the 1D End handle is glued to the inferior shape. To prove that the hierarchy is really there, I've used thicker lines and bigger fonts for higher-level boxes. Regardless, this diagram is still a mess and needs to be cleaned up.

If I knew in advance all the boxes needed for this diagram, the Dynamic Grid, AutoConnect could have helped me keep order as I drew. However, I was working quickly and adding boxes as they popped into my head. This is a perfectly valid and organic way to work in Visio.

You could try tidying up using Auto Align & Space, as I've done in Figure 5.14. You see that some *order* is gained, but the overall *meaning* still isn't clear.

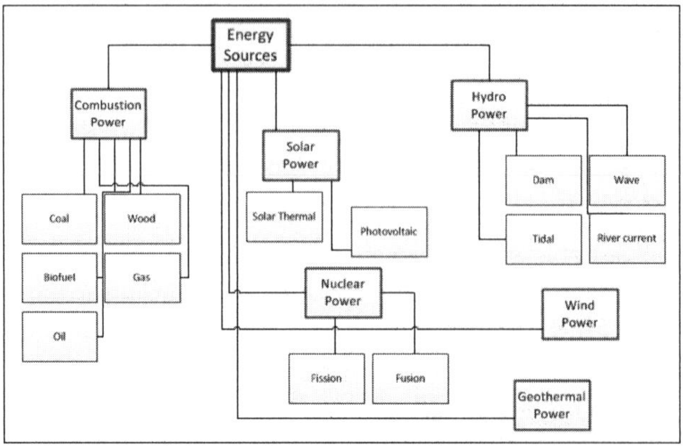

Figure 5.13 *A well-connected diagram that desperately needs layout.*

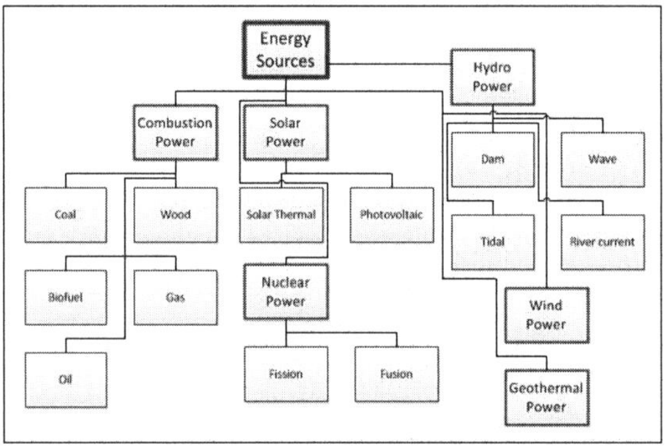

Figure 5.14 *Auto Align & Space makes the diagram neater, but the hierarchy is still not apparent, and the connectors are still spaghetti-like.*

The trick, then, is to use Visio's layout features, which you find in the Layout group on the Design tab. Figure 5.15 shows the heretofore messy energy diagram laid out using the Hierarchy style, chosen from the Re-layout Page gallery.

Now, the meaning and hierarchy of the diagram are clearly visible. The only complaint is that it is a bit wide for such a small number of shapes—this fairly simple diagram now spills over onto three pages.

In Figure 5.15, notice the Compact Tree layout styles, located just below the Hierarchy options. Compact tree styles work very nicely for this diagram, as Figure 5.16 demonstrates. This is an improvement over the previous one because all the information fits nicely on one page and is more easily seen at a glance.

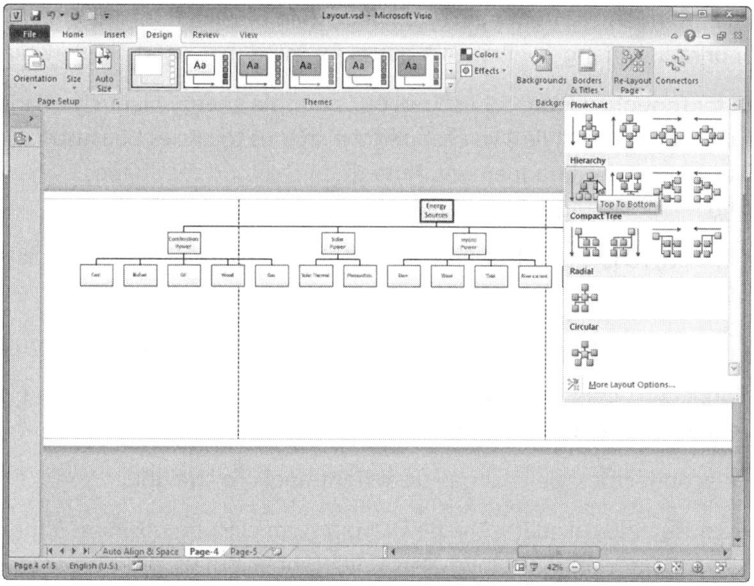

Figure 5.15 *Choosing the Hierarchy layout style from Visio's layout gallery arranges shapes in an org chart fashion.*

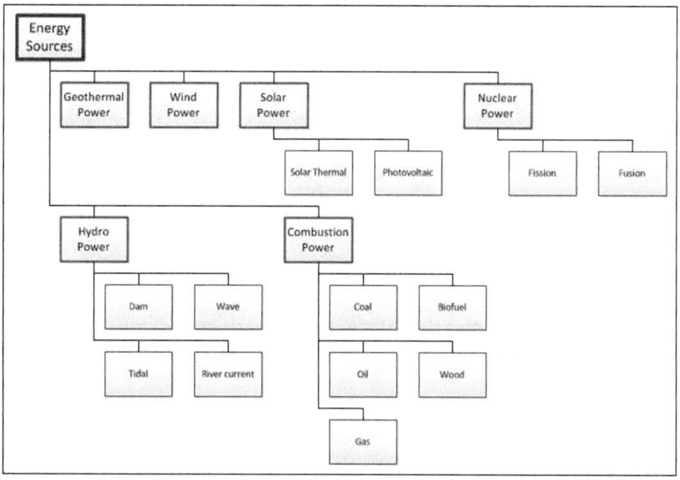

Figure 5.16 *The Compact Tree layout style does wonders for the energy sources diagram.*

Notice the Radial and Circular groups at the bottom of the Re-layout Page gallery. A circular arrangement might also work for a diagram like this, although I find that circular or radial arrangements work better for mind maps and network diagrams.

As food for thought, Figure 5.17 shows our example energy hierarchy diagram laid out using the Circular style. I've changed the shapes to circles because I think it looks better with this arrangement. Note that I changed the shapes by hand; there's no magic "change shape" feature.

Before I go on, I'd like to call attention to a few points about the circular layout in Figure 5.17:

- The arrangement takes up more space than the Compact Tree layout.
- Connectors cross over nodes (the circles), so a bit of hand tweaking is required to perfect the diagram.
- The connector style changed from right-angle to straight.
- Because Visio calculates the new layout from existing positions, repeatedly clicking Circular layout gives you a different layout each time. Some might frown on this inconsistency; others might enjoy the game of chance!

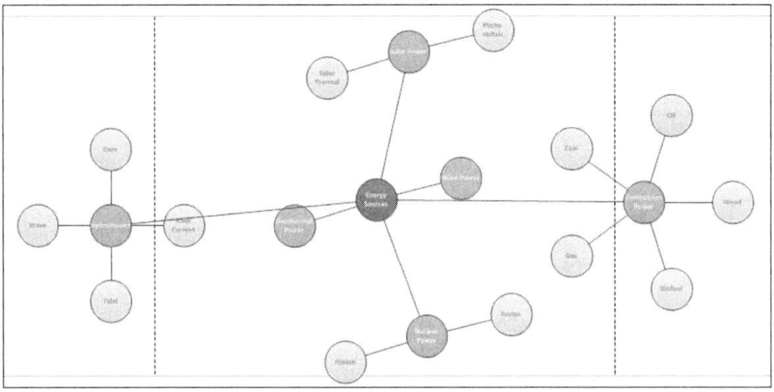

Figure 5.17 *The energy sources diagram with a circular layout and a change in shape style. For extra clarity, darker shapes are higher in the hierarchy.*

SHOW ME **Media 5.4—Experimenting with Layout in Visio 2010**
Access this video file through your registered Web Edition at ***my.safaribooksonline.com/9780132182683/media.***

Laying out connected diagrams in Visio is theoretically a matter of clicking a button or two. Take a moment to try it for yourself and see how it saves you time, but pay attention to the glitches you run into along the way as well.

LET ME TRY IT

Experimenting with Layout

1. Start a new diagram using the Network, Basic Network Diagram template.
2. Add a Server shape to the page and type **Department Server** for its text.
3. Drop Laptop Computer, Cell Phone, and PDA shapes on the page and type some descriptive text—for example, **Cell phone** and **PDA**.

   Note that all these shapes are not on the same stencil, so you have to click the various stencil tabs to find them all.
4. Connect the Laptop to the Cell Phone and PDA. For this example, make sure that you connect from higher-level shapes to lower-level shapes.

   Although networks don't necessarily have a hierarchy like an org chart, think of connecting from the bigger piece of equipment to the smaller. This will help you to experiment with and understand Visio's layout functions later on.
5. Connect the server to the laptop shape.
6. Duplicate the laptop, cell phone, PDA, and associated connectors several times. You can do this by selecting them all at once, copying and then pasting them repeatedly.
7. Connect the server to each of the new laptop shapes you created. Your diagram should look similar to Figure 5.18. Note the three groups of equipment, all connected to the server
8. The connectors are drawn over the network equipment, so send them all to back. The network shapes have connection points on each side, plus one in the middle. It is easy to (accidentally) create point-to-point glue connections with these shapes (instead of dynamic glue). As a result, connectors might be on top of shapes, so the diagram looks sloppy. If you've created dynamic glue connections, you won't have this problem.
   a. Select all the connectors by clicking Home, Select, Select by Type.
   b. Click Shape Role and check only Connectors.

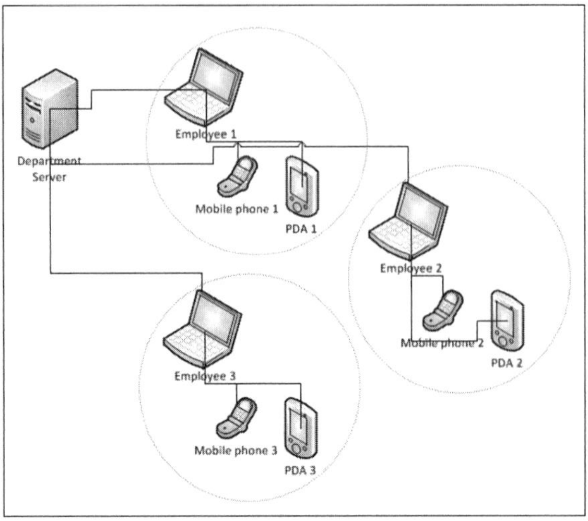

Figure 5.18 *A server haphazardly connected to three groups of employee equipment.*

c. Click OK. All the connectors in the page should be selected.

d. Send them to back by pressing Shift+Ctrl+B or using the button in the Home, Arrange group. All connectors should now be behind the network shapes.

9. Experiment with various layouts available in the layout gallery. On the Design tab, click the Re-layout Page drop-down button in the Layout group. Notice that as you mouse over each item in the gallery, Live Preview shows you how the new arrangement will look.

10. If you can't see the different layouts very well, be sure to zoom out.

11. Try the Circular layout style. I think it shows this network very clearly, as you see in Figure 5.19.

12. Try the Hierarchy or Flowchart styles also. Notice that they have multiple choices for direction of flow. The Flowchart, Left to Right layout works nicely. It offers space for the text, and the text doesn't overlap the connectors very much.

13. Save the diagram as **Ch05 Layout.vsd** so that you can use it in future examples.

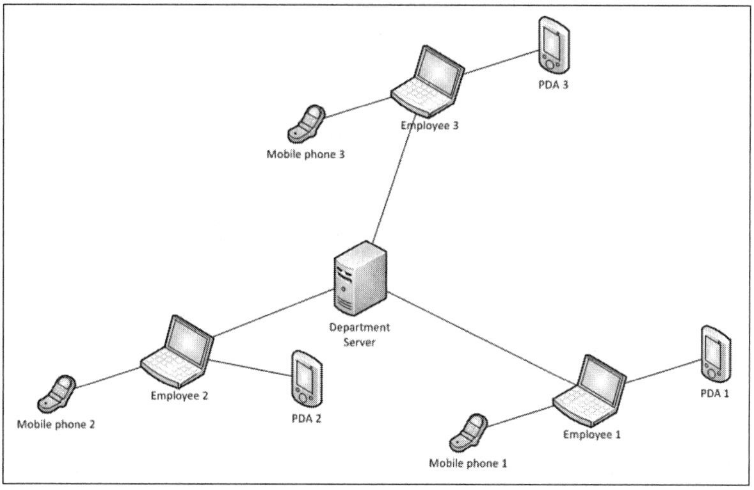

Figure 5.19 *The Circular layout style applied to the mini network.*

Fine-tuning Layout

The Re-layout button gives you quick access to several preconfigured layout styles. However, you can fine-tune the results by digging into three different dialogs, full of layout and connector settings just waiting to bewilder you.

LET ME TRY IT

Improving Layout

1. Open Ch05 Layout.vsd.
2. Apply the Flowchart, Top to Bottom layout style to the diagram. This layout looks like an org chart and is fairly orderly, but it could be improved. As Figure 5.20 shows, text is hard to read because of interference with connectors, and the spacing feels a bit cramped.
3. Give the text an opaque background so that it obscures the connectors.
   a. Select all the shapes in the diagram.
   b. On the Home tab, click the dialog box launcher for the Font or Paragraph group and then click the Text Block tab in the pop-up dialog.

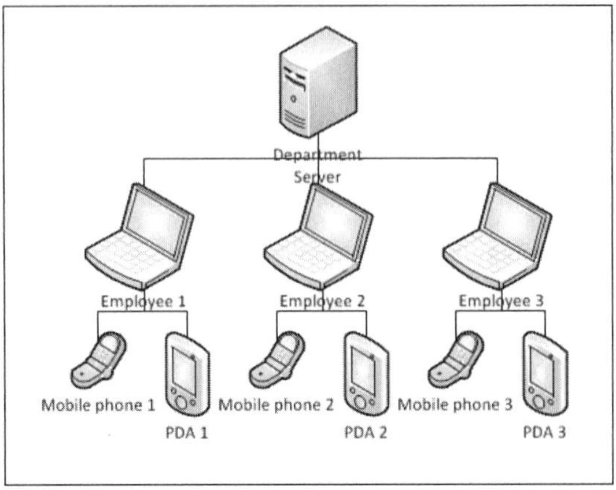

Figure 5.20 *The network diagram with the Flowchart, Top to Bottom layout style. Text and spacing could be better, though.*

c. Click Solid Color and select white from the drop-down color list.

   These settings might already be set, depending on the primary selection, because connectors already have opaque text backgrounds. Regardless, be sure to click them both so that Visio knows you intend to make a change.

d. Click OK. The text blocks now have white backgrounds that obscure the connectors, as shown in Figure 5.21. If all connectors haven't been sent to back, they might be on top of the shape's text and still be in the way.

4. Increase the spacing between shapes. The diagram is still cramped, and the opaque text makes connectors hard to see in some cases.

   a. Click the dialog box launcher for the Layout group (on the Design tab). The Page Setup dialog appears, showing the Layout and Routing tab. Take a moment to become utterly confused by all the settings!

   b. Click the Spacing button near the lower-right corner of the dialog. The Layout and Routing Spacing dialog appears, showing four pairs of horizontal and vertical spacing options.

   c. Because you want more space between the shapes, change the values under Space Between Shapes. Enter **0.75 in.** for the Horizontal value and **0.5 in.** for the Vertical.

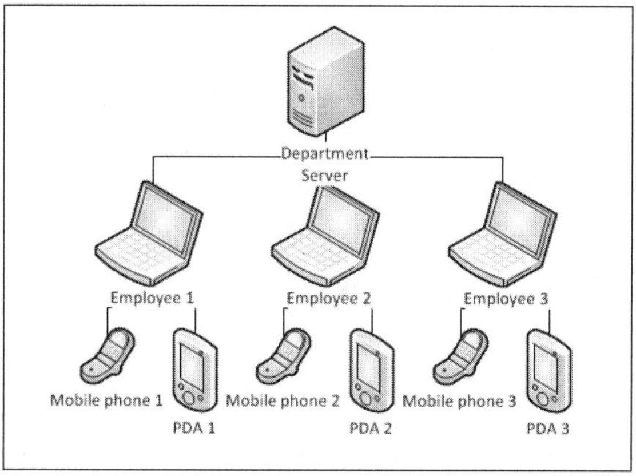

Figure 5.21 *White text backgrounds obscure connectors and make reading easier.*

d. Click OK twice to get back to the diagram. Notice that nothing happens. You have to use Re-layout to get the changes to take effect.

e. Click the Re-layout Page drop-down and notice that the current layout setting is highlighted in orange. Click it again to tell Visio to lay out the diagram using the new settings. The shapes are arranged in the same style, but with more space between them, as shown in Figure 5.22. You see that text is more readable, connectors are clearer, and the diagram is easier on the eyes in general.

5. To give the diagram a more network-ish feel, make the connectors straight. In the Layout group (Design tab), click the Connectors drop-down button and choose Straight Lines. All connectors on the page change from right-angled to straight, as shown in Figure 5.23.

6. Experiment further with layout. Move shapes around on the page manually and then click Re-layout to see what happens.

Visio has a plethora of ways to fine-tune and tweak layout and connector style settings. Describing all of the options and settings would take many pages and bore you to tears. My best advice is to know where the options are, watch the following Show Me video, and take some time yourself to experiment with how layout settings affect the look of your diagrams.

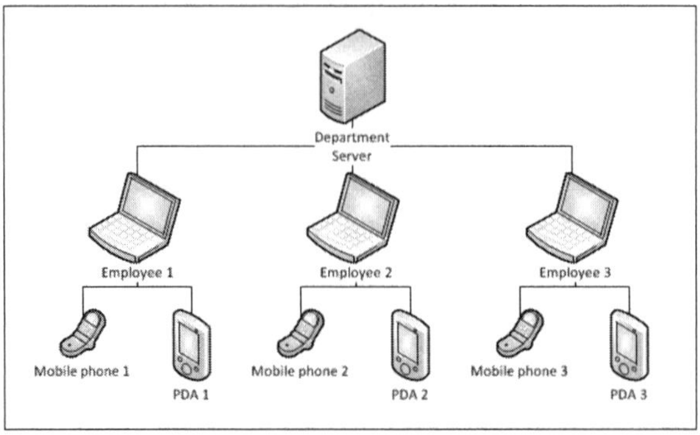

Figure 5.22 *Increased spacing between network shapes makes text easier to read and connectors easier to follow.*

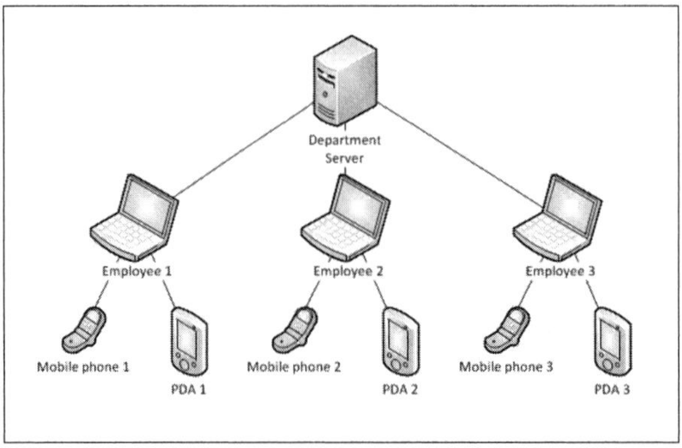

Figure 5.23 *Mixing layout styles by applying straight lines to a flowchart layout.*

Here are the places you will find layout and routing settings:

- Layout & Routing tab in the Page Setup dialog
- Spacing dialog, accessed via the Layout & Routing tab in the Page Setup dialog
- Configure Layout dialog, which you get to by clicking "More Layout Options..." at the bottom of the Re-layout Page drop-down gallery
- Re-layout Page and Connectors drop-down buttons in the Layout group on the Design tab

SHOW ME **Media 5.5—More Layout Settings**
Access this video file through your registered Web Edition at ***my.safaribooksonline.com/9780132182683/media.***

Summary

In this chapter, you learned many ways to arrange and align shapes as well as how to lay out connected diagrams. You saw how the Dynamic Grid helps you to maintain order while you draw, while Auto Align & Space and Re-layout Page help you clean up afterward. You learned that Auto Align & Space and Re-layout Page are aimed primarily at connected diagrams, whereas the Dynamic Grid, ruler, grid, and guides can be applied more generally.

You also explored various styles for laying out a connected diagram and how to manipulate some of the variables to fine-tune that layout.

In this chapter, you delve into nooks and crannies of SmartShapes and learn to find all that a shape can be. You also explore techniques for quickly and efficiently working with shapes so that diagramming with Visio becomes a fluid and natural endeavor.

6

Working with Individual Shapes

You'll get a lot more out of Visio if you can manipulate shapes like a pro. Several useful techniques for moving, copying, and positioning shapes can speed up your drawing, and shapes can have custom features that can help you make your drawings richer and more valuable.

Copying and Duplicating Shapes

Whether I'm making a simple matrix of boxes, an array of servers, or a seating chart for the next concert, I copy shapes constantly. You, too, should be able to copy shapes quickly and without thinking.

Several ways exist to create copies of existing shapes, including the following:

- Ctrl+drag creates a copy of selected shapes at the point where you release the mouse button.
- Copy and paste. You probably already use Ctrl+C and Ctrl+V to do this. You can also use the Ribbon, where the Home tab has the Clipboard group, which contains several copy, cut, and paste-related functions.
- Duplicating via Home, Clipboard, Paste, Duplicate, or Ctrl+D. Duplicates are offset right and down from the original shape.

In Visio 2010, pasting copied or cut shapes has several subtle behaviors that can be confusing at first but can work to your advantage once you understand them.

If you copy shapes and then paste them to a new page using the Ribbon or keyboard shortcuts, they will be pasted at their original location. This is great if you have elements like title and border shapes that need to be repeated on every page in the document but can't be placed on a background page. If the location is not in the current window, Visio pans to the location so that you aren't left wondering where your shapes went. If you paste to the same page in this manner, the new shapes are slightly offset from the originals, just like with duplcate.

If you right-click and choose Paste, shapes will be pasted right where the mouse cursor is.

Constraining Drag and Repeating Copies

I'm a big fan of Ctrl+dragging shapes because it allows me to keep my attention on the drawing instead of looking for copy/paste commands or keys. This capability becomes even more useful when you know the constraining and repeating features.

While Ctrl+dragging a new shape, you can constrain its position to the horizontal or vertical by holding the Shift key as you drag. You start with Ctrl+drag and then press the Shift key during the drag. While Shift is pressed, you are able to move only left and right or up and down. This makes creating neat and tidy rows or columns a snap.

The Repeat button is right next to the Undo button in the Quick Access Toolbar. After you create a copy of a shape, you can click the Repeat button to make more duplicates. I use the shortcut key F4 instead of clicking the Repeat button, but the effect is the same.

Using Ctrl+drag, Shift+constraining, and the Repeat feature, you can create arrays of shapes in an instant!

SHOW ME **Media 6.1—Quickly Copying Shapes to Create a Matrix in Visio 2010**

Access this video file through your registered Web Edition at ***my.safaribooksonline.com/9780132182683/media.***

LET ME TRY IT

Creating a Table of Boxes

Although Word and Excel are arguably better tools for creating tables, you will find yourself creating matrices of shapes in Visio from time to time. Trust me; I've seen it again and again. Practice your new skills and see whether you can whip out a matrix in record time.

1. Create a new, blank drawing.
2. On the View tab, make sure that the ruler and grid are visible and that the Dynamic Grid is turned off.
3. Return to the Home tab and get the Rectangle tool (or press Ctrl+8).
4. Draw a rectangle that is big enough to hold a few words of text. Notice how you can snap to the grid while drawing. Make your rectangle something like 1.0″ × 0.5″. If you're working in metric, approximately 25mm × 10mm will work. The size doesn't need to be exact, but it helps if the rectangle is a nice grid-fitting size.
5. Switch back to the Pointer tool (Ctrl+1).
6. Create a duplicate of your shape via Home, Clipboard, Paste, Duplicate or Ctrl+D.
7. Move the new shape into position directly to the right of the original. Notice how the grid makes it easy to position the shapes right up against one another.
8. Continue the row by creating a copy of the second box. Hold down the Ctrl key and then click+drag a new shape to the right. As you drag, press Shift to constrain the new shape in the horizontal direction.

You must press Shift *after* you start the Ctrl+drag. If you press Shift before, the zoom-in magnifying glass cursor appears, and you are not able to select the shape.

9. With your newest shape still selected, press F4 several times. You should see a neat row of shapes, as shown in Figure 6.1. Alternatively, you can repeat the copies using the Repeat button in the Quick Access Toolbar.

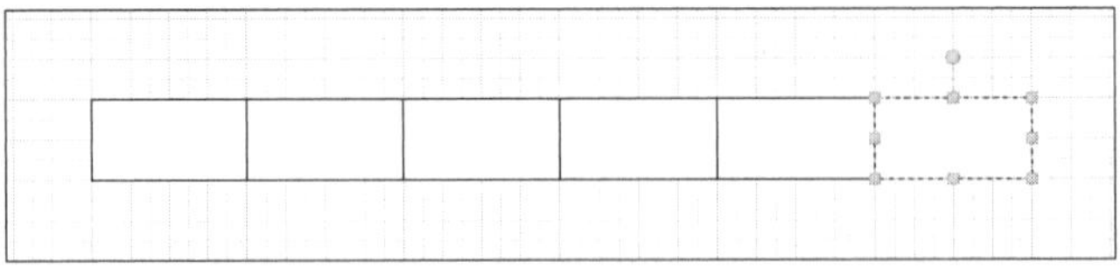

Figure 6.1 *A row of boxes created using duplicate, Ctrl+drag, Shift+constraining, and F4 repeating.*

10. Create a new row for your table. Select all the boxes in the row, hold down the Ctrl key, and start dragging in the downward direction. After you start dragging, press the Shift key to keep the new row aligned with the old. When you release the mouse button, you should have a new row.

11. With the new row of boxes selected, press F4 several times. Voilà! New rows of boxes are created instantly! Hold on to this drawing for a moment, as we'll continue modifying it in the next exercise.

LET ME TRY IT

Quickly Formatting a Table of Boxes

In the last exercise, you used Visio's repeating functions and copying shortcuts to create a matrix of boxes that has several columns and several rows. Now you quickly format the table using similar shortcuts.

1. Add some placeholder text to all the shapes in your table. Select the top-left box in the matrix and then type **TODO**.
2. Select every shape in your table by using the Pointer tool to drag a rectangle around all shapes in the matrix.
3. Press F4 to repeat the last operation, which was adding the text. Every shape in your table should now display the word *TODO*. See how powerful and quick F4 can be?
4. Select the top-left box again and give it a light-gray fill color.
5. Select the top row of boxes and the left column of boxes. To do this, hold down the Shift key and then drag two rectangles around the header row and left column.
6. Press F4 to repeat the fill formatting operation. Your header row and column boxes should now all be gray, as shown in Figure 6.2.
7. Select all the boxes in your table and copy them.
8. Add a new page to your document by clicking the Insert Page tab at the bottom of the window.
9. Experiment with pasting a copy of the table into the new page. Right-click and choose Paste. The table appears centered where you clicked.
10. Add another page, then paste by using Ctrl+V. The table appears in the same location where it was located on the original page.

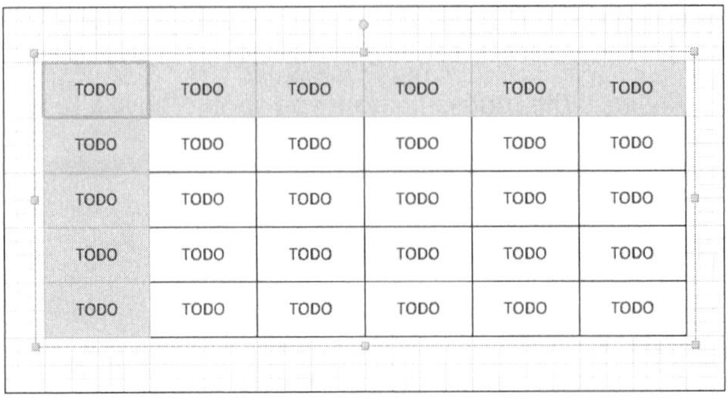

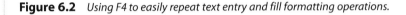

Figure 6.2 *Using F4 to easily repeat text entry and fill formatting operations.*

TELL ME MORE **Media 6.2—Tabbing Between Shapes**
Access this audio file through your registered Web Edition at ***my.safaribooksonline.com/9780132182683/media.***

USING ADD-ONS TO COPY SHAPES

If you are using the Pro or Premium editions of Visio 2010, you have two add-on utilities that make it easy to precisely duplicate shapes. To use them, go to the Macros group of the View tab and click the Add-ons drop-down. Expand the Visio Extras menu and then look for Move Shapes and Array Shapes.

Both add-ons have fairly simple interfaces, which you should be able to figure out. Move Shapes can move or duplicate shapes in the horizontal and vertical directions or at an angle over a distance.

Array Shapes is perfect for creating the matrix of shapes like you did in the last two exercises. The trick is to select "Between shape edges" and set the row and column spacing to zero.

Resizing and Rotating Shapes

By now, you have probably resized and rotated a shape or two. After all, you just select a shape and pull on the blue things! Here are a few tips that will give you finer control over resizing and rotating, and round out your knowledge of the process.

Resizing 2D Shapes

When you select a 2D shape, you see the eight square resizing handles around the perimeter of the shape. Pulling the center handles resizes the width or the height of the shape independently. If you pull on the corner handles, the aspect ratio of the shape is maintained.

You can override this corner handle behavior by holding down the Shift key. When you do this, you can independently size the width and height of the shape at the same time. This shifty behavior is the reverse of what you might have experienced in other Microsoft Office applications where you have to press Shift to preserve the aspect ratio of objects.

Some Visio shapes have locked aspect ratios because the shape designer thought it was important to preserve the width-to-height ratio. In these cases, the Shift trick doesn't have any effect.

Resizing 1D Shapes

When you resize 1D shapes, such as connectors, lines, or Block stencil arrows, you manipulate the two endpoint handles. Dragging these handles effectively changes the angle and length of the shape at the same time.

You can constrain this angle to be perfectly horizontal, vertical, or along a 45-degree increment by holding the Shift key as you drag an end.

Rotating 2D Shapes

You've likely noticed the "lollipop" handle that appears atop selected 2D shapes. This is the rotation handle that lets you spin the shape.

You can control the granularity of the rotation by moving the cursor closer or further from the center of rotation. When you are very close to the center, the rotation snaps to 5-degree increments. When you are far from the center, the snap is in 0.1-degree increments. You can watch the Angle field in the status bar at the bottom of the window to see the angle value change.

As soon as you mouse over the rotation handle, you see the rotation point appear. This is commonly called the shape's *pin* by Visio aficionados. It serves as the center of rotation for the shape, as well as the insertion point when the shape is dragged from a stencil. Ninety-nine percent of Visio shapes have the pin at the center, but you can freely move it to a different location. Figure 6.3 shows a practical application of moving the rotation point.

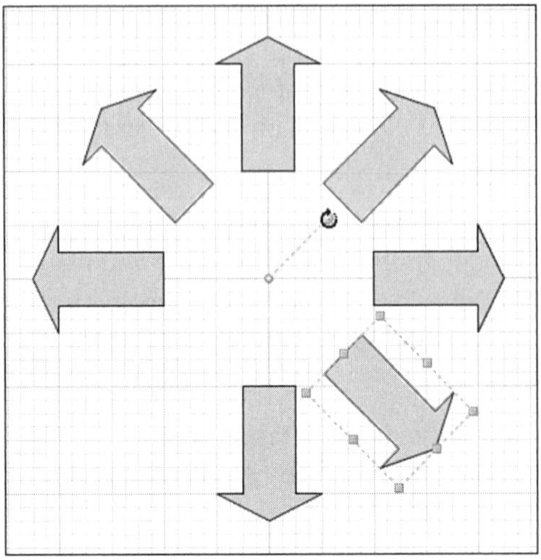

Figure 6.3 *A circular array of arrows is created by offsetting the rotation point, duplicating the shape several times, then rotating close to the pin to snap to 5-degree increments.*

LET ME TRY IT

Creating a Radial Array of Arrows

Figure 6.3 combines a number of techniques described so far to create a nice, radial array of arrows. Give it a try!

1. Create a new diagram using General, Block Diagram template.
2. On the View tab, make sure that the grid is visible.
3. From the Blocks stencil, drag out the "2D single" shape and zoom in on it.
4. Select the shape and mouse over the "lollipop" rotation handle.
5. When the rotation point appears, grab it and move it off the left side of the shape, but keep it vertically centered, as shown in Figure 6.3.
6. Make a copy of the shape, exactly on top of itself. To do this, select the original shape and start dragging it. Then press the Ctrl and Shift keys. Ctrl causes a copy to be made, and Shift constrains movement so you can easily drop the copy right on top of the original.

7. Make six more copies of the shape by pressing the F4 key six times. This repeats the last duplication operation. You should now have eight arrows, all directly on top of each other so it looks like only one arrow.
8. Select all the shapes by dragging a selection rectangle around them. Notice the heavy magenta outline for the selection highlight. This indicates more than one shape is selected.
9. Click an empty space on the diagram to deselect all shapes. Now drag all eight shapes to different locations—just to verify that you really have eight shapes.
10. Press Ctrl+Z repeatedly to undo the movements of the shapes in the last step. Do this until all are back on top of each other and it looks like just one arrow on the page.
11. Rotate each arrow into position. Select one shape at a time. Rotate it by pulling on the "lollipop" handle. Keep the cursor close to the rotation point so that you get the 5-degree snapping. Watch the angle in the status bar and rotate the shapes to 45-degree multiples: 45°, 90°, 135°, 180°, –135°, –90°, and –45° degrees.

One last rotation tip: If you find yourself frequently rotating shapes in 90-degree increments, you can quickly rotate counterclockwise by pressing Ctrl+L and clockwise by pressing Ctrl+R.

Formatting Individual Shapes

If you want to change the general look of your diagram, be sure to start with themes, as discussed in Chapter 2, "Working Around the Diagram." However, if you need to make specific changes to a shape or are creating your own library of symbols, Visio has a full set of formatting tools at your disposal.

Changing Line, Fill, and Text Attributes

You can't help but notice Visio's formatting controls. They are similar to what you would find in Word or Excel and located in similar places. The Home tab on the Ribbon has the Font, Paragraph, and Shape groups. Right-clicking any shape pops up a mini-toolbar that gives you quick access to popular formatting features, along with cascading menus to access just about everything else.

The best way to get good at formatting is to start a blank drawing, draw some rectangles, and then start clicking the controls on the Home Ribbon or right-click the mini-toolbar.

Which Formatting Attributes Can Be Edited?

Visual attributes fall into four formatting groups: Line, Fill, Shadow, and Text. While the list of possibilities is too long to show here, the best way to learn them is to play around and experiment.

There are formatting dialogs for each group that help you to get a good overview of available options, and make many related changes at once. For Text attributes, use the dialog box launcher buttons in the lower-right corner of the Font and Paragraph groups on the Home tab. For Fill, Shadow, and Line dialogs, click the corresponding drop-down button in the Shape group, then pick the Options item at the end of the list.

Take a moment to explore these dialogs to see all the formatting options available. Draw a few rectangles on a blank page and format the living daylights out of them!

SHOW ME **Media 6.3—Formatting Shapes in Visio 2010**
Access this video file through your registered Web Edition at ***my.safaribooksonline.com/9780132182683/media.***

LET ME TRY IT

Using Formatting Dialogs to Change Many Settings at Once

1. Start with a new, blank drawing.
2. Draw a rectangle on the page, and type **Using Microsoft Visio 2010** on it. Keep the shape selected, but switch back to the Pointer Tool.
3. Change fill formatting for the shape using the Fill dialog. On the Home tab, in the Shape group, click the Fill drop-down and then choose Options at the bottom of the list. The Fill dialog appears.
4. Choose different values for color, pattern, transparency, shadow style, shadow color, shadow pattern, and shadow transparency. After each change, click Apply and see how the shape changes without leaving the dialog. Click OK when you are ready to exit.
5. Compare the many options in the Fill dialog to the smaller set that is available in the Fill drop-down in the Shape group. Right-click the shape and notice that the same Fill drop-down is available from the mini-toolbar.

6. Notice that the Ribbon and context menu options give you Live Preview as you move the mouse over various options. In the dialog, you have more choices and can change many settings at once, but you don't get Live Preview.
7. Change line and shadow formatting similar to how you changed fill attributes in steps 3 and 4. The Shape group has drop-down buttons for Line and Shadow; these both have Options at the bottom which launch detailed dialogs.
8. Note the line and shadow options available directly from the Ribbon and via right-clicking and compare them to the options available in the dialogs.
9. Explore text formatting options by clicking the dialog box launcher in the Font or Paragraph groups. You see the Text dialog, which has six different tabs for formatting the Font, Character, Paragraph, Text Block, Tabs, and Bullets of your shape's text.
10. Note that you can format individual words and characters for the shape's text. To get into text edit mode, simply double-click the shape or select the shape and choose the Text tool from the Tools group on the Home tab. Then you can select portions of the text as you would in Word and format them.

Curing Menu Cascade-itis

Visio 2010 reduced toolbar clutter by combining toolbar buttons with cascading menus. I find the right-click mini-toolbar wonderfully convenient, and most of the formatting options come with live preview, which is an extra bonus.

If, however, you are making lots of formatting edits, frequent cascading is tiring. For example, I often find myself changing the color, weight, pattern, and arrowhead style of a line. This requires four separate, multilevel trips into the Line drop-down.

In the last exercise, you saw how the Line, Fill, Shadow, and Text dialogs enable you to make multiple changes at once. If you are in the middle of a formatting frenzy, using these dialogs is often faster and easier. For all but the text options, however, you still have to expand a drop-down list just to get to the dialogs. You can speed up the process by customizing the Ribbon or Quick Access Toolbar so that you can directly access the dialogs with one mouse click.

LET ME TRY IT

Creating a Custom Ribbon Tab for Quick Line, Fill, and Text Editing

1. Start with a new, blank drawing.
2. Draw a few test rectangles on the page. Add some text to the shapes. Play with formatting the shapes via the controls on the Home tab or by right-clicking.
3. Change the line color, line weight, and line pattern for a shape using the Line drop-down and cascading into the Weight and Dashes items. Imagine doing this many times. Feel the pain.
4. Right-click any area on the Ribbon and choose Customize the Ribbon.
5. In the Customize Ribbon dialog, click the New Tab button on the lower right. Notice that a new tab and new group are added to the list. Controls on a tab must be in a group.
6. Right-click New Tab and choose Rename. Change the name to **Using Visio**.
7. Similarly, rename New Group to **Format**. Make sure Format is highlighted in the list.
8. In the Choose Commands From drop-down list, pick All Commands.
9. Select Fill Options... in the commands list and then click Add >>. Fill Options is added to your custom Format Group on the right.
10. Similarly, add the items: Shadow Options, Line Options, and Text to your custom group. If you make a mistake, select an item in the Main Tabs list on the right and then click the Remove button.
11. Change the position of the Using Visio tab by selecting it and then pressing the up or down arrow on the right of the dialog box.
12. When you are satisfied with your changes, click OK. You should see your new Using Visio Ribbon tab, as shown in Figure 6.4. Clicking the buttons in your new Format group instantly launches the Line, Fill, or Shadow options dialogs.

If you don't want to bother creating a new menu tab, you can add the same items to the Quick Access Toolbar. If you look closely at the top-left corner of Figure 6.4, you can see I've done this already. To add these buttons, just right-click on the Fill

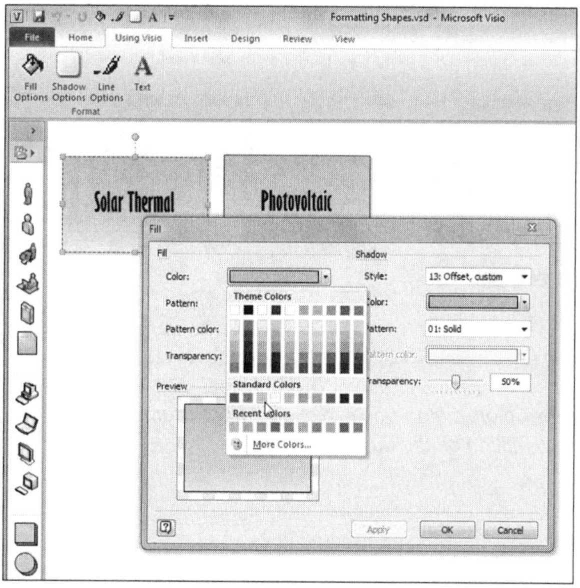

Figure 6.4 *The custom-built Using Visio Ribbon tab relieves the suffering caused by frequent cascading through Fill, Line, and Shadow drop-downs.*

Options, Shadow Options, and Line Options menu items and then choose Add to Quick Access Toolbar.

Finding More Options

If you can't find a button for something you want to change, there are two things to look for that lead you to more options. First is dialog box launcher buttons that you see in the lower-right corner of some Ribbon groups like Font and Paragraph. Second is menu items that end with "dot-dot-dot." The ellipsis always means that a dialog with more options will appear when you click it.

In your exploration of shape formatting features, you've probably already seen More Colors..., Fill Options..., More Lines..., More Arrows..., Line Options..., Shadow Options..., all of which lead to detailed settings dialogs for customizing your shapes.

One example that you see multiple times is More Colors... This menu item pops up the Colors dialog, which has two nifty tabs for picking just the right color. You can see it in Figure 6.5.

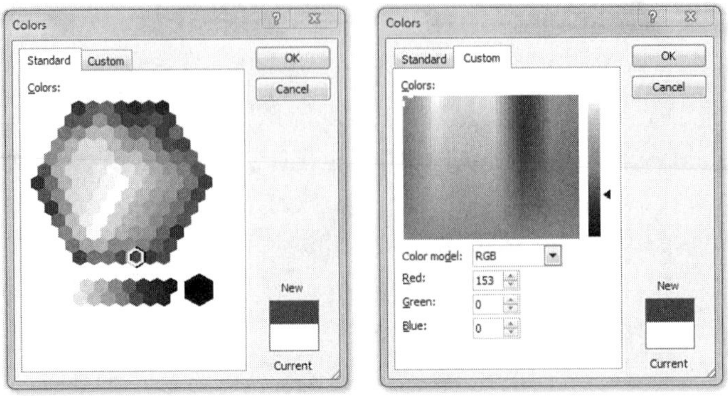

Figure 6.5 *In the Colors dialog, you can choose from a large set of predefined colors or choose from over 16 million on the Custom tab.*

The Colors' Custom tab is handy if you're working with designers in your art department and need to match specific, corporate colors. Custom colors that you pick or define show up in the Recent Colors area of the various formatting drop-downs, but this list changes: as you use new colors, older colors drop off the end.

To save custom colors, you can create a simple rectangle or circle and apply the color to the shape. Then you can use the Format Painter control from Home, Clipboard to apply it to other shapes. You can save these custom color shapes as masters in your Favorites stencil (see Chapter 2, "Working Around the Diagram") or just put them on another page in the document.

Formatting Groups

As you learned in Chapter 3, "Organizing and Annotating Diagrams," Visio shapes can be comprised of many shapes grouped together. Complicated shapes can be built by grouping simpler pieces together and nice effects created by layering shapes on top of one another.

When you select a group and apply formatting, Visio applies it to the group and all its submembers. This can either save you lots of time or totally ruin your shape!

To complicate matters, some grouped shapes have built-in protection and intelligence to better handle this all-at-once formatting. The discrepancy in behavior can be confusing, so it's important that you understand what is going on.

Figure 6.6 contrasts "intelligent formatting" behavior versus "dumb formatting" behavior for several grouped shapes.

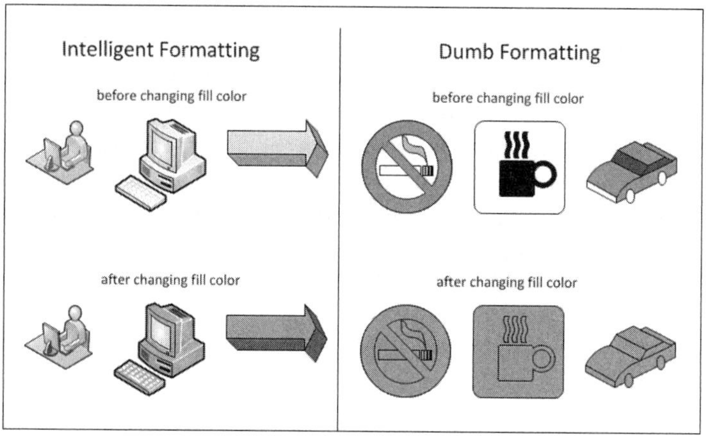

Figure 6.6 *The grouped shapes on the left react better to a change in fill color than the groups on the right.*

See that all of the subshapes in the groups on the right get blasted with a darker fill color? All subtlety and differentiation are lost when the new fill color is applied. The shapes on the left behave so well that it is hard to even notice that the color was changed.

Unfortunately, the dumb behavior is the default in Visio. If you draw your own shapes using the drawing tools and then group them together, your groups react to formatting in this way. The intelligent shapes in Figure 6.6 were created by shape designers who employed techniques beyond the scope of this book (but hinted at in Chapter 11, "Developing Custom Visio Solutions").

You will encounter both types of behavior. Indeed, all the shapes in Figure 6.6 come from stencils that ship with Visio.

To avoid ruining grouped shapes, you can subselect individual members and format them. Subselecting is as easy as clicking on the group, pausing a split second, and then clicking again on a part.

For example, in Figure 6.6, you could subselect the coffee cup icon and change it to a deep brown color, while leaving the background rectangle white.

Yet one more wrinkle in this story is that some shapes are locked against subselection. The intelligent shapes in Figure 6.6 don't allow subselection at all—but then again, you don't really need to subselect the items since they handle formatting so well. The shapes on the right, however, are not protected, so you can freely select and alter individual subshapes.

You will eventually run into groups with subshapes that you want to individually change but are locked against subselection. In this case, you can open the group to work with the individual subshapes inside. Just right-click the shape, choose Group, and then choose Open *Shapename*. In the group-editing window that appears, you can directly access the subshapes. Here, you can make formatting changes to the pieces. One last warning, however. Shape designers can lock down formatting on subshapes of groups, too, so you still might not be able to change the subshapes! It doesn't hurt to try, though.

Setting Default Formatting

You can set the default line, fill, and text attributes for shapes created with the drawing tools. Just choose settings from the Fill, Line, Shadow, Font, and Paragraph controls while no shapes are selected in your diagram.

For example, choose the color red from the Fill drop-down with no shapes selected. Now when you use the Rectangle tool or Ellipse tool to draw a shape, it is filled with red.

Unfortunately, these settings are forgotten when you close the drawing file, but this capability can be a real timesaver during an intense drawing session. Also note that these settings have no effect on masters dropped on your page—only new shapes you create using the drawing tools.

Working with Text

When it comes to shape text, there are two things to think about: the characters and the text block that contains them. You edit text in Visio similarly to the way you edit text in Word or Excel. The text block, however, is the region of a shape that the text occupies. You could compare text blocks to paragraphs or sections in Word, but they are really a feature unique to Visio shapes.

In this section, you look at how to manipulate text blocks and shape text, and explore a few other text-related issues while you're at it.

Creating and Editing Text Blocks

A *text block* is a region on a shape that holds text. By default, this region is exactly the same size as the shape itself, but it doesn't have to be. If you look at shapes like those in the workflow or network equipment stencils, you see text blocks that are below the shape.

All Visio shapes contain text blocks by default. If you draw a rectangle, you can type text directly on to it. If you group several shapes together, the group has its own text block, as does each subshape inside the group.

Figure 6.7 shows the Phone call shape from the Flowchart, Workflow Objects stencil. In the left window, you see the resize handles for the shape itself. In the right window, you see resize handles for the text block.

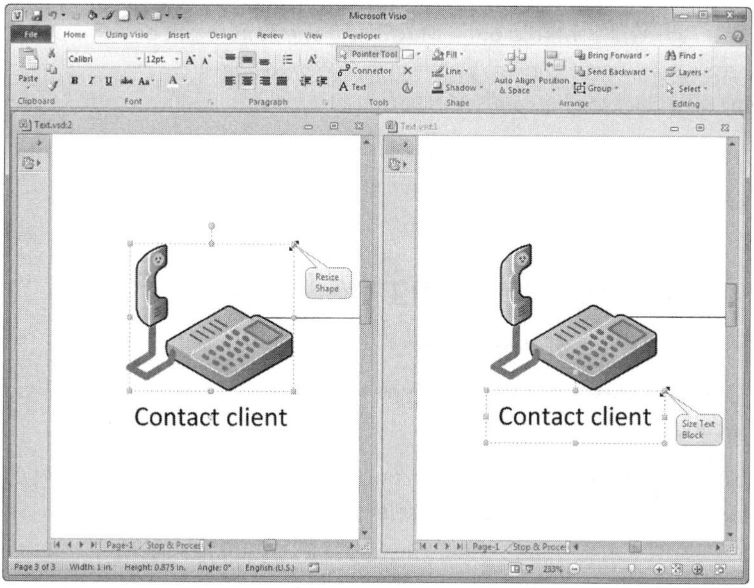

Figure 6.7 *The selection rectangles for the Phone call shape. On the left, the shape is selected using the Pointer tool; on the right, it is selected using the Text Block tool.*

There are two tools for working with text: the Text tool and Text Block tool. Both are found in the Tools group of the Home tab. They have similar names and similar icons. The Text tool has a big A, and the Text Block tool has a smaller A with a circular arrow around it.

You can use both tools to create text anywhere on the page. Click a blank region of the page or drag out a rectangle and then start typing. You just created a text shape.

I call it a "text shape" because what you really did is create a no-fill, no-line rectangle with text in it. You could just as easily draw a box with the Rectangle tool, type in some text, and apply no-line and no-fill styling to achieve the same result. Conversely, you can apply line and fill styling to your new text shape and make it look as though it was drawn with the Rectangle tool. There isn't really a separate text entity in Visio. If you are editing text in Visio, you are editing the text of *some shape*.

The two text tools differ in behavior when you click on existing shapes, however. The Text tool simply enters text-editing mode, so you edit, format, add, and delete words and characters. The Text Block tool enables you to resize, reposition, and rotate the text block. You saw the Text Block tool in action in Figure 6.7.

SHOW ME **Media 6.4—Modifying the Text Block of a Shape**

Access this video file through your registered Web Edition at ***my.safaribooksonline.com/9780132182683/media.***

LET ME TRY IT

Modifying a Text Block Using the Text Block Tool

1. On a new, blank drawing, draw an oval using the Ellipse tool.
2. Type some text on the shape. Type enough text so that the text wraps to a second line.
3. On the Home tab in the Tools group, select the Text Block tool and click on your shape. Notice that all the selection handles look the same as when you draw the shape or when you select it with the Pointer tool.
4. Pause your cursor over the selection handles and the "lollipop" handle atop the shape. Notice the word balloons that appear: "Size Text Block" and "Rotate Text Block." These ToolTips are helpful reminders that you have the Text Block tool and are working with the shape's text block, not the shape itself.
5. Change the size of the text block. Grab any resizing handle and move it. Notice that the text block resizes, but the ellipse is unchanged. You are only editing the text block. Make the text block wider. Notice that you can make it wide enough so that the text no longer wraps to a second line. This is one reason you might want to edit a shape's text block.

6. Move the text block. Position the cursor over the blue dashed outline of the text block. When you see the crosshair cursor, click and drag the text block around. It can be anywhere on or outside the shape.

7. Rotate the text block by moving the mouse cursor over the "lollipop" handle. When you see the circular arrow cursor, click and drag to rotate the block. Note that the closer you are to the center of rotation, the coarser the rotation—just as when you rotate shapes. Figure 6.8 shows the rotated, resized, translated text block for an ellipse shape.

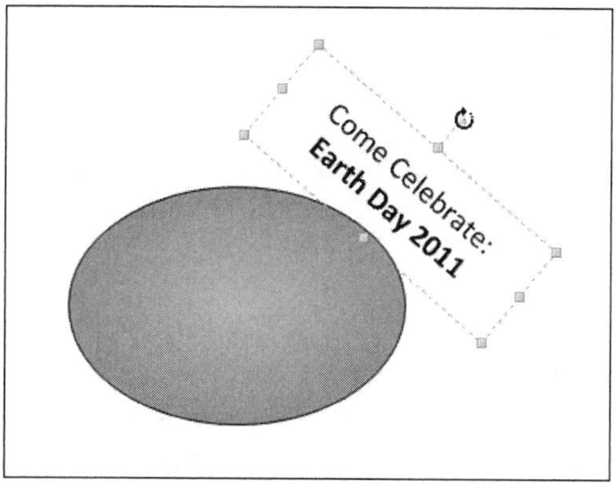

Figure 6.8 *Using the Text Block tool to manipulate a shape's text block.*

8. Switch back to the Pointer tool and select your shape. Notice that the shape handles match the size of the shape, as expected, independent of those of the text block.

USING TEXT WITH CONTROL HANDLES

Now that you've worked your way through text block training, let's discuss an easier way to move the text block. You may have noticed small, yellow diamond handles in the middle of text blocks on *some* Visio shapes Most of Visio's network shapes have this feature, but you won't see the control handle unless the shape has some text.

Pulling on such a control handle moves the text of the shape without the need to switch to the Text Block tool, as shown in Figure 6.9.

You usually find these text-positioning control handles added to shapes where it doesn't make sense to have text inside the shapes, such as the network shapes I mentioned earlier. They aren't a built-in Visio feature, but are added by shape developers to make things easier for you. Note that text control handles don't help you to rotate the text block. Also notice that the text blocks expand automatically as you add more text. If you need new lines, you'll have to manually press Enter, as the text never wraps by itself.

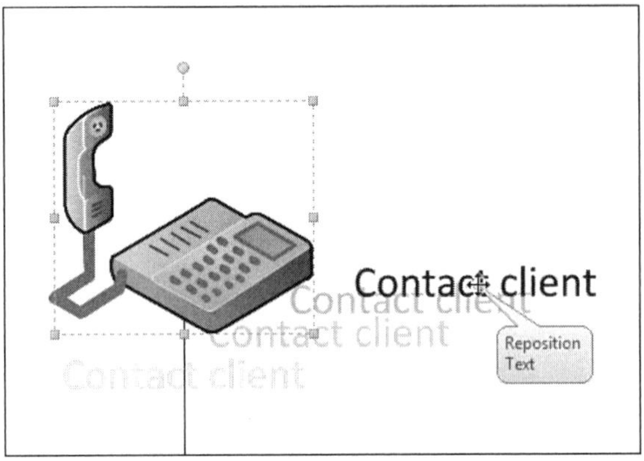

Figure 6.9 *Many of Visio's shapes have built-in control handles for easily moving the text block of a shape. Here, you can quickly move the text out of the way of the outgoing connector.*

Editing and Formatting Text

After a hard day of moving text blocks around, you might eventually want to type in some actual characters and format them.

Editing and formatting text in Visio isn't much different than in any other Microsoft Office application. You can see that a good deal of the Home tab is dedicated to text-formatting controls, and there are plenty of options in the right-click mini-toolbar as well.

What's more interesting are the Visio-specific quirks involved with text editing, which you investigate next.

Getting Into Text Edit Mode

The trick with shape text is getting into "text edit mode" so that you can get your mouse on individual words and characters. When you first add text to a shape, you simply select the shape and start typing. This naturally puts you in text edit mode until you deselect the shape. But how do you edit text that is already there? There are several ways to get into text edit mode to edit preexisting text:

- Select a shape using the Text tool.
- Select a shape with any tool; then press F2.
- Double-click a shape. Text editing is Visio's default behavior, but shape developers can override it, so not every shape will enter text edit mode via double-click.

Once in text edit mode, you can select runs of characters and format them, edit them, or delete them. Once finished, exit text edit mode by clicking a blank area on the page. If you want to keep the shape you are working on selected, press Esc instead.

GETTING INTO TEXT EDIT MODE FOR SUBSHAPES IN GROUPS

The easiest way to get into text edit mode for subshapes in a group is to subselect them with the Pointer tool and then press F2.

Although using the Text tool is the official way to edit text in Visio, it can be cumbersome when working with subshapes. First, you click on the group, which opens the text edit window for the group. If the text block obscures the subshapes (which it often does), it is impossible to get at the subshapes. You can then press Esc to reveal the subshapes, and finally click on one of them to open its text edit window. Like I said, cumbersome!

I personally almost never use the Text tool. I just double-click shapes or select and press F2. It's much quicker and easier, once you're used to it.

Formatting Text

When you're in text edit mode, you can type, copy, paste, delete, and format ranges of characters as you would in any word processor.

Inside a shape's text edit window, the world looks a bit different, as Figure 6.10 illustrates.

In Figure 6.10, notice the following:

- There is a standard text ruler control. It lets you specify left, right, first, and hanging indents as well as tab stops. If you don't see the ruler, right-click while editing text and check Text Ruler in the menu.

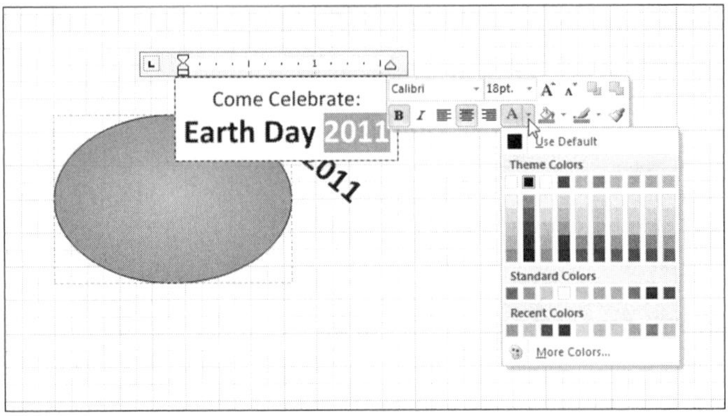

Figure 6.10 *Text edit mode for a shape with rotated text and mixed text formatting. The mini-toolbar appears automatically when editing text, you don't have to right-click to see it as you do when just editing shapes.*

- Text is edited right-side up, even though the text block is rotated on the shape. Although this causes some weird flashing, it's easier than twisting your head to read the text.
- Selected ranges of text can be formatted by right-clicking or by using the controls in the Ribbon.
- The selection handles for the shape are not visible. Only the thin, blue dashed outline of the shape's alignment box is visible, along with a second dashed outline around the text block.

Tabs and Alignment

The text ruler allows you to specify tab stops for neatly formatting columns of information. Just click anywhere on the ruler to insert a new tab. Existing tabs can be dragged to new positions. To delete a tab, drag the marker off the ruler and release the mouse button.

At first, you might conclude that tabs don't work properly in Visio, The problem is that most Visio shapes have center-aligned text, and center-aligned text doesn't work well (or make much sense) with tab stops!

If you need tabs for your shape text, right-align or justify-align the whole paragraph. Your tabs should look just fine once you've fixed the paragraph alignment.

Text Block Backgrounds

Sometimes your shape text is on top of geometry or other details that make the text hard to read. For that reason, a text block can have its own background color that obscures objects behind it and makes text easier to read.

In Figure 6.11, you see that the text for both the line and connector has an opaque white background. For lines and connectors, this is the default, since the text is very likely to be on top of the line.

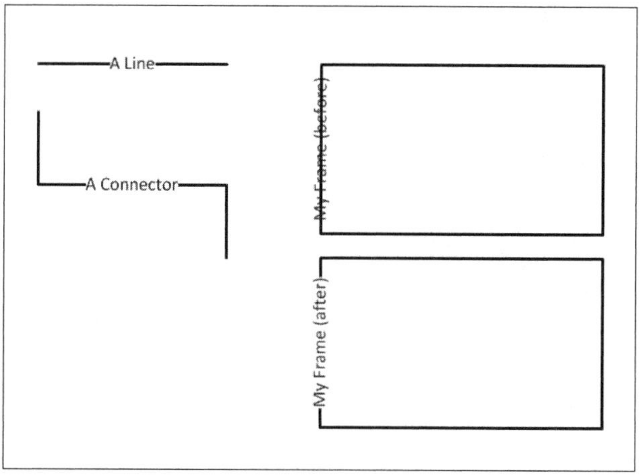

Figure 6.11 *Text on lines and connectors has an opaque background by default, but some shapes don't.*

For rectangles, text doesn't have a background color by default, since the text is usually in the middle of the shape. In Figure 6.11, I've moved and rotated the text to the left side of the rectangle to create a low-budget container. On the top rectangle, you see how hard it is to read the text. The bottom rectangle is easier to read because an opaque, white background was added to the text.

To add background fills to text blocks, click the dialog box launcher for the Font or Paragraph group. In the dialog, select the Text Block tab. In the Text Background area, select a color from the drop-down control that matches the background of your drawing, and then click OK. Your text will be easier to read.

Text Resizing Behavior

A common complaint from Visio users is that "my text is resizing improperly!" This problem stems from the fact that some text is informational and some text is graphical. Figure 6.12 illustrates the problem.

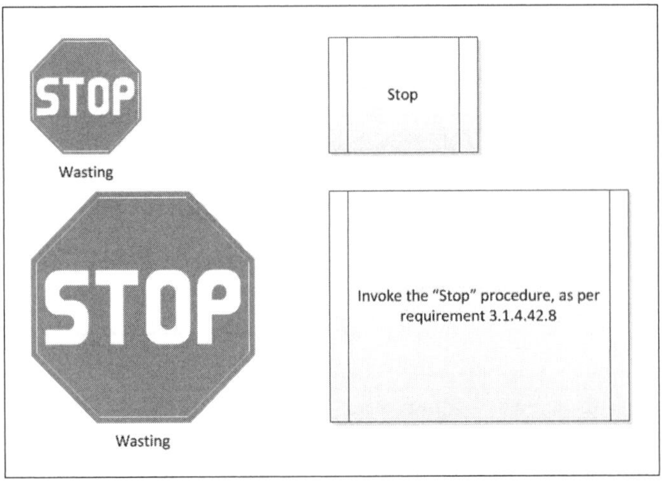

Figure 6.12 *Graphical text should resize with a symbol. Informational text should not.*

For the Stop Sign shape, S-T-O-P is part of the graphic. The text below the Stop sign serves as a caption and is informational—not part of the symbol. If the shape is resized, S-T-O-P resizes too, but the caption does not.

All the text on the Process shape is informational. You make the Process shape bigger when you need space for more text. The text on most Visio shapes behaves this way.

In this example, S-T-O-P isn't even editable text. It is four shapes drawn to look like the letters, so they naturally resize with the rest of the shape.

When you use advanced techniques, it *is* possible to create editable text that resizes with a shape, but a description of that process is beyond the scope of this book. For the über-curious, I'll reference two articles on the topic:

Text Resizing with ShapeSheet Formulas http://www.visguy.com/2007/08/21/text-resizing-with-shapesheet-formulas/.

Resize Text with Metafiles http://www.visguy.com/2007/08/24/resize-text-with-metafiles/

LET ME TRY IT

Creating Fixed, Graphical Text That Resizes with a Shape

If you have a fixed set of letters like S-T-O-P in the Stop Sign shape, you can convert them to a graphical block that stretches like a shape. Just follow these steps:

1. On a new, blank drawing, create a text block using the Text or Text Block tool. Alternatively, draw a rectangle and format it with no line and no fill.
2. Type the letters for your text.
3. Format the font, color, and style for your text.
4. Copy the shape to the Clipboard.
5. Right-click anywhere on the page and choose Paste Special.
6. In the dialog, choose As Picture (Enhanced Metafile) and click OK. A new shape appears with the text that you copied.
7. Verify that the text size grows with the shape by pulling on the resize handles.
8. Verify that you can't edit the text. Select the shape and type. The new shape has its own text block, unrelated to the graphical characters.
9. Change line, fill, and text formatting attributes for the shape. Notice that the text maintains the same font, color, and fill. Only the outline and background of the shape change. This is another limitation of this technique.
10. Group the new shape with other shapes to create a new shape.
11. Resize the new group and verify that your text grows with the shape.

Using Special Shape Features

Visio shapes are often referred to as SmartShapes because shape designers can add functionality to make them more useful. A lot of these extra goodies go undiscovered, however, because users don't know where to look.

This section gives a rundown of the bonus features that a shape might possess and shows you where to find them.

Right-Click Actions

One of my favorite tips for Visio users is to "right-click shapes like there's no tomorrow!" The context menu is one of the first places to look to find custom actions that have been added to a shape.

Custom actions can trigger textual and graphical changes to the shape, show and hide elements, change the way a shape resizes, pop up dialogs, and even communicate with add-ins.

Figure 6.13 compares the right-click menus of four sample shapes.

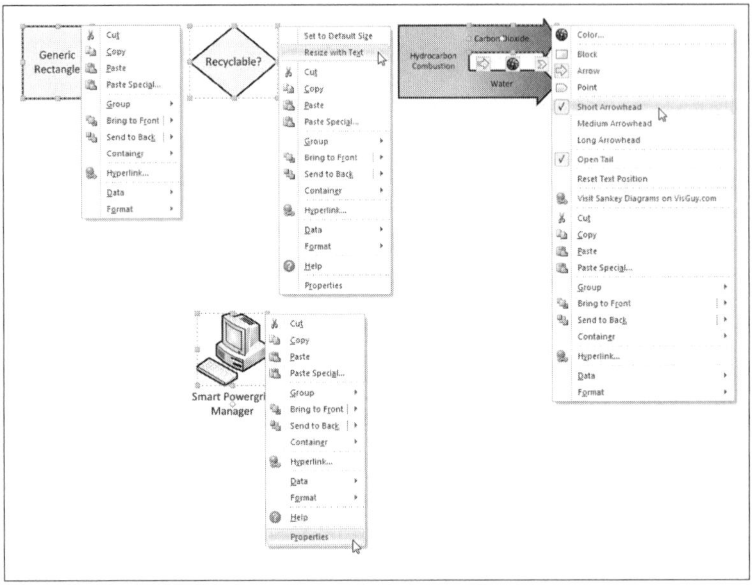

Figure 6.13 *Right-click context menus reveal additional functionality for SmartShapes. Typical locations for custom actions are at the top and bottom of the menu.*

The first rectangle in Figure 6.13 shows the unaltered menu for a default Visio shape. Compare it to the other three, which have custom menu items—most of which are at the top of the menu. Sometimes, custom items appear at the bottom, as the two shapes with "Properties" illustrate.

Shape Data Fields

By now you are well aware that Visio shapes can contain data. Many of the shapes that come with Visio are already populated with Shape Data fields.

If you want to see Shape Data fields, the Shape Data window needs to be visible, and one or more shapes must be selected. If the window isn't visible, just right-click a shape and choose Data, Shape Data. Alternatively, use the Ribbon and go to View, Show, Task Panes, Shape Data.

You learn more about working with data in Chapter 7, "Working with Data." For now, understand that Shape Data fields hold data that can be purely informational or can affect the appearance of the shape (see Figure 6.14). You can manually edit fields or link them to external data. And you can visualize shape data using Data Graphics if you have Visio Pro or Premium.

Figure 6.14 *Visio network shapes carry lots of Shape Data fields that store information about the hardware and the organization, but don't affect appearance. The Sankey diagram arrow below has Shape Data fields that control its appearance.*

Control Handles

Control handles are little yellow diamonds that appear when you select a shape. You use them to adjust graphical bits of a shape. Figure 6.15 illustrates several ways in which shapes use control handles.

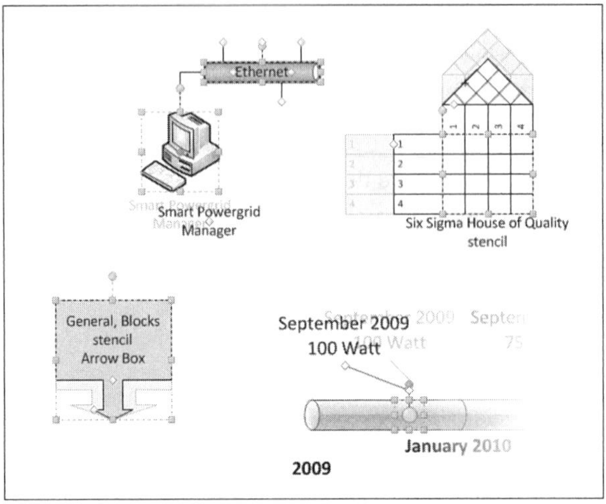

Figure 6.15 *Visio shapes employ control handles so that you can visually change more than just the width, height, and angle of a shape.*

When you move the mouse cursor over a control handle, you see a crosshairs cursor, which indicates that you can drag the handle to a new location. If you pause for a moment, you might also see a ToolTip that suggests the purpose of the control handle.

Some control handles are constrained to move only horizontally or vertically, and some can glue to connection points of other shapes.

In Figure 6.15, you see control handles for repositioning text, adjusting arrow sizes, resizing row and column headers, and pulling extra connectors out of the Ethernet bar.

Hyperlinks

Shapes can have hyperlinks that link to other pages, other documents, or web pages. Visio shapes can have multiple hyperlinks, which are accessed by right-clicking.

Figure 6.16 shows how the cursor changes when you mouse over a shape that contains one or more links. It also shows how multiple links are presented in the right-click context menu.

Adding hyperlinks to shapes is quite easy.

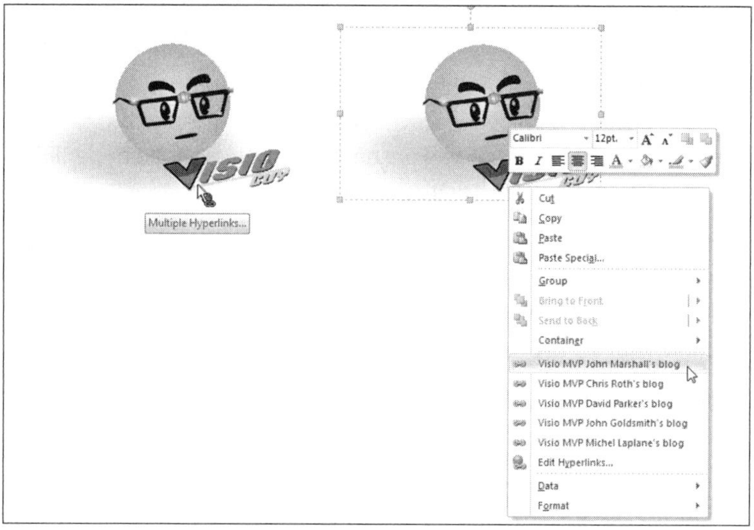

Figure 6.16 *The cursor changes when your mouse cursor is hovering over a shape that contains one or more hyperlinks. Ctrl+Click or right-click to follow one.*

LET ME TRY IT

Adding Multiple Hyperlinks to a Shape

1. Start a new drawing using the Basic Network Diagram template.
2. Rename Page 1 as **Overview**.
3. Insert a new page and rename it as **Network 1**.
4. Drop a Server or PC shape onto the Network 1 page.
5. Show the Shape Data window for the shape and edit the Manufacturer field to **Dell**.
6. Add a link to the shape that jumps to the Overview page. Right-click on the shape and choose Hyperlink. Alternatively, go to Insert, Links, Hyperlink.
7. In the Hyperlinks dialog, leave the Address field blank because this is for linking to web pages and other external documents. Instead, click the Browse button next to the Sub-address field. This lets you choose other pages within the document. Select Overview and click OK.

8. Change the Description field to Overview Page; then click OK. When you hover over your shape, you should see the Globe+chain cursor that indicates the shape has a hyperlink. Right-click the shape, and you should see the Overview Page midway down. Click on this to verify that the link jumps to the Overview page. For shapes that have single hyperlinks, Ctrl+clicking jumps immediately to the link location.

9. Because the equipment's manufacturer is Dell, add a link to Dell's home page. Return to the Network 1 page and select your PC shape again. Edit the hyperlinks by pressing Ctrl+K, or use the methods described in Step 6 to get there.

   Click New to create a new link. Type **www.dell.com** in the Address field and **Dell Home Page** in the Description field; then click OK.

10. Right-click the shape and check that you have two links: Overview Page and Dell Home Page. Click on Dell Home Page. Your default browser should open to Dell's main web page.

You can envision using links to more easily navigate complex documents that contain many pages and to tie shapes to useful documents such as instruction manuals and specifications.

You can also add hyperlinks to several shapes at the same time. Just select a bunch of shapes and then use your favorite method for inserting links. All the selected shapes receive the same hyperlinks that you create in the dialog.

Action Tags

Action Tags are similar to custom right-click actions except that you access them by clicking drop-down buttons that appear on or around a shape (see Figure 6.17).

Double-Clicking

Most Visio shapes enter text edit mode when you double-click them. However, you might run into shapes that do other things when double-clicked—especially if you use shapes created for early versions of Visio. For example imagine an electrical switch symbol where the switch opens and closes when you double-click the shape.

Since the advent of Shape Data fields, right-click actions, and action tags, using double-click to alter a shape has become unnecessary. This is good because it takes the guesswork and surprise out of exploring shape behavior. But you will occasionally run into fancy double-click behavior if you use old shapes from Visio tricksters sharing their home-spun SmartShapes on the Web.

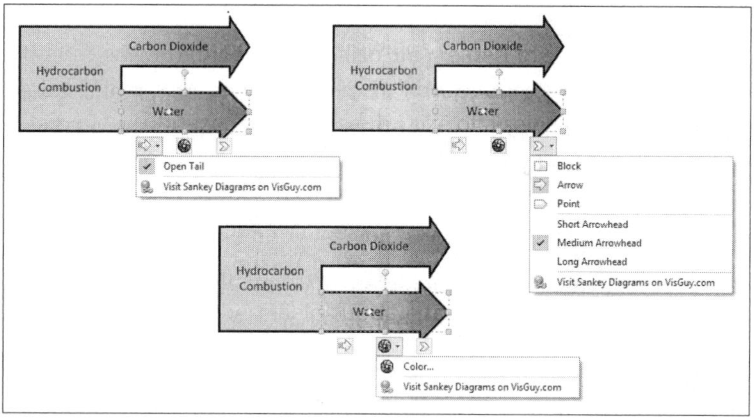

Figure 6.17 *Action Tags add context to special actions by locating items closer to the parts of shapes they affect. Here, the Sankey arrow shape has three Action Tags. Head and tail-related functions are at either end, while general formatting options are located in the middle Action Tag.*

Importing Graphics

In today's computing environment, no application is an island. You need to take advantage of the Web and the immense resources it offers. Fortunately, you can import bitmap images, vector art, and even CAD drawings into Visio.

Using Images as Shapes in Visio

Diagrams don't have to be just black-and-white boxes and lines, and you don't have to spend lots of time drawing objects that have already been created.

Importing Images

You can bring images into Visio in many ways. You can insert, copy/paste, drag from Windows Explorer, or import using File, Open. Using File, Open or Insert, Illustrations, Picture, brings up an open file dialog that lets you browse to a file. You see a file-type filter drop-down in the lower-right corner that tells you which image formats Visio supports:

- Graphics Interchange Format (*.gif)
- JPEG File Interchange Format (*.jpg;*.jpeg)
- Portable Network Graphics (*.png)

- Tagged Image File Format (*.tif; *.tiff)
- Windows Bitmap (*.bmp;*.dib)

If you import using File, Open, you create a new document containing just the imported image. Using Insert, Picture adds it directly to the drawing you are editing, which is usually what you want.

Working with Images

After you import an image, you manipulate it as you would any other Visio shape. You can add text to it, resize it, rotate it, and format the line style of its outlining box.

When you select an image shape, you also see the contextual Picture Tools Ribbon tab. Its controls enable you to tweak the brightness and contrast of the image, compress its size within the Visio file, and crop the image to just the region you want to show. Figure 6.18 shows a photo of a sign from Hong Kong's subway being edited with these tools.

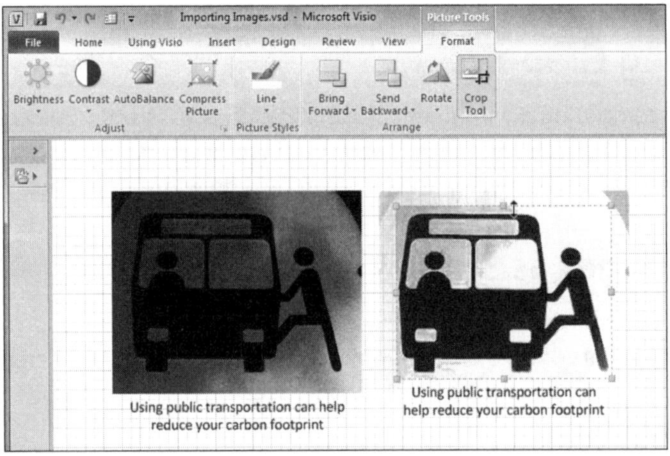

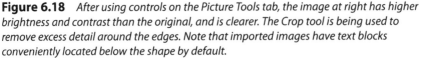

Figure 6.18 *After using controls on the Picture Tools tab, the image at right has higher brightness and contrast than the original, and is clearer. The Crop tool is being used to remove excess detail around the edges. Note that imported images have text blocks conveniently located below the shape by default.*

The Crop tool lets you focus on part of the image by changing the "viewport," so to speak. When you crop an image, you are shrinking the portion of the image that is shown within the shape's alignment box, not deleting portions of the picture. You can later uncrop to re-reveal these hidden parts.

For more image-related controls, click the dialog box launcher in the Adjust group on the Picture Tools tab. There you can tweak gamma, transparency, denoise, sharpen, and blur settings.

You can use images to create interesting and attractive backgrounds by lightening them with transparency and then blurring them.

Controlling Image Size

Photos taken by modern digital cameras have a very high resolution, which means lots of dots, and large file sizes. Using high-resolution photos in your Visio diagrams can hurt performance and bloat file size.

Resizing an imported image-shape so that it is smaller doesn't reduce the amount of data. A 6MB photo will have 6MB of data no matter how big or small you stretch it.

Often, imported images are used as iconic shapes, such as equipment photos for network diagrams. Since the size of these shapes is relatively small, you don't need super-high resolution photos to ensure quality output.

Fortunately, the Picture Tools tab has the Compress Picture button that helps. Located in the Adjust group, it offers nifty options for making images more efficient. You can reduce the size of the image using the slider control or just downsize the resolution to screen, web, or printer resolution. If you have heavily cropped the image, you can also discard the hidden portions and save even more space.

Reducing the resolution of your image speeds Visio performance and reduces file size at little or no cost to the visual quality of your document.

COPYING AND PASTING IMAGES CAN BE INEFFICIENT!

The easiest way to get an image into Visio is to copy and paste. Use Google or Bing to locate an image on the Web, right-click it to copy, and then paste it into your Visio drawing. Simple!

However, the copy/paste process seems to be inefficient and can make your file sizes explode. I found an image on the Web that occupied 12KB of disk space when saved to a file. Inserting it (from the file) added 49KB to the Visio document.

But copying and pasting directly from the browser into my drawing added a whopping 402KB to my diagram!

If you have a diagram containing lots of images, and it seems to be reacting or loading very slowly, take a few moments to use the Compress Picture feature to lighten the load!

Handling Bitmaps and Jaggies

Because images are built up from lots of dots, the bigger you make them, the more dots you need so that they print smoothly. You just learned about reducing file size by compressing images. Before you go on an image-reducing binge, consider how the image will be used in your diagrams.

Figure 6.19 shows the get-on-the-bus image at two sizes. On the left, it is about 1-inch wide—a great size if it is to be used in a flowchart or some other type of connected diagram. At this size, the image looks and prints just fine.

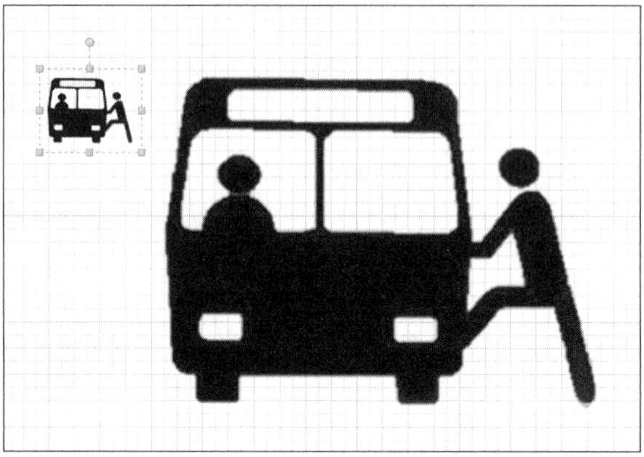

Figure 6.19 *An imported image at 1.6 inches and resized 500%.*

On the right, the image is five times bigger. If the bus graphic were intended to be used at such a large size, it would be inadequate. You can see the "jaggies" and degradation that appear when the image is stretched. In this case, too much image compression is undesirable.

Removing Rectangular Backgrounds from Images

If you take another look closely at Figure 6.18 you see that the image has a rectangular background that muddies its appearance and clashes with the white background of the drawing page. This is a drawback of importing images into your drawings. The rectangular blocks often have distracting background details that detract and distract from your work.

Compare Figure 6.18 with Figure 6.19. In Figure 6.19, the bus graphic no longer has a rectangular background. You can see the grid around the edges and even through the windows! This image has a transparent background and a non-rectangular outline. It looks and feels more like a real Visio shape.

I removed the background using the Background Removal Tool that comes with PowerPoint, Excel and Word 2010. Unfortunately it isn't integrated with Visio 2010, but it is easy enough to import an image into one of the other Microsoft Office 2010 applications, remove the background, and then copy the image over to Visio.

Properly removed backgrounds make image-based shapes look more professional. Without the distracting backgrounds, your diagrams appear cleaner. Also, you can place shapes closer together because the rectangular backgrounds no longer interfere with each other.

You can read about using the Background Removal Tool in this article: Remove Backgrounds From Images With Office 2010! http://www.visguy.com/2009/11/11/remove-backgrounds-from-images-with-office-2010/

Adding Clip Art to Your Diagrams

You don't have to leave Visio to access a library of images and vector-based line art. Head over to the Insert tab, click Clip Art in the Illustrations group and you see the Clip Art task pane. This gives you access to a searchable library of quality photos and illustrations which can be added to your diagrams by dragging and dropping.

The Clip Art task pane has a search field which makes it easier to find just the graphic you're looking for. You can refine your search to look for all media types or any combination of illustrations, photos, videos, or audio. In Figure 6.20, you see the result of a search on "Wind power," which returned photos and vector illustrations. A few of the results have been dragged into a drawing, where they instantly become Visio shapes in your diagram.

There is undoubtedly a setup option or two for installing or not installing clip art locally on your system when you install Visio and Office. This is probably a non-issue, though, because there is a check box to "Include Office.com Content" box. Checking this option allows you to access the latest and greatest clip art stored and organized on Microsoft's servers.

If you want to have access to a search result in the future but fear you might be offline when the time comes, right-click an item in the Clip Art task pane and choose Make Available Offline. This opens a dialog that enables you to save the item to your local clip art store, so it is always accessible.

If you are looking for vector art that you can pull apart and edit in Visio, search for illustrations only. Since illustrations are vector based, you can ungroup them and use the pieces in for your own custom Visio shapes. Figure 6.21 shows the dissection of a piece of clip art.

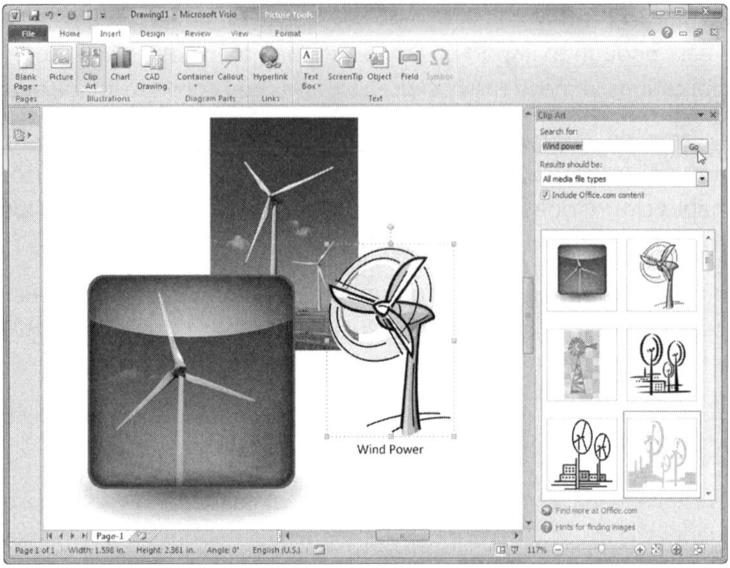

Figure 6.20 *Simply drag clip art search results from the task pane into your drawing.*

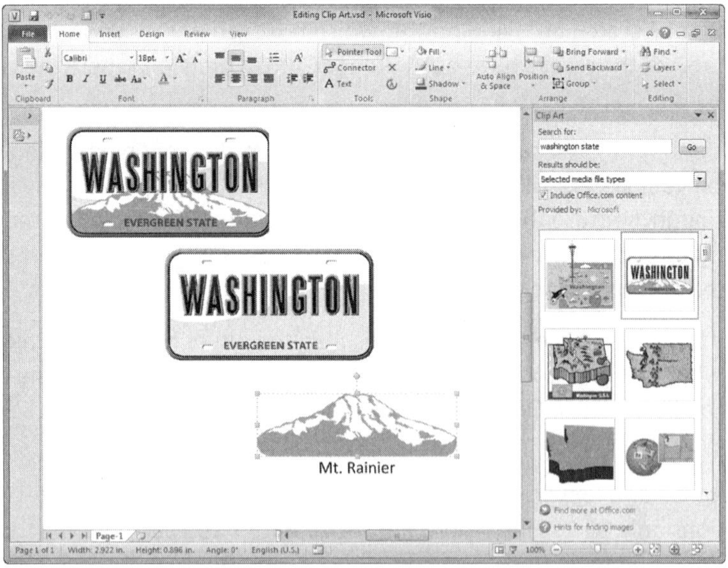

Figure 6.21 *An imported Office.com illustration clip art is ungrouped. This converts it to a collection of Visio shapes which you can access individually. Here, the Mt. Rainier graphic is swiped from a Washington State license plate illustration.*

Adding Excel Charts to Your Diagrams

If you have Microsoft Excel 2010 installed on your system, the Chart button appears to the right of the Clip Art button on the Insert tab. This feature enables you to quickly add Excel charts and associated data to your diagram. The effect is the same as copying a chart from Excel and pasting it to Visio, which is arguably an easier way to go about it.

Figure 6.22 shows five versions of an Excel chart embedded in Visio. Although creating an Excel chart is the subject for another book, there are a few points to note when working within Visio.

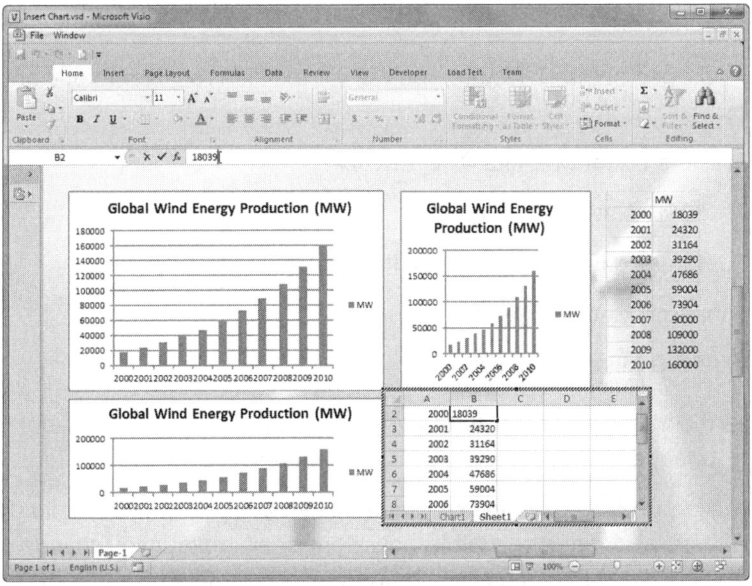

Figure 6.22 *Five copies of an Excel chart inserted in Visio. All have different sizes, the data for one is being edited, and the data for another is being shown as a table instead of a chart.*

- The lower right chart object has been activated for in-place editing by double-clicking. Once opened, Visio's Ribbon is replaced by Excel's until you finish editing. In fact, you don't even see the chart, because the data tab (Sheet1) has been selected, and values are being edited.
- To finish in-place editing, click a blank area in the drawing or press the Esc key. If you exit editing while the data tab is active, you will see a table in Visio rather than a chart, as the "MW" table in the top-right corner shows.

- When charts are resized, they do so intelligently. Notice how the three charts—which have identical data—aren't simply stretched or squished. Fonts aren't warped, the title text wraps, the chart labels rotate to best fit the space, and the number of grid-lines changes to fit the space.

If you don't like the cramped environment of in-place editing, right-click a chart and then choose Chart Object, Open. This pops up the chart in a separate Excel window, where you can make changes as you normally would. When you're done, close the Excel window.

Importing Vector Graphics

Just as you can import bitmap images, you can also import a variety of vector-based graphics files.

Using File, Open or Insert, Picture, you can set the file-type filter to one of these formats:

- Scalable Vector Graphics (*.svg;*.svgz)
- AutoCAD Drawing (*.dwg;*.dxf)
- Compressed Enhanced Metafile (*.emz)
- Enhanced Metafile (*.emf)
- Windows Metafile (*.wmf)

Because these files are vector-based, you don't have to worry about jaggies on resizing, opaque blockish backgrounds, or compression.

After you import a graphic, you can add text to it as you would any Visio shape. The vectors themselves are inaccessible, however. For example, if you change the fill color, you just set the color for the background rectangle, which usually isn't what you intended.

If you don't need to alter the colors or bits of an imported graphic, just leave it alone. If you do need to modify pieces, you can convert the graphic to Visio-native objects. Just right-click and choose Group, Ungroup.

This conversion isn't always perfect and comes with occasional oddities. Sometimes you might get duplicate shapes: one for the outline of an object and one for its fill. Sometimes gradient fills end up as hundreds of thin rectangles. In addition, advanced, unsupported effects from SVG files can end up as bitmaps.

Importing AutoCAD Drawings

Visio is a great tool that touches many different disciplines. It's no replacement for CAD, but it does work great *with* CAD. One typical example is with floor plans and office layouts. A CAD program like AutoCAD is better at creating precise drawings of a building's shell and structure—the walls, support pillars, doors, windows, and so on.

When it comes to arranging furniture, cubicle walls, fixtures, computer equipment, and personnel shapes in a drawing, however, Visio excels. Such tasks are probably a poor use of a CAD professional's time anyway, and any Visio user can drop couches and chairs onto a page and arrange them!

AutoCAD is expensive and has a steep learning curve, whereas Visio is cheaper and easier to learn. As a result, an interesting symbiosis has evolved where CAD and Visio users can work together. The makers of Visio used to talk about *CAD adjacency*, which I think is a great term to describe Visio's relationship with CAD.

In this scenario, Visio users can open AutoCAD files, mark them up with ideas, add furniture, equipment, and other shapes to them, then export the result back to AutoCAD format. The engineering department can continue working within AutoCAD but benefit from the additions made by the Visio users.

With Visio 2010, you can import and save CAD files from AutoCAD 2008. You can control the visibility of CAD layers as well as change their colors. Plus, you can snap to objects in the imported CAD object. And this can all be done without converting the object to Visio vectors, although that is an option, too.

LET ME TRY IT

Inserting an AutoCAD File

1. Start a new Office Layout drawing from the Maps and Floorplans template category.
2. On the Insert tab, click CAD Drawing. The Insert AutoCAD Drawing dialog appears. Note that the file filter is pre-set to AutoCAD Drawing (*.dwg;*.dxf) in the lower-right corner of the dialog.
3. Your Visio 2010 installation should have a sample AutoCAD file handy, located in this directory:

   C:\Program Files\Microsoft Office\Office14\Visio Content\1033

   (The last number in the path might be different if you are using a language version other than U.S. English. Browse to this folder.)

4. The file BLDGPLAN.DWG appears in the dialog. Select it and click Open.
5. The CAD Drawing Properties dialog appears, as shown in Figure 6.23.

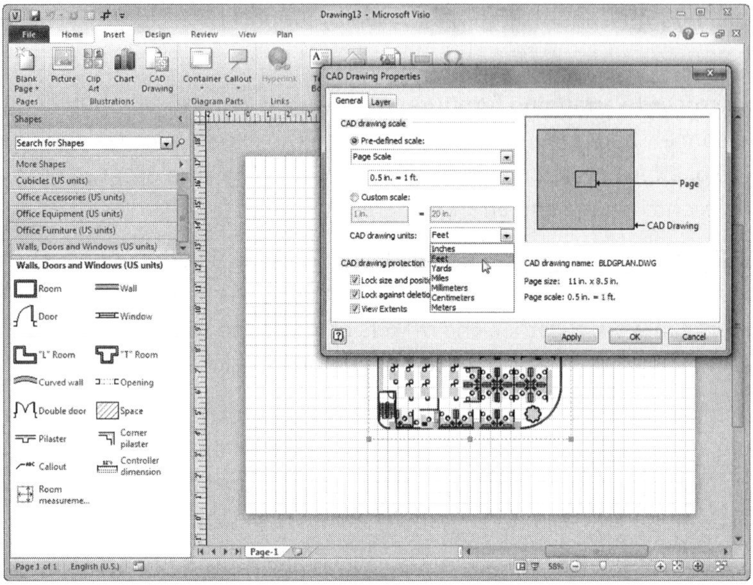

Figure 6.23 *Inserting an AutoCAD file into a Visio drawing.*

6. Set the CAD Drawing Units to Feet. AutoCAD drawings don't specify which units the drawings are in, so unfortunately you have to know this information in advance. If you don't know, try asking the file's creator. You can also use trial and error; the usual suspects are inches, feet, millimeters, and meters. If one doesn't work, try another.
7. In the dialog, notice the preview area on the right. It shows that the CAD Drawing is much larger than the page as a result of choosing Feet for the drawing units. This is similar to the Page Setup dialog's preview that shows the relationship between printer paper and drawing paper.

   It looks as though you should adjust the drawing scale here to get the CAD drawing to fit on the page. But don't change any settings here because they don't work. You'll fix the drawing scale in a minute. Just click OK for now.
8. The building plan is now inserted into your drawing, and it is much larger than the drawing page. Try zooming out to see the whole plan.

9. Click on the building plan object. Notice that it has gray resize handles indicating it is locked against resizing. Notice also that it can't be moved or deleted either.
10. With the CAD object selected, check the size of the object by looking at the status bar. The CAD object is 98ft 9in x 99ft. This size seems reasonable for this office plan, so we just need to change the scale so that it fits the drawing page.
11. Change the drawing scale. Right-click on the page tab and choose Page Setup. On the Drawing Scale tab, choose a Civil Engineering scale of 1″ = 20″ 0″ and then click OK. The drawing scale changes, and the page is now big enough for the CAD object. However, the office plan object is now off-center.
12. Right-click the CAD object and choose CAD Drawing Object, Properties to bring up the CAD Drawing Properties dialog again. Alternatively, you can just double-click the CAD object.
13. Uncheck Lock Size and Position; then click OK.
14. Move the CAD object to the center of the drawing page. Because it is important that the CAD object not accidentally be resized, revisit the dialog and relock the object's size and position.
15. Hold on to this drawing. We'll continue working on it in the next exercise.

LET ME TRY IT

Manipulating an Imported AutoCAD Drawing and Adding Furniture

1. CAD files often use layers to organize their elements. With CAD objects, you can toggle visibility and change the line color and weight for layers. Try this by bringing up the CAD Drawing Properties dialog again. This time, click the Layer tab.
2. Turn off the layer for furniture by clicking the Visible column next to layer 12 (Layer 12 is the furniture layer, determined by trial-and-error.) Click Apply to test your changes without leaving the dialog. The chairs and tables disappear from the CAD object.
3. Try turning off the computer equipment layer. This is cleverly named 7.
4. You can crop CAD objects so that only a certain region is visible by using the Crop tool, but you can't crop the CAD object when it is locked. Return

to the CAD Drawing Properties dialog, as you did in the last exercise and unlock its size and position.

5. To crop the CAD object, you need the Crop tool. But it only appears on the Picture Tools contextual tab when an imported image is selected, so you can't get to it.

   Luckily, there's a keyboard shortcut for the Crop tool. Press Shift+Ctrl+2, and your mouse cursor changes to the Crop tool.

6. Drag a selection handle of the CAD object so that only part of it shows, as illustrated in Figure 6.24.

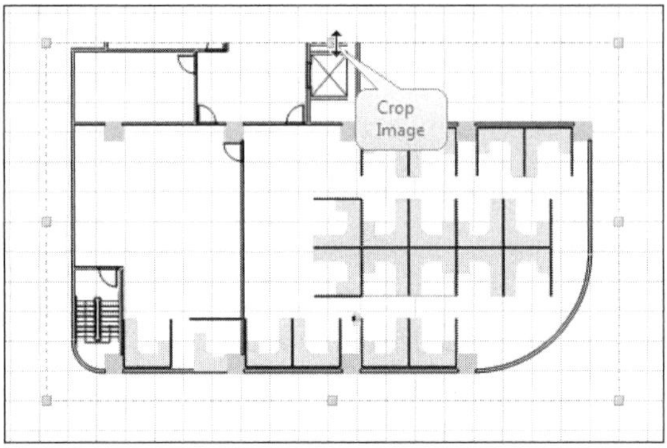

Figure 6.24 *Cropping an imported AutoCAD object.*

7. Relock the size and position of the CAD object.

8. Because you started with the Office Layout template, you have several stencils at your disposal. Drop some plant shapes from the Office Accessories stencil or add your own conference tables and sofas from the Office Furniture stencil. Notice that the shapes drop at a reasonable size compared to other details of the floor plan. This is further verification that you have set the drawing scale correctly.

9. Save the drawing as a CAD file using File, Save As.

10. In the Save dialog, set the file type filter to AutoCAD Drawing (*.dwg;*.dxf), browse to a target directory, enter a name for the file, and then click Save.

    You have just modified the original AutoCAD file and appended Visio shapes to it. You can now send it to AutoCAD users, and they will be able to open it and work with it. You can try re-importing it to see how it looks, or if you know someone with AutoCAD on their PC, try sending them the file.

If you have a library of symbols that were created for AutoCAD, you might wonder if you can convert it into a Visio stencil. Well, there is an add-on that does just this! Go to the View tab, click the Add-ons button, and navigate to Visio Extras, Convert CAD Library.

Visio 2010 even comes with a sample CAD library to test. You can try converting the valves in symbols in the following file:

C:\Program Files\Microsoft Office\Office14\Visio Content\1033\BLOCKS.DWG

Summary

In this chapter, you learned about the essentials for working with individual shapes.

You learned how to efficiently resize, reposition, and duplicate shapes; the ins and outs of formatting shapes and groups; and the difference between text and text blocks.

You saw that shapes can have a variety of extra features, and you learned where to look for them. You can discover a lot about shapes by experimentation and have hopefully developed the habit of pulling on handles, right-clicking, double-clicking, and looking for Shape Data fields.

Finally, you explored integrating non-native graphics such as bitmap images, clip art, charts, and AutoCAD files with Visio.

In this chapter, you learn how to use Shape Data fields, add new ones to shapes, link them to external data sources, create reports that tally them, and apply graphical adornments that visually highlight data.

7

Working with Data

The ability to work with data makes Visio special. With data, diagrams become more than just pictures, transforming into interactive data-entry surfaces, configuration and estimating tools, status dashboards, and visual inventory systems.

Many Visio shapes come prepopulated with fields, and you can add your own. After shapes have Shape Data fields, you can fill them out one by one or link them to external sources.

With a data-filled diagram, you can apply visualizations to get a dashboard overview and run reports to tally the information.

Some of the data-related features discussed in this chapter are available only in the Premium and Pro editions of Visio 2010. I re-iterate this point where appropriate, so be on the lookout if you are using Visio Standard. I don't want you madly searching for features that you don't have!

Introducing Shape Data Fields

Many Visio shapes already contain Shape Data fields, ready and waiting for your data. Whether or not these fields are right for your business, they let you quickly see the kinds of data you can attach to shapes.

Exploring Shape Data

Get a feel for Shape Data fields by looking at the fields in flowchart and network shapes.

LET ME TRY IT

Exploring Shape Data Fields

1. Choose Flowchart, Basic Flowchart to start a new drawing.
2. Drag any shape onto the page and inspect its Shape Data fields.

   The Shape Data window normally resides on the left side of the drawing window, docked above or below the Shapes window. As you can do with most task panes, you can tear it off from the left and float it or dock it to another side.

   If you don't see the Shape Data window, you can make it visible in the following three ways:

   - Right-click any shape and choose Data, Shape Data.
   - Go to View tab, Show, Task Panes, Shape Data.
   - Go to the Data tab (Pro and Premium only), Show/Hide, Shape Data Window check box.

   With the Shape Data window visible, you need only select shapes in the drawing window to see their Shape Data fields.

3. With your flowchart shape still selected, note the different Shape Data fields. Most flowchart shapes have seven fields: Cost, Process Number, Owner, Function, Start Data, End Date, and Status. They are blank by default, just waiting for you to fill them out with your business-specific information.
4. Inspect the data fields for network equipment. Open the Computers and Monitors stencil. You can access it via More Shapes, Network, Computers and Monitors.
5. Drag a few network equipment shapes onto the page. Network shapes have quite a few more fields than the flowchart shapes. Figure 7.1 contrasts flowchart and network Shape Data fields.

   You can see that the flowchart fields are process related, and the network fields relate to hardware, software, and facilities management.

6. Select two or more flowchart shapes. Notice that their fields still appear in the Shape Data window. The reason is that they have the same set of fields.

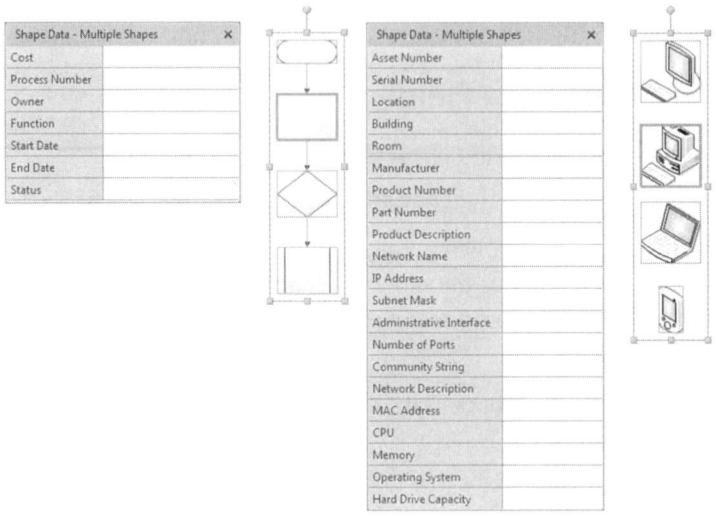

Figure 7.1 *Built-in Shape Data fields for flowchart and network shapes. Note that this image is a composite; only one Shape Data window exists per drawing window.*

7. Select a flowchart shape and network shape. The Shape Data window is empty. Because flowchart and network shapes have no properties in common, the Shape Data window punts and displays no fields. Shape Data only shows fields that the selected shapes have in common. However, shapes that have no data fields are ignored from this consideration. In Figure 7.1, note that the connectors between the flowchart shapes are also selected. Because they have no data fields, they don't interfere with this common-properties calculation.

8. Set a value for multiple shapes at once. Select several flowchart shapes. In the Shape Data window, enter **Bob** for the Owner field.

9. Click on each flowchart shape separately. Notice that each shape received the value Bob for its Owner property. You can set fields for many shapes in one fell swoop!

10. Note the different types of data that Shape Data fields can hold. Select a flowchart shape and enter some sample data for each field in the Shape Data window. Figure 7.2 shows how different data types present different input controls.

    Visio has some rudimentary data validation that enforces correct entries. For example, in the Currency field, you must enter a number or a currency value.

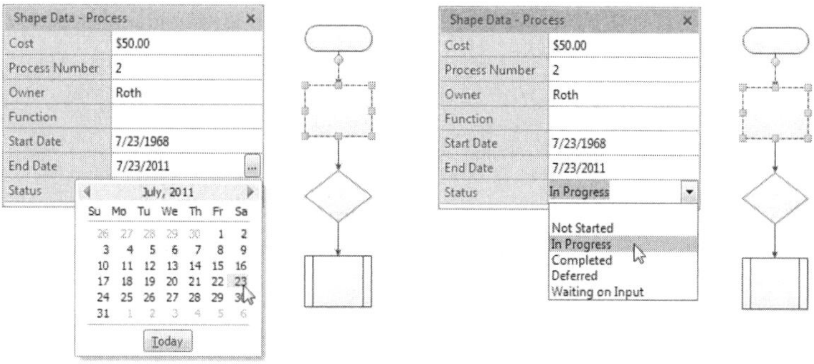

Figure 7.2 *Custom controls make data entry easier for certain data types.*

So you can enter 1.50, $1.50, or EUR 1.50, but not Bob. Process Number must be a number, but Owner and Function can contain any text. The two date fields must have date values. Status is a variable list; you can pick from the drop-down list or enter a new value.

Types and Uses of Shape Data

Shape Data in flowchart and network shapes is purely "data behind the shape." The fields have no effect on how the shapes appear but are useful for reports and interaction with the drawing. (They can be visualized using Data Graphics, which I discuss toward the end of the chapter.)

Contrast this with Figure 7.3, where you see space planning shapes that graphically change depending on Shape Data values. This figure shows window and door shapes from the Walls, Shell, and Structure stencil (Accessed via: More Shapes, Maps and Floor Plans, Building Plan).

In Figure 7.3, the actual sizes of the shapes are affected by the Window Width and Door Width field values. Because the drawing is scaled, you can work in real-world units and choose typical door and window sizes from the pick lists.

Interestingly, the two door shapes come from the same master. The result of picking different door types and changing the opening percentage is shapes that are quite different in appearance. Because SmartShapes can be configured in so many different ways, the number of masters in stencils is vastly reduced. Other graphics programs supply hundreds of door symbols, but Visio has only a few—and these have hundreds of possible configurations thanks to Shape Data.

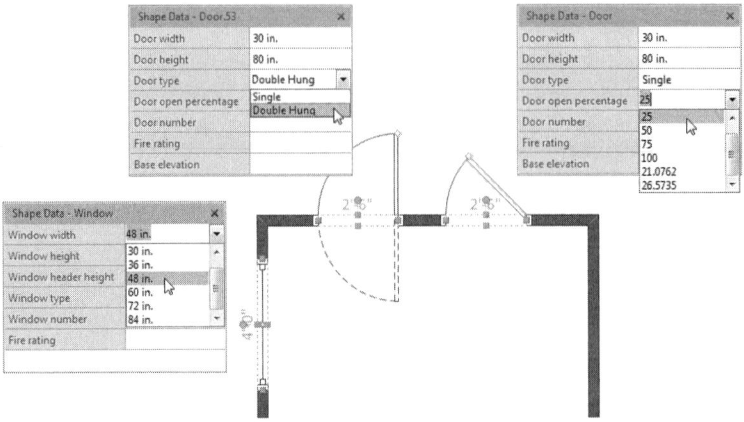

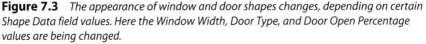

Figure 7.3 *The appearance of window and door shapes changes, depending on certain Shape Data field values. Here the Window Width, Door Type, and Door Open Percentage values are being changed.*

Adding Shape Data fields to shapes is easy to do, and you learn how in just a bit. But making shapes visually respond to Shape Data, like the Door and Window shapes in Figure 7.3, requires advanced skills. I touch on how to do this Chapter 11, "Developing Custom Visio Solutions," but most Visio users use prebuilt SmartShapes; they don't create them.

TELL ME MORE **Media 7.1—Turning Many Symbols into One Shape Using Shape Data**

Access this audio file through your registered Web Edition at ***my.safaribooksonline.com/9780132182683/media.***

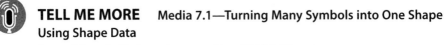

Creating and Using Shape Data Fields

You can add Shape Data fields to any Visio shape. The fields can hold several different types of data, and you can save sets that you've defined and apply them to other shapes all at once.

SHOW ME **Media 7.2—Creating Shape Data Fields in Visio 2010**

Access this video file through your registered Web Edition at ***my.safaribooksonline.com/9780132182683/media.***

Adding Simple Data Fields

Adding basic Shape Data fields is a snap using the Define Shape Data dialog. Let's jump in and give it a whirl!

LET ME TRY IT

Adding Shape Data Fields to a Shape

1. Start a new, blank drawing.
2. Rename Page-1 to **Light Bulbs** and then save it somewhere convenient as **Ch7 Shape Data.vsd**. You will use this file throughout the chapter.
3. Draw a circle on the page and add a bit of line and fill formatting so that it isn't *too* boring. I'll call this a *light bulb* shape. I know it's not much of a light bulb, but it will do for learning purposes.
4. Right-click the light bulb and choose Data, Define Shape Data. Alternatively, if the Shape Data window is visible, select a shape, right-click the Shape Data window, and then choose Define Shape Data. The Define Shape Data window appears.
5. Create a field to hold the bulb's power rating.
   a. In the Label field, type **Power (Watts)**.
   b. Change the Type to Number.
   c. You can choose a number format by clicking the arrow to the right of the Format field.

      Light bulbs are rated in whole-number wattages, so you don't need decimal places. Some options for units are provided, but Visio understands only linear or angular units; there's no choice for power units in the list.

      You can specify custom prefixes and suffixes in the Format field, however. For the Power field, enter **#\ \W** in the Format box. The pound symbol tells Visio to repeat the full nondecimal part of the number, and the backslashes tell Visio to append the next character. So you are appending a space and a *W* to denote Watts.
   d. Set the default by typing **100** in the Value field.
6. Now add a Model field.
   a. Click New at the bottom of the dialog. You see Power in the list of fields, plus a new "Property2", which is highlighted.

b. In the Label field, type **Model**.

c. Leave the Type as String.

d. Make a placeholder for the default value by typing **<model>**. Figure 7.4 shows how the dialog should appear.

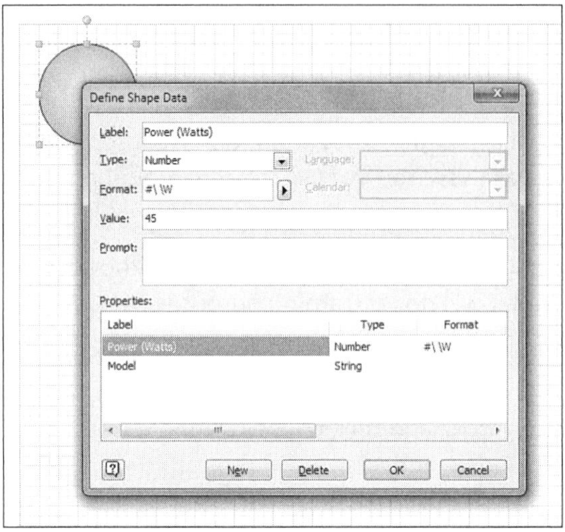

Figure 7.4 *Two new Shape Data fields being defined using the Define Shape Data window.*

7. Click OK. With the bulb selected, note that the Shape Data window displays the two fields you just created.

8. Make a few copies of the light bulb and experiment with changing the Shape Data values. Notice what happens if you try to enter non-numerical text in the Power field.

9. Save the drawing and keep it open for the next Let Me Try It.

Choosing Shape Data Field Types

You just created Shape Data fields of type string and number. Be aware that Shape Data fields can hold eight different data types of data. Here's a rundown of the different data types you can specify for your fields:

- **String**—This data type holds general text information.
- **Number**—This data type can be pure numbers, such as 1 or 3.14159265358, or number-unit pairs, such as 1.5 in. or 38.1 mm.
- **Fixed List**—This data type provides a noneditable drop-down list of items.
- **Variable List**—This data type provides an editable drop-down list of items. You can select from the list or type in a custom entry.
- **Boolean**—This term is Geek-speak for true or false, which appear in a drop-down list for this data type.
- **Currency**—Entering a pure number for this data type results in your system's default currency being used, so 1.5 ends up as $1.50, for example. You can specify other currencies by entering the proper symbol or three-letter abbreviation before or after the number. Some common examples are EUR, GBP, JPY, CAD, AUD, CHF, HKD, CNY. No, Visio doesn't convert currencies, nor does it charge a service fee.
- **Date**—If you click the field for this data type, an ellipses (...) button appears, which lets you pick a date from a calendar control. Alternatively, you can type a date. Visio seems relatively good at recognizing date text. For example, I typed in Jul 23, 2011 and 2011.7.23, and Visio recognized them both, displaying 7/23/2011 after I pressed Enter. Visio takes your system's date settings into account too, so don't worry about having to view month-day-year if you're used to day-year-month.
- **Duration**—This data type relates to time but isn't a calendar value. Duration denotes elapsed time and is useful for timeline diagrams and other scheduling applications. For example, instead of Start Date and End Date fields, you could have Start Date and Duration fields. The End Date then could be calculated by adding the two together.

  If you enter a pure number, the default units are elapsed day, which appear as "ed." You can explicitly specify other durations: elapsed day, hour, minute, second, or week values. Just type these units after a number—ed., eh., em., es., or ew.—making sure to include the trailing period.

Creating Lists and Controlling Formatting

You can practice defining a few more of these data types by adding a drop-down list and a date value to the light bulb shape.

LET ME TRY IT

Creating Lists and Formatting Shape Data Values

1. Continue working with Ch7 Shape Data.vsd.
2. Make sure that you have several copies of the bulb shape.
3. Select all of them and then open the Define Shape Data window.
4. Add a fixed list type field with five choices. They appear in a drop-down list.
   a. Click the New button.
   b. Change Property3 to Bulb Type.
   c. Set the Type to Fixed List.
   d. In the Format field, type **CF;Halogen;Incandescent;LED;Other**. Notice that each item is separated by a semicolon. This is the way you indicate list items for Shape Data fields.
   e. Click OK. All the selected shapes now have a blank Bulb Type field, but their other data fields remain unchanged.
   f. Experiment with setting the Bulb Type value for individual shapes. Note the cool drop-down control that lets you pick from the list.
5. Select all the shapes again and open the Define Shape Data window.
6. Add a date type field and set the display formatting.
   a. Click the New button.
   b. Change Property4 to **Surveyed**.
   c. Set the Type to Date.
   d. In the Format cell, click the arrow button on the right. Note the variety of date formats.
   e. Select a date format that you like from the list. Notice that a format string is inserted as editable text in the Format field.

      For example, choosing "Sunday, October 03, 1993" results in a Format of "{{dddd, MMMM dd, yyyy}}". You can experiment with these codes and modify them to get options that aren't in the list.

I frequently work with Americans and Europeans, who can't agree where the month and day should be in date formats. To avoid confusion, I like to use a sortable date format. So I type a format string of "{{yyyy.MM.dd}}" which displays 1993.10.03 in the Shape Data window.

f. Click OK to accept the changes. The bulbs all have a new, blank "Surveyed" field.

g. Experiment with setting values for the Surveyed field. When you click the field, an ellipses (...) button appears. This lets you use the nifty calendar control that you saw in Figure 7.2. You can also type date text, which will be reformatted as soon as you press Enter or Tab away from the field.

7. Save the drawing. Figure 7.5 shows an example of how your shapes should look.

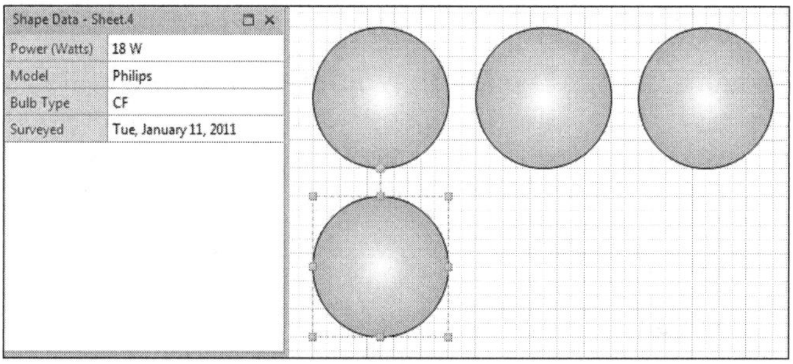

Figure 7.5 *The data-enabled light bulb shapes, now sporting four Shape Data fields.*

Saving Sets of Shape Data Fields

Now that you've toiled to create a set of Shape Data fields, you might want to save it so that you can apply it to other shapes.

You saw that you can edit Shape Data definitions for multiple shapes by selecting a bunch at once and going to the Define Shape Data window. A better way is to save a set of fields as a Shape Data Set.

LET ME TRY IT

Creating and Applying Shape Data Sets

1. Continue with Ch7 Shape Data.vsd.
2. Select one bulb shape.
3. Right-click the Shape Data window and choose Shape Data Sets. The Shape Data Sets window appears. It is a taskbar that remains open. You can float it anywhere or dock it to any side of the drawing window.
4. Note the Sample set that is already defined in the window.
5. Highlight Sample in the list and then click Define. The Define Shape Data window appears, exactly the same as it appears for shapes. You can inspect and edit field attributes for the set. Click Cancel for now, though.
6. In the Shape Data Sets window, click Add. The Add Shape Data Set window pops up.
7. Enter a name, such as **Light Bulb Properties**, as shown in Figure 7.6.

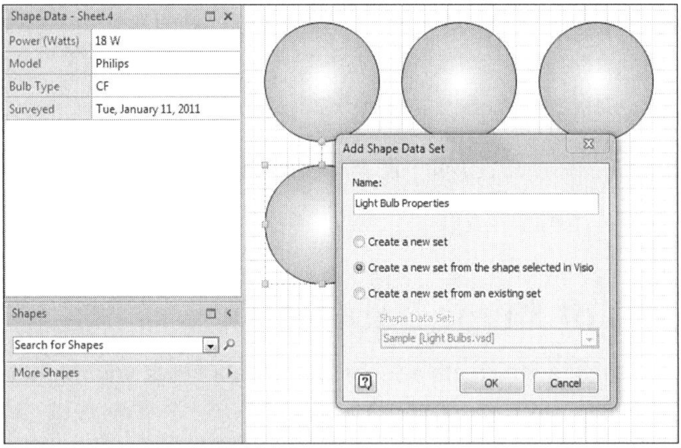

Figure 7.6 *Creating a new Shape Data Set from the existing fields in a shape.*

8. Check the Create a New Set from the Shape Selected in Visio radio button. Note that you could also create a new blank set or a new set based on an existing set.

9. Click OK. The new Shape Data set appears in the Shape Data Sets window.

10. Inspect the new set and check default values. I created this set from existing fields in a shape. The fields are correct, but the default values might not be right for generic application.

    a. Highlight Light Bulb Properties in the list.

    b. Click Define. The Define Shape Data window appears.

    c. Highlight each field in the Properties list and check the Value.

    d. Change any specific default values to something more generic. For Power, set Value to 0. For Bulb Type and Surveyed, leave Value blank, and for Model, enter **<model>**.

    e. Click OK to save your changes.

11. Take your Shape Data Set for a spin.

    a. Draw some rectangles on the page using the Rectangle tool.

    b. Select all the rectangles that you just added.

    c. In the Shape Data Sets window, check Light Bulb Properties and then click Apply. (Note: The check boxes allow you to apply multiple sets at once.)

    d. Check each shape to see that it has the Shape Data fields: Power, Model, Bulb Type, and Surveyed.

When you create a custom Shape Data Set, it isn't stored globally, so you don't have access to it when you work on another drawing. This sounds frustrating, but it's easy to transfer sets. Just copy a shape that has a Shape Data Set applied and paste it to your drawing. The Shape Data Set comes along for the ride.

So one quick way to bring sets into other drawings is to

1. Quickly draw a rectangle.
2. Apply all the Shape Data Sets that you want to transfer to the rectangle.
3. Cut the rectangle and paste it into other drawings.

You can even add this rectangle to your Favorites stencil for easy access in the future.

Displaying Shape Data in Shape Text

Having data behind shapes is useful if you're interacting with Visio. But if you need a printout or a quick overview, it's nice to be able to see the data at a glance.

I described how to insert fields in Chapter 3, "Organizing and Annotating Diagrams." Now that you know how to create Shape Data fields, you can show them off in the shape's text block.

LET ME TRY IT

Linking Text to Shape Data

1. Continue working with Ch7 Shape Data.vsd.
2. Select one of the light bulbs. It should have four data fields, filled with meaningful data.
3. On the Insert tab, click Field.
4. Select Shape Data from the Category list.
5. Choose Power and then click OK. The power value is displayed in the shape's text.
6. Note that the *W* is missing after the power value. This is special formatting for displaying the value in the Shape Data window, which unfortunately isn't picked up when you insert text. No worries, though. You can mix inserted fields with free-form text. Just place your cursor at the end of the line, then enter a space and a **W**.
7. Continue adding fields. Select the bulb again, press F2 to enter text edit mode, place the cursor at the end of the text, and then press Enter to start a new line.
8. Revisit the Insert Field dialog, but select the Model field this time.
9. In a similar fashion, add the Bulb Type to the last line of the text.
10. Verify that the shape's text is dynamic by changing Shape Data values. The text changes to reflect the new data.
11. Save your work for the next exercise.

Adding fields to shapes to display data is fairly easy, doing so to lots of shapes can become tedious. Right now, your drawing has numerous shapes with the same set of fields, but only one has text fields linked to data.

You would think that the solution is to copy the text from one shape and then paste to another shape. But this doesn't quite work. Your target shape ends up with nondynamic text that looks correct until you realize that changing the data doesn't change the text any more. Luckily, there is a solution.

1. Select a shape that has inserted fields.
2. Copy the *shape*. Copy the *whole shape;* not just the text inside the shape.
3. Select a target shape that has the same data fields.
4. Press F2 to enter text edit mode.
5. Paste.

Yes, you are copying a shape but pasting it into a text block. This tells Visio to work a bit harder and hook the text to the Shape Data. Figure 7.7 shows four different rectangles, with smart text displaying different data.

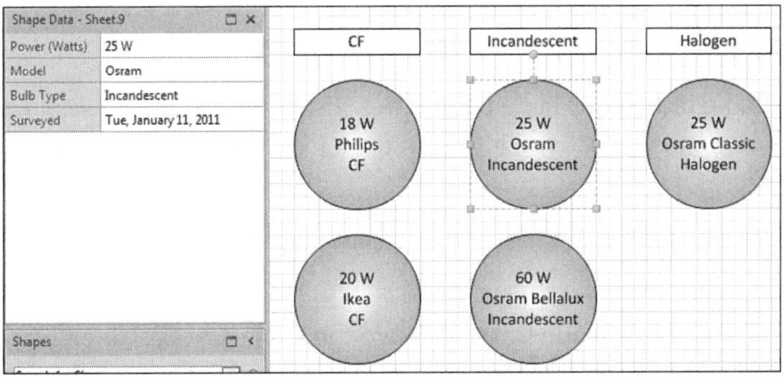

Figure 7.7 *Text fields displaying Shape Data values.*

If you have Visio Pro or Premium, an add-on makes it easy to configure shape text to display up to four Shape Data fields and to change them at any time.

The Label Shapes add-on can be found by going to View, Macros, Add-ons, Maps and Floor Plans, Label Shapes.

You can apply the smart text to a selection of shapes, all shapes on the page, or all instances of a particular master. Figure 7.8 shows the light bulbs being modified by the Label Shapes tool.

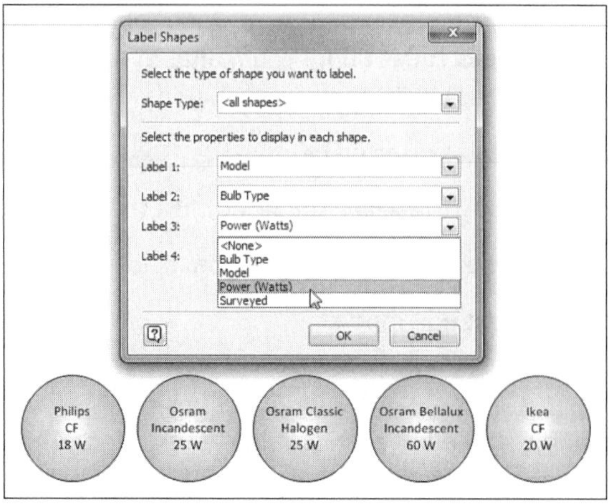

Figure 7.8 *For Premium and Pro owners, the Label Shapes add-on makes it easy to link text to Shape Data.*

Shape Data Labels versus Names

Shape Data fields actually have two names. Visio does its best to shield end users from this fact, but you will run into situations in which it helps to understand the nitpicky details.

Warning: This section is a bit technical, so you might choose to skip it or skim it quickly.

However, if you think Shape Data fields are the coolest, you plan on using them often in your Visio work, are interested in doing calculations with them, and want to link them to data using the Database Wizard, you need to understand how they are named.

Shape Data used to be known as Custom Properties until Visio 2007. You see vestiges of in the ShapeSheet, where you see that cells which hold Shape Data information are prefixed with "Prop." If you search the Internet for information on Visio Shape Data, you will run into the term "Custom Properties" in older articles, and will probably find more information if you include the term in your search.

When you define a Shape Data field, note that you enter its name in a field called "Label." If you turn on the Developer tab (via Customize the Ribbon), Visio switches to "developer mode" and adds extra elements to the user interface. In the Define Shape Data dialog, you see additional fields, one of which is the "Name" field.

Figure 7.9 compares the non-developer-mode dialog (left) with the developer-mode dialog (right).

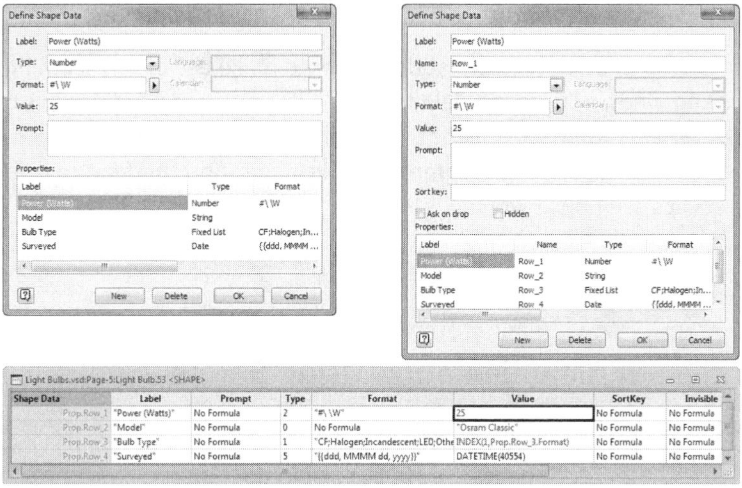

Figure 7.9 *The Developer-mode Define Shape Data dialog (right) shows more fields than the default. The ShapeSheet below shows the relationship between row Name and that of the Label.*

In Figure 7.9, take a look at the Name field that appears just below Label. The Name is the row name of the Shape Data field, as represented in the ShapeSheet.

The ShapeSheet is how a developer views Visio shapes. It is an Excel-like spreadsheet that lives behind every Visio shape and is discussed in Chapter 11, "Developing Custom Visio Solutions." Normally, you don't need to go into the ShapeSheet, and you should probably stay away from it. But I've already warned you that this was a technical section, so have a glance at the ShapeSheet at the bottom of Figure 7.9.

Even though I've given the data fields nice names like "Power (Watts)" and "Bulb Type", the fields are internally represented with dull automatic row names such as Prop.Row_1 and Prop.Row_3. You can see these row names in the developer version of the Define Shape Data dialog at right in Figure 7.9.

Visio tries to shield the average user from Row_1, Row_2, and Row_3 by showing only labels by default. However, if you try to map fields to a database using the (older) Database Wizard or try to do calculations with Shape Data fields, you run into them. This can make it hard to know what you're mapping or calculating. If you have Visio 2010 Standard, the Database Wizard is your only data-linking option, so you're even more likely to run into the problem.

Turning on the Developer tab on the Ribbon gives you a chance to change these names when defining Shape Data fields. For the light bulb shapes, you can change

Row_1 to Power_W and Row_3 to Bulb_Type, for example. Note that row names can't contain spaces, commas, colons, semicolons, and so on.

You don't have to be a ShapeSheet developer to make use of this seemingly obscure knowledge. The insert field function lets you create calculations based on Shape Data fields using the Custom Formula option. To create custom formulas, you need to reference the row names, not the labels. And this feature is too cool to ignore, so let's see how it works.

LET ME TRY IT

Creating a Simple Calculation Using Shape Data

1. Continue working with Ch7 Shape Data.vsd.
2. Turn on the Developer tab via Customizing the Ribbon.
3. Copy a light bulb shape and clear the text from it. (I do it like this: Select the shape, type space, Backspace, Esc. No more text!)
4. Bring up the Define Shape Data window for the shape.
5. So that you can better understand where the power row is, change the row Name field from Row_1 to **Power_W**. Then click OK to accept the change.
6. With the shape still selected, go to Insert, Field. The Insert Field dialog appears.
7. Select Custom Formula from the Category list.
8. In the Custom Formula field, type

   = Prop.Power_W/1000 & "kW"

   Notice that as you type **Prop**..., a drop-down list of Shape Data fields appears to assist you. Most of them still have "Row_" style names, but Prop.Power_W should be atop the list. The descriptive Shape Data labels are nowhere to be seen and you can see why changing row names is important.
9. After you enter the complete formula, click OK. The shape's text displays the kilowatts for the light bulb, calculated from the watts.

   Prop.Power_W refers to the value stored in the Shape Data field. You then divide it by 1000 using the division symbol. Finally, you concatenate (append text) the units by using the "&" character and the letters *kW*.
10. Change the Shape Data value of Power (Watts) to check that the text responds to data changes.

For the intrepid who would like a bit more control, there is a function that allows you to specify the formatting of calculations. To show two decimal units for the kilowatt value, you can enter the following formula:

FORMAT(Prop.Power_W/1000,"0.00")&"kW"

The Custom Formula field can accept any valid ShapeSheet formula, which you learn more about in Chapter 11, "Developing Custom Visio Solutions."

Creating Reports

Being able to store extra data behind Visio shapes extends the utility of drawings and makes them useful as interactive tools. The ability to report on this data adds even more value to Visio drawings.

For example, you can use the light bulb shapes as a "visual data entry system." Figure 7.10 shows the light bulb shapes being used in a "home energy inventory" diagram. I found it easier to make sure that I got every light in our house by going room by room and adding a light bulb shape for each actual light. Seeing an actual shape on the diagram in the proper room container was easier and less error-prone than managing an abstract matrix in Excel.

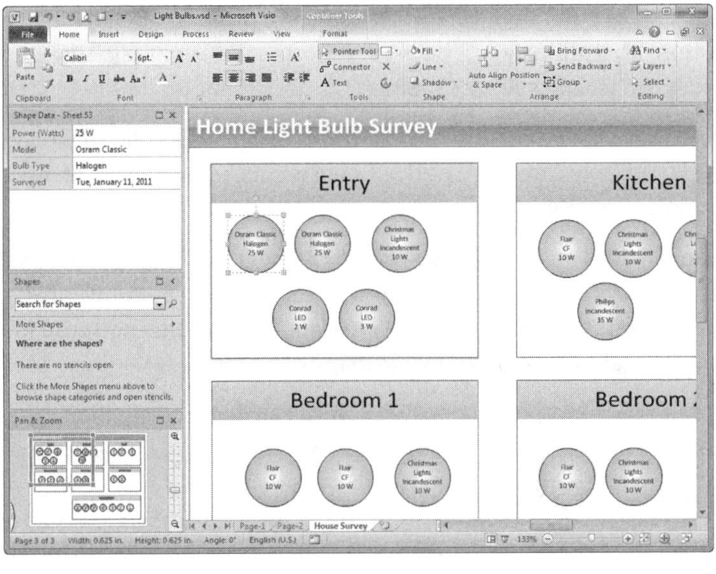

Figure 7.10 *Room-by-room inventory diagram showing types of light bulbs and their power usages.*

You could even go whole-hog by adding the light bulbs to an actual floor plan of your house and locating each bulb shape where a real-life lamp exists. This approach is great for big inventories, such as in an office space. For our small abode, however, the containers were sufficient.

Introducing the Report Definition Wizard

No matter what kind of drawing you've created, after you have shapes with data-filled fields, you might want to create a report. The simple light bulb shapes are a great place to start in getting to know how to do this.

LET ME TRY IT

Defining a Simple Light Bulb Inventory Report

1. Continue working with Ch7 Shape Data.vsd.
2. Add a new page and rename it to **Basic Report**.
3. Copy a shape from the Light Bulbs page and paste it to this page. Create several copies of it, each with different types, wattages, etc., to make the report more interesting.
4. On the Review tab, click Shape Reports. The Reports dialog appears.

   I personally think that Review tab is an odd place for the Shape Reports button. If you think you'll be using reports often, right-click the button and add it to the Quick Access Toolbar.
5. Note the solitary Inventory report shown in the report list. If you uncheck the Show Only Drawing-Specific Reports check box, the list of reports grows considerably.

   Visio includes many template-specific reports but filters the list by looking at the available Shape Data fields in the shapes of your drawing. Because Visio reports focus largely on Shape Data fields, there's no sense in listing reports that tally fields that your shapes don't have.
6. Start a new report definition. Click New. The Report Definition Wizard starts.
   a. Check Select Shapes on the Current Page.
   b. If your drawing contains shapes that aren't light bulbs, they will cause blank rows in the report. You can add a filter to the report to prevent this. Click Advanced. The Advanced filtering dialog appears.

c. Select Bulb Type from the Property list.

d. Select Exists from the Condition list.

e. Select True for the Value.

f. Click Add.

g. You can also add Power (Watts) Exists = True if you like, but for this exercise, it's probably not necessary.

h. Click OK to complete the filtering.

7. Click Next to get to the column-selection page of the wizard. You see a list of shape properties (in brackets), along with Shape Data fields that exist in shapes in the drawing. Here you can choose to report on the type of bulb and the energy use. Ignore the model and surveyed fields for now.

   Check Bulb Type and Power (Watts) and then click Next.

8. Enter a report title, such as **Light Bulb Power Use** and copy this text because you'll need it again for the report name. The report title shows in the generated table.

9. Ignore the Subtotals, Sort, and Format buttons for now and click Next.

10. In the "Save the report definition" screen, paste the report title into the Name field.

11. Check "Save in this drawing" and then click Finish. You return to the Reports starting screen. You see your new report in the list of reports, along with a location of "Visio Drawing," indicating that the report is stored in the drawing file itself. You can now run this report on any page that contains light bulb shapes.

12. Click Close for now, and save your drawing.

LET ME TRY IT

Running a Report

1. Continue working with Ch7 Shape Data.vsd, and go to the Basic Report page.

2. On the Review tab, click Shape Reports. The Reports dialog appears. Select Light Bulb Power Use in the list.

3. Click Run. The Run Report dialog appears, offering you choices on how to output the report.
4. Select Visio Shape as the target for the report. This generates an embedded Microsoft Excel object that lists the light bulb data for the current page.
5. Check Link to Report Definition and then click OK. The report runs, and a report shape is created with a listing of light bulb shape types and power ratings, as shown in Figure 7.11.

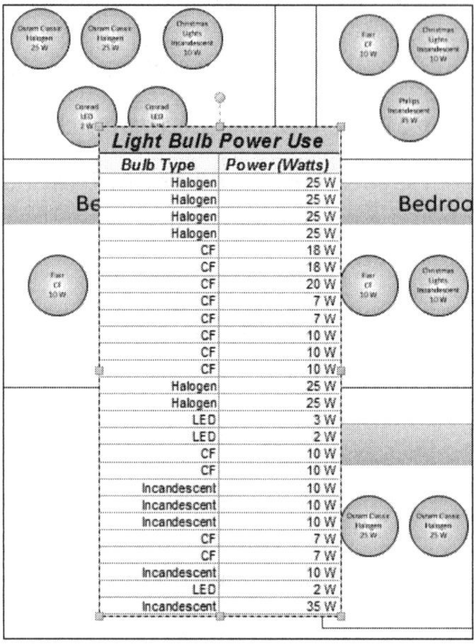

Figure 7.11 *The simple report definition lists an inventory of all the light bulb shapes, including their types and power ratings.*

6. Double-click the report shape. The report becomes an in-place activated Excel object. The Ribbon changes to Excel's Ribbon, and you can edit the individual cells of the report as you normally would in Excel.
7. Press Esc or click on a blank region of the page to exit Excel editing mode.
8. If you change the data in the drawing, you can rerun the report. Select one of the light bulb shapes in the drawing and then copy it a whole bunch of times.

9. Right-click the report shape and choose Run Report. The length of the report is much longer, reflecting all the extra shapes you've just created.
10. Save the drawing so you can continue using it.

Grouping and Totaling Items in a Report

You've just created a nice inventory of the light bulb shapes in your drawing and their associated data, but the report would be more informative if it grouped like items and showed totals. It would also be nice to make it portable, so that you can use it in other drawings.

LET ME TRY IT

Grouping Items in Reports

1. Continue working with Ch7 Shape Data.vsd.
2. Right-click the report shape that you created on the Basic Report page, and choose Update Report.
3. Select Light Bulb Power Use from the list and then click Modify.
4. Click Next twice until you see the Subtotals button and then click it. The Subtotals screen appears.
5. Choose Group By: Bulb Type so that like bulb types are listed together in the report.
6. Click OK, then Next, Finish, and Run to run the modified report. The report now has all bulbs grouped together by type, sorted alphabetically.
7. Save the drawing.

LET ME TRY IT

Adding Subtotals to Reports

1. Continue working with the Ch7 Shape Data.vsd drawing, and the report shape on the Basic Reports page.
2. Return to the Subtotals screen, as you did in steps 2, 3, and 4 of the previous exercise.
3. In the Subtotals list, check COUNT in the Bulb Type row, and check COUNT and TOTAL in the Power row, as shown in Figure 7.12.

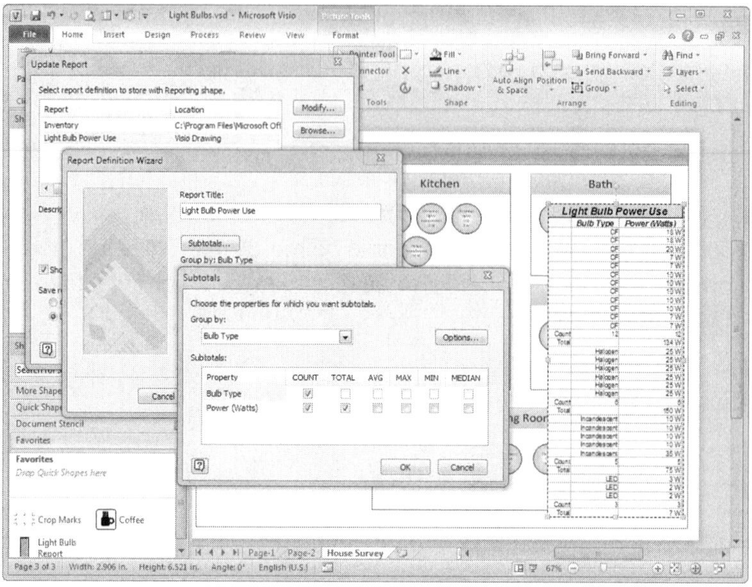

Figure 7.12 *Reports can be ordered using grouping, as well as subtotals.*

4. Click OK, then Next, Finish, and Run to run the modified report. You now see counts and totals, in addition to items grouped together. Figure 7.12 shows this version of the reporting shape on the right.

   The report is starting to look really useful, but it is still long. You can get rid of duplicate entries by adding a quantity column to the report.

5. Right-click the report shape and return to the Subtotals screen, as you've done before.
6. Click Options. The Options dialog appears.
7. Check Don't Repeat Identical Values.
8. Check Exclude Duplicate Rows in Group.
9. Check Show Grand Totals.
10. Click OK, then OK, Next, Finish and Run to execute the modified report. Figure 7.13 shows an example. Notice the Quantity column that enables duplicate items to be tallied in single rows.
11. Save the drawing.

Light Bulb Power Use			
	Bulb Type	**Power (Watts)**	**Quantity**
	CF	10 W	5
		18 W	2
		20 W	1
		7 W	4
Count	4	4	
Total		55 W	
	Halogen	25 W	6
Count	1	1	
Total		25 W	
	Incandescent	10 W	4
		35 W	1
Count	2	2	
Total		45 W	
	LED	2 W	2
		3 W	1
Count	2	2	
Total		5 W	
Grand Total		130 W	

Figure 7.13 *The report modified to show grand totals and not display duplicate values. Note the Quantity column appears to make up for suppressed duplicate values.*

LET ME TRY IT

Storing a Report Definition in a Report Shape

1. Continue working with the Ch7 Shape Data.vsd drawing and the report shape on the Basic Reports page.
2. Right-click the report shape and choose Update Report.
3. Under Save Report With, check Copy of Report Definition this time.

   This saves the modified definition of the report in the report shape itself. You can copy the report to other drawings, and the report definition comes along. You can even add the report to stencils in your Favorites and have them ready in an instant.
4. Click Run to rerun the report. The report looks identical to the last time you ran it.
5. Right-click the report shape and choose Update Report again. In the Update Report screen, notice the new entry in the list: "Definition Stored in Shape." This is a result of the change you made in step 2.

   Any changes you make to this report will be stored only in the report shape. The shape becomes the sole container of the report definition, and you won't see it in the list of reports when you click the Shape Reports button on the Review tab.

6. Save the drawing.

So far you've made heavy use of the options behind the Subtotal button. On the same screen as Subtotal, you also find the Sort and Format buttons. If you need to control the number of decimal places shown in a report, click the Format button. Behind the Sort button, you find more sorting options that you might want to investigate.

Using Reports with Other Documents

After you create a report and get it to look just right, you'll want to use it in other similar drawings and diagrams. Let's now take a quick look at one way to port the report to another drawing.

LET ME TRY IT

Transferring Reports to Other Drawings

1. Continue working with Ch7 Shape Data.vsd.
2. Select a few light bulb shapes and copy them to the Clipboard.
3. Start a new, blank drawing and paste the shapes to it.
4. Click Review, Shape Reports. Notice that Light Bulb Use report definition isn't in the list of reports. That report is stored in the other drawing (and a modified copy is stored in the report shape).
5. Close the Report window and then return to Ch7 Shape Data.vsd. (Press Ctrl+Tab or click the Switch Windows button in the lower-right corner.)
6. Select the report shape and copy it.
7. Return to the blank drawing and paste a copy of the report shape.
8. Right-click the report shape and choose Run Report. The report shape updates to show the light bulb shapes that you copied into the new drawing.

For portability and ease of modification, I prefer working with report definitions saved in report shapes. If you think you will want to send the output to Excel, HTML, or XML, however, shape-stored reports make this difficult. These formats are especially valuable for reports that are too large for a shape on the page.

A good workflow might be as follows:

1. Start by defining a drawing-stored report.
2. Experiment, tweak, polish, and perfect it.
3. Export it to a .VRD (Visio Report Definition) file. This is done on the last screen in the Report Definition Wizard, where the Finish button is located. Just check Save in a File, enter a path, and Visio spits out an XML-based definition of your report.

   Visio doesn't seem to remember the paths for saved reports, so you end up browsing to the save location every time you modify and run the report. You can avoid the browsing by working with a document-saved report until it is perfected.
4. When the definition is perfect, go to the Finish screen of the Report Definition Wizard and check "Save in a file" to export the report to a .VRD file. Having a report file is nice for backup purposes and for sharing with colleagues.
5. Run the report to a report shape and then update the shape so that the definition is saved in the report shape itself.
6. Add the report shape to your Favorites stencil, and re-use it whenever you want to add a shape-based report in a drawing.
7. Call up the report file when you need Excel, HTML, or XML output.

Linking External Data to Shapes

Shape Data fields are great in their own right, but if you already have a bunch of data somewhere else, the last thing you want to do is re-enter it. Luckily, Visio has a couple of ways to import data and stuff it into Shape Data fields:

- The venerable Database Wizard, which is available in all editions of Visio. It has many powerful features, including the ability to change data in Visio and push it back to the database. On the downside, it is harder to use, it's a bit complicated to understand, and data sources are harder to create.
- Link Data, which was introduced in Visio 2007, and is available only in Pro and Premium. Hooking into a simple data source such as an Excel spreadsheet is super easy, and linking to shapes is fairly intuitive. You can link data from multiple sources to a single shape, too. But the data goes only one way: from source to Visio. You can't push changes to Shape Data fields back to the database.

Preparing the Data

Before you start any data linking at all, prepare a data source in the form of a simple Excel spreadsheet. Continue with the light bulb theme by creating a list of bulbs with different characteristics.

LET ME TRY IT

Creating Data in Excel

1. Start Microsoft Excel and create a new, blank worksheet.
2. Create four column labels in the first row: ID, Model, Bulb Type, and Power (Watts).
3. Enter the data shown in Figure 7.14 in columns B, C, and D. You don't need to enter all of it, but do enter at least the first three or four rows. Column A is a calculation, so hold off on that for a moment.

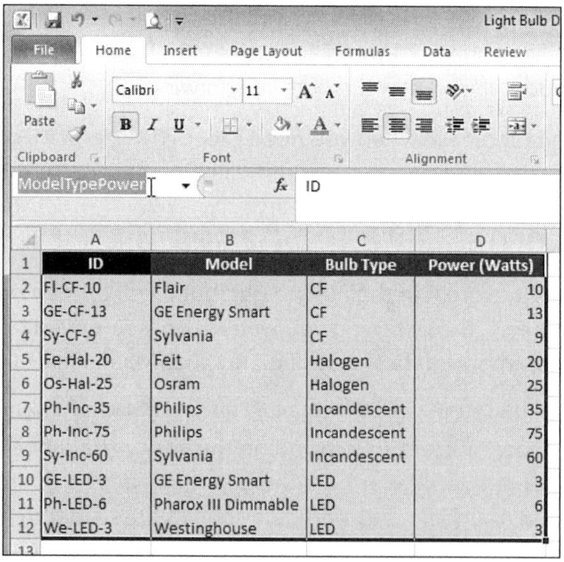
Light Bulb D
File
Home
Insert
Page Layout
Formulas
Data
Review
Calibri
11
Paste
Clipboard
Font
Alignment
ModelTypePower
ID
ID Model Bulb Type Power (Watts)
Fl-CF-10 Flair CF 10
GE-CF-13 GE Energy Smart CF 13
Sy-CF-9 Sylvania CF 9
Fe-Hal-20 Feit Halogen 20
Os-Hal-25 Osram Halogen 25
Ph-Inc-35 Philips Incandescent 35
Ph-Inc-75 Philips Incandescent 75
Sy-Inc-60 Sylvania Incandescent 60
GE-LED-3 GE Energy Smart LED 3
Ph-LED-6 Pharox III Dimmable LED 6
We-LED-3 Westinghouse LED 3

Figure 7.14 *Sample data for data linking in an Excel spreadsheet.*

4. You need unique IDs for each bulb. You could simply use the numbers 1–12, but the Database Wizard actually lets you choose records by picking

an ID. If you make IDs that hint at the actual bulb characteristics, picking is easier than simply looking at numbers.

In cell A2, enter this formula:

=LEFT(B2,2) &"-"& LEFT(C2,3)&"-"&D2

This takes the first two characters in columns B and C, adds a dash between them, and finally appends the power to the end. So a 10-watt compact fluorescent from Flair gets an id of Fl-CF-10.

5. Copy the formula in A2 to the rest of the cells in column A. Your spreadsheet should look something like that in Figure 7.14.
6. Give the data range a name.
    a. Select all the cells that contain values, including the column headers.
    b. In the Name box in the upper left corner just below "Clipboard", enter **ModelTypePower**, as shown in Figure 7.14. This will help the Database Wizard to find the data within the Excel file later.
7. Save the spreadsheet as **Light Bulb Data.xlsx** for future use.

Preparing the Light Bulb Shape for Data Linking

Before you link to the data, you can make a few changes to the light bulb shape that will make life easier later. First, rename the rows so that they match the labels, as discussed earlier in "Shape Data Labels versus Names." Second, turn the light bulb into a master shape.

These steps aren't absolutely necessary for data linking, but they provide good practice nonetheless.

LET ME TRY IT

Preparing the Light Bulb Master Shape

1. Continue working with Ch7 Shape Data.vsd.
2. Select a light bulb shape and set its data to empty or default values.
3. Rename the Shape Data rows so that they are more meaningful. This step is important if you are using the Database Wizard, less so for Link Data (Pro and Premium users).
    a. Make sure that the Developer tab is visible in the Ribbon.

   b. Select your light bulb shape and edit its Shape Data fields using the Define Shape Data window.

   c. For each field, replace the default row names with meaningful names. Replace Row_1, Row_2, Row_3, Row_4 with Power, Model, BulbType, DateSurveyed.

   d. Click OK to accept the changes.

4. Show the Document Stencil via More Shapes, Show Document Stencil. The local stencil for the document appears.

5. Drag the light bulb shape into the Document Stencil.

6. Click on your new master and change the name from Master.X to **Light Bulb DBW** (DBW for Database Wizard, which is the first method you use to link data).

7. Save the drawing.

Using the Database Wizard

If you have Visio Standard, the Database Wizard is your only choice for data linking. Although it is arguably more powerful and feature-rich than Link Data, it is more difficult to use and feels more developer-ish.

> If you have Pro or Premium and are in a hurry to get to data linking, you can skip this section and jump straight to "Using Link Data." Remember that you, too, can use the Database Wizard, and it can do some things that Link Data can't, such as two-way data linking, so you might want to revisit this section.

Because the database wizard uses ODBC to connect with data, you have to set up your Excel spreadsheet as an ODBC data source. This simply means you are telling the system which data driver to use for which file—kind of like hiring a bunch of interpreters to allow you to talk to the guy at the other end of the table.

SHOW ME **Media 7.3—Linking Shape Data Fields to External Data Using the Database Wizard**

Access this video file through your registered Web Edition at ***my.safaribooksonline.com/9780132182683/media.***

After the Excel file is set up as a data source, you can use it over and over for different Visio data-linking applications. But the first time through the setup seems like a lot of steps and can be a bit tedious, but bear with me.

LET ME TRY IT

Setting Up the Excel File as a Data Source

1. Continue working with Ch7 Shape Data.vsd.
2. Start the Database Wizard. On the View tab, go to the Macros group and click Add-ons, Visio Extras, Database Wizard.
3. Click Next to advance to the second screen.
4. Under Choose What You Want to Do, check Link Shapes to Database Records and then click Next.

   The first few steps of the Database Wizard actually deal with which shapes you will be linking. The data source setup comes just after that.
5. Under Choose the Shape Type for Which You Want to Define Links, select Master(s) on a Document Stencil. Click Next.
6. Select Light Bulbs.vsd for the drawing and Light Bulb for the master, as shown in Figure 7.15. Click Next.

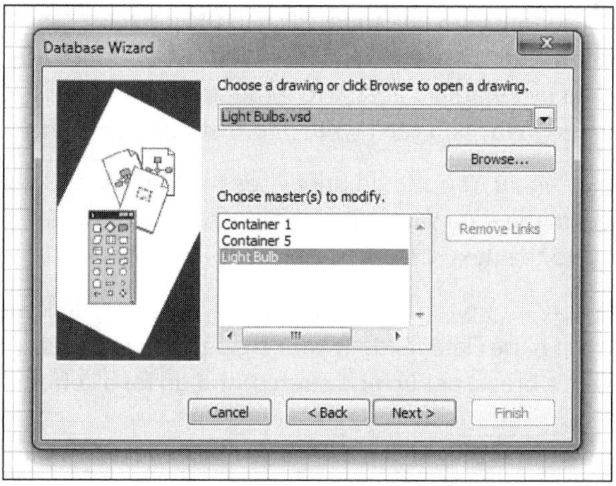

Figure 7.15 *Selecting the drawing and master shape to which you will link data.*

7. The next screen offers a list of available data sources. Your light bulb data isn't yet there, but this is where you set it up.

   Notice the item Visio Database Samples 2010 in the list box. When you install Visio, you get a sample set of data that enables you to experiment with data linking right away.

8. Configure Light Bulb Data.xlsx as a data source.

   a. Click Create Data Source.

   b. If you see the warning "You are logged on with non-Administrator privileges. System DSNs could not be created or modified," just click OK.

   c. For Select a Type of Data Source, choose User Data Source and then click Next.

   d. For Select a Driver..., choose Microsoft Excel Driver. Click Next.

   e. On the next screen, click Finish. The ODBC Microsoft Excel Setup screen appears.

   f. For Data Source Name, type **Light Bulb Excel Data**.

   g. Click Select Workbook, browse to the location of Light Bulb Data.xlsx, then select it, and click OK.

   h. Click the Options button to expand the dialog.

   i. Uncheck Read Only. This makes it possible to change values in the Visio diagram and write them back to the database. This is one of the powerful features of the Database Wizard, but notice that Read Only is checked by default. It is easy to forget to uncheck this and go crazy wondering why you can't write information back to the data source.

   j. Click OK again. You should briefly see the item Light Bulb Excel Data appear in the data source list before Visio automatically advances the wizard to the next screen.

9. You have now set up the data source and are ready to link the columns in Excel to the Shape Data fields in your shape. Leave the wizard running, exhale, take a break, get up and stretch, and go for a coffee.

> You can create and edit data sources outside Visio's Database Wizard as well. This is useful if you've already configured shapes or a drawing to work with a data source but have moved to a machine that doesn't have the data source

yet. You can separate the data source creation from the shape-linking. For Windows 7 users:

1. Go to the Windows Start menu.
2. Type **ODBC** in the Search field and press Enter.
3. Data Sources (ODBC) appears at the top of the list. Click it.
4. The ODBC Data Source Administrator dialog appears. Click the Add button to be taken through a similar set of setup steps as discussed previously.

Now that you have a data source, you need to map fields in the Visio shape to fields in the database so that the communication can begin.

LET ME TRY IT

Configuring Links Between Data and Shape Data

1. Continuing with the Database Wizard where you last left off, you should now be looking at the Choose Table screen, as shown in Figure 7.16.

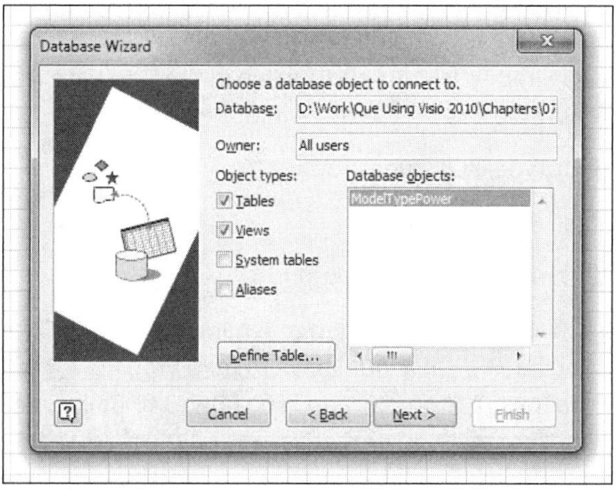

Figure 7.16 *After you set up the data source, the named range of cells shows up as a table in the Database Wizard.*

2. Notice the Database Objects list. You should see ModelTypePower. This is the named range of cells that you defined when you first created the Excel file. Select ModelTypePower and click Next.

3. For Choose the Number of Fields..., select 1 and then click Next. The ID field is sufficient to identify rows in our data.

4. For Choose the Primary Key Field..., select ID from the list and then click Next.

5. For Choose a Default Key Value..., click None instead of selecting an item from the list. The default light bulb shape won't be linked to any particular record in the data. The wizard advances to the next screen.

6. The Choose the Events and Actions... screen allows you to add and remove features from the data-linked shape's right-click menu. Uncheck Delete Shape and Database Record but leave the rest of the settings as they are. Click Next.

7. For Choose the Shape Cell to Be Used for Storing the Primary Key Field Value, select the default: Prop.ID.

   If you look at the drop-down list, you see the names of the other Shape Data fields that exist in the light bulb master. Even though you didn't add an ID field, the wizard creates it for you automatically. Click Next.

8. The Link ShapeSheet Cells to Database Fields screen is the place where you map shape data fields to columns in the Excel file. You work in classic "chooser" style, creating pairings by moving from left to right. So first, select a value in the Cells list and a value in the Database Fields list, and then click Add. Do this for the three light bulb values:

   a. Prop.BulbType, Bulb Type, Add.

   b. Prop.Model, Model, Add.

   c. Prop.Power, Power (Watts), Add.

9. Now you can see why you needed to rename the Shape Data field row names. If you hadn't, you would have to map Prop.Row_1 to Power (Watts), Prop.Row_2 to Model, and Prop.Row_3 to Bulb Type. It would be difficult to ensure that you properly mapped the right Shape Data fields to the right data fields.

   When all three fields have been mapped and appear in the Links column, as in Figure 7.17, click Next.

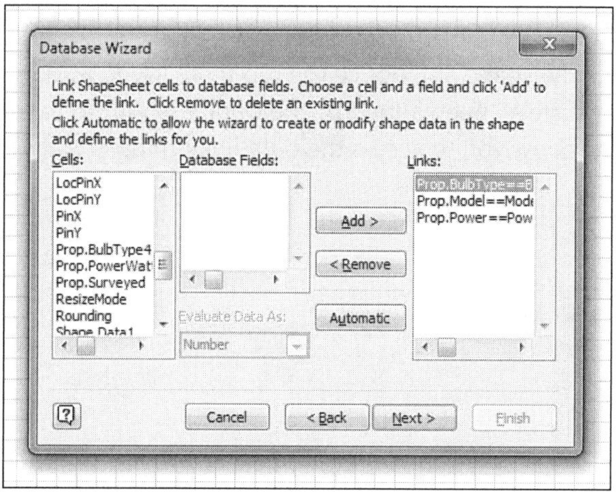

Figure 7.17 *Shape Data fields properly mapped to Excel data fields.*

10. Nod your head thoughtfully at the final summary screen and then click Finish. Congratulate yourself for your patience. Your Light Bulb master is now linked to the data in the Excel file.

11. Save the drawing.

I know that reading step-by-step procedures for using the Database Wizard is tedious at best, but after a few times through, you'll see that it's not difficult. Each step of the wizard reminds you what to do, so there isn't a lot that needs memorizing.

The trickiest part is remembering the Read Only setting when you set up the data source. This box is checked by default, which means you aren't able to change values in Shape Data fields and push them back to the database. This is fine for many applications, where you simply want to visualize existing data in Visio but not change it from within Visio.

LET ME TRY IT

Taking the Data-Linked Light Bulb Shape for a Spin

1. Create a new, empty page in your Ch7 Shape Data.vsd drawing and name it **DB Wiz**.

2. Drag the Light Bulb master from the Document Stencil and drop it on the page.

3. Right-click the shape and notice the top three items, as shown in Figure 7.18. They have all been added by the Database Wizard to the master shape, and allow you to access the data-linking features.

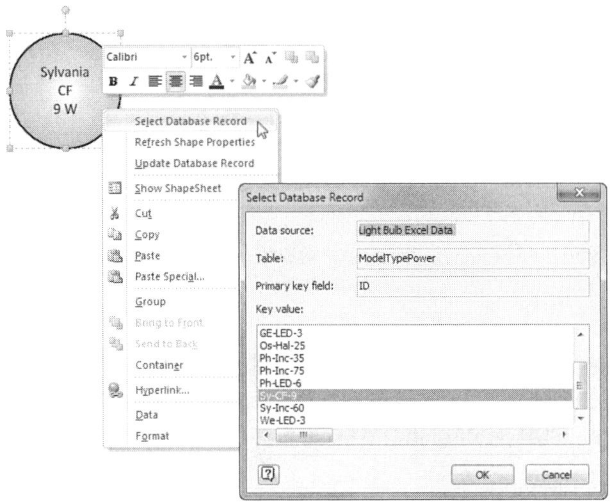

Figure 7.18 *Data-linked shapes have special right-click menu items for interfacing with the database. Clicking the first item launches the Select Database Record dialog.*

4. Choose Select Database Record. The Select Database Record dialog appears, showing a list of light bulbs by ID, as shown in Figure 7.18. This dialog comes from the Database Wizard and is your interface into the actual Excel data. You should recognize the list of IDs as the first column in the Excel file.

5. Choose a value from the list and then click OK. Notice that the fields in the Shape Data window now have new values. You can compare them with the values in the Excel file.

6. Notice also that the Light Bulb shape now has an ID Shape Data field. This field was added by the Database Wizard to hold the key that identifies the data record stored in the shape.

7. Open the Excel file and make a change. Make sure you change a record that is linked to a shape on the page. Append **XXXX** onto the model name.

For example, in Figure 7.18, change Sylvania to **SylvaniaXXXX** in the Excel file and then save the change.

8. Back in Visio, the Sylvania light bulb shape is now out of sync with the data. You can easily rectify this problem. Right-click shape and choose Refresh Shape Properties. The shape's Model value immediately updates to SylvaniaXXXX.
9. Make a copy of this shape.
10. Using the Shape Data window, remove XXXX from the Model name for just one of the shapes. You now have two shapes that are out of sync with each other, and one of them is out of sync with the database.
11. Right-click the modified shape and choose Update Database Record. If you heck the Excel file, you see that it now says Sylvania instead of SylvaniaXXXX.
12. The copied shape is still out of sync, however. Make several more copies of this shape. The Excel record and one shape in the drawing now say "Sylvania," but several shapes display "SylvaniaXXXX" in their Model field.
13. Right-click one of the copies and choose Refresh Shape Properties. The Model reverts to Sylvania, but the other copies still display XXXX, which is no longer in the Excel file. How can we refresh all of the shapes on the page at once?
14. You can easily refresh the whole drawing at once by:
    a. Making sure that no shapes are selected in the drawing window.
    b. Going to View, Add-ons, Visio Extras, and clicking Database Refresh. All of the out-of-sync copies are refreshed and no longer have XXXX in the model name.

You have now successfully created a data source, linked Visio shapes to rows in that data, and synchronized changes made to the data in both the data source and Visio. Congratulations!

You can change the data-linking settings for the Light Bulb master at any time. Just start the Database Wizard from the Add-ins menu and follow the screens. The wizard reads your shape, recognizes the settings inside, and presents them to you for modification in each screen.

For example, you can remove the data linking altogether by visiting the fourth screen in the wizard. As soon as you select the Light Bulb master from the list, the Remove Links button to the right is enabled, allowing you to remove the database connection to the shape. Figure 7.19 illustrates this.

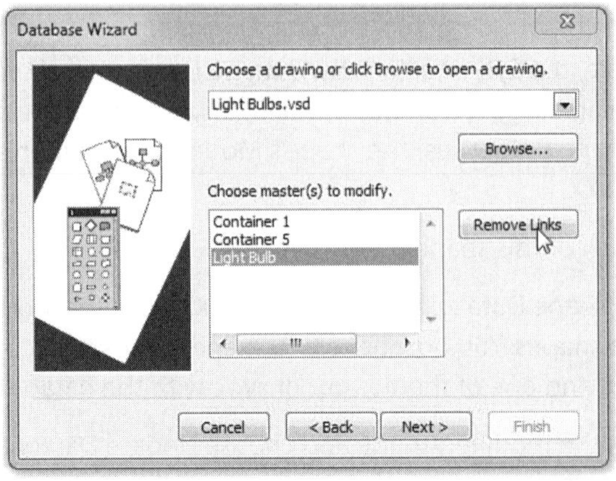

Figure 7.19 *Removing data links using the Database Wizard. The wizard recognizes existing settings inside the shape.*

Another modification that you might want to make is to add or remove some of the data-related right-click menu items from the shape.

You've just seen a brief glimpse of what the Database Wizard can do. Whether you have lists of network equipment or standard business processes stored in some database or spreadsheet, you can now quickly get that data into a Visio drawing, create an illustration of a system, and then generate reports when the diagram looks correct.

By linking shapes to data sources, you avoid tedious rekeying and enforce consistency by allowing only standardized or realistic sets of data. If GE doesn't make a 30,000W LED bulb, there's no chance of picking one when you select Database Record.

The Database Wizard can do a lot more, but I've run out of space for now. If you're still thirsty for knowledge, have a look at the Microsoft Office website:

"Linking Shapes and Drawings to Databases"

http://office.microsoft.com/en-us/visio-help/CH001019175.aspx

"About linking shapes to databases"

http://office.microsoft.com/en-us/visio-help/about-linking-shapes-to-databases-HP085050567.aspx

Using Link Data

If you have Visio 2010 Pro or Premium, you also have access to the Link Data feature. Using it is not only much easier than using the Database Wizard, but it gives you more data choices. In addition to OLEDB and ODBC data sources, Link Data can hook up to data stored in Excel, Access, SharePoint lists, and SQL Server.

Link Data works in only one direction: External data is brought into shapes, but shapes can't change external data. You can, however, link data from multiple sources to a single shape.

> If you're not sure which edition of Visio you have, take a quick look at the Ribbon. If you see the Data tab, then you have Visio Pro or Premium, and Link Data is available. You can also go to the Backstage area and click Help. In the upper-right corner, your edition is listed under Product Activated.
>
> If you have Visio Standard, then the next sections (until "Other Data-Enabled Solutions in Visio") don't apply.

SHOW ME **Media 7.4—Using Link Data to Link Data to Shapes**
Access this video file through your registered Web Edition at
my.safaribooksonline.com/9780132182683/media.

LET ME TRY IT

Preparing a Master for Link Data

1. Continue with Ch7 Shape Data.vsd.
2. Create a new, blank page and name it **Link Data**.
3. Copy a shape from the Light Bulbs page.

   Note: This shape shouldn't be an instance of any master; it still has the default internal row naming for its Shape Data fields (that is, Prop.Row_1, Prop.Row_2, and so on) and it doesn't have an ID field.
4. Clear or set generic values for the bulb's Shape Data fields.
5. Create a new master in the Document Stencil.
   a. Make sure that the Document Stencil is visible by checking More Shapes, Show Document Stencil.

b. Drag the light bulb shape into the Document Stencil.

c. Click on your new master and change the name from Master.X to **Light Bulb LD**.

You use this master with the Link Data features in the following steps. Unlike Light Bulb DBW, this master is not linked in any special way to external data.

Now you can import the Excel data. Instead of an elaborate (long!) set of steps to establish the connection, Link Data shows the data inside Visio in the External Data window and enables you to link to shapes using drag and drop.

LET ME TRY IT

Importing Data for Link Data (Pro and Premium Only)

1. Click the Data tab on the Ribbon.
2. Click Link Data to Shapes in the External Data group. The Data Selector window appears. You can see the Data Ribbon in Figure 7.20.

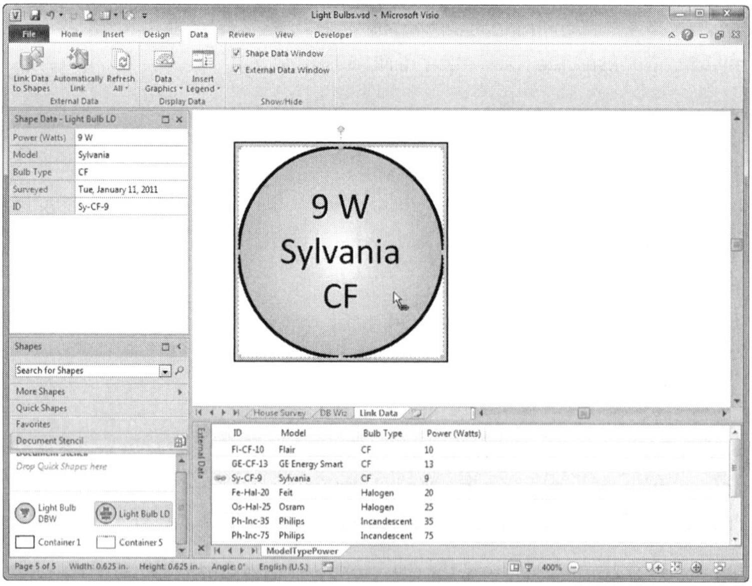

Figure 7.20 *The Data tab and External Data window are two key elements in Link Data. Here, you see a data record being dragged onto a shape. A data link is being created and is denoted by the special highlighting around the shape and the chain-link icon on the mouse cursor.*

3. Select Microsoft Excel Workbook and then click Next.

4. Browse to the location of Light Bulb Data.xlsx and then select it. Click Next.

5. For the worksheet or range, select ModelTypePower from the drop-down list. Notice that the Data Selector also sees Sheet1$ as a data range. If you use Link Data, you don't need to define a named range as for the Database Wizard, but it is nice to see a meaningful name nevertheless.

6. Make sure that First Row of Data Contains Column Headings is checked and then click Next.

7. In the Connect to Data screen, you can select columns and specific rows from the data source to import. For now, leave the default (All Columns) and (All Rows) settings as they are and then click Next.

8. In the Configure Refresh Unique Identifier screen, an ID field is recommended as the key into your data. Make sure that this is checked, click Next, and then click Finish.

The External Data window appears beneath the drawing window, filled with familiar data from the Light Bulb Data Excel file. Now you're ready to link the data to shapes.

LET ME TRY IT

Linking Data to Shapes Using Link Data (Pro and Premium Only)

1. Drag Light Bulb LD from the Document Stencil and drop an instance on the page.

2. Link a data row to a shape. Select a row in the External Data window and drag to the shape. Figure 7.20 shows this in action.

3. If you see some extra text and lines on your shape, a Data Graphic was probably applied. I discuss Data Graphics near the end of the chapter, but for now, remove them and turn off auto-application by doing this:

    a. Leave the data-linked shape selected.

    b. On the Data tab in the Display Data group, expand the Data Graphics drop-down, and click the item under No Data Graphic. The lines and text disappear.

    c. Turn off the automatic application of Data Graphics when data linking. Revisit the Data Graphics drop-down and uncheck Apply after Linking Data to Shapes at the bottom of the list.

4. In the External Data window, note the link icon next to the row that you just dragged. This indicates that one or more shapes in the drawing are linked to this row.
5. Practice tracing links between data rows and shapes.
   a. Create several copies of the data-linked light bulb shape.
   b. Deselect all shapes in the drawing.
   c. Right-click the linked row in the External Data window and then click Linked Shapes. You should see several entries.
   d. Click one of the subitems in the Linked Shapes menu. The corresponding shape is selected in the drawing window.
6. Unlink shapes and data.
   a. Right-click one of the data-linked light bulbs in the drawing window.
   b. Choose Data, Unlink from Row. The shape is no longer linked.
   c. Right-click the row in the External Data window and click on Linked Shapes. The list should have one fewer item.
   d. Alternatively, you can right-click a linked row in the External Data window and choose Unlink. This breaks links to all shapes at once.
7. Link multiple rows to multiple shapes.
   a. Select the Light Bulb LD master in the Document Stencil window.
   b. Hold down the Ctrl key and click on several rows in the External Data window so that multiple rows are highlighted.
   c. Drag the selected rows into the drawing window. An instance of the selected master is created for each row of data and linked to that row, as shown in Figure 7.21.
8. Save the drawing.

When you use Link Data, Visio tries to map the column names in your data source to the *Labels* of your Shape Data fields. If it finds a match, the Shape Data is linked to the database record. If not, Visio adds a new Shape Data field to your shape when you link.

This mapping is case sensitive. So if your Light Bulb shape has the *Bulb Type* field and your Excel sheet has a *Bulb type* column, no match would be found. Your shapes would end up with an extra (and unwanted!) *Bulb type* Shape Data field.

You see this with ID as well. The Light Bulb shapes have no Shape Data field for ID, but it is added automatically when you drag a record from the External Data window onto a shape.

Recall the earlier discussions about Shape Data row names like Prop.Row_1 and Prop.Row_2. With Link Data, you don't have to worry about this, since data is mapped to Labels, not internal ShapeSheet row names.

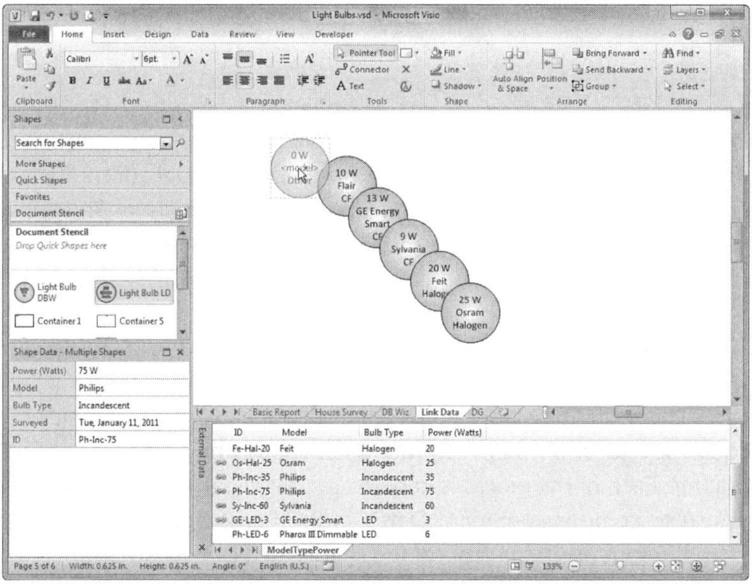

Figure 7.21 *Linking multiple rows to multiple shapes. Select a master first, select multiple rows of data second, and then drag and drop!*

Clearly, using Link Data is much easier than using the Database Wizard. The picture gets even prettier when you throw in Data Graphics, discussed in the next section.

Here are a few other things you can do with Link Data and the Data tab:

- **Refresh the data**—The Refresh All button provides some options for refreshing the data, when the external data changes. You can set the refresh to happen at specific time intervals, choose to overwrite changes to Shape Data with values from the data source, and be presented with refresh choices whenever the document is opened.

- **Automatically link**—If you have shapes that represent real-world objects, they might naturally have IDs that can be used to automatically pick up imported data using Auto Link. A classic example is a map of the United States. It makes sense to give each state shape a Shape Data field that holds the state's name. Auto Link then can use this name to correctly map each shape to a record in a data set concerning states. The Automatically Link button leads you through a series of steps to properly match an identifying Shape Data field with a key in the data.
- **Use additional data**—You can import more than one data source using Link Data to Shapes. Each source shows on its own tab in the External Data window.

Introducing Data Graphics

If you have Visio 2010 Pro or Premium, you have another fantastic option for working with Shape Data: Data Graphics. Data Graphics are visual adornments that bring Shape Data out in the open by making it visible and visual. You apply Data Graphics to shapes so that you can visualize the data behind them without having to modify the shapes.

What Is a Data Graphic?

Figure 7.22 shows a single Light Bulb shape with a single Data Graphic applied to it. Although several adornments surround the shape, they are all part of a single Data Graphic. Each of the pieces is known as a Data Graphic item. A single Data Graphic can be composed of many Data Graphic items, and the items can be located at different positions around the shape. So a Data Graphic is a predefined set of visualizations that bring Shape Data to the surface.

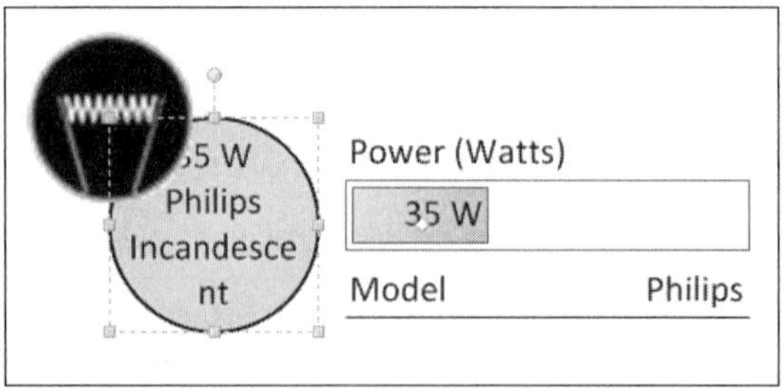

Figure 7.22 *A Light Bulb shape with a Data Graphic applied. An icon tells you the Bulb Type, the bar's length shows you the Power rating, as does the circle's fill color. Finally, a text callout shows the Model information.*

As Figure 7.22 hints, the four types of Data Graphic items are as follows:

- Text callout
- Data bar
- Icon set
- Color by value

The Data Graphic applied to the Light Bulb in Figure 7.22 uses all four of them. Color by value isn't really a graphical adornment. It changes the hue or shade of a shape, depending on the value of a Shape Data field. Color by value is similar to what you might know as a "heat map."

Figure 7.22 is nice, but Data Graphics make much more sense if you see them applied to numerous shapes, with differing data. Figure 7.23 shows several Light Bulb shapes, all with the same Data Graphic applied to them. Note how the different parts change for each bulb (and, therefore, each set of data).

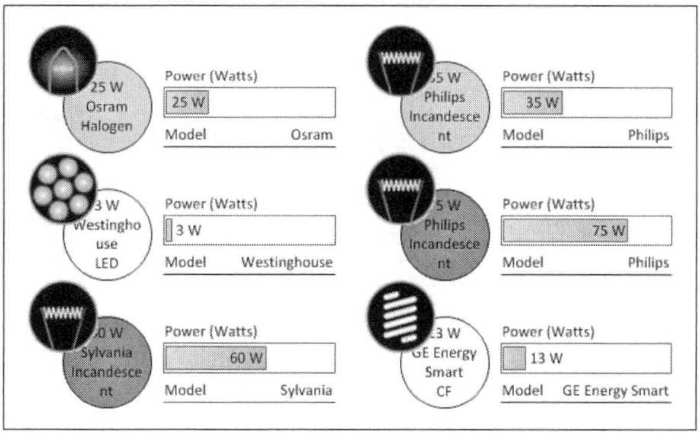

Figure 7.23 *Several Light Bulb shapes with the same Data Graphic applied. Icons change, bars grow longer and shorter, color intensity varies, and text displays the model. It's easy to see the bulbs that use more energy by looking for darker shades or longer bars.*

You can start to imagine the possibilities: opening a network diagram every day, refreshing the data, and noting which servers display an alert icon when there's a problem. Or perhaps you might want to analyze a process flow by color-coding processes according to duration or cost. Those over a threshold could, for example, turn red, making them instantly identifiable.

Creating Data Graphics

Creating your own Data Graphics is a simple process that involves mapping Shape Data fields to Data Graphic items. One issue to keep in mind is which types of data work best with which types of items. Data bars and color by value are best used with numerical values. Text callouts obviously are best for textual descriptions and names. Icon sets work well for data that fits a small number of distinct regions such as "pass" and "fail" or "low," "medium," and "high."

To get you up and running, Visio provides you with the premade text callouts, data bars, and icon sets shown in Figure 7.24.

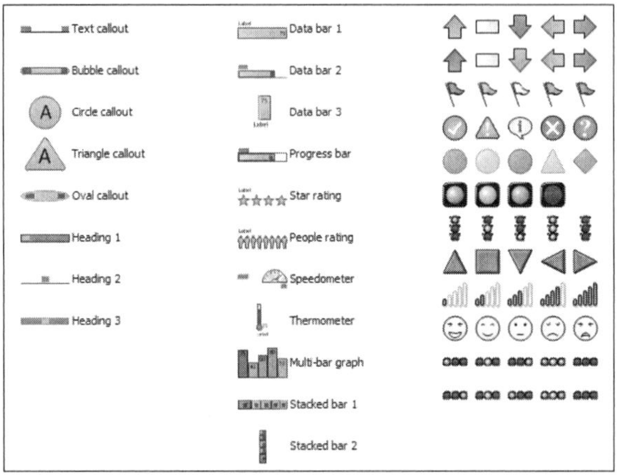

Figure 7.24 *Visio comes with several built-in styles of text callouts, data bars, and icon sets.*

The first time I saw the choices shown in Figure 7.24, I couldn't wait to try them out. So dive in now and create your own Data Graphic without further ado!

SHOW ME **Media 7.5—Creating and Applying Data Graphics**
Access this video file through your registered Web Edition at
my.safaribooksonline.com/9780132182683/media.

LET ME TRY IT

Creating a Custom Data Graphic

1. Continue with Ch7 Shape Data.vsd.
2. Create a new, blank page called DG and drop a few Light Bulb shapes on it. Make sure they have different information either by manually editing the Shape Data fields or using Link Data methods described in the previous section.
3. Go to the Data tab, expand the Data Graphics gallery, and then click Create New Data Graphic. The New Data Graphic dialog appears, with no items in it.
4. Click New Item. The New Item dialog appears.
5. For the Data field, choose Power (Watts), and for Displayed As, choose Data Bar. Pick any style of bar you would like from the Style drop-down.
6. Notice the Details section, which allows you to fine-tune the look and behavior of the data bar. For now, focus on the minimum and maximum values. In this case, 0 and 100 are good choices for light bulbs, but make sure that your bulbs fall within this range and use it fully. If your maximum Wattage is only 30, you might change the maximum value to that number instead.
7. Leave the default settings for Position, which governs where on the shape the Data Graphic Item will be located. You can come back and experiment with this later.
8. Click OK to exit the New Item dialog. You see your new item displayed in the list, summarizing that Power (Watts) is being displayed as a data bar.
9. Click New Item again; then choose to display Bulb Type as an icon set. Pick any style from the drop-down and then look at the Rules for Showing Each Icon section. This section allows you to specify when to show each icon from the set.
10. Icon sets can display up to five icons, representing five different values. Amazingly, you have exactly five different types of Bulb Types: CF, Halogen, Incandescent, LED, and Other.

    Unfortunately, Visio doesn't pick up on the fact that Bulb Type is a fixed list and offer a convenient drop-down list for the conditions. You have to type **CF**, **Halogen**, **Incandescent**, **LED**, and **Other** into the far-right field for each icon. Do this now and make sure that the condition is "equals" in the middle drop-down for each icon. Figure 7.25 shows how it should look.

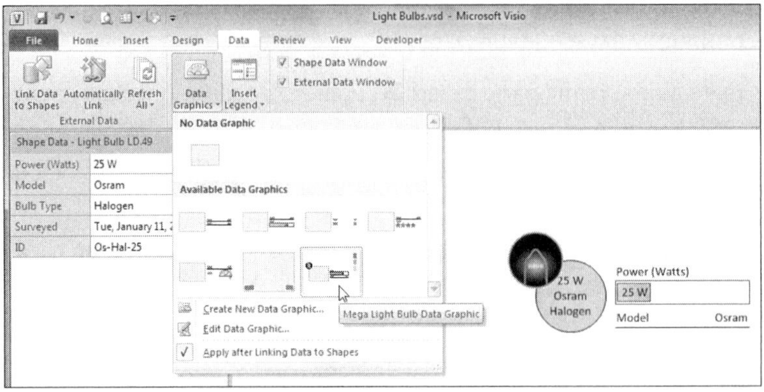

Figure 7.25 *Pausing over an item displays a Data Graphic's name. Here, you apply the Mega Light Bulb Data graphic to a Light Bulb shape.*

Click OK twice to exit the dialogs for creating your new Data Graphic. You see your new item in the Data Graphics drop-down gallery on the Data tab.

11. Rename your Data Graphic. The Data Graphics drop-down is purely visual, but the icons you see aren't always clear enough—especially if you define several similar Data Graphics.

    If you pause the mouse pointer over an item, a ToolTip appears showing the name. Visio gives Data Graphics odd default names, but you can choose your own. Figure 7.26 shows the application of the Mega Light Bulb Data Graphic, which loudly hints that I created and named it myself!

    Rename your new Data Graphic by right-clicking it and choosing Rename. If you've just added the Data Graphic, it should be the last one in the list.

12. Save the drawing, as usual.

> You can create custom Data Graphic items, but this is a task for a developer. If you are a technical type and find Chapter 11, "Developing Custom Visio Solutions," fascinating beyond words, be sure to search the Internet for "Building Custom Data Graphics for Visio 2007." This search will take you to an MSDN article that offers all the details on building custom items.

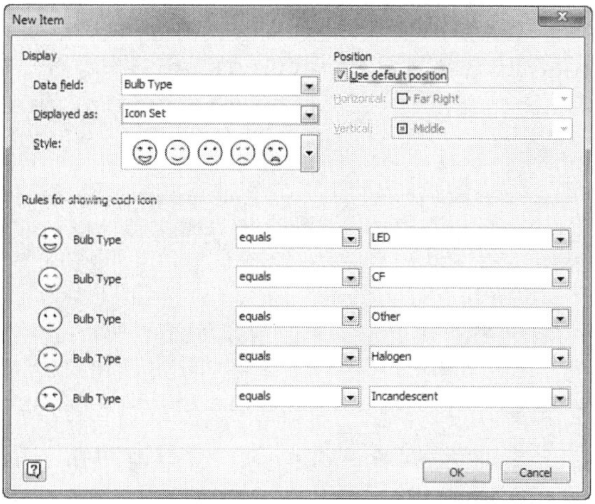

Figure 7.26 *Setting conditions for a smiley face Icon Set that visually depicts bulb types.*

Applying Data Graphics to Shapes

Applying Data Graphics to shapes is simply a matter of selecting the shapes you want and then picking Data Graphics from the Data Graphics drop-down list. You probably figured this out from Figure 7.26, where you renamed the Data Graphic.

The Data Graphics gallery is wired with Live Preview, so you can pause over an item, and Visio shows you how it will look in the drawing window before you click. This capability is especially helpful if you've created several similar Data Graphics. You can use Live Preview to help in choosing the right one.

Of course, you can remove Data Graphics at any time by selecting shapes and choosing the top item in the gallery, just under No Data Graphic. All Data Graphics are removed from the selected shapes.

Another helpful feature enables you to find the shapes that are using a particular Data Graphic. Just right-click on any item in the gallery and click Select Shapes That Use This Data Graphic. Any shapes on the page that use that particular Data Graphic are selected. You can now easily apply a different Data Graphic to just these shapes or clear the Data Graphic by applying No Data Graphic.

CREATING CUSTOM ICON SETS

You might have noticed that the icon set used for the Light Bulb shape in Figures 7.22 and 7.23 does not appear in the list of built-in icon sets shown in Figure 7.24.

This is a custom icon set that I built using a free online tool located here: http://visiotoolbox.com/IconSet.aspx (or search for "Visio Icon Set Builder")

All I had to do was draw five icons (yes, I used Visio) and then export each icon as a PNG, GIF, or JPG image. Then I uploaded the icons using the interface on the website. The tool immediately returns a Visio drawing containing the icon set, which is built into a dummy Data Graphic and applied to a rectangle.

Just copy this rectangle into another drawing, and you'll have the icon set at your disposal. It shows up in the Style drop-down when you choose Display as Icon Set.

If you are totally fascinated by Shape Data, Visio's data linking capabilities, and Data Graphics, and you see huge potential for how you could enhance your workflow with data-enabled, visual solutions, you might want to check out the following book, from fellow Visio MVP David Parker:

Visualizing Information with Microsoft Office Visio 2007 by David Parker, from McGraw-Hill Osborne.

This book is aimed at power users and developers. Although it contains lots of Visual Basic code samples, you do not have to be a programmer to benefit from reading it. You can learn plenty about data linking and Data Graphics even if you skip the code sections.

Other Data-Enabled Solutions in Visio

In this chapter, I've focused heavily on Shape Data fields and how you create, populate, and link them to other sources. But Visio is full of data-aware solutions that go beyond this. Here's a quick rundown of templates that enable you to import, export, and work with external data:

- **Brainstorming Diagrams,** or "mind maps," enable you to export diagram data to an XML format and also create diagrams by importing properly formed XML. Data could be theoretically generated by some other tool and then rendered in Visio for the visual.

- **Organization Charts** enable you to create reporting structures by importing data from text files, Org Plus files, Excel, Microsoft Exchange Server, or any ODBC-compliant database. You can also export data from org charts that you've created and save them as Excel, text, or comma-separated value (CSV) files.
- **Pivot Diagrams** (Visio Pro and Premium only) import your own data from Excel, Access, SharePoint lists, SQL Server, SQL Server Analysis Services, and other OLEDB or ODBC data sources and then view hierarchical tree-like diagrams. You can group and total the data visually—essentially the visual counterpart to Excel's pivot tables.
- **Process Flow and Piping and Instrumentation** are engineering templates that come with tools to help you track components and trace connections. They also have several prebuilt reporting shapes for generating equipment, pipeline, valve, and instrument lists automatically.
- **Microsoft SharePoint WorkFlow** (Visio Premium only) enables you to author a SharePoint workflow in Visio and export it to a format that SharePoint Designer 2010 can import. In Designer, the flow can be further edited and then executed in SharePoint.
- **Space Plan** (Pro and Premium only), Office Plan's bigger brother, is actually a mini Facilities Management solution. It contains tools to help you track the locations of people, offices, and equipment. You can import lists of room numbers and then simply place data-linked rooms onto a floor plan. You can import other people and asset-related data and have that data linked to shapes as well. Finally, several predefined report shapes are provided for tallying space, assets, and move information.
- **Calendar** enables you to import calendar data from an Outlook profile. You don't have to re-create information that you've already entered in Outlook. However, you can annotate a calendar that shows any period of time with Visio graphics. Plus, printing is easier from Visio than from Outlook's calendar.
- **Gantt Chart** enables you to import and export project scheduling data from Excel, text, and Microsoft Project files.
- **Timelines** aren't explicitly data enabled. You can, however, use the Link Data to Shapes features in Pro and Premium to import data that contains Start date and Task Name information. This can be linked to Milestone shapes, which automatically position themselves based on the date information.
- **Database Model Diagrams** (Pro and Premium only) enable you to document and design databases using IDEF1X and relational notation styles. You can reverse engineer existing databases or import ERwinERX files and Visio Modeler IMD files.

- **Web Site Map** crawls existing web pages and diagrams their link structure automatically.
- **Callout Shapes that report Shape Data** The Callouts stencil accessed via More Shapes, Visio Extras has three interesting shapes: "Custom callout 1", "Custom callout 2" and "Custom callout 3". When you point one at a target shape which contains Shape Data fields, the Configure Callout dialog appears, which lets you choose which Shape Data fields in the target to display in the callout.

Summary

This chapter described the essentials for working with individual shapes. You saw that Shape Data can enhance shapes with data behind the scenes, but also can be used to affect the appearance of shapes. You learned not only how to create and use Shape Data fields, but also how to manage sets of them using Shape Data Sets.

After placing real data behind shapes in a diagram, you discovered Visio's reporting features (hiding on the Review tab), and saw how to define reports and save them in various locations.

You also practiced importing data from real-world sources and linking it to Shape Data fields using the Database Wizard and Link Data. Visio Pro and Premium users saw how to put visuals to that data by defining Data Graphics and applying them to shapes.

Finally, you got a glimpse of the breadth of data-enabled applications that are included with Visio.

This chapter is a potpourri. Unfortunately, I don't have space to delve into the details for every template, shape, and add-on. But I hope that you say, "Aha, just what I needed!" at least a few times before you reach the end!

8

Tips for Creating Specific Types of Diagrams

By now, you've seen plenty of Visio's features. You know to be on the lookout for custom right-click menu items, yellow control handles, and Ribbon tabs that bring extra functionality to shapes and templates.

To complete the story, you need a bit of wholistic wisdom to accompany those features. The aim of this chapter is to briefly share some in-depth features and techniques for using a selection of Visio's templates and shapes.

Tips for Creating Process and Flowchart Diagrams

Throughout this book, I've already covered the main features you need to complete your flowcharts. Following are a few less-than-obvious tips and tricks to put in your flowcharting toolbox.

Working with Autoresizing Flowchart Shapes

Many of the masters on the Basic Flowchart Shapes and the various BPMN stencils have a nifty behavior that automatically expands the shapes vertically as you type in more text. This feature is useful and cool, but it exhibits some confusing quirks:

- The shapes have two custom right-click actions: Resize with Text and Set to Default Size. You can see them in the menu shown in Figure 8.1.
- Resize with Text resets the autostretch behavior—if it has been deactivated. For example, manually stretching the shape turns off autostretch. Right-click to turn it back on.
- Set to Default Size restores the shape to its original width and height. I actually wish more shapes had this behavior built in.
- The menu items appear only when they can be asserted. For example, Resize with Text isn't visible if the shape is already resizing with text.

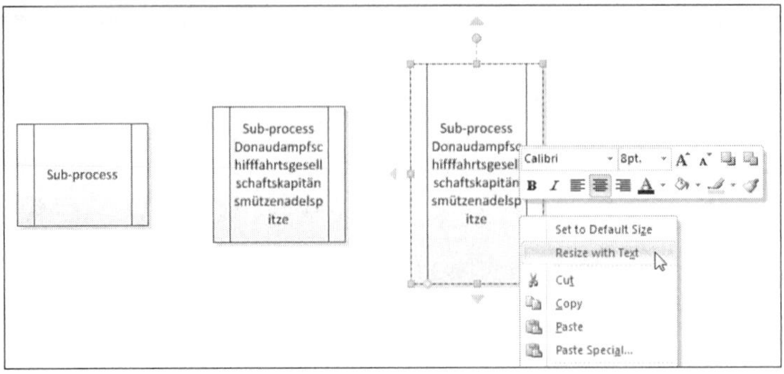

Figure 8.1 *Autoexpanding flowchart shapes and their mysterious right-click actions. The right-most shape has been manually resized by the user, so both menu items appear.*

- If you copy a shape from one on the page, instead of dragging from the stencil, the autostretch behavior gets deactivated for some reason. Furthermore, if you right-click this copy, you don't see the Resize with Text option *until* the text in the shape exceeds the height of the shape. Strange.
- Resetting a shape to its default size doesn't reactivate Resize with Text. And Resize with Text reappears only after it's too late—that is, when the text is bigger than the shape.

Odd as the behavior is, it seems less ridiculous after you've tried it yourself. Take a moment to play with the flowchart shapes, fill them with text, remove the text, and copy them. Just make sure that you right-click after every modification and notice the items that appear or disappear from the top of the menu.

Connecting to Decision Shapes

Visio's Re-layout Page functionality helps make sense of connected diagrams that have turned into spaghetti. However, Visio's layout algorithms are applied rather academically; they don't take into account what people typically do with particular shapes.

A prime example is the Decision diamond shape used for conditional branching. If you're like me, you probably use the Decision shape like the first example in Figure 8.2.

All these shapes are connected using dynamic glue, and everything looks fine, unless you click Re-layout Page on the Design tab.

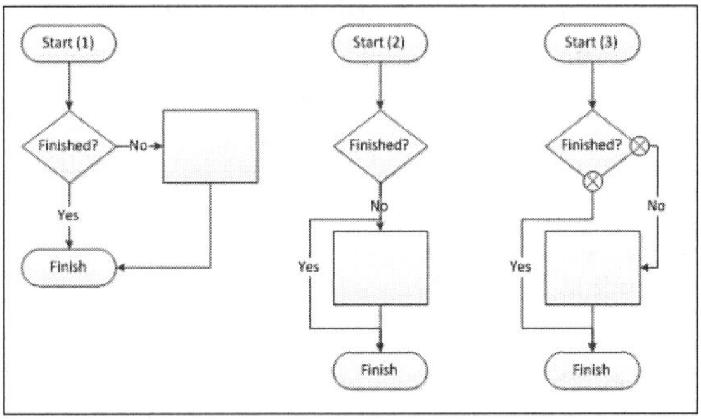

Figure 8.2 *Autolayout does silly things to Decision shapes in flowcharts. The (X) symbols in the third example show where connectors are attached to specific connection points using point-to-point glue.*

The result is the middle flowchart in Figure 8.2. Although evenly spaced and orderly, the flowchart is very difficult to read and doesn't follow the traditional right-angled layout that folks traditionally use with decision diamonds.

The third example in Figure 8.2 partially fixes the situation. The Yes and No connectors now use point-to-point glue to explicitly connect to the bottom and right sides of the Decision shape.

Point-to-point glue doesn't solve the problem entirely, but it does result in a more readable flowchart.

If you really want to keep the nice, right-angled branching that you started with, forget Re-layout Page altogether and rely on the Dynamic Grid and Auto Align & Space to keep things tidy but where you want them. Or be prepared to do some cleanup after clicking re-layout.

Creating Subprocesses to Drill Down to Details

When a flowchart gets too complicated, you might consider simplifying it using subprocesses. This means moving a series of steps to another page, replacing them with a Subprocess shape in the original flow, and then linking that Subprocess shape to the details page.

In this way, users can easily understand the top level of a flow but still drill down to explore the finer details on the subprocess page if they want.

Creating subprocesses is highly automated in Visio Premium, but Standard and Pro users can still do it by hand. Yes, *Using Microsoft Visio 2010* is here to save the day and show you how to create subprocess systems in just a few steps.

SHOW ME **Media 8.1—Creating a Subprocess Using Visio Standard and Pro**

Access this video file through your registered Web Edition at ***my.safaribooksonline.com/9780132182683/media.***

LET ME TRY IT

Creating Subprocesses the "Hard Way"

1. Select a set of shapes in an existing flowchart that you want to turn into a subprocess.
2. Cut them from the diagram. The shapes disappear into the clipboard ether, and Visio removes any dangling connectors.
3. Click the Insert Page tab to create a new page and give it the name of the subprocess.
4. Paste the cut shapes onto the new page.
5. On the original page, add a Subprocess shape in the gaping hole left by the shapes you cut in Step 2.
6. Type the name of the subprocess into this shape. It's a good idea to match this text to the name of the new page.
7. Add incoming and outgoing connectors to the Subprocess shape, so that it is connected to the original flow.
8. Give the Subprocess shape a hyperlink that links to the subprocess page.
   a. Select the Subprocess shape.
   b. Press Ctrl+K to quickly get to the Hyperlinks dialog. (Or use Insert, Links, Hyperlink.)
   c. Use the Subaddress Browse button to choose the subprocess page as the link's target. Visio calls links within the same document subaddresses. The top-most Address field is for links to external documents and web pages
   d. Add a meaningful description if the name of the subprocess page isn't enough to understand where the link will take you.
   e. Click OK. Your Subprocess shape now has a hyperlink that jumps to the subprocess page.
9. Congratulate yourself on saving $200–$500 by not purchasing Visio Premium!

If you *didn't* save any money and have Visio Premium, be sure to check out the Process tab on your more-expensive Ribbon. There you'll find the Subprocess group, which contains three buttons for your subprocessing enjoyment:

- **Create New**—Creates a new page with a name that matches the text of the selected shape. The shape gets a hyperlink to the new page. You then diagram the detailed steps of the subprocess on the newly added page.
- **Link to Existing**—Links a selected shape to an existing page that already contains detailed process steps. This is essentially creates a hyperlink straight from the drop-down list. Very convenient!
- **Create from Selection**—Does everything you did in the preceding Let Me Try It with one click of the mouse. It copies selected shapes to a new page, replaces them with a Subprocess shape, and links this shape to the new page. It even connects the new Subprocess shape to the original flowchart. However, you have to manually change the name of the subprocess page and the text of the Subprocess shape. Microsoft should have popped up a dialog to ask for the name of the subprocess. Nevertheless, this is a huge timesaver for you frequent flowcharters.

Managing Swimlanes and Phases in Cross-functional Flowcharts

Cross-functional flowcharts provide a useful variation on the age-old flowchart by letting you categorize steps in lanes and phases. They have some user-interface enhancements that make life easier but might throw off your Visio intuition a little bit.

SHOW ME **Media 8.2—Using the UI Enhancements for Cross-functional Flowcharts**
Access this video file through your registered Web Edition at ***my.safaribooksonline.com/9780132182683/media.***

Adding Lanes and Phases

You can add swimlanes to a diagram in several ways. You can drag Swimlane masters from the stencil, click Insert, Swimlane on the Cross-functional Flowchart contextual Ribbon tab, or click the blue insertion arrows that appear when you pause the mouse pointer over either end of a swimlane, as shown in Figure 8.3.

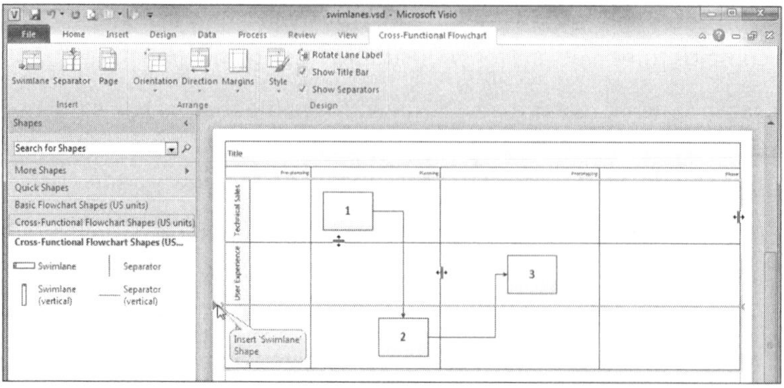

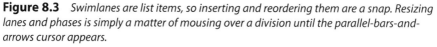

Figure 8.3 *Swimlanes are list items, so inserting and reordering them are a snap. Resizing lanes and phases is simply a matter of mousing over a division until the parallel-bars-and-arrows cursor appears.*

A swimlane is a container, so flowchart shapes inside a lane move with it when you reposition it. The Title shape is a container, too. However, it is specially designed to contain a list of swimlanes. Remember from Chapter 3, "Organizing and Annotating Diagrams," that lists make it easy to insert and reorder members.

You add phases by dragging the Separator master or by clicking Insert, Separator on the CFF tab. Phases are not list items, so they are more difficult to reorder. If you make them wider or narrower, shapes that come after will shift forward or backward automatically, which saves the need to manually adjust shapes.

Resizing Lanes and Phases

Unlike most Visio shapes, you don't have to select lanes or phases to resize them. Instead of pulling on selection handles, you can resize them similar to the way you resize rows and columns in Excel. Pause the mouse pointer over any division until you see the reposition break cursor, which appears as two parallel bars and two arrows. Figure 8.3 is a composite which shows three examples.

When you add a separator to create a phase, Visio divides the available space at the point you drop the shape. When you widen a phase, however, everything after the phase shifts, too. This often causes the flowchart to spill over onto a new page. If you want to keep to one page, you have to go to the end and make the last phase narrower to compensate. Not hard, but potentially annoying.

Contextual Ribbon Tab

The Cross-functional Flowchart tab has some neat functionality that you should explore. There's a style gallery for quickly changing the overall appearance of the chart. You can reverse the direction of flow or transpose the whole diagram between the horizontal and the vertical. You can save space by turning off the title bar, and you set text for each lane so that it is right-side-up and easier to read.

Numbering Shapes

If you like to have your process steps numbered, automated help is hiding in the wings. The Number Shapes add-on has myriad options to help you get your numbering just right.

You find the add-on by going to View, Macros, Add-ons, Visio Extras, Number Shapes. The add-on presents a single screen with a General and Advanced tab, both full of useful options.

You can number your shapes automatically or manually click on them in the order you want. You can set the step interval, define a prefix, opt to continue numbering new shapes added to the diagram, number shapes only on specific layers, and choose whether to add the numbering before or after the existing shape text.

Validating Diagrams

If your wallet is feeling empty and you are the proud owner of Visio Premium, you have yet another bit of powerful technology at your disposal: the ability to validate diagrams for correctness and consistency.

Figure 8.4 shows a simple flowchart that has a few mistakes. The Process tab's Check Diagram button is expanded to reveal that you are validating the diagram using the Flowchart rules set.

Visio 2010 Premium comes with three rule sets, which are loaded with the corresponding templates: Flowchart Rule Set, BPMN, and SharePoint Workflow.

Custom rule sets can be built and imported into documents. They don't even have to be process-diagram specific. Visio validation is still in its infancy, but huge potential exists here for creating valuable Visio-based solutions.

Defining and managing rules are still tasks for developers. Microsoft has laid the groundwork, but there aren't a lot of custom solutions that use the technology yet. If you are excited about the potential of validation and want to get your developers

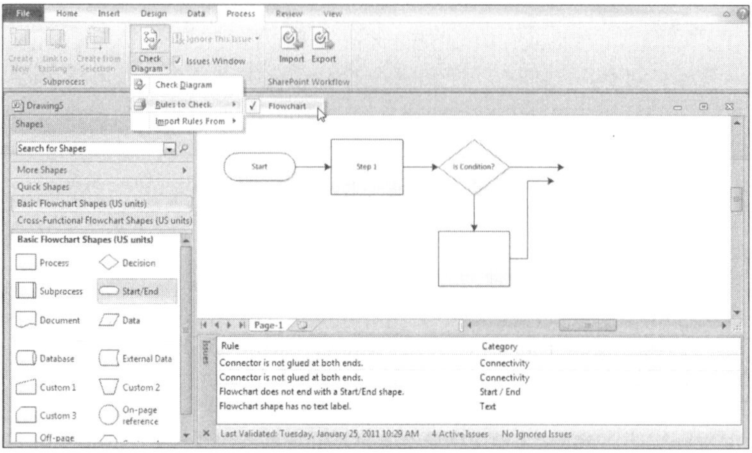

Figure 8.4 *This basic flowchart has a few defects. Visio 2010 Premium knows what they are!*

involved, order a few copies of this book for them, written by fellow Visio MVP David Parker:

- *Microsoft Visio 2010 Business Process Diagramming and Validation*, from Packt Publishing.

You might also find the book's companion website interesting:

- http://visiorules.com.

Business Process Diagrams (BPMN) and SharePoint Workflows

If you have the Premium edition of Visio 2010, be advised that you have two advanced flowcharting templates at your disposal. The BPMN Diagram and Microsoft SharePoint Workflow templates both appear under the Flowchart category in the Choose a Template page.

BPMN Diagrams

The BPMN Diagram template supports the Business Process Modeling Notation 1.2 standard. The shapes that come with this template not only have the proper BPMN look, but also contain appropriate Shape Data fields. They also have custom right-click menu items for fine-tuning shapes to more specialized purposes. All this, along with the BPMN rule validation discussed in the preceding section, and Visio 2010 Premium goes a long way toward helping you create BPMN-compliant diagrams.

For more information, see "BPMN Support in Visio 2010:"

http://blogs.msdn.com/b/visio/archive/2009/12/03/bpmn-support-in-visio-2010.aspx

SharePoint Workflows

With the SharePoint Workflow template, you can diagram a SharePoint workflow in Visio. Then, using the Export button in the SharePoint Workflow group on the Process tab, you can export your work to a VWI (Visio Workflow Interchange format) file. This VWI file can be imported and understood by SharePoint Designer 2010, where you can further edit the workflow and finally run it in SharePoint.

Tips for Creating Network Diagrams

Visio does a good job at two types of network diagrams: logical network diagrams and rack equipment elevation drawings. Let's look at a few tips for both kinds.

Logical Network Diagrams

Visio's logical network shapes, such as those found on stencils like Computers and Monitors, Detailed Network Diagram, Network and Peripherals, Servers, and so on, have a 3D or isometric style.

If you connect them with straight connectors, diagrams look okay. But if you use right-angled connectors, diagrams don't quite look right. The middle example in Figure 8.5 shows this awkwardness.

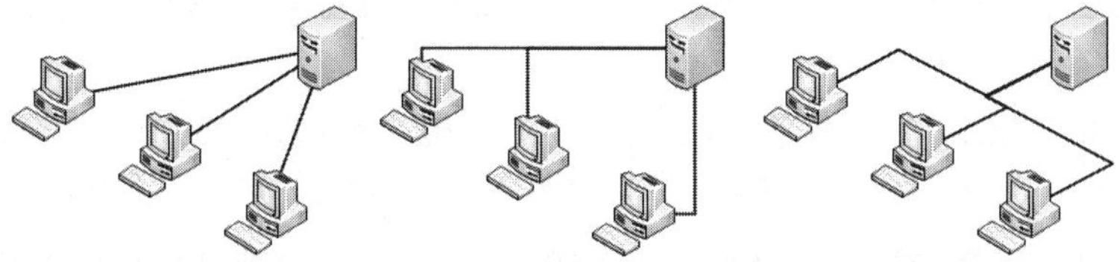

Figure 8.5 *A simple network diagram using Visio's Straight and Right Angle connectors and Visio Guy's Oblique connector.*

The connectors in the right-most example of Figure 8.5 do look correct, however. If you want to create network diagrams that look like this, go to my website, where you can download "Oblique Connectors for Your 3D Diagrams" for free. Here's the address:

http://www.visguy.com/2007/10/29/oblique-connectors-for-your-3d-diagrams/

If you are a Pro or Premium user, you can really enhance your logical network diagrams. You can use Link Data and Data graphics, as discussed in Chapter 7, "Working with Data," Data Graphics to really enhance your drawings by highlighting details without obscuring the landscape of the network.

Rack Diagrams

Rack diagrams (available in Pro and Premium) depict scaled elevation views of actual closet racks and equipment. The shapes used in these diagrams are accurately drawn, and they snap into racks in a manner similar to real world hardware.

If you have only Visio Standard, you can still get a feel for rack diagrams. Open the IT Asset Management sample drawing, which we've used many times throughout this book. To find rack-mounted equipment shapes, look at pages 2 and 3.

Placing and Attaching Rack Shapes

The equipment shapes for Visio rack diagrams are 1D shapes. Normally, 1D behavior is reserved for lines, arrows and connectors where "begin" and "end" are defining characteristics of the shape.

A rack equipment shape, therefore, seems an unlikely candidate for 1D-ness. However, the ends of 1D shapes glue nicely to connection points. And shapes for the racks themselves can be built with lots of connection points located exactly where the screw holes in real racks are. For this reason, Visio rack equipment shapes evolved as 1D shapes.

Figure 8.6 shows a rack with several pieces of equipment glued to it. If the rack is moved, all the equipment moves with it, thanks to the glued 1D handles.

You might think that Containers could do this job rather well, and you might well be right. But rack equipment diagrams have existed since the very early versions of Visio when 1D shapes and connection points were the best option. Containers are new in Visio 2010, so it remains to be seen whether rack solutions get updated and improved. Since there is a huge volume of existing third-party network equipment shapes, it might be more trouble than it's worth.

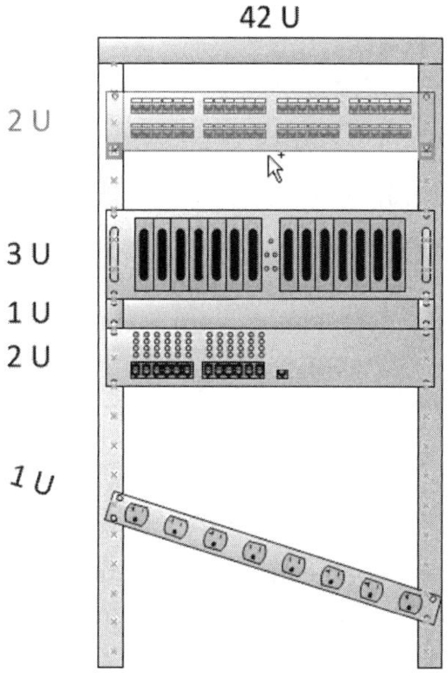

Figure 8.6 *A Patch Panel being glued to a rack. Note the connection points located at standard rack units along both rails. Some joker has glued the Power Strip crooked by regluing one end.*

In Figure 8.6, the "2U," "3U," "1U," and so on text denotes how tall each piece of equipment is in "rack units." Rack guys think in terms of rack units because they mount everything to rack chasses, which are drilled with standard-spaced holes. You can turn off this text by right-clicking any shape.

If you'd rather label rack units using a dimension line, you may be interested in the "Rack Unit Dimension Line" shape, available for free from Visio Guy at

http://www.visguy.com/2007/04/01/rack-unit-dimension-line/

Finding Rack Equipment Shapes

With rack diagrams, the name of the game is realistic-looking shapes. With folks who make rack diagrams, it seems the more accurate and more beautiful the shape, the better!

Visio comes with a smattering of general-purpose shapes. But many sources of manufacturer-specific shapes exist out on the Web. Some even sell a subscription service so you get the latest shapes when new products are released.

Following are a few places to look. There are free stencils, for-sale products, and free samples to get you interested in the commercial offerings.

- **Visio Café**—www.visiocafe.com
- **NetZoom**—Visiostencils.com
- **Visimation**—www.shapesource.com
- **John Marshall's Visio Download Sites**—http://visio.mvps.org/3rdparty.htm

Another tip is to look at network equipment manufacturers' websites. Many firms commission Visio shapes to represent their product lines and then give the shapes away free—or at least to their customers for free.

Tips for Creating Block Diagrams

Visio has several templates for creating block diagrams, and you can even create fairly attractive ones using just the humble Rectangle tool and a bit of formatting finesse. This section points out a few features that you might not discover on first look and points out a few graphical techniques for making your block diagrams more snazzy.

Blending Block Shapes Together

The Block Diagram template in the General template group has some nice block-and-arrow shapes for diagramming all manner of systems, architectures, flows, and anything that you can call a "block diagram."

Whether you use the normal, flat shapes or the 3D "raised" block shapes, your diagrams will look better if you know how to blend shapes together. You can open many of the arrow and bar shapes so that they appear to blend with adjacent shapes.

Figure 8.7 shows a raised block arrow's right-click menu. Choosing Open Tail removes the line from the tail, and creates a small, filled tab that obscures the outline of the adjacent shape.

You need to be sure that the arrow shape is on top of the adjacent shape for this trick to work, though. This is easily accomplished by right-clicking the arrow again and choosing Bring to Front.

If you later pull the arrow away from the other shape, you can close the tail by right-clicking and choosing Close Tail.

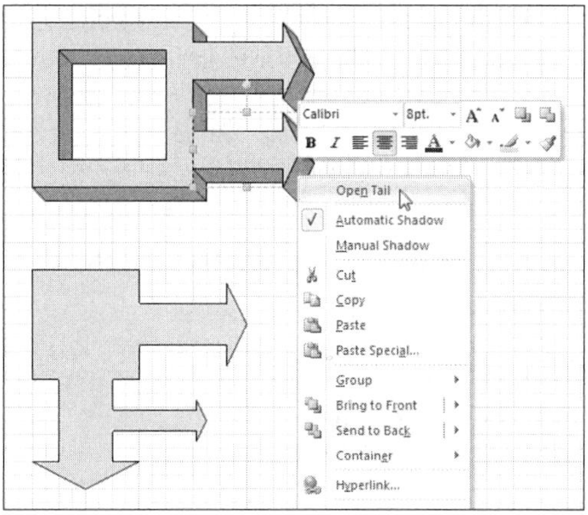

Figure 8.7 *Right-clicking block diagram arrow shapes reveals the Open Tail item, which helps blend shapes together. Make sure that you bring the arrows to the front, though.*

The shapes on the Blocks Raised stencil have specific shapes for left, right, up, down, horizontal, and vertical orientations. You would think that you could simply rotate these shapes, but don't! If you rotate them, the 3D extruded portion of the shapes won't look correct. Use the specific shape for the direction you are working with.

3D Perspective Block Diagrams

The General template category contains the Block Diagram with Perspective template. The shapes in this template one-up the Blocks Raised shapes by venturing into the third dimension in a more realistic fashion. They appear to converge at infinity, which can make for some interesting diagrams.

To effectively use these shapes, you need to keep a few concepts in mind:

- The purple crosshairs shape with the "V.P." text is the vanishing point. This is the virtual "point at infinity" toward which the shapes converge. You can freely move the vanishing point around to change the perspective of the whole diagram.
- The V.P. shape doesn't print, so don't worry about it ruining your handouts at the next meeting.
- You need to be good at managing the Z-order of the shapes (see Chapter 5, "Aligning, Arranging, and Laying Out Shapes") so that shapes don't appear to be on top of each other. Be ready to send shapes to back or bring them to

front at a moment's notice (Ctrl+Shift+F and Ctrl+Shift+B for shortcut fans). If you move the vanishing point, you may need to change the z-order of your shapes because some may wrongly appear on top of others.

- Each shape has the Shape Data field Depth. A depth of 100% means the shape will extrude all the way to the V.P. A depth of 10% means the shape is fairly shallow.
- You can select multiple shapes and set their depths at the same time using the Shape Data window.

Figure 8.8 shows a sample Block Diagram with Perspective, including shapes with varying depths, and one Z-order mistake.

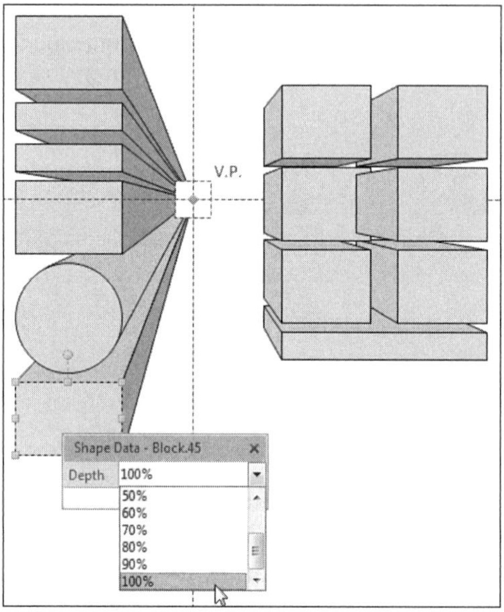

Figure 8.8 *Use Shape Data to set the depth of perspective block shapes from 10% to 100%. The shapes on the left have 100% depth; those on the right have 10%. Note one box on the right that needs to be sent backward.*

Corner Rounding and Other Tips for Architecture Block Diagrams

I see a lot of "system architecture drawings" that use boxes within boxes within boxes to show the components and structure of a system. Figure 8.9 shows an example that conceptualizes Visio's bits and pieces.

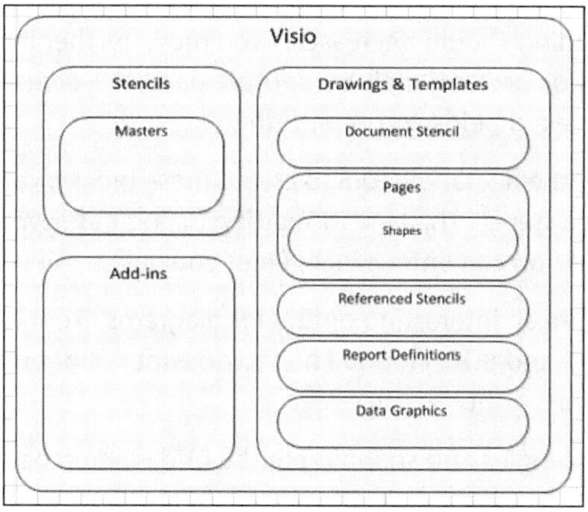

Figure 8.9 *A block diagram of Visio elements that could be improved.*

Figure 8.9 is rather lackluster and contains graphical shortcomings that I often see. Contrast it with Figure 8.10, which is more attractive and easier to read.

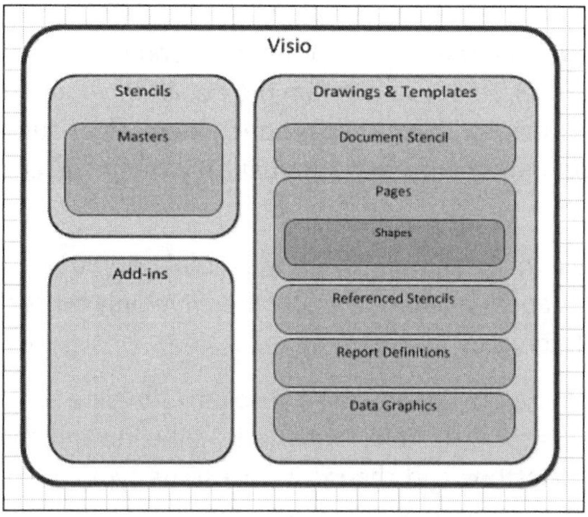

Figure 8.10 *Corner rounding should be large for outer shapes, but small for inner shapes so that curves appear parallel. Line weight and shading can also be used to accentuate hierarchy and structure.*

Here are five tips for sprucing up system architecture block diagrams.

- Corner rounding should decrease as you move further inside the diagram. The boxes look better if their borders are parallel. Decreasing corner radii as you move inward helps accomplish this.
- You can use the Rectangle tool to create these blocks; you don't have to use a shape from a stencil. The Line formatting dialog has several corner rounding choices, plus you can enter exact values yourself.
- Containers are an interesting option for diagrams like this. I used containers in Figures 8.9 and 8.10. I found I had to do a lot of fidgeting with them to get them sized just right.
- Drawing rectangles and snapping to the grid worked best for me. You might find this attack easier than using Containers.
- Varying fill color, line weight, and font size can make the hierarchy more apparent and easier to look at. You don't have to vary all of them, and Figure 8.10 is admittedly a bit overdone, but I wanted to illustrate the point.

Tips for Creating Timelines

The Timeline template (File, New, Schedule, Timeline) is great for sketching out quick schedules with a medium to light amount of detail.

You start with a timeline shape, set its date span, and then choose the size of intervals to mark and label. Then you diagram the details of your plan by adding milestone and interval shapes. These shapes attach themselves automatically to the Timeline and reposition themselves automatically when you change their date values.

If you look at the stencil that opens with the template, you see a selection of 22 timeline-related shapes. In reality, though, there are only three shapes: Timelines, Milestones, and Intervals.

The reason is that you can change the style of any timeline shape by right-clicking or by changing a Shape Data field. Right-click a timeline and choose Set Timeline Type. Select any milestone and change its Milestone Type property. Similarly, interval shapes have the Set Interval Type menu item and Shape Data field.

Figure 8.11 shows three copies of the same timeline diagram. Pay particular attention to the look of the timeline bar and the style of the intervals and milestones. None of the shapes were deleted or replaced. They were simply altered by changing their Type properties.

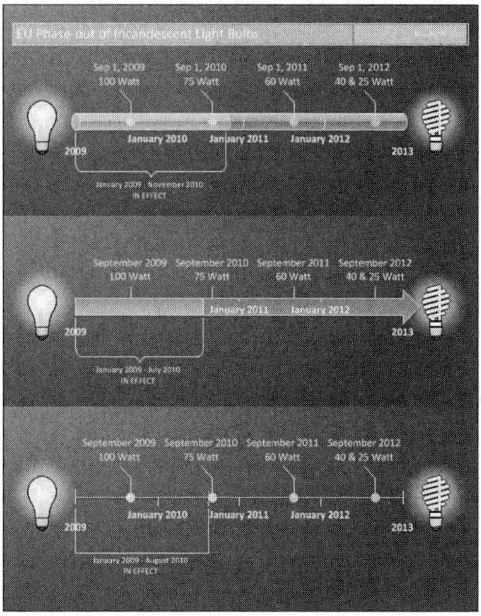

Figure 8.11 *The same timeline copied three times, but the style of timeline, interval, and milestone was changed. Shape properties allow you to easily change the look of timeline shapes without redrawing.*

Being able to change the type is a big time saver. Without such a mechanism, you would have to delete the original shape, drop a different style master, and then re-enter the data and any other options you might have set.

Tips for Creating Organizational Charts

The Business template category contains two items for creating org charts: Organization Chart and the Organization Chart Wizard. The wizard template presents you with some dialogs that help you import data and generate an org chart automatically.

Both templates load an add-in that gives you extra functionality that assists you not only in generating a chart, but also rearranging, promoting, and deleting employees. The automatic features are cool, but they force you to use Visio differently and ignore certain conventions that you're used to by now.

Drawing and Editing Org Charts by Hand

Let's build a simple org chart and see how the add-in functionality makes things easier for us. In this exercise, pay particular attention to the notes about how org chart manipulation differs from typical connected diagrams.

LET ME TRY IT

Creating a Very Basic Org Chart

1. Start a new Organization Chart drawing. The template is located in the Business template group.
2. Drag an Executive shape onto the page. The first time you drop an org chart shape, a small animation plays, showing you how to build an org chart. For now, nod and smile and click OK.
3. Type two lines of text: **Bill Jobs**, **CEO**.
4. View the Shape Data window for the shape. Org chart shapes have five default Shape Data fields: Department, Telephone, Name, Title, and E-mail.

   Note that even though you typed text only into the Executive shape, its Name and Title fields magically contain "Bill Jobs" and "CEO." This is the org chart add-in at work behind the scenes. It is not normal Visio behavior to set Shape Data from text typed onto shapes.
5. Change the values for Name and Title in the Shape Data window. See that the text in the shape updates? This two-way data entry and display is special to the org chart solution.
6. Drop several Manager shapes on top of the Executive shape. Note how they automatically are connected and aligned below the Executive.

   Unlike other Visio diagrams, you don't need to use the Connector tool or AutoConnect to get your org charts completed.
7. Set the text for each Manager shape. Type something simple like **Mgr1**, **Mgr2**, **Mgr3**.
8. Save the org chart file for use in the next exercise.

Creating an org chart is as simple as dragging and dropping on top of other shapes. And the synchronization between text and Shape Data fields is also quite handy. Next, you learn how to lay out subordinates, set chart-wide options, and where to look to discover more features.

LET ME TRY IT

Extending a Very Basic Org Chart

1. Continue using the org chart you created in the last Let Me Try It.
2. Drop six Position shapes on top of Mgr2. They orient themselves below Mgr2 but are spread out in a very wide formation.
3. You can change the way Mgr2's subordinates are arranged. Right-click Mgr2 and choose Arrange Subordinates. The Arrange Subordinates dialog appears.

   The org chart add-in offers special layout functionality, so you don't use Visio's normal layout functionality (Design, Re-layout Page) with org charts.

   You can also rearrange shapes using controls in the Layout and Arrange groups on the Org Chart contextual tab.
4. Click the first option in the Side-by-side group and then click OK. The six Position shapes are neatly arranged in two vertical columns below Mgr2.
5. Move the whole chart. Select the CEO shape and move it. Notice that the whole organization moves with it. You don't have to select all the shapes!
6. Give Mgr2 a demotion. Select Mgr2 and drag it on top of Mgr1. Mgr2 becomes a subordinate of Mgr1, and Mgr2's subordinates descend the corporate ladder with their boss, as shown in Figure 8.12.
7. Click the Org Chart contextual Ribbon tab. The tab contains a superset of the options available by right-clicking org chart shapes. The controls are divided into five groups: Layout, Arrange, Picture, Synchronize, and Organization Data.

   A lot of functionality is available here, and I don't have space to cover it all right now. So take some time to explore the options. Be sure to pause over each control because the ToolTips are very informative and explain each feature well.
8. Change the data displayed on all the org chart shapes. Click Display Options in the Organization Data group on the Org Chart tab. The Options dialog appears.

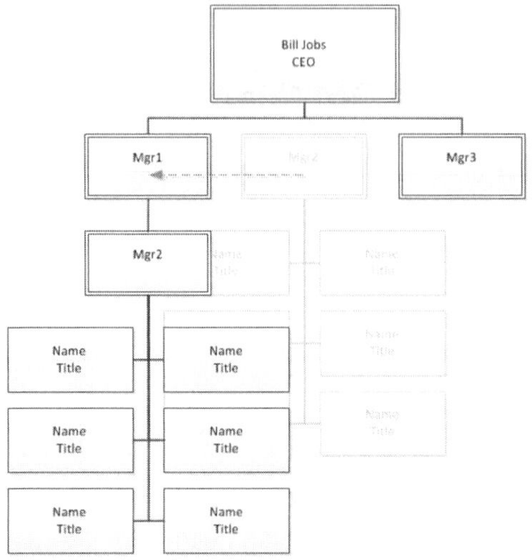

Figure 8.12 *Mgr2 hasn't been performing. Demoting him, along with his whole team, is a simple matter of dragging and dropping.*

9. Click the Fields tab. Here, you can customize the data displayed in the org chart shapes. Check Department in addition to Name and Title (which are already checked) and then click OK. All the org chart shapes now display Department in their third line. Note: "Department" is the default value for the Department field. Normally, you would assign real values for the Department field.

Generating Org Charts from Data Using the Wizard

You can also generate an org chart automatically by importing data from a database, text file, or Excel spreadsheet.

About Org Chart Data

The data doesn't have to be related to personnel; it can be any hierarchical system. What's most important is that each record in the data has a unique ID, and every record except the top-most person or thing must have a reports-to ID that is the same as one of the IDs.

Figure 8.13 shows data that represents the Energy Sources hierarchy that I've used several times in this book. We've seen it illustrated with nested containers, but an org-chart style diagram works just as well.

	A	B	C	D	E
1	ID	Name	ReportsTo	Notes	Renewable
2	1	Energy Sources			Yes
3	2	Wind Power	1		Yes
4	3	Solar Power	1		Yes
5	4	Hydro Power	1		Yes
6	5	Geothermal Power	1		Yes
7	6	Combustion Power	1		Yes
8	7	Nuclear Power	1		Yes
9	8	Photovoltaic	3		Yes
10	9	Solar Thermal	3		Yes
11	10	Dam	4		Yes
12	11	Tidal	4		Yes
13	12	Wave	4		Yes
14	13	Oil	6		No
15	14	Wood	6		Yes
16	15	Coal	6		No
17	16	Gas	6		No
18	17	Biofuel	6		Yes
19	18	Fission	7		No
20	19	Fusion	7	Not yet feasible	Yes
21	20	River current	4		Yes
22					

Figure 8.13 *Org chart data for a nonemployee hierarchical system.*

The columns in your data do not require special names because the Org Chart Wizard enables you to specify which columns contain the ID and Reports To information.

Also, the wizard enables you to import extra data, which gets stored in the Shape Data fields of the position shapes. Looking at the data in Figure 8.13, you can see that it makes a lot of sense to push the data in the Name, Notes, and Renewable columns into your shapes.

Figure 8.14 shows the result of importing the data in Figure 8.13. Instead of a nested-container block diagram, the energy sources have been arranged in org chart fashion. The Notes and Renewable information has been imported as well; you can see it in the Shape Data window.

The little circles in Figure 8.14 are Data Graphics (discussed in Chapter 7, "Working with Data"). These make use of the otherwise invisible Shape Data stored in each shape, and bring a pretty face to the value of the Renewable field. A check mark shows whether the value is Yes; an X, whether the value is No.

After you've run through the Org Chart Wizard several times, you might start wondering about automation, especially if you're generating charts from the same data source, using the same options, over and over.

Good news! You can generate org charts automatically "from the command line." Instead of running the wizard, you execute a batch file that tells the wizard which options you want in advance.

The following article describes all the command-line switches and other details for making this happen.

"Make Visio organization charts from personnel files"

http://office.microsoft.com/en-us/visio-help/make-visio-organization-charts-from-personnel-files-HA001077464.aspx

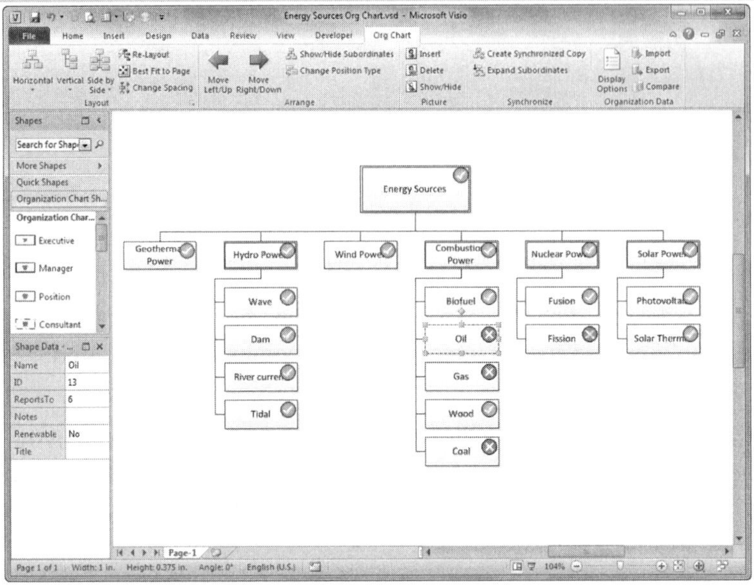

Figure 8.14 *The Energy Sources data imported via the Org Chart Wizard. Note the extra Shape Data fields Notes and Renewable have been added.*

Limitations of the Org Chart Wizard

Although the Org Chart Wizard has lots of nifty features, it also has a few limitations.

- Shapes are placed in random order when you import data. Alphabetically sorting by employee name in Excel won't give you a sensible layout in Visio, unfortunately.
- You can round-trip an org chart: import from data, modify it, export it to a data file, then re-import it. But fancy customizations like arrangement styles, colors and other formatting, photos added to position shapes, and layout order are not preserved. Only the raw data and relationship information is exported.

Using Walls, Windows, and Doors in Office and Space Plans

Many of the templates in the Maps and Floor Plans group open with the Walls, Doors, and Windows stencil. This library contains shapes for drawing exterior and interior walls, and the windows and doors that perforate them.

These shapes come with extra functionality that make them easier to work with. If you are familiar with the automated features, you won't find yourself fighting against them; you can let them do a lot of mundane work for you.

The key behaviors that you will encounter can be summed up as follows:

- Wall, window, and door shapes are all highly configurable via right-clicking and Shape Data fields. Don't look for hundreds of different symbols, look at the configuration options for the basic type of object.
- Doors and windows automatically align to walls when dropped on or near them, and stay glued when walls are moved.
- Walls automatically extend to other walls when brought within a small distance of each other.
- Wall intersections and corners heal automatically, so you don't have to worry about line removal.

SHOW ME **Media 8.3—Using Walls, Windows, and Doors in a Visio 2010 Office Plan**

Access this video file through your registered Web Edition at ***my.safaribooksonline.com/9780132182683/media.***

LET ME TRY IT

Creating Building Plans Using Wall Shapes

1. Start a new Office Layout drawing.
2. Create a rough building outline using the Line tool. It can be any shape; have fun and go wild! But be sure to draw it in the counterclockwise direction, though.
3. Leaving the outline shape selected, go to the Plan contextual Ribbon tab and click Convert to Walls. The Convert to Walls dialog appears.

4. In the dialog, select Exterior Wall, check Add Dimensions, check Delete under Original Geometry; then click OK. You should see something like Figure 8.15.

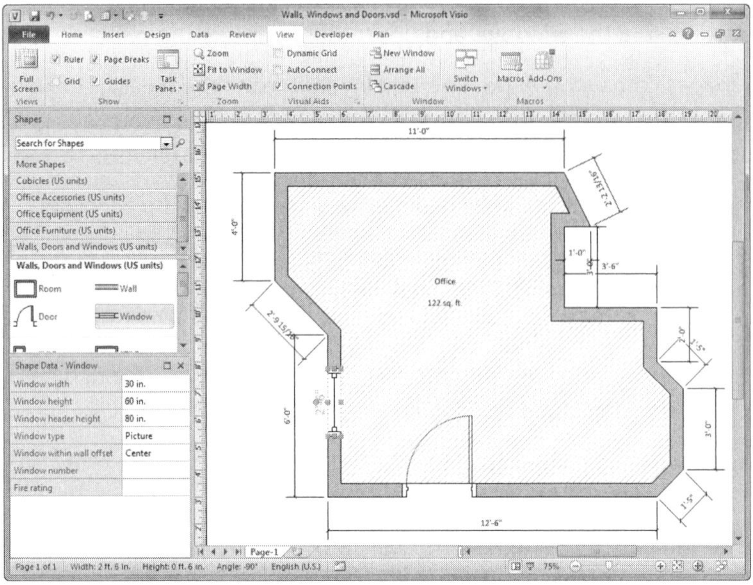

Figure 8.15 *A polyline created by the Line tool is converted to walls and dimension lines. By drawing the outline counterclockwise, you ensure that the dimension lines are on the outside of the space.*

If you had drawn the building in the clockwise direction, the dimensions would have appeared on the inside of the building, a minor nuisance or blessing, depending on your point of view!

5. Explore the new shapes. Each wall segment and dimension line is a separate shape. The dimension lines are glued to the walls. If you change the length of a wall, the dimension line changes with it, and the dimension's readout updates to show the actual length.

6. Select a wall shape. Note that it has Begin and End handles as well. It too is a 1D shape.

7. Note that dimension text appears on the wall when a wall shape is selected. This is a visual aid to help you keep the length of the wall in mind, but it goes away when you deselect the shape. If you need dimensions in printed output, use dimension line shapes.

8. Pull one end of a wall away from a corner so that the end is dangling in free space. See how the open ends of the walls magically heal so that the black outline goes around the ends?

9. Move the wall end back to the corner where it originally was. Notice that the black outline magically re-heals at the corner joint. You don't see any inappropriate lines.

10. View the Shape Data window for the selected wall shape and experiment with the properties. Note that some affect the look of the wall, whereas others are purely informational. These might be useful in reports or for construction details.

11. Drop another Wall shape from the stencil in the middle of the outline. Notice that it doesn't automatically come with an attached dimension line. Experiment with moving the ends close to other walls and notice how the wall automatically jumps to intersect and heal with those walls.

12. Save the drawing for use in the next exercise.

Now that you know how to work with the supersmart wall shapes, it's time to learn how to add windows and doors to your plan. In the next exercise, you also see how to automatically create space shapes that are great for analyzing floor area and tracking facilities.

LET ME TRY IT

Using Window, Door, and Space Shapes with Walls

1. Continue working with the drawing you created in the last exercise.

2. Drag a Window shape onto the plan and drop it on a wall that runs vertically. Notice that the window automatically rotates to match the orientation of the wall. Also, note the red handles on the selected window shape. These indicate that it is glued to the wall.

3. Verify this glue by moving the wall onto which you dropped the window. The window moves with the wall. Undo this step to restore the integrity of your beautiful outline.

4. Change the thickness of the wall using the Wall Thickness Shape Data field. The thickness of the window changes with the wall. The window is truly integrated with the wall in an intelligent way.

5. Experiment with the width of the window. You can change it manually by dragging its selection handles. You can also select or enter values in the Window Width Shape Data field.

6. Drop a Door shape on another wall. It auto-orients and glues to the wall. It has features, data fields, and behavior that are very similar to the window shape.

7. Notice the yellow control handle on the Door. Use it to actually open and close the door! You can use the Shape Data field Door Open Percentage to open and close the door as well.

8. Right-click the door and notice the Reverse Left/Right Opening and Reverse In/Out Opening options. You don't have to rotate or flip the doors once they're attached to walls; just use the flip features.

9. Drop a Space shape in the middle of your plan. You see a cross-hatched rectangle that displays name and area. You want this shape to match the outline of your building plan and accurately reflect the area of the space.

10. Right-click the Space shape and choose Auto Size. The Space shape magically morphs to fit the interior of your plan's outline, and the area value updates. This is also shown in Figure 8.15.

    Space shapes take ordinary floor plans into the realm of facilities management systems. If you look at the Shape Data for the Space shape, you see fields like Name, Space ID, Department, Phone Number, Occupancy, Capacity, and Zones. These can be used to tie the space to people and equipment shapes and then used in reports. If you have Pro or Premium, you can color spaces according to data using the Data Graphics feature.

11. Go to Home, Editing, Layers, Layer Properties to bring up the layers dialog. Notice that the shapes are pre-assigned to several useful layers like Building Envelope, Dimensions, Door, Space, Wall, and Window. These layers are great for reducing complexity and preventing modifications. For instance, while you are working on spaces, you might choose to hide the Dimensions layer and lock the Building Envelope layer so that you don't accidentally move any walls, windows, or doors.

I could go on and on about Floor Plans, but I think that's a good introduction. If you're thirsty for more, be sure to check out the Display Options button on the Plan tab. This dialog enables you to fine-tune the overall look of your drawing; the settings apply to everything on the page.

Dimension Lines

Dimension lines made a brief appearance in the preceding section on walls, windows, and doors. Whether you are creating floor plans or other measured or scaled technical drawings, you need to understand how to use the dimension line shapes.

If you go to More Shapes and expand the Visio Extras group, you see three dimensioning stencils:

- Dimensioning—Architectural (US units)
- Dimensioning—Engineering (Metric)
- Dimensioning—Engineering (US units)

All three stencils actually contain the same set of shapes. The only difference is the default units that they display and the style of arrow used between extension lines.

With these dimensioning shapes, you can do things such as dimension the part shown in Figure 8.16.

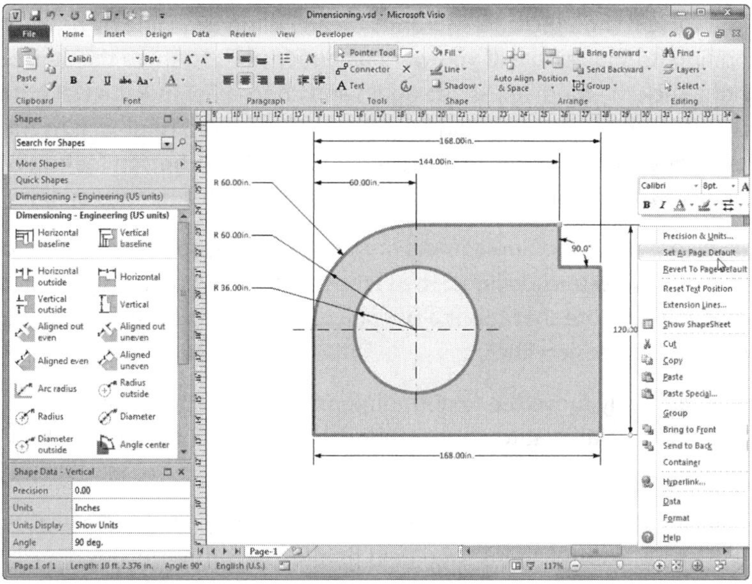

Figure 8.16 *A fully dimensioned mechanical part, using Visio's dimensioning shapes. Note the Shape Data and right-click items for the selected dimension line.*

Dimension lines are pure Visio shapes, not a special built-in feature. They don't use any special add-ons to get the job done. You position them using 1D endpoints and control handles, and you configure them using Shape Data or by right-clicking.

It is difficult to explain how to use them in text, so I recommend watching the following video.

SHOW ME **Media 8.4—Using Dimension Lines**

Access this video file through your registered Web Edition at ***my.safaribooksonline.com/9780132182683/media.***

Keep in mind these basic principles when using these shapes:

- All dimension lines are 1D shapes. The 1D ends are the more important handles, so place these blue handles first. Tweak the yellow control handles afterward to fine-tune each shape.
- Snapping is important. You turn on snapping options via View, Visual Aids, Dialog box launcher. I recommend snapping to Shape geometry, Shape vertices, Shape intersections, and Connection points.
- You can set the precision and units for any dimension line by right-clicking or editing its Shape Data. If you want all dimensions to share the new settings, right-click the modified shape again and choose Set as Page Default. This updates a page-wide setting for precision and units. Think of it as the "make everybody look like me" feature. There is no Ribbon button for editing the page's precision and units. You have to go through a dimension line.
- If you are dimensioning corners or interior spaces, you might want to turn off one or both extension lines. The Extension Lines right-click menu item helps you do this. Note that this is a per-shape setting; no page-wide application exists for extension lines.
- You can freely move the text for dimension line shapes. If you'd like to put it back in its default, automatic position, however, right-click and choose Reset Text Position.
- You can add text before or after the dimensioning number. To ensure that you don't destroy the inserted field that displays the size, double-click the shape, or press F2 to get into text-edit mode. Then you can place the cursor before or after the dimension and freely add text.

Dimension line shapes aren't hard to use, but they do take some practice and experimentation. If you get one in too sorry a state, just delete it and start over!

Summary

In this chapter, you learned some less-than-obvious techniques for creating flowcharts, swimlane diagrams, network diagrams, block diagrams, timelines, org charts, and floor plans; plus you learned how to use the dimension line shapes.

You learned that some templates are actually complete solutions that load extra add-ins to assist your drawing. Sometimes this automated assistance requires you to use Visio in non-standard ways. The org chart add-in helps you to connect and arrange subordinates as well as import external data. Timelines automatically position milestones and intervals based on the dates you input. And walls, windows, and doors have automated help for positioning, intersecting, and space definition.

You saw that you can go to the Internet to get specially designed shapes for free and for purchase. And I hope you learned about a diagram type or two that you didn't know Visio could do but are now inspired to use in your daily work!

Fortunately, Visio has plenty of options to help you get the perfect printed output. In this chapter, you explore several scenarios and the locations of the settings and options for getting the right printout.

9

Printing

The paperless office is a noble goal, but we are tactile creatures. Sometimes there's no substitute for a paper in one hand and a red pen in the other!

In addition to correcting and reviewing, there are plenty of other reasons for printing. Maybe you need handouts or large-format posters for your next meeting, or plans for builders and installers in the field. Maybe your audience doesn't have Visio or even the free Visio Viewer installed. Perhaps you don't want people to manipulate your work or "borrow" its contents. Or if you don't have the option to publish your diagrams to the web or SharePoint site, then printed output might be the best way to share your ideas.

Printing Basics

One-page documents using built-in templates generally print just fine on typical office printers. Visio's built-in templates are configured to match standard office paper: the U.S. Units templates for letter-sized paper and the Metric Units templates for A4.

Printing from the Backstage Area

To start printing, the first place to go is the Backstage area. Let's look at the basic options behind File, Print.

LET ME TRY IT

Exploring Basic Print Options

1. Start a new drawing from Sample Diagrams. Choose the IT Asset Management sample. This drawing has three pages; a logical network diagram, and two physical rack layouts, which are scaled drawings. Figure 9.1 shows an overview of all three pages.

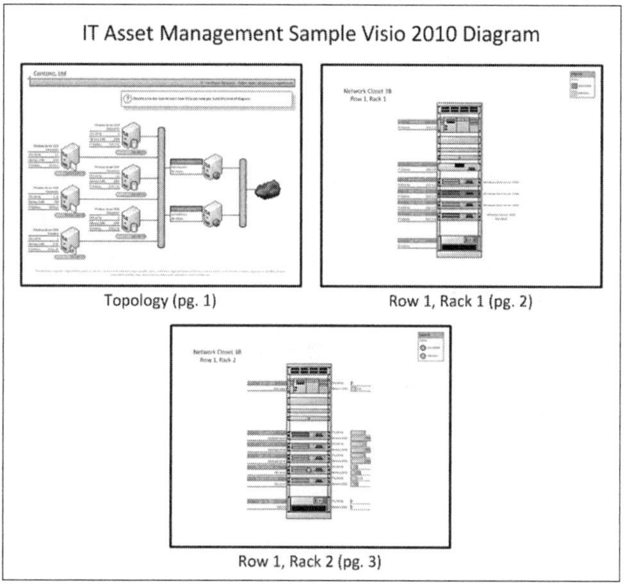

Figure 9.1 *The three pages of the IT Asset Management drawing.*

2. To explore the print options for this document, click File, Print. You see the Backstage Print screen with three options—Quick Print, Print, and Print Preview—as shown in Figure 9.2.

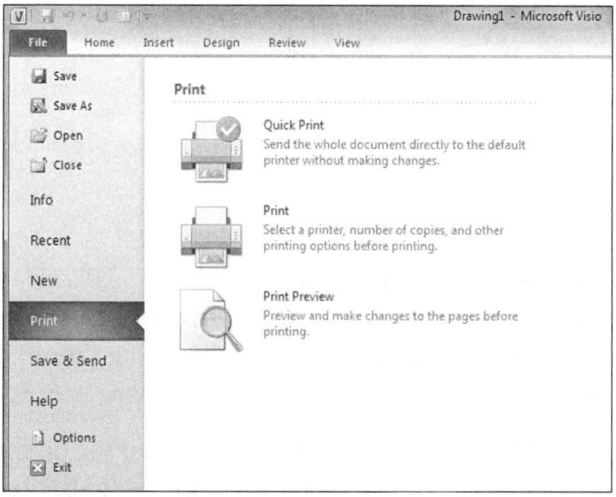

Figure 9.2 *Print options in the Backstage area.*

3. The top button, Quick Print, prints to your default printer without asking questions. No dialogs, no choices, just print. If you want to test printing from Visio, go ahead and click it. If you're a paper-saver, skip this step.

   I rarely use this button because I like to review what I'm about to print. I've had too many experiences of sending what I thought was a small print job to the printer, only to end up with a whole stack of wasted paper.

   Another caveat: The Quick Print caption says that it sends the whole document to the default printer, but my experience is that it sends only the current page to the printer.

4. Click the Print button to open a standard Print dialog, as shown in Figure 9.3. It contains options for choosing a printer, along with which pages and how many copies to print.

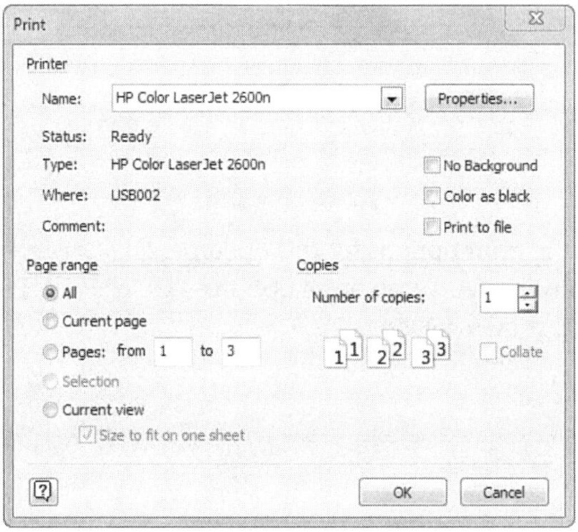

Figure 9.3 *Visio's Print dialog.*

   Note that you can choose Current View under Page Range to print exactly what is shown in the current drawing window. This is a Visio user favorite, which was missing from earlier versions of Visio. Just zoom in on a detail that you want to print and use this option. No more Print Screen key!

5. Click the Properties button in the Print dialog. You see options for your printer. The dialog that appears varies from printer to printer and contains printer-specific features and options.

I frequently visit Printer Properties to print multiple pages on a sheet of paper and to specify duplex printing. Because most of the printing I do is "rough draft" printing, I like to save paper. Figure 9.4 shows the settings for my HP printer.

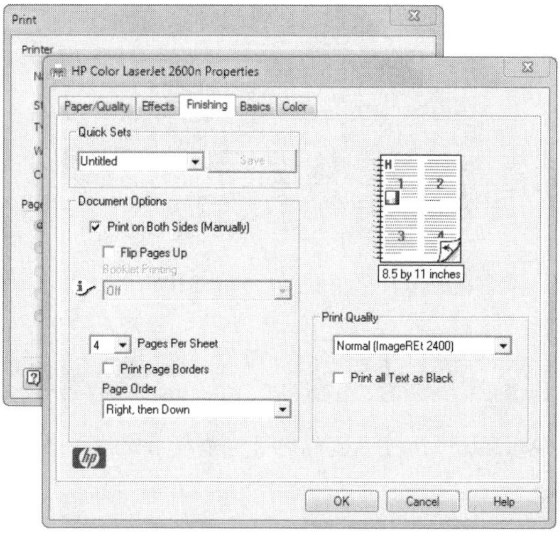

Figure 9.4 *Specifying four pages per sheet and duplex printing for an HP LaserJet 2600n printer.*

6. Return to File, Print by cancelling the dialogs, and click Print Preview. You see the Print Preview view of your document, as shown in Figure 9.5.

   Print Preview looks like a normal drawing window, but there are some key differences:

   a. The Ribbon has only one tab: Print Preview.

   b. You can access all pages via tabs, but you can't make edits or select shapes.

   c. The mouse cursor is a magnifying glass that enables you to toggle between fit-to-page and 100% zoom levels by clicking.

   d. Stencils and other task panes are hidden.

   e. The grid is hidden (unless you've chosen to print the grid via Page Setup, Print Setup, Print gridlines).

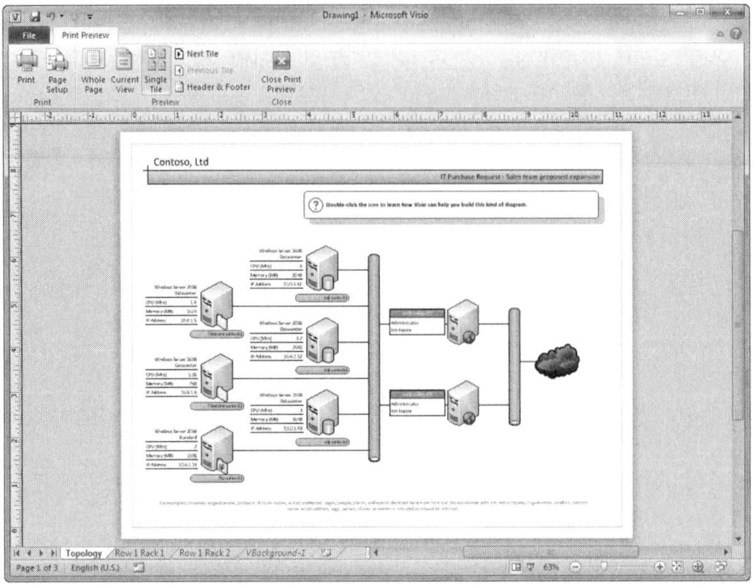

Figure 9.5 *Print Preview for the IT Asset Management sample drawing.*

7. Save this drawing as **Ch09 Printing IT Assets.vsd** so that you can use it in future exercises.

Print Preview

For your sample drawing, Print Preview looks pretty much as it does in the drawing window. Because all three pages are landscape oriented, on standard office page sizes, this is expected.

Print Preview's usefulness is more apparent when you have drawings that are tiled across several sheets of paper, have odd page sizes, or have multiple pages with mixed orientations.

SHOW ME **Media 9.1—Exploring Print Preview**
Access this video file through your registered Web Edition at ***my.safaribooksonline.com/9780132182683/media.***

So let's experiment and make the sample's Print Preview more interesting.

LET ME TRY IT

Exploring Print Preview

1. Continue using the file Ch09 Printing IT Assets.vsd that you created earlier.
2. Go to File, Print Preview.
3. Note that Print Preview has a Print button, which is the same as the one you see in the Backstage area.
4. Print Preview also has a Page Setup button, seen in previous chapters, that lets you configure many different page settings. This is the same Page Setup that you access by right-clicking page tabs or access from the Design tab.
5. Say you want to blow up a drawing to make a poster, but you don't have a large-format printer. You can magnify the printed size of the current page, and tile it across several sheets of printer paper. You don't have to alter the drawing at all!
    a. Click Page Setup and find the Print Zoom section of the Print Setup tab.
    b. Set the page to Fit to 3 Sheets Across by 3 Sheets Down. Note how the preview area on the right gives you an idea of how the page will print.
    c. Click OK to return to the Print Preview window. Notice the dashed lines dividing the page into nine sections. These are page tiles and indicate that this drawing will print across nine sheets of paper. Each page tile represents one piece of printer paper. After you print, you can trim the pages and tape them together.
6. Experiment with the Whole Page and Single Tile buttons.

    In Whole Page view, notice the red rectangles that appear around page tiles when you move the mouse cursor. When you see a red rectangle, clicking zooms in to show just a page tile up close. Clicking a second time zooms out again. You can check individual page tiles to see whether important information falls near the edge of the tile and might get lost when you cut and paste the sheets together.
7. Experiment with the Next Tile and Previous Tile buttons. They cycle through all the page tiles for your document and show you what will come out of the printer.

The IT Asset Management document has 3 pages plus one background page. Because of the modified Fit To settings for the first page, it now prints on 11 sheets. The background page doesn't print, and Next Tile stops short of the background page.

Note also that Fit to 3 x 3 affected only the first page in the document. The other two pages will still print on one sheet of paper each.

8. Click the big, red Close Print Preview button to return to the normal Visio environment.
9. Go to page 2 of the document—Row 1, Rack 1.
10. Change the orientation of the drawing to Portrait. On the Design tab, click the Orientation button and choose Portrait. The drawing page becomes vertically oriented and some of the shapes fall outside the page border. You can reposition the shapes so that they are on the paper and centered if you like.
11. Return to Print Preview. As you flip through the page tiles, see how page 2 is now oriented to landscape? The Orientation button handles the rotation of both the Visio page and printer paper.

    If you change a page's orientation using the Page Setup dialog, you need to make changes on the Print Setup and Page Setup tabs; otherwise, the printer and page settings won't agree.

I always start with Print Preview because I like to resize drawings to odd page sizes. If you anticipate creating complex documents that have multiple pages with different sizes, scales, or orientations, you should always start with Print Preview before you print.

You can speed up the process by adding Print Preview to the Quick Access Toolbar.

LET ME TRY IT

Adding Print Preview to the Quick Access Toolbar

1. Click the Customize Quick Access Toolbar drop-down arrow in the top-left corner of Visio's main window.
2. Select Print Preview from the list. You should now see the Print Preview icon—a sheet of paper with a magnifying glass.

Now you don't have to go to File, Print every time you want to print or check how your document will print.

The only remaining reason to go to the Backstage area is for Quick Print (which isn't very quick if you have to go the Backstage area). If you use Quick Print frequently, you can add it to the Quick Access Toolbar too. It is one of the standard items in the drop-down list; located immediately above Print Preview.

Experimenting with Printing Without Wasting Trees

Whether you are learning the ins and outs of Visio's complex printing features or configuring a complicated document for output, wouldn't it be great to test printing without wasting paper?

You've just seen how easily a 3-page document can turn into 11 pages of output. Clearly, Visio's print options are numerous, and the potential to mess up print jobs for complex documents is there.

Luckily, in addition to Print Preview, you have another way to protect the forests. You can print to a file instead of to an actual printer. When you print to a file, you create a PDF or XPS (Microsoft XML Paper Specification) file. This file contains a sheet-by-sheet picture of your print job, which you can view in the appropriate viewer, and decide whether or not to print.

SHOW ME **Media 9.2—Testing Print Settings by Printing to PDF or XPS Files**

Access this video file through your registered Web Edition at ***my.safaribooksonline.com/9780132182683/media.***

LET ME TRY IT

Testing Print Settings by Printing to File

1. Continue using the file Ch09 Printing IT Assets.vsd that you created earlier.
2. Go to File, Print and then click Print. Alternatively, if you added Print Preview to the Quick Access Toolbar, click it and then click Print on the Ribbon.
3. Choose a PDF or XPS printer instead of a physical printer. In the Name drop-down of the Print dialog, choose Microsoft XPS Document Writer, as shown in Figure 9.6.

   Note that Office 2010 and Visio 2010 install the Microsoft XPS Document Writer and XPS Viewer by default. You might not have these utilities if your IT department has decided not to install them.

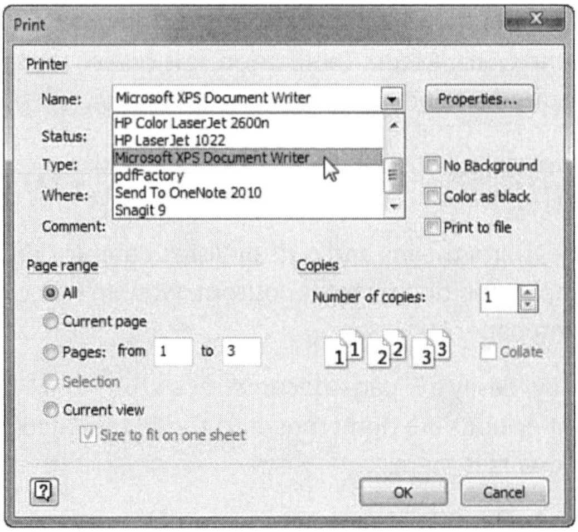

Figure 9.6 *Choosing a print-to-file printer driver. Note the other "virtual printers" in the list: pdfFactory, Send To OneNote 2010, and Snagit 9 (a screen-capturing utility).*

4. Click OK. You are prompted to choose a location and name for the XPS file that is about to be created. Choose an easy-to-remember location, such as your desktop; enter a name; and then click Save. A new XPS file is created.

5. Using Explorer, browse to the location of the saved XPS file and then double-click the file. It opens in the XPS Viewer, and you can examine each sheet of paper that your print settings create.

You can use this XPS file to check that your Visio document will print as expected then print from Visio, or you can print directly from the XPS Viewer itself.

Printing to files is a great way to learn how to print with Visio because you are able to double-check complex jobs. You can also create print jobs when you are working away from your printer.

If you like working like this, consider making the Microsoft XPS Document Writer your system's default printer so that you don't have to choose it in the Print dialog every time. Be aware that setting the default printer affects all your applications, not just Visio, so you might not want to do it. However, the change is easy to do and easy to undo, so it's worth exploring.

LET ME TRY IT

Setting the Default Printer (Windows 7)

1. Click the Windows Start button in the lower-left corner of your screen.
2. Select Devices and Printers in the menu. The Devices and Printers window appears.
3. Expand the Printers and Faxes area and locate the Microsoft XPS Document Writer item.
4. Right click the icon and select Set as Default Printer, as shown in Figure 9.7.

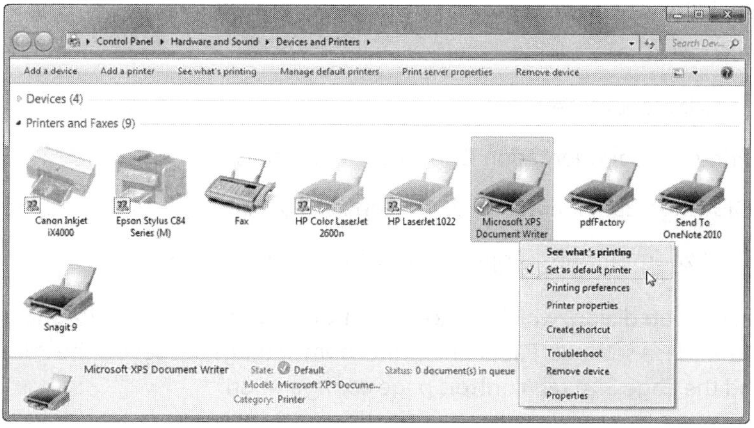

Figure 9.7 *Setting the default printer to the XPS Document Writer.*

The XPS Document Writer is now your default printer. If you choose Quick Print now, the XPS Document Writer is used, so you won't burn any paper without a chance to stop. When you click Print, the XPS Writer is already selected in the printer list, saving you that step each time.

To restore your normal default printer, just follow the steps in the last exercise, except right-click on the physical printer to set it as default.

Understanding Printing

By now, you've noticed that several independent factors influence your printed output. If you understand them, you will have an easier time solving printing problems and properly printing your diagrams.

Keeping Print Variables in Mind

First, notice the vocabulary. The words *printer*, *paper*, and *sheet* are used for the physical output. The words *drawing* and *page* are used for the virtual canvas inside Visio.

You also need to keep the following variables in mind for each page in your document. They can be adjusted in numerous ways, offering rich and complicated printing possibilities:

- Printer paper size
- Drawing page size
- Printer paper orientation (Landscape or Portrait)
- Drawing page orientation (Landscape or Portrait)
- Print zoom settings (Adjust to % or Fit to *X* by *Y* sheets)

The Page Setup dialog, which is accessible from many places in Visio, enables you to control these settings. Paper and print zoom settings are set on the Print Setup tab, and the Page Size tab controls page configuration.

On the Ribbon, the Design tab also has the Page Setup group, which enables you to set orientation and size. These controls differ from the Page Setup dialog in that they set the size and orientation for both printer paper and the page at the same time. This capability is a great convenience but can be confusing if you are accustomed to setting paper and page settings independently via Page Setup.

TELL ME MORE **Media 9.3—Don't Resize Shapes, Configure Printer Settings!**

Access this audio file through your registered Web Edition at ***my.safaribooksonline.com/9780132182683/media.***

If you use the Page Setup dialog to independently size and orient page and paper, you might occasionally configure a mismatch. A common misstep is to have paper and page settings with different orientations.

Visio helps in two ways. First, the Print Setup and Page Size tabs in the Page Setup dialog have preview areas on the right that illustrate the relationship between page and paper.

Second, when you send the job to the printer, Visio will warn you about mismatched orientations with this pop-up:

"One or more drawing pages is oriented differently from the printed page setup. Click OK to print your drawing across multiple pages. To match orientations, change the printed page orientation."

This warning enables you to cancel the print command and reconfigure your settings before any paper is harmed.

Looking at a Complicated Print Job from a Simple Document

The IT Asset Management sample drawing is a fairly simple document with three pages (see Figure 9.1), all of which are oriented horizontally and have typical page and paper sizes.

By playing with paper and page sizes and orientations, you can create a complicated set of printings, such as the example shown in Figure 9.8, without altering the shapes in the drawing.

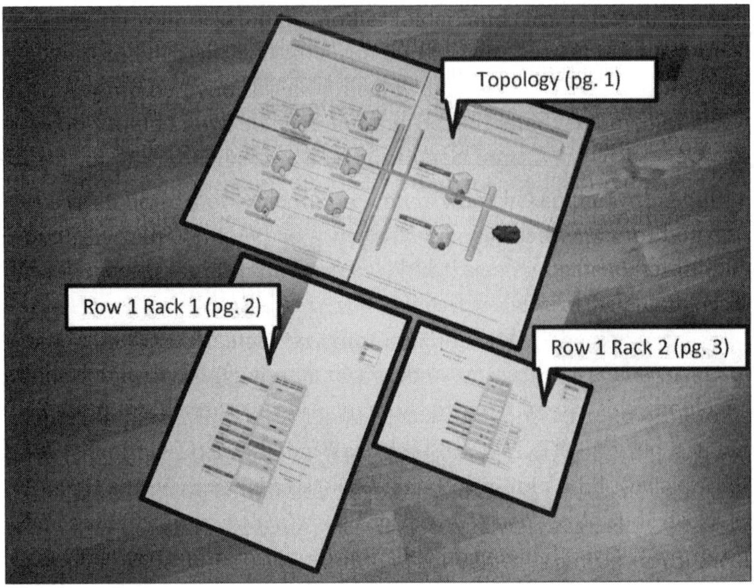

Figure 9.8 *After manipulating printer and page settings, the IT Asset Management sample's three pages printed on six sheets of paper with various sizes and orientations.*

Let's go over each page shown in Figure 9.8, look at the paper and page settings, and point out interesting features for each case.

Page 1: Topology	
Scale	1:1
Paper size	A4
Paper orientation	Landscape
Page size	Letter
Page orientation	Landscape
Print zoom	Fit to two sheets across by two sheets down

Page 1 is enlarged and spread across four sheets of paper. Because I am an American living in Germany, I still like to work with U.S. Units templates, but I print on metric-sized paper. Notice in the preceding table that the page is Letter-sized, but the paper size is A4. A4 is a metric size that is very close to Letter (see the note at the end of this section for more information on paper sizes around the world).

I used the Print Zoom setting to spread it across four sheets of paper. With some scissors, tape, and a bit of patience, I can piece together a large rendition of the Topology page.

Page 2: Row 1 Rack 1	
Scale	1:12
Paper size	A3
Paper orientation	Portrait
Page size	Letter
Page orientation	Portrait
Print zoom	Fit to one sheet across by one sheet down

For page 2, I changed settings for both page and printer paper. First, I set the page orientation to Portrait but left the page size as Letter. I then set the paper size to A3, Portrait. A3 paper is twice the size as normal office paper and similar to US Tabloid size paper.

It's important to note that the printer paper is much bigger than the page size. The Fit to 1 Sheet Across by 1 Sheet Down print zoom setting effectively magnifies the output, doing its best to fit the page contents to the paper.

If your printer has several trays that can hold different-sized paper, you might be able to send the whole document to one printer in one step. For this example, however, I had to print each page separately. Page 1 and page 3 went to my normal laser printer, but page 2 was sent to my large-format inkjet.

Page 3: Row 1 Rack 2	
Scale	1:12
Paper size	A4
Paper orientation	Landscape
Page size	Letter
Page orientation	Landscape
Print zoom	Fit to one sheet across by one sheet down

The last page has pretty much an unchanged setup, except that the page size is Letter and the printer paper is A4. Although these are nearly the same size, Print Zoom still plays a small role.

If I use Adjust to 100% instead of Fit to 1 Sheet Across by 1 Sheet Down, I get two pages, one of which is blank. The Fit To setting squeezes the fatter Letter-sized page onto the skinnier A4 paper, with a slight reduction in size to make it work. Using 100% tells Visio that you don't want any resizing to happen in the printout, and the slight mismatch between A4 and Letter results in page tiling.

Another option is to change the drawing page size to A4, too. Because no details of this drawing are against the edge of the page, this is a harmless modification. Matching page size and paper size simplifies things and reduces confusion.

The standard paper size in the United States is called Letter and is 8.5 × 11 inches. In the rest of the world, A4 is common, measuring 210 × 297 millimeters.

To put the most common paper sizes in perspective, U.S. Letter is 0.2 inches (6 mm) wider than A4 paper, but 0.7 inches (18 mm) shorter.

If your company has offices across the globe, it may be helpful to know about the paper sizes that your overseas colleagues use.

Sheet-size Name	U.S. Units (inches)	Metric Units (mm)
Letter or A	8.5 × 11	216 × 279
Legal	8.5 × 14	216 × 356
Tabloid or B	11 × 17	279 × 432
C	17 × 22	432 × 559
D	22 × 34	559 × 864
E	34 × 44	864 × 1118
A4	8.3 × 11.7	210 × 297
A3	11.7 × 16.5	297 × 420
A2	16.5 × 23.4	420 × 594
A1	23.4 × 33.1	594 × 841

Headers and Footers and Print Margins

Print Preview is the place to edit and see headers and footers. Just click the Header & Footer button on the Print Preview Ribbon. The information and fields that you can add to headers and footers are discussed in Chapter 3, "Organizing and Annotating Diagrams."

Inside the Header & Footer dialog, you see two Margin fields for controlling the distance of the header and footer from the top and bottom of the page, respectively. These settings are independent of the print margins. Although it is nice to have headers and footers as out of the way as possible, make sure that you don't get too close to the edges of the paper; otherwise, they get cut off by the printer.

You can set print margins via the Page Setup dialog. Just go to the Print Setup tab and then click Setup. The Print Setup dialog appears and contains left, right, top, and bottom print margin fields. The default values are 0.25 in. or 6.28 mm. Your actual printer might have different capabilities. Visio does its best to understand the specified printer's capabilities and not let you set smaller values than the printer can handle. In Print Preview, you see a border around the page that represents the print margins. This is a helpful guide when checking header and footer margins and checking whether details of your drawing are likely to be cut off by the printer.

The print margins are also visible in the drawing window if page breaks are turned on. Go to View, Show and check the Page Breaks box. Figure 9.9 shows print margins in the drawing window, as well as the settings in the Print Setup dialog.

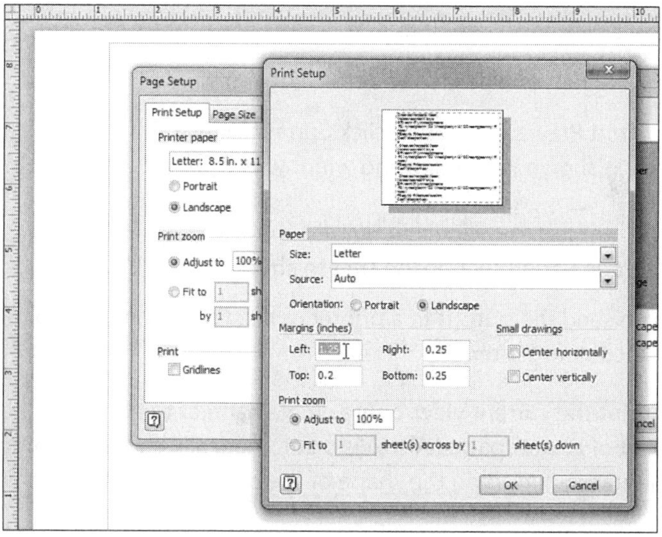

Figure 9.9 *Going wild with print margins in the Print Setup dialog.*

If you are printing drawings that are tiled across multiple sheets of paper, you actually want your print margin values to be a bit larger than your printer's limit so that you get some overlap from tile to tile. Having this overlap makes it easier to trim each sheet and paste them together.

Printing Scenarios

Visio's print, print zoom, and page settings offer innumerable combinations for getting drawings onto paper. Examining all the variations is mind-numbing and could possibly prevent you from reaching the next chapter.

Instead, let's look at a few scenarios and discuss what it takes to get the proper output for each of them.

Printing Part of a Diagram

While you work, you zoom in and out, and pan around to get a better view of specific parts of your drawing. You can print any view of your diagram—exactly what is showing in the drawing window, and you can have it fill up an entire sheet of paper so your output is as easy to see as possible.

LET ME TRY IT

Printing the Current View

1. Start with any Visio drawing.
2. Zoom and pan to a particular detail that you would like to print.
3. Go to Print Preview and then click Current View. You should see roughly what was shown in the drawing window before you entered Print Preview.
4. Click Print. The Print dialog appears.
5. In the Page Range section, be sure to check Current View.
6. You can send the output to a printer or just test by printing to the Microsoft XPS Document Writer.

When you print the current view, only a single page of the document is printed, on a single sheet of printer paper. Also, Visio automatically chooses a landscape or portrait orientation based on the shape of the current drawing window.

Selectively Printing Elements in a Drawing

You've seen how you can print the current view, but there are a few other granular options for printing subsets of a Visio drawing.

Printing Specific Pages

The Print dialog's Page Range section enables you to print the current page or a range of pages by specifying starting and ending page numbers. However, you can't print disjointed ranges of pages like you can in Word.

Printing Background Pages

Normally, background pages don't explicitly print on separate sheets; they accompany the foreground pages to which they are assigned. However, you can print a background page by selecting its page tab in the drawing window and then selecting Current Page in the Page Range section of the Print dialog.

Printing Selected Shapes

You can print just the shapes that are selected in the active drawing window. To do this, choose Selection from the Print dialog's Page Range section.

Oddly, this option doesn't work if you go through Print Preview; Selection is disabled via this route. You have to use the Backstage area and go to the Print dialog via File, Print, Print.

Printing Shapes by Layer

In Chapter 3, "Organizing and Annotating Diagrams," we discussed assigning shapes to layers and setting various attributes for those layers. One layer property is Print, which you can check or uncheck via Home, Editing, Layers, Layer Properties.

Layers that have their Print property deselected do not print, which is useful for simplifying drawings, focusing on specific details, or hiding sensitive data.

You can also show and hide shapes of a layer using the Visible layer property. It is important to note, however, that invisible layers still print unless their Print attribute is unchecked. This can lead to unwanted surprises, so be sure to check Print Preview first.

Printing Gridlines

If you like to see the grid while you work, you can turn it on via View, Show, Grid. You can also see gridlines in your printed output. On the Print Setup tab of the Page Setup dialog, notice the Gridlines check box in the bottom-left corner. Check this option to make the grid print.

Printed gridlines are great if you plan to pencil in some details on your hard copy. They also help you estimate the sizes of objects in scaled drawings, as well as align things horizontally and vertically.

Saving Ink by Not Printing Backgrounds

Fancy backgrounds and themes add flair to your drawings but use up a lot of printer toner. You can ease the load on your printer when printing drafts by turning off background page printing.

The Print dialog has a No Background check box in the top-right corner. Check this option to omit background pages from your print job.

Printing Tiled Drawings

You've learned how to enlarge printed output by tiling a single page across several sheets of paper.

If you create flowcharts and other connected diagrams using the AutoSize feature, you have a sort of flipped situation. As your diagram grows, your drawing is tiled across several drawing pages, and will print on several sheets of paper by default.

When you print such a diagram, you may choose to accept the defaults and piece the tiled sheets of paper together, or you might want to shrink the whole diagram to print on one sheet of paper.

LET ME TRY IT

Printing Drawings with Multiple Page Tiles

1. Start a new diagram using Network, Basic Network Diagram template.
2. Drop a Server shape in the middle of the page.
3. Use AutoConnect to join two more servers to the first: one to the right and one below.
4. Drag the server on the right to the edge of the page until AutoSize inserts a new page tile. (AutoSize is on by default for the Basic Network Diagram template.)
5. Similarly, drag the bottom server down until AutoSize adds another page tile beneath the original. Figure 9.10 illustrates how the diagram looks. Note that your drawing now spans four page tiles.
6. Go to Print Preview.

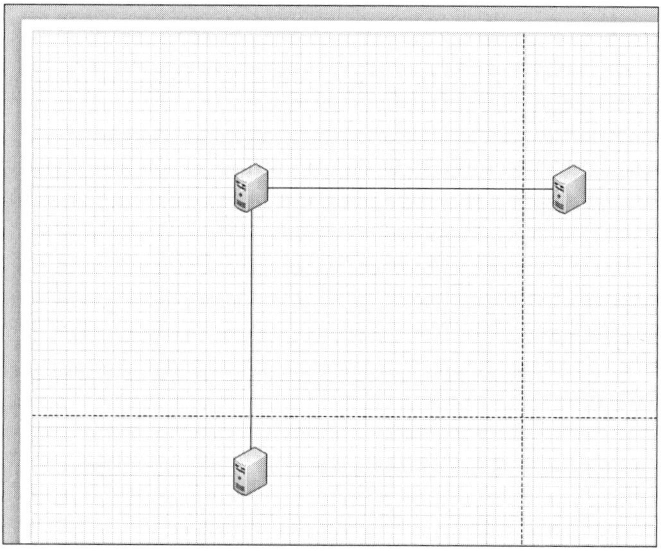

Figure 9.10 *A simple network diagram, spread across four page tiles. Dashed lines indicate where the tiles fall, and the printed pages overlap.*

7. Click the Whole Page button. You see dashed page-break lines that indicate your drawing will print on four sheets. Move the mouse cursor across the page and notice the four red highlight rectangles that appear. Click any tile to zoom in on it. Click Whole Page to zoom back out. If you print this drawing, your output will be tiled across four sheets of paper, as expected.

8. Click the Page Setup button. In the Print Zoom section, set the output to Fit to 1 Sheet Across by 1 Sheet Down and then click OK. Back in the Print Preview window, notice that the page-break lines are now gone. Your four-page diagram is reduced to print on just one sheet of paper.

9. Click Page Setup again. In the Print Zoom section, select Adjust to 100% and then click OK. The page-break lines reappear, and your drawing again is set to print across four sheets of paper.

AutoSize enables you to work freely, expanding the drawing surface for you automatically as you draw. You don't need to worry about the size of the drawing surface or the size of your shapes because you can enlarge or reduce at print time instead.

Understanding How AutoSize Affects Printing and Backgrounds

You should be aware of a few things about AutoSize, however, especially if you add backgrounds and titles to your drawings.

- Visio expands the titles and backgrounds to fit the entire drawing page surface, but sometimes there are problems like the one shown in Figure 9.11.

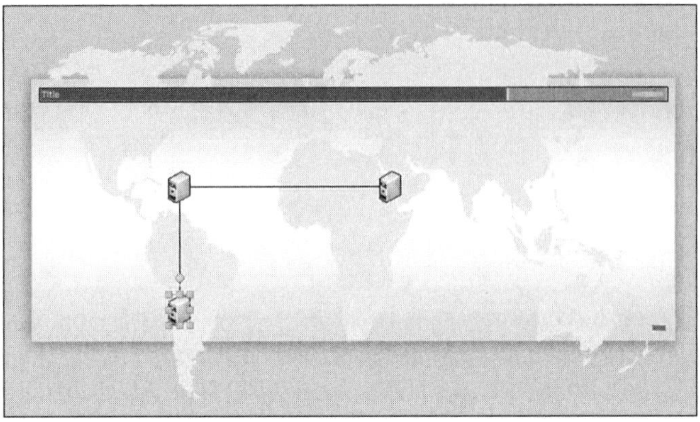

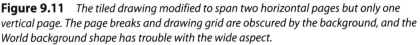

Figure 9.11 *The tiled drawing modified to span two horizontal pages but only one vertical page. The page breaks and drawing grid are obscured by the background, and the World background shape has trouble with the wide aspect.*

- Backgrounds obscure page breaks and the grid.
- Page breaks are obscured by backgrounds in Print Preview as well, but you can use the Single Tile, Next Tile, and Previous Tile buttons when you aren't sure how the drawing will be tiled.
- Shapes on or near page breaks are printed on multiple sheets, as shown in Figure 9.12. Because you need to trim away the blank margins on some of the sheet, Visio prints with extra overlap so that you can be less precise in your cutting.
- Page tiles are smaller than the chosen printer paper size in order to account for margins and page-tiling overlap. In Figure 9.12, you see page breaks for a drawing that is tiled across letter-sized paper (8.5 × 11 inches), but the tiles themselves are smaller because Visio takes the print margins into account. In fact, if you have more than three tiles in any direction, the inner tiles are smaller than the outer tiles because they have overlap on both sides.

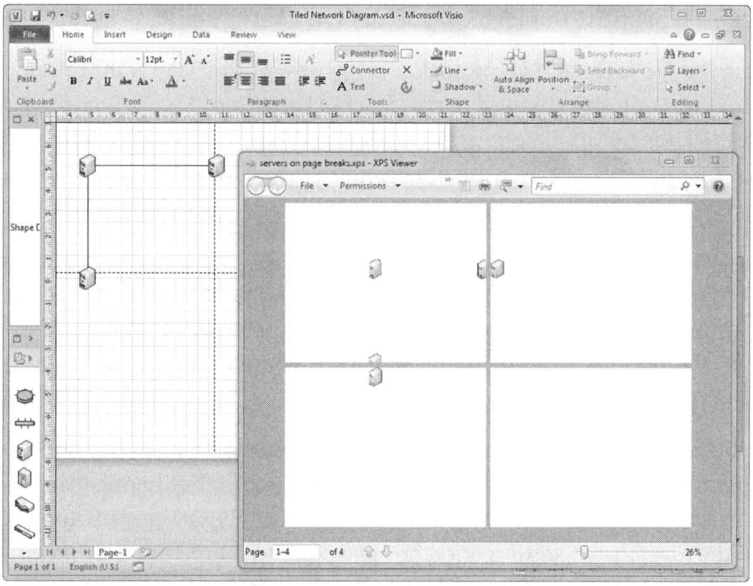

Figure 9.12 *Viewing tiled output in the XPS Viewer. Notice that shapes near page breaks are printed doubly to make trimming and assembling the separate sheets easier. Because most printers can't print to the very edge of the paper, some of the detail near the edges won't print at all, so the overlap isn't as extreme as it appears.*

Printing Complex, Mixed-Orientation Drawings

You may have a complex drawing with multiple pages, different scales, different page orientations, different sizes, and different background pages. I often see Visio files that represent a "project" of drawings. They typically include the following:

- A title page explaining the purpose, conventions, and symbols of the drawing. These are usually unscaled, with landscape orientation.
- A few pages of floor plan layouts showing equipment locations, wiring paths, lighting, and other technical details. These are usually scaled, with landscape orientation.
- Several pages of detailed drawings showing elevation views of rack-mounted equipment and other gadgetry. These scaled drawings usually have portrait orientation.
- All pages in the drawing that require a common frame, title, title block, and company logo. These details are often on a single background page shared by the rest of the document.

Visio can handle printing such a document, but you should take extra care to inspect each page in Print Preview and double-check your Page Setup settings.

Because the file represents a project of drawings, you usually want to print each page on the same size sheet of paper. So check the Print Setup, Printer Paper setting in the Page Setup dialog for each page in the document. (If your printer has multiple paper trays, you may be able to send mixed-size pages to the same printer.)

If you have mixed landscape and portrait page orientations across pages, be sure that the Print Setup and Page Size settings for orientation agree for each page. The Page Setup dialog has preview areas for both of these tabs that make it obvious when orientations differ, and you receive a last-chance warning just before printing if orientations don't match.

After you've verified that the printer paper is the same for all pages and orientations match, you can decide how to print each page to that paper. If all your pages have the same size, you don't need to worry about this. Otherwise, turn your attention to the Print Zoom setting and choose Adjust to 100% (or other zoom) or tile the drawing using Fit to *X* Sheets Across by *Y* Sheets Down.

Printing Any Size Drawing on Any Size Paper

A friend of mine who works at Microsoft is a big fan of Visio and occasionally writes about it in his blog: Saveen Reddy's blog. (http://blogs.msdn.com/b/saveenr/) He uses Visio as a tool for quickly getting his thoughts and ideas diagrammed and regularly brings the printouts to team meetings for discussion and brainstorming.

Interestingly, he never worries about the page size of his Visio drawings at all. He freely drags, drops, connects, and tweaks shapes all over the place and then resizes the page to fit the content, using one of the following methods:

1. Turning on AutoSize from the Design tab. Visio automatically adds and removes full page tiles as the diagram grows or shrinks.
2. Clicking the Size drop-down on the Design tab and choosing Fit to Drawing at the bottom of the list. The page contracts or expands to tightly enclose all details.
3. Manually resizing the page by holding Ctrl while dragging an edge of the page, which you learned about in Chapter 2, "Working Around the Diagram."

As you can easily guess, his page sizes rarely match any existing printer paper size. Because Saveen understands how printing works in Visio, however, this isn't a problem.

When it's time to print, he uses only the Print Setup tab in the Page Setup dialog. There, he chooses a paper size that matches his target printer and sets the Print Zoom to Fit to 1 Page Across by 1 Page Down. He can send his output to a normal office laser printer for personal use or to a large-format plotter to create a poster for his next meeting.

Figures 9.13, 9.14, and 9.15 illustrate this process for a very tall drawing.

I call this method of working the "Saveen method," but you might call it the "Don't worry about page size" method. If the actual, physical size of your printed document isn't important, and you don't have style requirements or corporate standards for page sizes, borders, and title blocks, this is a great way to work.

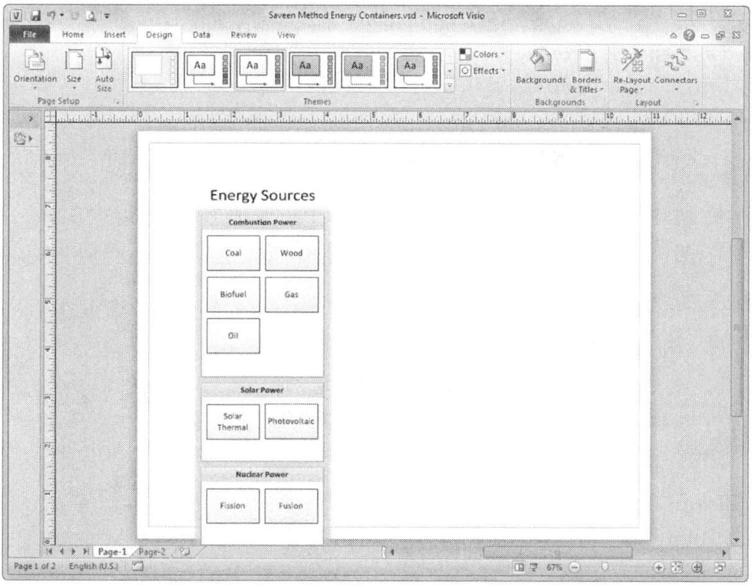

Figure 9.13 *The Energy Sources diagram has been rearranged to a very tall format and doesn't fit on the page any more.*

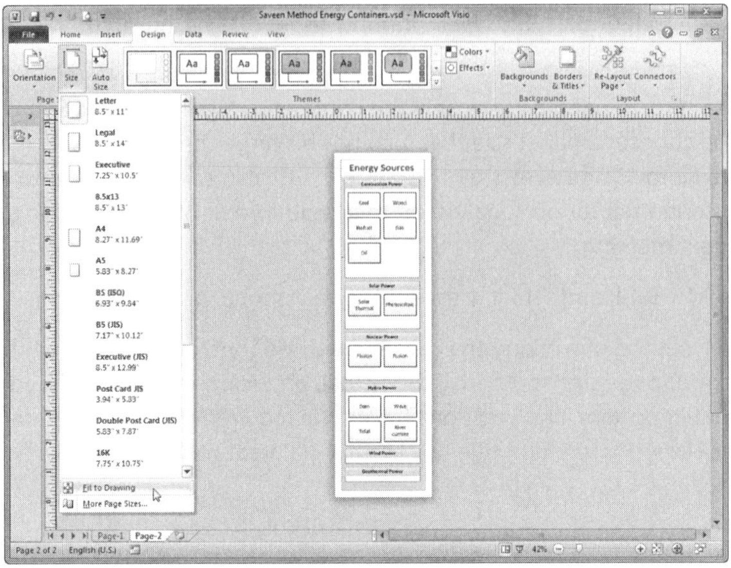

Figure 9.14 *A quick visit to the Design tab and click of Size, Fit to Drawing expands the page to tightly enclose the content.*

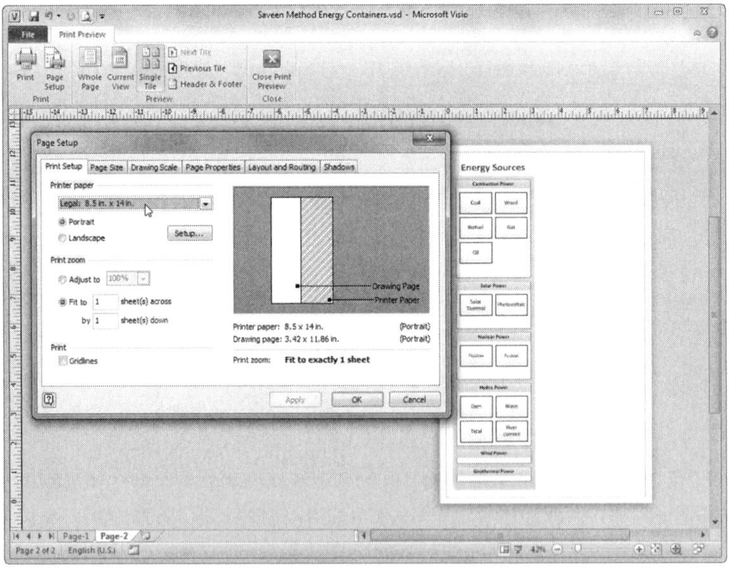

Figure 9.15 *In Print Preview, the Page Setup dialog is used to print the page to legal-sized paper. Print Zoom is set to 1 Sheet Across by 1 Sheet Down, and Visio scales the drawing to fit the paper.*

Printing Multiple Drawings on a Single Sheet

When you have photos developed or professionally printed, you receive a proof sheet with thumbnail images of every photo in the batch. You might want to do something similar with Visio.

You've seen that you can tile one page across several sheets of paper. But how do you print several pages on one sheet of paper?

Although there is no explicit feature for doing this, there are several strategies for getting it done:

1. Use your printer's features to print multiple pages per sheet.
2. Copy and paste each page to a new document.
3. Export or copy each page as an image or metafile and then import or paste into a new document.

Using Printer Features

Not all printers have the same features, but many have the option to print multiple pages on one sheet of paper. For example, my HP LaserJet 2600 lets me print 1, 2, 4, 6, 9, or 16 pages per sheet. To do this, I go to the Print dialog, click Properties, click the Finishing tab, and then choose a number from the Pages Per Sheet drop-down list.

Pasting Multiple Pages on a Single Page

You can copy each page and then paste it into another document. Although this sounds simple enough, many problems can surface:

- To fit several pages onto one page, you need to resize each page's contents after pasting. SmartShape behavior can actually get in the way of mass resizing, and create quite a mess.
- Connectors might reroute, causing more mess.
- Individual pages can have different theme effects, theme colors, backgrounds, and titles. Pasting all to the same page forces them to share the same combination, which might not be what you want.
- Pages might have different scales. A single page can have only one scale, so scale-related conflicts might arise.
- Resizing an entire page's elements doesn't resize font sizes. When you reduce the size of a pasted drawing, the shapes shrink, but the text doesn't.

Using an Export Format

The most flexible way to create a proof sheet is to convert each page into a metafile and then import each object into a blank drawing. Since metafiles are "dumb graphics," you can freely resize each one without encountering the problems described previously.

SHOW ME **Media 9.4—Creating a "Proof Sheet" for a Multi-page Document**

Access this video file through your registered Web Edition at ***my.safaribooksonline.com/9780132182683/media.***

LET ME TRY IT

Printing Multiple Pages on One Sheet of Paper Using Copy and Paste

1. Start a new drawing from the IT Asset Management sample.
2. Start a new, blank drawing.
3. Tile the two drawing windows so that you can see both at the same time. Go to View, Window, Arrange All to do this.
4. Go to the first page in the IT Asset Management sample. Make sure that no shapes are selected.
5. Right-click a blank area on the page and select Copy. This copies all the page's graphics plus any background-page details to the Clipboard.
6. In the blank drawing, right-click the page and choose Paste Special. The Paste Special dialog appears.
7. Choose Picture (Enhanced Metafile) from the list and then click OK. The copied page is pasted as a single vector-graphic object that you can freely resize. You won't have any of the resizing problems that you might have found if you had pasted the data as Visio objects.
8. Repeat steps 4 through 7 for each page in the IT Asset Management drawing until you have three objects in the new drawing.
9. The page shapes are likely too big for the drawing page and need to be reduced. Press Ctrl+A to select all the shapes and then drag a corner handle of the selection to reduce the size of all three page shapes at the same time.

10. Neatly rearrange the shapes on the page so that each page shape is clearly visible, as shown in Figure 9.16.

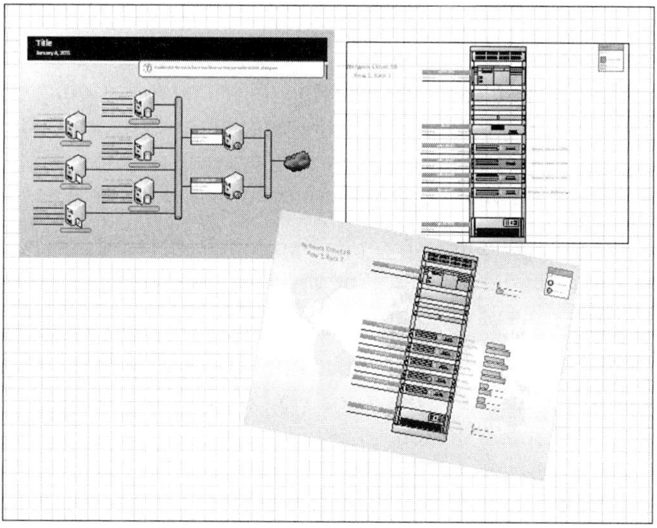

Figure 9.16 *The three IT Asset Management pages copied and then pasted as metafiles in a blank drawing. Note the different backgrounds and titles. Page 3 is rotated, just because you can!*

11. Print to a printer or file as desired.

Another way to achieve the same result is to export each page to a file, using the Save As dialog and choosing the file type Enhanced Metafile (*.emf).

Although this is more labor-intensive, you may have other uses for the exported graphics such as maintaining a time snapshot for your drawing, or using the graphics in other documents.

Metafiles are a good choice for exporting and importing pages because EMF or WMF files are vector formats. When you export (or copy) each Visio page, Visio behavior is stripped out, and only the pure graphical detail is preserved. When you re-import (or paste special) the metafiles, then resize them, the graphics and text will resize equally and print smoothly.

Printing Scaled Drawings at Reduced Size

Scaled drawings are often designed to be printed out on large-format paper, such as C-, D-, E-, A3-, A2-, or A1-sized sheets. These drawings can be very detailed and are used on construction sites; the larger size makes them easier to use in this environment.

You still might need to print them out in the office on regular, office-sized paper. You can do this by using the Print Zoom settings in the Page Setup dialog. The Adjust to % or Fit to *X* Sheets Across by Y Sheets Down settings make it a snap to print a large-format drawing page onto a small sheet of paper.

When you reduce a scaled drawing, it is important to note that scale notations on the drawing are no longer accurate. Better yet, use a physical scale symbol that visually shows the scale of the drawing.

The More Shapes, Visio Extras, Annotations stencil has two scale-indicating shapes that you can use in your scaled drawings. Figure 9.17 shows the Drawing Scale and the Scale Symbol shapes in action.

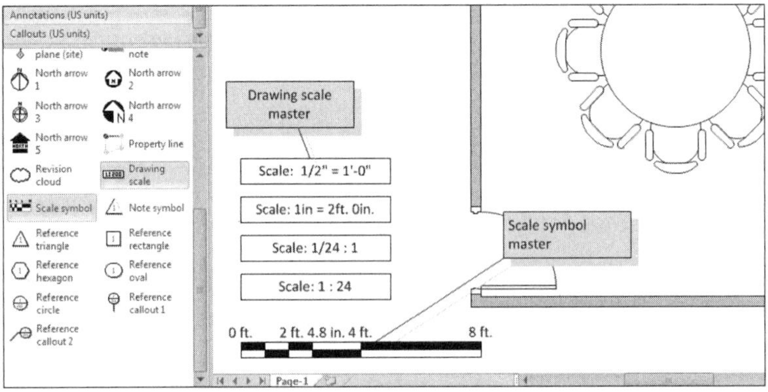

Figure 9.17 *The Drawing Scale shape numerically notes the scale of the drawing in several styles. The Scale Symbol shape visually illustrates it. Both automatically pick up the scale of the drawing page.*

In Figure 9.17, four variations of the Drawing Scale shape are shown. You can choose the text that is displayed by right-clicking the shape. Because the scale information is numerical, it is inaccurate if you reduce the drawing at print time.

A better choice is the Scale Symbol. Because it physically illustrates the drawing scale, it is still accurate in reduced printouts.

If you have used the Drawing Scale shape and want to indicate that the scale information is wrong, consider using another shape from the Annotations stencil. The Rounded Stamp and Angled Stamp masters, as shown in Figure 9.18, are great for making eye-catching notes.

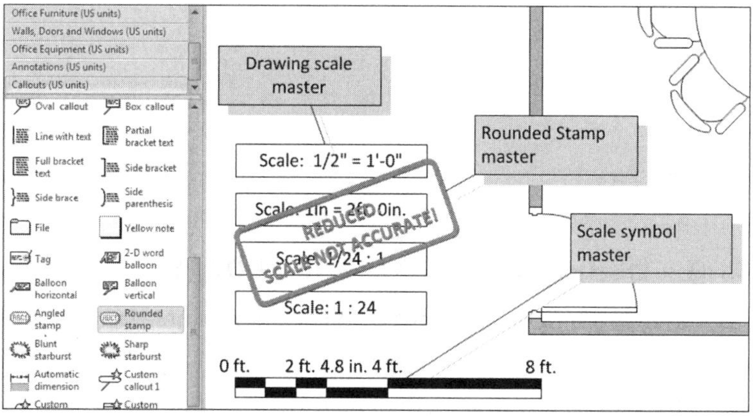

Figure 9.18 *The Rounded Stamp shape makes an eye-catching indication that the scale numbers aren't accurate for reduced-to-print output.*

Printing High-Quality Materials

You've worked all night and created a perfect, beautifully formatted Visio diagram that has lots of color, good-looking themes, gradient fills, and transparency. Your company's leaders are so impressed that they want to use your diagram for a brochure and poster at the next trade show. What do you do to get a good result?

There are a number of issues that can stand in the way of getting great output, suitable for distribution to the public. Among these are

- Your print shop or service bureau might not have Visio and isn't able to read your VSD file. Because Visio evolved as an office app, it doesn't have the print-production pedigree that applications such as Adobe Illustrator or Adobe Photoshop have.
- Some printers have trouble printing gradient fills and transparency from Visio.
- PDF exports can experience similar problems with gradients and transparency.

I've used Visio to create shiny business cards, posters, and brochures, and I've run into all these problems. The solution I use is simple and crude but effective: export your file as a high-resolution bitmap image.

Visio is a vector-based graphics program, and vectors print smoothly, using the full resolution of the printer. Bitmaps are collections of dots that get uglier as you blow them up, so exporting to an image seems to go against the whole purpose of using vectors in the first place.

The secret is to export an image that has the same resolution as the target printer. Since the printer can't print any better than that anyway, the bitmap will print well.

LET ME TRY IT

Exporting a High-Resolution Bitmap Image

1. Start with any sample document from File, New, Sample Diagrams, or open a document that you've created.
2. Go to the page that you want to print. Exporting to an image works for only one page at a time.
3. Make sure that no shapes are selected if you want the whole page to be exported. If you want to export just a portion of the diagram, select the shapes you want.
4. Click File, Save As. The Save As dialog appears.
5. Choose a location for the file and give it a name, such as **High-Res-Visio-Export.bmp**.
6. In the Save As Type drop-down, select Windows Bitmap (*.bmp, *.dib) and then click Save. The BMP Output Options screen appears.
7. In the Resolution section of the dialog, select Custom and enter the resolution of your target printer. You can check your printer's documentation or call your print shop and ask for a sufficient resolution. In Figure 9.19, 600 × 600 dots, or pixels/inch, has been entered.
8. Click OK to save your export. A very large BMP file is created in the location you specified. You can now send this file to the printer and be assured of high-quality printed output.

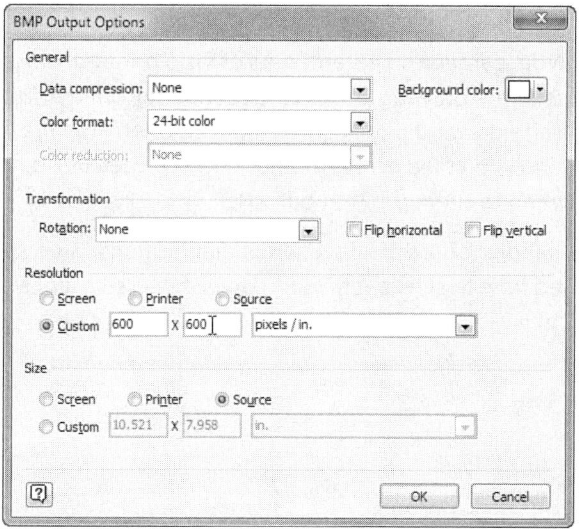

Figure 9.19 *Exporting a page as a bitmap image. Note the custom resolution is set to a respectably high 600 × 600 dpi (dots per inch).*

The BMP file format doesn't use any compression algorithms, as JPG, GIF and PNG do, so the file size will likely be huge. As an example, I exported the Topology Page in the IT Asset Management sample at 600 x 600 dpi. The file size was 88 MB! BMPs retain full-fidelity, so they're still a good choice. The other formats can lose detail and introduce unwanted artifacts in the interest of file compression, so they might not print as well.

If your USB key isn't large enough for such a file, never worry. Bitmaps zip well. That 88 MB file zips to just 915 KB, making transportation and e-mailing practical. To compress, just right-click the file, then choose: Send To Compressed (zipped) Folder.

The resulting file will be readable by any print shop around, and the resulting output will be suitable for public distribution and display.

Summary

In this chapter, you learned the ins and outs of Visio printing. Most importantly, you saw that the size of the drawing page is independent from the size of the paper in the printer. Any size drawing page can be reduced or enlarged to fit onto any size sheet of paper and even tiled across multiple sheets. There is no need to modify shapes in a drawing to serve printing purposes.

You also saw a handful of practical scenarios that demonstrated specific printer settings and learned how to selectively print pages, selected shapes, background pages, shapes on layers, and gridlines.

This chapter explores how you can address all these issues with just a few mouse clicks!

10

Sharing, Publishing, and Exporting Visio Diagrams

Now that you've crystallized your thoughts so eloquently in a well-honed Visio diagram, it's time to get the word out. After all, you want to communicate visually; now is the time to share your visualizations with others.

Visio offers a slew of ways to distribute and share your creations. When choosing one, consider your audience. Should they be able to edit the diagram or not? Do they have Visio installed on their PCs? Should they receive a copy as an email attachment or access the file from a centralized Internet or intranet location? If you are distributing read-only information, does your audience need to interact with the document, for example, by viewing Shape Data, accessing multiple hyperlinks, searching, zooming, and panning?

Sending Visio Files in Email

If you want to quickly zap a copy of a diagram to colleagues, the Send Using E-mail function makes it super easy.

LET ME TRY IT

Sending a Visio File via Email

1. Start with an open Visio document that you want to send. Try from File, New, Sample Diagrams if you just want to run a quick test.
2. Go to the Save & Send panel in the Backstage area. In this chapter, you spend most of your time here, so take a moment to look at all of the Save & Send options.
3. Under the Save & Send column in the left side of the panel, click Send Using E-mail. The right column changes to display four large "Send Using e-mail" buttons: Send as Attachment, Send a Link, Send as PDF, and Send as XPS.

4. Choose one of the options by clicking one of the big square buttons on the right:

   a. To send a copy of the actual Visio file, click Send as Attachment. The recipients receive a Visio file that they can open and edit, independent of the copy on which you are working. If they make changes that you need to re-incorporate into your drawing, you have to do this manually. Visio has no easy way to merge different versions of a file. To eliminate double efforts, you might suggest the recipients use markup to note needed changes instead of editing the document directly.

   b. Send a Link is likely disabled, unless you are editing a file that is saved on the network. This option not only keeps the email size down, but also ensures that everyone is working on the same file. Use this strategy if two or more people need to edit the drawing, and be sure to save your drawing to the network first.

   c. To send a noneditable (or, "not easily editable") snapshot of your document, choose Send as PDF or Send as XPS. PDF is Adobe's ubiquitous portable document format with which you are surely familiar. XPS is Microsoft's XML Paper Specification format that creates portable, printable files that are similar to PDFs.

   A new email window pops up, with your file (or link) attached, and the Subject field filled out with the name of the document.

5. Edit the To, CC, Bcc, and message body fields as you normally would and then send the email.

Sending as PDF or XPS directly within Visio is a great timesaver. It eliminates the traditional steps of saving the file, browsing to it in Explorer, and then copying the file into an email. You don't have to manage copies of PDF or XPS files at all!

Creating Web Pages from Visio Drawings

Visio offers an interesting option for sharing noneditable versions of your diagrams. Saving your diagram as a web page creates dynamic web pages that render high-quality vector-based graphics; support multipage documents; and allow users to pan and zoom, view Shape Data, and search for text.

When this option works, it is fantastic. Unfortunately, there are a few glitches that can mar the experience, as you see later.

Saving as Web Page

The sample IT Asset Management drawing is a great place to test the web export capabilities. This document has multiple pages, shapes with hyperlinks to those pages, plus many shapes with Shape Data fields.

SHOW ME **Media 10.1—Saving a Visio Document as a Web Page**
Access this video file through your registered Web Edition at ***my.safaribooksonline.com/9780132182683/media.***

LET ME TRY IT

Saving a Visio Drawing as a Web Page

1. Start with a copy of the IT Asset Management sample drawing, which you find under File, New, Sample Diagrams.
2. Note the server shapes on the Topology page have hyperlinks that link to the other pages in the document. To follow them, right-click the shapes and choose the link item or hold down the Ctrl key and click a shape.
3. Add several more hyperlinks to the top-left server on the Topology page (this will make the web-export exercise more interesting):
    a. Select the shape and press Ctrl+K to get to the Hyperlinks dialog. Note that a Row 1 Rack 2 link already exists.
    b. Click New. A new hyperlink item appears and is selected.
    c. Enter **www.visguy.com** in the Address field.
    d. Click New again.
    e. Enter **www.lenovo.com** in the Address field.
    f. Click OK. The server shape now has three hyperlinks—one within the document and two that go out to Internet sites.
    g. Ctrl+click the server shape and note the special "multihyperlink" pop-up that appears. You see something similar to Figure 10.1.
4. Save your modified file as **IT Asset Management SAW** (SAW = Save As Web).
5. Export the file as a web page. Go to File, Save & Send, and then click Change File Type. The right-side of the panel displays a wide assortment of output types, which are shown in Figure 10.2.

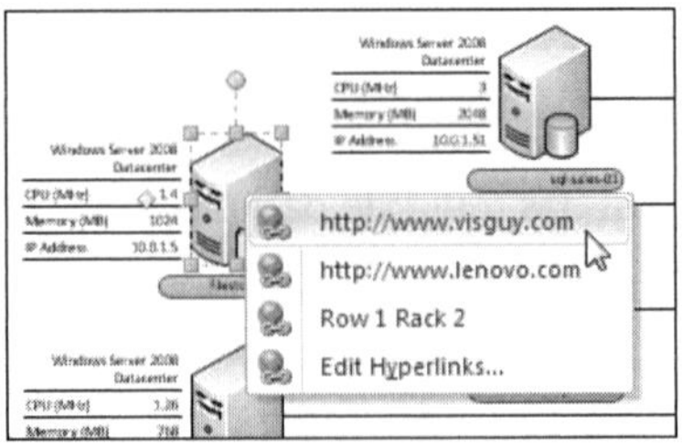

Figure 10.1 *Ctrl+clicking a shape with multiple hyperlinks presents a nifty pop-up for choosing the link to follow.*

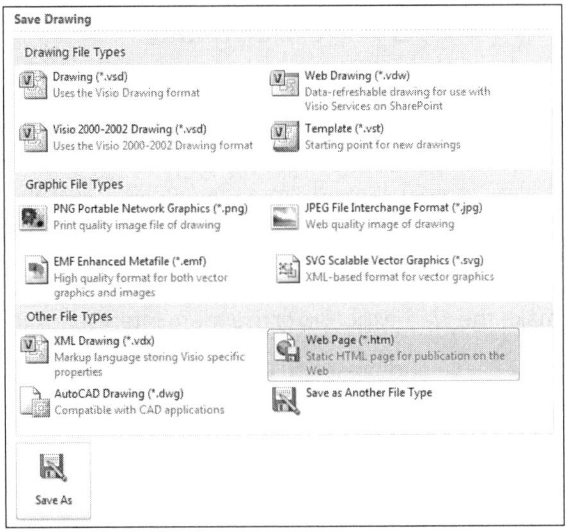

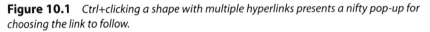

Figure 10.2 *Save & Send's Change File Type option offers many possibilities for saving and exporting Visio diagrams. Note that Web Drawing (*.vdw) is available only in Premium and Pro and relates to Visio Services for SharePoint 2010. For this exercise, we want "Web Page," not "Web Drawing."*

Take a moment to study the Save Drawing file types; you see this screen several more times in this chapter.

6. Double-click Web Page (*.htm). The Save As dialog appears with the Save as Type set to Web Page (*.htm;*.html).

7. Browse to a suitable location on your hard drive and save the file as **IT Asset Management SAW** and then click Save.

The Save as Web page status window appears for a few moments as Visio exports the diagram. Then your default browser opens to reveal the exported web pages. Figure 10.3 shows what you might initially see.

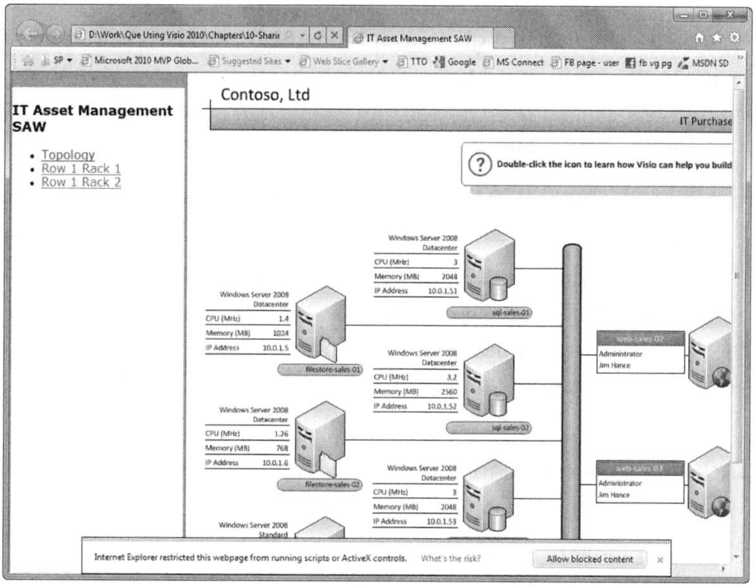

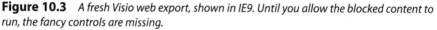

Figure 10.3 *A fresh Visio web export, shown in IE9. Until you allow the blocked content to run, the fancy controls are missing.*

You can also use File, Save As to create a web page. Just select Web Page (*.htm;*.html) in the Save As Type drop-down. You might find this faster than the whole File, Save & Send, Change File Type, Web Page chain described previously.

Saving a file as a web page doesn't save the actual Visio drawing! If you've made changes in Visio, be sure to save the drawing as you normally would.

Exploring Visio-Generated Web Pages

After Visio has created web pages from your documents, you're in for an interesting treat. Visio adds extra controls to the web pages that enable you to do all sorts of interesting things. First, though, you have to jump through a few hoops!

LET ME TRY IT

Exploring Visio-Generated Web Pages

1. Figure 10.3 shows a first glimpse at Visio's web output. Take a moment to examine the result. You can navigate between pages using the three links on the left, which is pretty cool. Your multi-page documents get exported into a single mini-website.

   The drawing crowds the browser window, though, and you have to use the scrollbars to see everything. Don't worry; it gets better.

2. If you're using Internet Explorer, you see a warning about restricting scripts and controls. On my machine, using the IE9 beta, the warning appears at the bottom of the window and says: "Internet Explorer has restricted this webpage from running scripts or ActiveX controls." Older browsers might display a similar warning in a bar at the top of the window.

3. Click Allow Blocked Content or similar to ignore the warning to let the special content run.

4. You might run into one more hurdle. If you don't have the Silverlight plug-in installed for your browser, you see a message like "To enable full functionality such as Pan and Zoom, click here to install the Silverlight plug-in." Click the link and install the Silverlight plug-in.

   Silverlight is a Microsoft technology similar to Adobe Flash. The plug-in is small, installs in seconds, and is nothing to fear.

5. Finally your web page transforms into something much friendlier looking, as shown in Figure 10.4.

6. Note the controls in the column on the left. Each blue heading can be collapsed or expanded to hide or show controls and information. You see Go to Page, Pan and Zoom, Details, and Search. Note the scroll bar for the left panel, which lets you access off-page controls.

7. Experiment with Go to Page, which is now a sleek drop-down list. Select one of the three pages from the list and then click the green arrow to the right.

8. Click your browser's Back button to return to the Topology page.

9. Click on the top-left server shape. You jump to another page. This is the shape to which you added three hyperlinks. Notice that you didn't get a choice of which link to jump to. This is a bug in the product, discussed later.

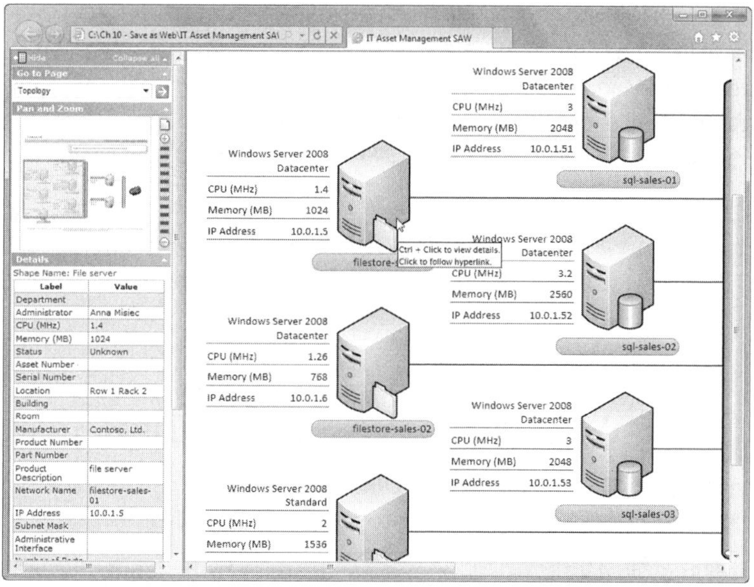

Figure 10.4 *With content unblocked and Silverlight installed, the Visio Web page displays helpful controls in the column on the left.*

10. Click the Pan and Zoom control. This is similar to the Pan and Zoom control in Visio itself. You resize the red rectangle to zoom in or out and drag the rectangle around to pan. You can also click anywhere between the + and – icons on the right to zoom in and out, or fit the entire drawing to the browser window by clicking the sheet of paper icon.

    Notice also that no matter how far in you zoom, text and graphics remain smooth. This is one of the signature features of Visio's web export: it displays a vector representation of your drawing, not a bitmap. If the diagram was displayed as a bitmap image, zooming would show magnified dots resulting in a jagged representation. Vectors are mathematical descriptions of graphics and utilize the full resolution of the screen, no matter the zoom.

11. The Details control enables you to examine Shape Data fields. To view Shape Data, hold down the Ctrl key while clicking a shape in the browser. In Figure 10.4, the Shape Data for the server in the top-left corner is showing.

12. Collapse the Details area by clicking the little arrow on the right end of the blue bar.

13. Notice the Search Pages field. If you expand the Advanced item, you see a long list of options that hint at what can be searched. You see that a shape's text, name, and data fields are all candidates for searching—another cool feature! However, due to yet another frustrating bug, you get almost no search results for this particular drawing. More on this in the next section as well.

If you copy the web page and supporting files to a network location, users who access the page won't see the warnings discussed in Steps 2 and 3, and will see the web page and useful controls in all their glory.

Fine-tuning Web Pages and Battling Bugs

If you need to support multiple hyperlinks in your Visio-generated web pages, use the Search feature, or customize the web pages, this section is for you.

Microsoft improved Visio 2010's save as web features by updating the behind-the-scenes technology. The new export saves vector data in the new and widespread XAML format instead of VML (Vector Markup Language—a dead-end Microsoft format that never caught on, elicits snickers from techies, and is supported only by Internet Explorer).

In the browser, the Silverlight plug-in renders this XAML data in vector format and creates the fancy controls in the left sidebar. Silverlight is a modern technology, similar to Flash that works in all major browsers. Older versions of Visio required IE in order to get the advanced features for web exports.

Customizing Web Page Output

You can tweak the way your web pages look in many ways...*unless* you have the Standard edition. Figure 10.5 contrasts the web export Save As dialogs for Visio Standard and for Visio Pro/Premium at the time of writing. You can see that Standard is missing the Change Title and Publish buttons. Microsoft did not intend to limit web page customization to its higher-paying customers, but an odd set of conditions led to this unfortunate bug.

Change Title enables you to change the title of the output web page. Publish takes you to a two-tab dialog full of options for choosing which controls to show, which pages to export, whether to append reports, how to organize the output files, and which output formats and resolutions to use. You can even specify custom web page hosts and style sheets!

Figure 10.6 shows the Save as Web Page dialog, which you see if you click the Publish button. Figure 10.7 shows the Advanced tab of this same dialog.

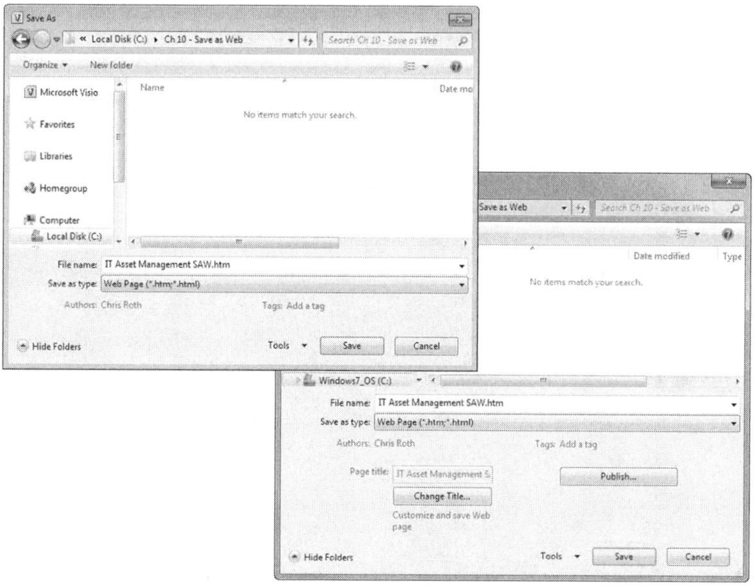

Figure 10.5 *Visio Standard's Save as Web Page dialog is unintentionally missing the Change Title and Publish buttons that Visio Pro and Premium have.*

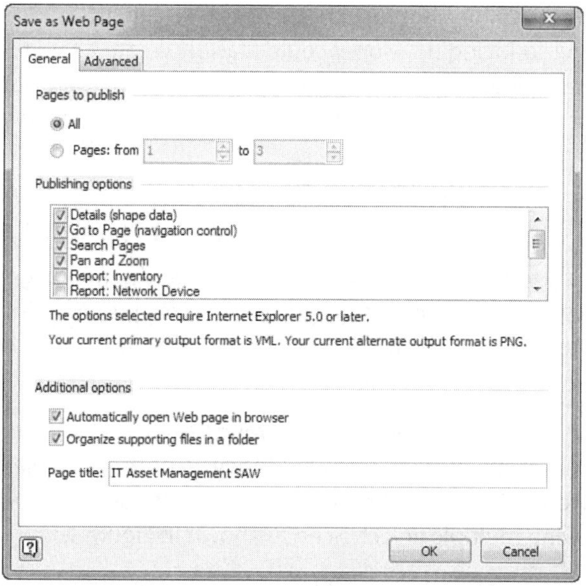

Figure 10.6 *The General tab of the Save as Web Page dialog, which you can get to only if you have Pro or Premium.*

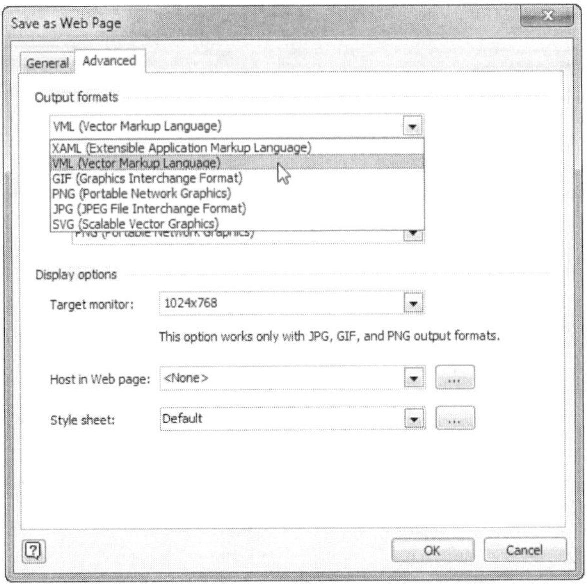

Figure 10.7 *On the Advanced tab of the Save as Web Page dialog, you can choose output formats among other things. Notice that the old VML format is still an option.*

Standard users can either pray for an update from Microsoft or hope for a utility from the Visio community. Because the Save as Web functionality in Visio is programmable, a Visio-loving developer could feasibly create a tool that lets Standard users manipulate all the web customization options. Until then, Standard users have to accept the default settings when saving Visio drawings as web pages.

Getting Multiple Hyperlinks to Function

The default Visio web export uses the fancy XAML/Silverlight combo. If shapes have multiple hyperlinks, only the first link is used in the web page. If you absolutely need to support multiple hyperlinks on shapes, go to the Publish options, click the Advanced tab, and choose the older VML as the output format. Figure 10.7 shows this being done.

By using VML, you are encouraging an old format that is supposed to go away. You also limit your users to Internet Explorer (if they want the multiple hyperlinks to work). But it works! When you click a shape in the browser window, you see a small pop-up displaying multiple link choices, as shown in Figure 10.8.

Note that choosing VML is a "sticky setting." The next time you export web pages, VML is the default. Be sure to change the setting back to XAML if you only wanted VML temporarily.

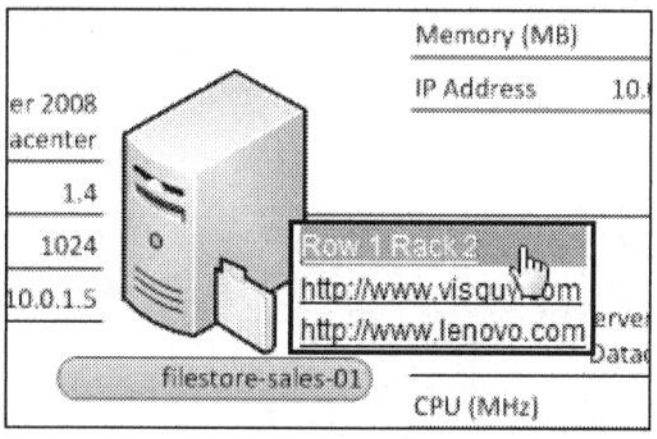

Figure 10.8 *Multiple hyperlinks work if you export using VML instead of XAML. However, Standard users can't get to this option, unfortunately.*

Getting Search to Work

The IT Asset Management and Visio's network shapes in general have a problem that make the web search function not work properly. To get an idea of how Search Pages are intended to work, let's create a simpler example.

SHOW ME **Media 10.2—Searching Web Pages**
Access this video file through your registered Web Edition at ***my.safaribooksonline.com/9780132182683/media.***

LET ME TRY IT

Saving a Visio Drawing as a Web Page

1. Start a new, blank drawing.
2. Draw a circle, square, and diamond shape.
3. Type the text **circle**, **square**, and **diamond** into the corresponding shapes.
4. Give each shape a different fill color.
5. Select all three shapes and add the Shape Data field "Color" to them. (Recall Chapter 7, "Working with Data," for how to add Shape Data fields to shapes.)
6. For each shape, type a descriptive name for the shape's color into the Color Shape Data field. For example, I colored the circle, square and diamond gray, blue and black. Then I entered the values "Gray," "Blue" and "Black" in their Color fields.

7. Save the drawing as a web page. A browser window opens showing the exported diagram. You see something like Figure 10.9.

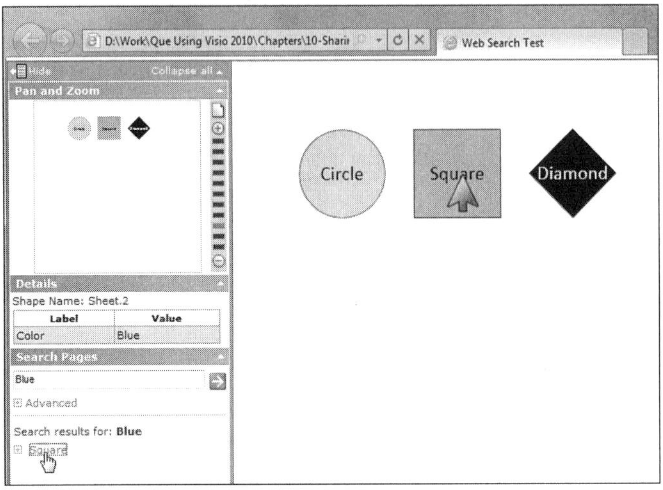

Figure 10.9 *A simple drawing saved to web. The Details pane shows the Shape Data for the Square. A temporary arrow appears to visually highlight a search result on "Blue."*

8. Type **Circle** into the field under Search Pages. Then click the green arrow or press Enter to perform the search. One search result appears below.
9. Click the Circle item in the Search Results area. An arrow appears over the circle for three seconds, indicating the location of the shape. If the shape is off the screen, the drawing is panned to bring the shape into view.
10. Ctrl+click the square shape. You see its Shape Data in the Details area on the left, also shown in Figure 10.9. You can also search on Shape Data values.
11. Type the square's value for Color into the Search Pages field and then press Enter. In Figure 10.9, a search for "Blue" results in one result: the Square shape.
12. Click on Square in the results area. An arrow temporarily highlights the square shape.
13. Type **Color** into the Search Pages field and press Enter. You see the message "No matches found in the results area." Only Shape Data values are searched, not field names.

You can see that Search Pages is a nifty and useful feature!

If you try search with a web export of the IT Asset Management drawing, however, you encounter problems. Very few searches will be successful, even though you search for data that is in the diagram.

The problem is with the network shapes used in the diagram. At some point in history, they were assigned to layers, then these layers were removed. This left a sort of "empty layer artifact" behind that oddly causes problems with Search Pages.

You can quickly simulate this with your simple circle-square-diamond drawing if you follow these steps:

1. Duplicate the diamond shape and leave it selected.
2. Assign it to a layer called "Bug." (Remember assigning layers from Chapter 3, "Organizing and Annotating Diagrams": Home, Edting, Layers, Assign to Layer will get the job done!)
3. Duplicate the new diamond shape (which is on the Bug layer).
4. Remove this diamond from the layer by unchecking Bug in the Assign to Layer dialog. Note that your drawing now has three diamond shapes. One was never on a layer, one is on the Bug layer, and one has been removed from the Bug layer.
5. Save the drawing as a web page. The browser opens with your new creation.
6. Type "Diamond" into the Search Pages field and press Enter. Only two results for Diamond appear, even though three shapes clearly say "Diamond."

I tried to fix the IT Asset Management drawing by assigning all shapes to a dummy layer. This got me plenty of search results, but the highlighting arrow never appeared when I clicked a search result item. If the result was on another page, at least that page would be brought into view. So adding the layer only half-fixed the problem.

If I changed the output format to VML and assigned all the network shapes to a layer, the search worked, and the highlighting arrow appeared.

It's sad that such bugs exist to tarnish what is a really cool web export feature. But knowing about these bugs is better than getting stuck in a loop, wondering if you have done something wrong. (I've done my best to point out the problems.)

If you need multiple hyperlinks in your web pages, switch the default format to VML and tell your users to use Internet Explorer. If your need search to work, try the XAML output format first. If it doesn't work, switch to VML. If you have Visio

Standard, you can't change the export options and will have to wait for an update or some other workaround.

And lest we forget, the Go to Page, Pan & Zoom, and Details controls are bug-free and add wonderful functionality to your web pages. You get these by default, no matter which edition of Visio you have, and they work in any major browser that has the Silverlight plug-in installed.

Saving as PDF or XPS Files

Earlier, you saw how easy it was to mail a Visio document as a PDF or XPS document. If you want to hold on to actual copies of these files, Save & Send helps you out again.

PDF and XPS files are high-quality documents that are essentially read-only because most people don't have editors for them. They are great for distributing to folks who don't need to edit your content or who don't have Visio. PDF and XPS files look the same on most computers because, for example, they preserve font information. Even if the recipient's system doesn't have a font that you used, it appears properly in the PDF or XPS document.

Because these files are unlikely to be altered, they offer a great way to preserve historical snapshots of documents that you frequently edit. They can be more compact than Visio files. For example, the IT Asset Management Visio file is around 900KB. When saved as PDF or XPS, it's around 360KB.

Hyperlinks are preserved in the final output—even links that go to other pages within the document. If a shape has multiple links, however, only the first one is used.

LET ME TRY IT

Saving a PDF or XPS Document

1. Start with any drawing you want to see in PDF or XPS form.
2. Go to File, Save & Send.
3. Click Create PDF/XPS Document in the Save & Send area. The Create PDF/XPS button appears on the right.
4. Click Create PDF/XPS button. (Tip: You can save a step by double-clicking Create PDF/XPS Document in step 3.)

The Publish as PDF or XPS dialog appears. It's similar to a typical Save As dialog but has a few options at the bottom.

5. Choose to save either a PDF or XPS document by making a choice from the Save as Type drop-down list. If you have time, try repeating the following steps for both PDF and XPS.
6. Note the Optimize For settings and click the Options button. The Options dialog appears, which enables you to specify specific pages to export, include backgrounds, remove or include document information, and perform a few other tasks. You can make changes here and click OK, or just click Cancel.
7. Browse to a suitable location, give your PDF or XPS file a name, and then click Publish. If you left the Open File After Publishing box checked, the exported document opens for inspection.

The Save & Send panel provides a friendly interface for perusing and choosing different export options. Big, fat buttons, colorful icons, and helpful text make for a pleasant experience, especially when you are doing something for the first time.

The downside is that for PDF and XPS documents, it always suggests your Documents folder as the place to save the output. If you're like me, you want to save the PDF or XPS file in the same directory where the drawing is saved. Having to browse back to that location to save is annoying.

Luckily, most of the options in Save & Send can be accessed via File, Save As dialog. Instead of clicking several buttons as you do via Save & Send, you just pick a Save As type from the drop-down list. When you use Save As, the default folder is the same as that of the current Visio drawing, so you don't have to do any browsing!

Saving Visio Files in XML Format

Visio drawings, templates, and stencils can be saved in an XML format that is useful for a number of reasons. As an end user, you probably won't find this capability very exciting, but your IT and Development departments might be interested, so be sure and mention it to your nearest techie.

XML is an open format that uses structured text to define data. Because it is plain text, XML is human readable (but not easily readable), and developers can access, edit, compare, and filter the information programmatically. An aspiring programmer can extract information from Visio XML drawings or even generate them without using Visio at all.

You can save Visio files in XML format via File, Save As, or File, Save & Send, Change File Type. In the Save As dialog, look for the options XML Drawing, XML Stencil, or XML Template, depending on the file you are trying to save. Instead of .VSD, .VST, and .VSS extensions, files saved in XML format have the extensions .VDX, .VTX, and .VSX.

There is an option to save drawings in Visio XML format by default. Go to File, Options, Save. In the Save Documents area, you see the Save Files in This Format drop-down list, where you specify Visio XML Document as the default.

Saving Files in Older Visio Formats

If you have colleagues or customers using older versions of Visio, they might not be able to open your Visio 2010 documents. Using Save As or Save & Send, you can save documents in the Visio 2000–2002 format. Just look for Visio 2000–2002 Drawing (*.vsd) in the Save options.

So that you don't forget that you have done this, Visio reminds you every time you save thereafter. When you save the document, the Save Options dialog pops up, asking you to choose between the Current Visio Format and Visio 2002 Format.

If you choose Current Visio Format, the file becomes a Visio 2010 drawing again, and you won't see the pop-up anymore.

If you choose Visio 2002 Format, you (frustratingly) see the pop-up every time you save, along with the reminder that "Saving in the Visio 2002 format may result in the loss of attributes unique to the current format."

Because of this minor annoyance, I work in the newest format and save a copy to the older format just before sending the file to a customer. I typically add the suffix "(2000)" to the filename to keep things clear. In this manner, older versions of the file are essentially exports. I don't work in the older format.

If you frequently need to save to the older format, you can tell Visio to do it by default. Go to File, Options, Save and notice the Save Files in This Format drop-down list. Choose Visio 2002 Document to set the default.

When you save to an older format, you won't likely lose any of the graphics in your diagram. What's missing is the ability to manipulate the shapes using the latest technology. For example, your drawing might use Visio 2010's containers and callouts (see Chapter 3, "Organizing and Annotating Diagrams"). Saving it to an older format won't destroy the containers and callouts. But users of Visio 2000 or 2002 won't get the automated benefits that these shapes have.

Using Visio Graphics with Other Applications

If you want to use your Visio diagrams in other applications, your best bet is to try copy and paste first. If you are using Microsoft Office applications, this approach usually works fine, but there are some subtleties to keep in mind.

Copying from Visio

If one or more shapes are selected when you copy, only those shapes get pasted into the target document. If no shapes are selected, the entire page is copied—including any backgrounds and titles.

If you want all the shapes on the page, but not the background, select all of the shapes on the page and then copy. You can select all shapes via Ctrl+A or Home, Editing, Select, Select All.

Default Paste Behavior

If you copy Visio shapes to the Clipboard and then paste to an Office application, you see different default behavior, depending on the app. Table 10.1 shows how several Office apps handle the pasting of Visio data.

Table 10.1 Default Pasting Behavior of Visio Clipboard Data in Microsoft Applications

Application	Default Paste Behavior
Excel 2010	Embedded Visio object
Outlook 2010	Embedded Visio object
OneNote 2010	Metafile
PowerPoint 2010	Bitmap image
Publisher 2010	Embedded Visio object
Word 2010	Embedded Visio object

Embedded Visio objects contain all original Visio data, and can be edited in-place within the host application. Since the Visio information is there, you can modify the drawing using Visio features, but without leaving the host application. Just double-click on the Visio object to activate "in-place editing." To exit the editing session, click outside the object in the host document.

Metafiles are vector objects, so they print smoothly and have transparent backgrounds, but they don't contain any Visio-specific data. You *can* edit them, but you first have to convert them to Microsoft Office drawing objects. As a metafile, Visio SmartShape behavior, Shape Data fields, and other characteristics that make Visio graphics special are removed from the object.

Bitmap images are collections of dots that degrade in quality if you stretch them, like digital photos. They also have a solid background that can look clunky if the host document has a different-colored background.

Using Paste Special and Matching Themes Across Applications

If you don't like the default format that paste offers, you can specify it using Paste Special. In Office 2010 applications, just click the drop-down arrow below the Paste button and choose Paste Special. A dialog pops up, enabling you to choose exactly the format you want.

For example, in Word, Paste Special gives you these options when the Clipboard contains Visio data:

- Microsoft Visio Drawing Object
- Device Independent Bitmap
- Picture (Enhanced Metafile)

If you want to tweak the diagram within the host application, choose Visio Drawing Object. At any time, you can double-click the Visio object, and an in-place editing session starts. The Ribbon switches to Visio, and you have Visio functionality at your disposal. Click outside the Visio object to end the session and return to the host application.

If you don't need to edit the object, pasting as Picture is usually sufficient. Bitmaps often don't look as nice, especially if the background colors don't match.

SHOW ME **Media 10.3—Matching Themes When Copying Visio Graphics to PowerPoint**

Access this video file through your registered Web Edition at ***my.safaribooksonline.com/9780132182683/media.***

Figure 10.10 shows a simple Visio diagram pasted into PowerPoint in six different ways.

Let's go over the differences between the items. The first three objects in the top row were copied from a Visio drawing that had the no theme applied.

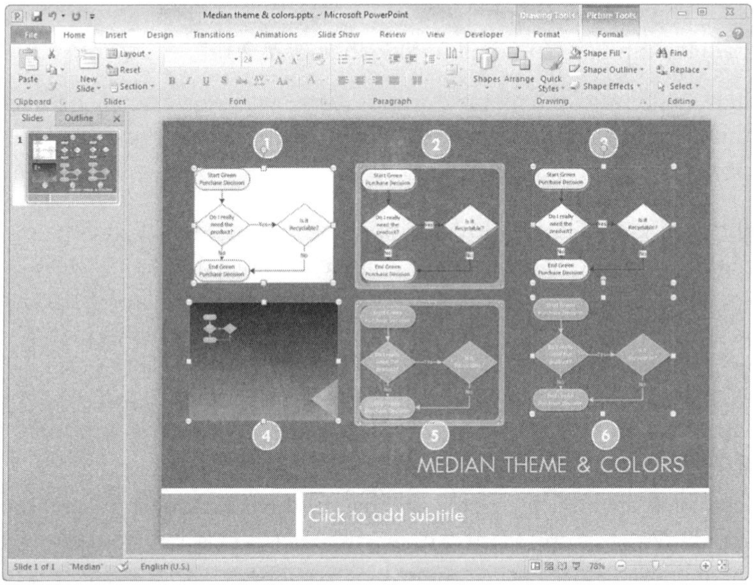

Figure 10.10 *A Visio flowchart pasted into PowerPoint in six different ways.*

1. This item is a Bitmap, as per PowerPoint's default paste. You see the ugly white background that sticks out like a sore thumb!

2. This item was pasted as a Visio object, using Paste Special. It has a transparent background and vector-based data that stretches and prints nicely. The text background on the connectors is white, though, which doesn't match well with our PowerPoint theme.

3. This item was pasted as a metafile (aka: "Picture"). It can't be edited in-place, but it appears identical to item 2.

   Items 4, 5, and 6 in Figure 10.10 were copied from Visio after a color theme was applied. The PowerPoint file uses a theme called Median. In Visio, on the Design tab, the Colors drop-down just to the right of the theme gallery also contains an item called Median. This makes it easy to match colors across Office applications.

4. This item was copied from Visio with no shapes selected. So all shapes on the page, plus the background, came along for the ride. It was pasted using the default behavior (bitmap). It looks better than item 1 because of the matching theme colors, but including the Visio background looks odd inside of PowerPoint.

5. This item was pasted as a Visio object, just like item 2. See what a difference applying matching theme colors in Visio before copying makes? This item looks much better in our slide than item 2.

6. Item 6 is pasted as a metafile, just as item 3 was. Again, applying Median theme colors in Visio before copying hugely improves the look of our pasted object.

Take one last look at Figure 10.10 and note the different selection handles used by PowerPoint. Objects that are bitmaps or metafiles have the same style of selection handles, which you see for items 1, 3, 4, and 6. Items 2 and 5 are embedded Visio objects and have a fancy frame around them. This frame indicates that they are rich embedded objects that can be edited in-place.

Using Visio Graphics Outside Office

If you are using an application that isn't part of the Office suite, you might not be able to paste Visio graphics into it. If general pasting fails, look to see whether the application has a Paste Special option and experiment with the different formats that it offers. If no Paste Special function is available, your last resort is to export your Visio diagram to a vector or bitmap format and then try importing it into the application.

Exporting Visio Graphics to Other Formats

If you are working with other desktop applications—especially from the Microsoft Office suite—the easiest way to transport a Visio graphic to another document is to copy and paste.

If the copy-and-paste approach doesn't work, or you need to upload a file to a blog or to Facebook, for example, you can try exporting to a file.

Exporting from Visio generally follows this flow:

1. Choose what to export. As mentioned, only selected shapes are exported. If no shapes are selected, the whole page, including backgrounds and titles, is exported. Most of the formats handle only one selection or page at a time, but PDF, XPS, and Web Page handle multiple pages.

2. Choose a format in the File, Save As dialog, or via File, Save & Send, Change File Type.

3. Depending on the target format you select, watch for options at the bottom of the Save As dialog.

4. Choose a name for the file and location and then click Save or Publish.
5. Before the file is created, you might see an options dialog. For example, the image formats enable you to choose a background color, color depth, dots-per-inch resolution, and a few other settings. Choose your options and then click OK.
6. Your exported file gets created.

Exporting to PDF or XPS bucks the trend by not looking at the selected shapes. Instead, all pages are exported by default. If, however, you click the Options button in the Save As dialog, you can specify to export the Selection.

Saving Bitmapped Images

If you need graphics for a web page or blog entry or to share on your favorite social networking site, images are your best bet.

Bitmapped images are made up of a fixed number of dots, like a photo. If you stretch them, their quality degrades. However, they are generally fine for onscreen purposes.

Supported Image Formats

Visio can export images in BMP, GIF, JPG, PNG, and TIF formats. These days, JPG and PNG seem to be the most common. When you want to export, be aware that the type description and file extension don't always match, which can make it tricky to find what you're looking for. For example, you might be looking to export Visio graphics as a bitmap or BMP file. But this file type is listed way at the bottom under Windows Bitmap (*.bmp, *.dib).

GIF and PNG images are interesting because they support transparent backgrounds.

JPG images enable you to control the amount of compression. More compression means smaller files, but a lower quality image. In some cases, the decrease in quality is negligible and is worth the space savings.

BMP is a raw format that produces large files but doesn't throw out any detail in the name of smaller file size. Recall in Chapter 9, "Printing," that you learned how to export a very high-resolution BMP to take to a print shop.

Image Output Options

When you are exporting Visio graphics to image formats, an Output Options screen appears immediately after you finish with the Save As dialog. This enables you to fine-tune your exported image. Figure 10.11 shows the options for PNG export.

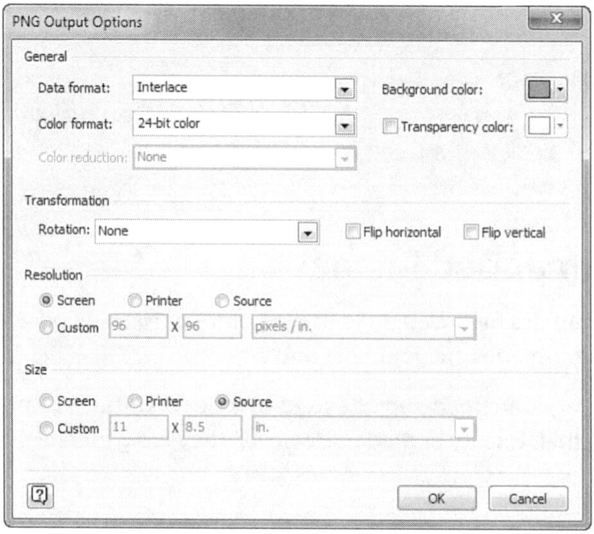

Figure 10.11 *The PNG Output Options screen gives you control over how your Visio graphics are exported. Option screens for JPG, GIF, and BMP are similar.*

The settings you are most likely to tweak are Background Color, Transparency Color, and Resolution.

Exported images are always rectangular. Any blank space between shapes is filled with a background color, which is white by default.

Say your blog has a magenta background color (shudder!). If you export an image using the default settings, you get a rectangular image with a white background. This sticks out loudly on your magenta web page. If you choose a background color of magenta, your image blends nicely with your blog's color scheme.

Alternatively, you can draw a magenta rectangle in Visio, place it behind the shapes that you want to export, and include this rectangle in the export. Because no empty space exists between your shapes, the background color setting becomes meaningless but the end result is the same.

If you export to PNG or GIF, you can also select a transparency color. Say your blog's background has a gradient fill. In this case, any background color chosen during export still shows up as an ugly block, because the blog's background isn't uniform, but the image's background is. If you choose a transparency color, your exported image can appear borderless and nonrectangular.

Figure 10.12 shows two PNG images against a complex background (exported from Visio, then reimported as images.) The image on the left used a transparent color of white. The background nicely shows through, but dithering has muddied the shape edges and the Yes/No text. Close, but not perfect.

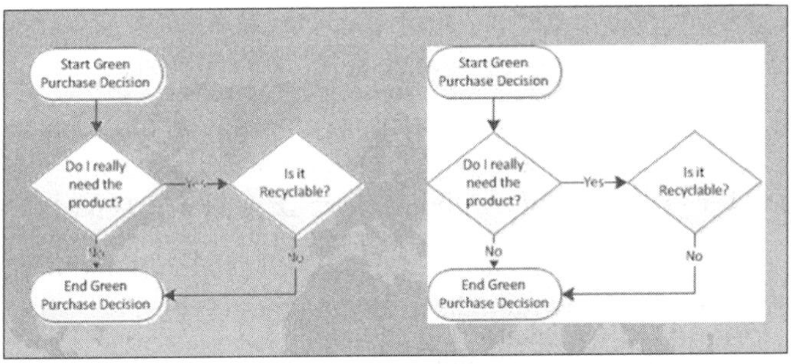

Figure 10.12 *Two images on top of a complex background. The image on the left was exported with white as the transparent color. The image on the right used white as the background color.*

The image on the right used white as the background color. The image is clearer, but the stark white block is rather alarming and doesn't blend well with the background at all.

If you are interested in more information on removing backgrounds, be sure to review "Removing Rectangular Backgrounds from Images" in Chapter 6, "Working with Individual Shapes."

For onscreen applications such as presentations and web pages, Screen resolution is usually sufficient. If you need high quality that matches the resolution of your printer, however, check the Printer button under Resolution, or select Custom and enter a high number such as 600 × 600 or 1200 × 1200.

If you use Visio to create lots of images for web sites, application user interfaces, or other projects, you might quickly tire of visiting the Save As dialog.

Luckily, Visio can be programmed using the VBA macro language (discussed more in Chapter 11, "Developing Custom Visio Solutions"). If you visit my website, there is an article that contains macro code to help you export all pages in a document as images.

See: Export All Pages in Document

http://www.visguy.com/2006/09/18/export-all-pages-in-document/

Saving to Vector Formats

If you want to use Visio graphics in another vector-editing program such as an illustration or CAD application, you can first try to copy and paste. If that doesn't work, try exporting the file to one of the three vector-based formats that Visio supports.

In the Save As dialog, there are seven items, but they add up to three basic types: SVG files, AutoCAD files, and metafiles. Here are the options:

- Scalable Vector Graphics (*.svg)
- Scalable Vector Graphics—Compressed (*.svgz)
- AutoCAD Drawing (*.dwg)
- AutoCAD Interchange (*.dxf)
- Compressed Enhanced Metafile (*.emz)
- Enhanced Metafile (*.emf)
- Windows Metafile (*.wmf)

Exporting to vector files is similar to how you export to image formats. Selected shapes are exported, or the whole page is exported if no shapes are selected. Multipage documents are not exported as with PDF and XPS, however. Also, you won't see any options dialogs with these vector formats, since vector data is resolution-independent and background colors don't apply.

SVG is an XML-based standard that has been around since 1999 and has a following that spans many computing platforms. Visio does not support SVG 100% because SVG can do some things that Visio can't, so be on the lookout for the occasional oddity. If you are exchanging graphics with your art department, and the staff uses Adobe Illustrator, SVG is a good route to take.

You can test your SVG export by opening it in a browser. A quick test on my machine reveals that IE9, FireFox 3.6, and Chrome 8 can display SVG files. IE8 doesn't support it directly, but there is a discontinued plug-in from Adobe, available here: http://www.ieaddons.com/en/details/Time_Savers/Adobe_SVG_Viewer/

Architects and engineers use AutoCAD to create precise 2D and 3D technical drawings. It has been around since 1982. You might recall our discussion in Chapter 6 about importing AutoCAD drawings as backgrounds for placing furniture and equipment. A classic workflow goes like this: A technical department creates a floorplan in AutoCAD and then sends it to the facilities management people. Using Visio, they add equipment, furniture, cubicle walls, and the like and then re-export to AutoCAD format and send it back to the technical guys.

You heard about metafiles in the earlier discussion on Paste Special. WMF is an older form of metafile; EMF, the newer. With EMF, exported graphics have higher quality, but some older apps might understand only WMF.

> Any format that you can export to can also be imported into Visio. You can import other file types using File, Open. The Open dialog has a drop-down filter that lets you find files of specific types more easily.
>
> Also, the Illustrations group on the Insert tab contains the Picture button. This presents a dialog that is almost identical to the Open dialog.
>
> The primary difference between Open and Insert is that Open creates a new Visio document with the imported graphics, whereas Insert drops the file into the current drawing.

Working with SharePoint

One of the selling points of Microsoft Office is its great integration with SharePoint, and Visio is no exception. In Visio 2010, you don't even have to go to SharePoint to work with documents in SharePoint document libraries.

Working with Files in Document Libraries

Let's create a document, save it to a SharePoint document library, and look at revisions. For this exercise, you need to know the address of a SharePoint document library, and it should have versioning switched on. If versioning isn't on for your library, some of the steps below won't work, but you'll get the picture if you follow along.

LET ME TRY IT

Saving and Editing Visio Documents in SharePoint

1. Start with a new, blank drawing.
2. Draw a rectangle near the top of the page and type **SharePoint** on it.
3. Go to File, Save & Send, and click Save to SharePoint. The right side of the panel shows you any recent locations that you might have browsed to, plus a Browse For a Location button.
4. Double-click Browse For a Location. The Save As dialog appears.
5. In the File Name field, paste the address to your SharePoint site.

   For example, I have a SharePoint site on Microsoft Online. The address to the document library looks something like this: https://blahblahblahmicrosoftonlinecom-1.sharepoint.microsoftonline.com/SharedDocuments, ("blahblahblah" is the fictitious part of the address and would be your name or your company's name).

   Paste the address into the File Name field and then press Enter. After a few moments, you should see a view of the document library, with a listing of any files that are in it.
6. Type a name for your file, such as **Ch10 SharePoint**, and then click Save.

   After a few moments (depending on your connection speed), your document is magically saved to the cloud. Note the window title changes from Drawing1 to Ch10 SharePoint—another clue that your document has been saved. You have saved the document directly to SharePoint; you didn't need to save it to your hard drive first and then upload it later.
7. Now let's experiment with check-out and versioning. Click File and go to the Info panel. Because this document is saved in SharePoint, you see two SharePoint-related buttons that aren't normally on the Info panel: Check Out and View Version History.

   Click Check Out. SharePoint alerts you that it is saving a copy of the document to the SharePoint drafts folder so that you can edit the document offline. Click OK.

   The Check Out button turns into a Check In button, and red text tells you that this is now a Checked Out Document. Nobody else with access to the document library can make changes to this file as long as you have it checked out.

8. Click Home to return to the drawing window.

9. Give the rectangle a fill color—something gaudy like bright orange!

10. Return to the Info panel and click Check In, Check In. In the Check In dialog, decide how you want to version the file and add a comment, such as **Changed color to orange**. Check the Keep the Document Checked Out After Checking In This Version box, as shown in Figure 10.13. Click OK to finish the check-in process.

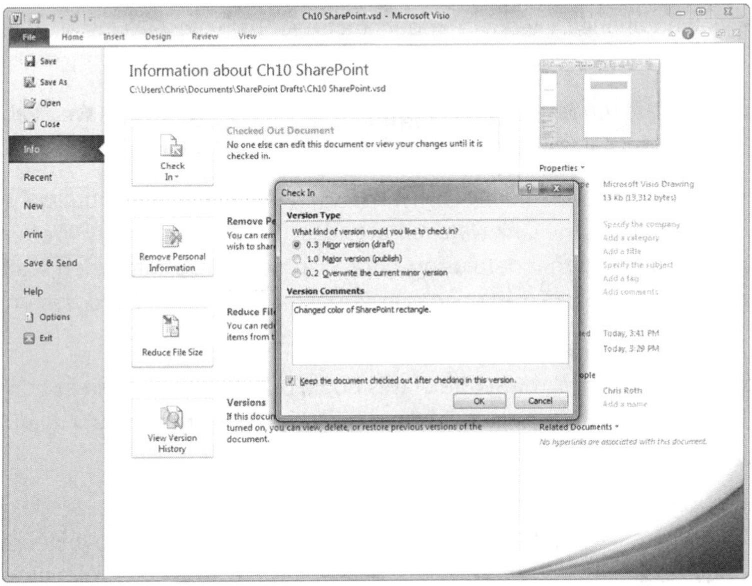

Figure 10.13 *Checking in a file using the Info panel in Backstage. You can enter comments describing changes and decide whether the change represents a major or minor change.*

11. Return to the document and move the rectangle to the bottom of the page. Repeat the check-in process from step 10 adding an appropriate comment and keeping the document checked out.

12. Return to the document and make the rectangle's font size much bigger. Check in the document after commenting, but this time, don't keep it checked out. The document is checked in, and the Check In button reverts to the Check Out button

13. Click the View Version History button on the Info Panel. You see a dialog titled Versions Saved for Ch10 SharePoint.vsd, which shows a list of the modifications and check-ins that you just made. You can view older versions of the document, and even restore older states as the current state if you don't like a modification that was made.

Introducing Visio Services for SharePoint 2010

Visio Premium users are able to interact with SharePoint in a new and exciting way. They can author and publish data-connected Visio diagrams to SharePoint, which can be viewed online by team members that needn't have Visio installed on their systems.

The drawings are rendered using Silverlight, similar to the Save as Web Page feature discussed earlier, so users can zoom and pan the drawings smoothly.

The real benefit is in data connectivity, however. Drawings that contain shapes linked to data (using the Link Data features described in Chapter 7, "Working with Data") and displaying that data using Data Graphics will update when that data changes. Visitors can use these pages as visual dashboards to check system status and so on.

Visio Services is beyond the scope of this book, but it represents an exciting new direction for Visio and Visio-authored content. If you are interested in learning more, here are a few articles to check out:

- Embedding a Web Drawing in a SharePoint Page http://blogs.msdn.com/b/visio/archive/2009/11/05/embedding-a-web-drawing-into-a-sharepoint-page.aspx
- All Visio Services posts on Visio Insights http://blogs.msdn.com/b/visio/archive/tags/visio+services/
- Dave McMahon: Visio Services in SharePoint 2010—Part 1 http://davemcmahon81.wordpress.com/2009/12/17/visio-services-in-sharepoint-2010-%E2%80%93-part-1/
- Chak's Corner: SharePoint 2010: Visio Services http://www.chakkaradeep.com/post/SharePoint-2010-Visio-Services.aspx
- Visio World Cup This site is an actual Visio Services example that you can interact with online. It deals with 2010's World Cup (Soccer) and during that tournament, the data was updated after each match. Now the data is fixed because the tournament is over, but the site is still interactive, and you get a feel for what is possible with Visio Services for SharePoint 2010. http://www.visioworldcup.com/SitePages/default.aspx

Cleaning Up Documents

Before you share a Visio document, you might want to change or remove certain bits of sensitive in-house information and reduce the file size as much as possible. The Info panel in the Backstage area offers several functions to help you do this.

Setting Document Properties

When you click the Info tab in the Backstage area, you see something like Figure 10.14, which shows two big buttons for removing information and reducing file size, along with summary of information fields under Properties on the right.

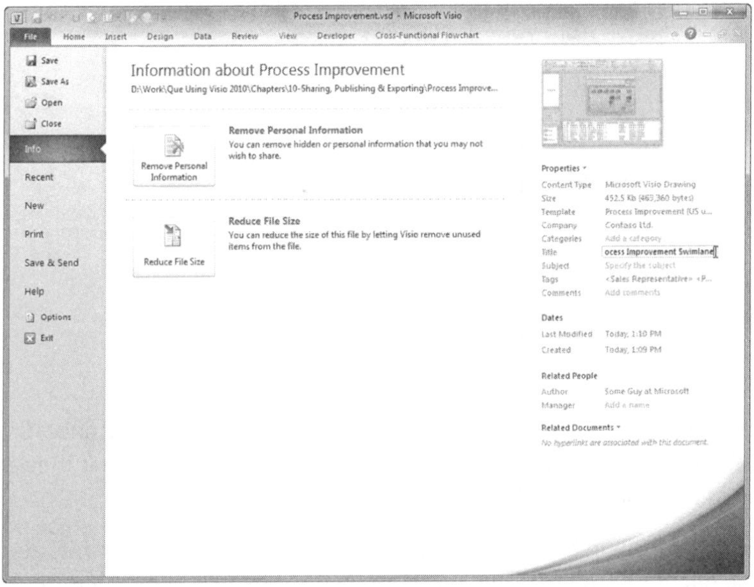

Figure 10.14 *The Info panel in the Backstage area. Several of the fields on the right can be edited in-place.*

If you've used Microsoft Office for a long time, you might be used to editing document properties such as Author, Title, Company, Categories, and so on via a pop-up accessible from File, Properties.

With the new Backstage area, it took me awhile to notice that you can actually edit several of these fields in-place. Just mouse over the fields on the right; orange highlights around a field indicate that it is editable. In Figure 10.14, the Title field is being edited.

You can still access the "old" properties dialog by clicking the little Properties item just under the preview thumbnail and choosing Advanced Properties. The pop-up dialog also has a few more fields and settings than are shown in the Info panel.

Removing Personal Information

Before you email a document outside the company, you might want to erase some of those document property fields, along with other information. On the Info panel, click the Remove Personal Information button. The Remove Hidden Information dialog appears, with the Personal Information tab active.

Which Information Gets Removed?

The Personal Information tab has a few check boxes that enable you to clear quite a bit of information from your document:

- File properties (author, company, manager, and so on)
- Reviewer comments
- Reviewer marks and pages
- Stencil file paths
- Template filename
- Validation issues and time stamp
- External data sources

We discussed reviewer comments in Chapter 3, "Organizing and Annotating Diagrams," in the section on Markup and Review. It's easy to forget that they are present if you've turned them off.

Stencil file paths and template filenames could give someone an unwanted look into the directory structure of your PC or your company's infrastructure.

Although validation issues can be generated only by Visio Premium, they might still take up space in a document, even if it is being edited in Standard or Pro.

External data was discussed at the end of Chapter 7, "Working with Data," where you learned about the Link Data feature available in Pro and Premium. Visio files with linked data keep the data links and display a copy of the data, even if the data source isn't present. If such a document is opened and edited in Standard, the data is not visible, but it isn't forgotten. If the file is the forwarded to a Pro or Premium user, that user can see the data in the External Data window. For this reason, the Remove Data from External Sources Stored in the Document check box is especially important. You don't want the wrong people to see data about employee performance or salaries, for example.

Which Information Isn't Removed?

Determining which information isn't removed is the tricky bit, of course. Shape Data fields aren't erased, even when data sources are removed from a document. If you've populated an org chart with salary data, people can still see this data by inspecting the Shape Data fields for shapes. Data Graphics applied to such shapes reveal this data visually as well.

If you've used callouts or text blocks to add comments to a drawing, Visio isn't able to remind you to remove it. So if you add a comment to a callout attached to a process shape that says "Duration should be 3.5 hours, but Bob needs 6," information removal won't catch it.

Multipage documents can be dangerous, too, because the tabs can sometimes be off the edge, out of sight and out of mind. Make sure that you haven't retained any "junk" or "test" pages unintended for external eyes.

TELL ME MORE **Media 10.4—Unremoved Personal Information Horror Stories**

Access this audio file through your registered Web Edition at ***my.safaribooksonline.com/9780132182683/media.***

Reducing File Size

The second tab in the Remove Hidden Information window is the File Size Reduction tab. You can also jump straight to it by clicking the Reduce File Size button in the Info panel.

The things that you can clean up to make your Visio file smaller include

- The preview picture
- Unused master shapes
- Unused themes, data graphics, and styles
- Inactive validation rule sets

The preview picture usually isn't a huge detail, especially with today's large hard drives. But unused masters, themes, data graphics, and styles can really add up.

Validation rule sets are a feature that is useful only to Visio Premium users, but the rule sets can still take up space in a document, even if it is being edited in Standard or Pro.

Remember from Chapter 2's discussion about the Document Stencil that masters dragged into a drawing get copied to the local Document Stencil. Even if the shape is deleted from the page, the master remains. Cleaning up unused masters can make a huge difference.

I've seen files from customers that contain, say, a simple flowchart. A simple diagram, but the file is a whopping 3MB! What often happens is that they experiment with every shape they can get their mouse on. They drop one, play with it, explore its features, and then delete it. But it remains in the Document Stencil.

The File Size Reduction tab is very informative and tells you how many unused objects you have, so you can tell whether you have a cluttered document before you commit to removing the items.

Reducing your Visio file sizes not only helps keep your hard drive free, but also keeps you on the happy side of folks to whom you mail attachments. These features are a great addition to Visio and well worth learning.

Summary

In this chapter, you learned how to share Visio diagrams in many different ways, as well as the nuances involved with preparing diagrams for distribution.

You saw how Visio saves you time by allowing you to send files as attachments directly from within the Visio user interface.

Visio graphics can be used with other applications via cut and paste or by exporting to various image and vector formats. Complete documents can be exported as PDF or XPS files and even as mini websites. Unfortunately, a few bugs in the Save as Web Page feature mean you need to stay on your toes when creating web pages with Visio 2010.

Visio content can easily be used in PowerPoint presentations, and using matching themes can make the transition from Visio to PowerPoint more eye-appealing and professional looking.

Visio 2010 works well with SharePoint document libraries. You can open, save, check in, and check out documents from the Backstage area, without leaving the Visio interface. Visio Premium users can author and publish live, data-connected drawings straight to SharePoint. These drawings are updated when data changes and can be viewed and interacted with by users who don't have Visio.

Finally, you learned how to edit document properties, remove sensitive information before sending it out to nonprivy recipients, and reduce file size by removing unnecessary, unused clutter.

index

Symbols

A

B

D

G

H

I

S

T

U

V

W

X

Z